Oxford AQA History

A LEVEL AND AS
Component 2

The English Revolution 1625–1660

Judith Daniels

SERIES EDITOR
Sally Waller

OXFORD
UNIVERSITY PRESS

Great Clarendon Street, Oxford, OX2 6DP, United Kingdom

Oxford University Press is a department of the University of Oxford. It furthers the University's objective of excellence in research, scholarship, and education by publishing worldwide. Oxford is a registered trade mark of Oxford University Press in the UK and in certain other countries

© Oxford University Press 2015

The moral rights of the authors have been asserted

First published in 2015

All rights reserved. No part of this publication may be reproduced, stored in a retrieval system, or transmitted, in any form or by any means, without the prior permission in writing of Oxford University Press, or as expressly permitted by law, by licence or under terms agreed with the appropriate reprographics rights organization. Enquiries concerning reproduction outside the scope of the above should be sent to the Rights Department, Oxford University Press, at the address above.

You must not circulate this work in any other form and you must impose this same condition on any acquirer

British Library Cataloguing in Publication Data
Data available

978-0-19-8354-727

Kindle edition: 978-0-19-8363-835

10 9 8

Paper used in the production of this book is a natural, recyclable product made from wood grown in sustainable forests. The manufacturing process conforms to the environmental regulations of the country of origin.

Printed by CPI Group (UK) Ltd, Croydon CR0 4YY

Links to third party websites are provided by Oxford in good faith and for information only. Oxford disclaims any responsibility for the materials contained in any third party website referenced in this work.

The author thanks her inspirational colleagues at George Abbot School for their encouragement, Dr Alice Eardley for her input and the team at OUP for their helpful advice. Huge appreciation must go to her lovely husband Paul and spectacular children. This book is dedicated to her mum and dad.

Approval message from AQA

This textbook has been approved by AQA for use with our qualification. This means that we have checked that it broadly covers the specification and we are satisfied with the overall quality. Full details of our approval process can be found on our website.

We approve textbooks because we know how important it is for teachers and students to have the right resources to support their teaching and learning. However, the publisher is ultimately responsible for the editorial control and quality of this book.

Please note that when teaching the AQA A Level History course, you must refer to AQA's specification as your definitive source of information. While this book has been written to match the specification, it does not provide complete coverage of every aspect of the course.

A wide range of other useful resources can be found on the relevant subject pages of our website: www.aqa.org.uk.

Please note that the Practice Questions in this book allow students a genuine attempt at practising exam skills, but they are not intended to replicate examination papers.

Acknowledgements

The publisher would like to thank the following for permission to use their photographs:

Cover: Mary Evans Picture Library; **pxii**: Pictorial Press Ltd/Alamy; **p1**: ACTIVE MUSEUM/Alamy; **p3**: 19th era/Alamy; **p10**: Steve Vidler/Alamy; **p12**: Victoria & Albert Museum; **p16**: Mike Booth/Alamy; **p20**: TopFoto; **p23**: Bridgeman Art Library; **p24**: PRISMA ARCHIVO/Alamy; **p28**: Dan Kitwood/Getty Images; **p29**: (l) National Trust Photographic Library/Bridgeman Art Library, (r) Norwich Castle Museum and Art Gallery/Bridgeman Art Library; **p32**: Mary Evans Picture Library/Alamy; **p37**: Georgios Kollidas/Alamy; **p39**: Antiquarian Images/Alamy; **p45**: The Art Archive/Alamy; **p46**: Universal History Archive/Getty Images; **p49**: Nottingham University Library; **p56**: SuperStock/Alamy; **p57**: Photoshot/Getty Images; **p62**: Peter Horree/Alamy; **p64**: Timewatch Images/Alamy; **p65**: Bridgeman Art Library; **p67**: Classic Image/Alamy; **p70**: Fotomas/TopFoto; **p72**: INTERFOTO/Alamy; **p76**: Luigino Visconti/Lebrecht Music and Arts; **p81**: National Library of Medicine; **p85**: 2003 Topham Picturepoint/TopFoto; **p86**: The Mineralogical Record; **p87**: Universal History Archive/Getty Images; **p89**: Universal History Archive/Getty Images; **p91**: World History Archive/Ann Rona/Age Fotostock; **p97**: Hulton Archive/Getty Images; **p98**: The Gallery Collection/Corbis UK Ltd.; **p99**: SFL Travel/Alamy; **p100**: IAM/AKG-images; **p105**: Lebrecht Music and Arts Photo Library/Alamy; **p106**: Private Collection/Bridgeman Art Library; **p109**: Walker Art Gallery, National Museums Liverpool/Bridgeman Art Library; **p110**: Mary Evans Picture Library; **p118**: IMAGE ASSET MANAGEMEN/Age Fotostock; **p121**: Timewatch Images/Alamy; **p122**: Thom Atkinson/Gallery Stock; **p127**: Heritage Image Partnership Ltd /Alamy; **p129**: Private Collection;/Bridgeman Art Library; **p132**: Pictorial Press Ltd/Alamy; **p133**: 2013 Culture Club/Getty Images; **p135**: John Noott Galleries/Bridgeman Art Library; **p137**: Derek Mitchell/Alamy; **p138**: Westminster Assembly/Wikipedia Commons; **p141**: AA World Travel Library/Alamy; **p144**: Chronicle/Alamy; **p145**: Stefano Baldini/National Portrait Gallery, London, UK/Bridgeman Art Library; **p146**: Heritage Image Partnership Ltd /Alamy; **p149**: British Library Board/TopFoto; **p150**: liszt collection/Alamy; **p151**: Collection of the Earl of Pembroke, Wilton House, Wilts./Bridgeman Art Library; **p154**: (l) The Granger Collection/TopFoto, (r) Jansos/Alamy; **p156**: Universal History Archive/Getty Images; **p159**: WorldPhotos/Alamy; **p162**: Christopher Barnes/Alamy; **p163**: National Army Museum/Art Archive; **p165**: Hulton Archive/Getty Images; **p167**: Mary Evans Picture Library/Alamy; **p170**: (l) Ashmolean Museum, University of Oxford, UK/Bridgeman Art Library, (r) Mary Evans Picture Library; **p172**: Hulton Archive/Getty Images; **p173**: Timewatch Images/Alamy; **p176**: Archive Photos/Getty Images; **p184**: John Lilburne/Wikipedia Commons; **p186**: Universal History Archive/Getty Images; **p188**: Hulton Archive/Getty Images; **p193**: Hulton Archive/Getty Images; **p195**: DeAgostini/Getty Images; **p205**: TopFoto; **p209**: GL Archive/Alamy; **p211**: Nate D. Sanders Auctions; **p212**: Niday Picture Library/Alamy; **p214**: Stapleton Collection/Corbis UK Ltd.; **p215**: The Art Archive/Alamy

Page 48 artwork by Roger Wade-Walker; other artwork by OKS and OUP.

Artwork by OKS and OUP.

We are grateful to the authors and publishers for use of extracts from their titles and in particular for the following:

Barry Coward: LONGMAN ADVANCED HISTORY STUART ENGLAND 1603-1714 1st Ed., © 1997, Pearson Education Ltd., pp 64, 114. Reprinted by permission of Pearson Education Ltd. **Tristam Hunt**: The English Civil War At First Hand Copyright © Tristam Hunt 2002. Reproduced by permission of Tristam Hunt c/o Georgina Capel Associates Ltd, 29 Wardour Street, London W1D 6PS. **Andrew Marvell**: The Prose Works of Andrew Marvell: 1676-1678 Volume 2 Copyright © 2003 by Yale University Press. All rights reserved. Reproduced by permission. **John Stephen Morrill and Christopher W. Daniels**: Taken from Charles I (Cambridge Topics in History) from British History Online http://www.british-history.ac.uk/cal-state-papers/venice/vol19/pp9-24. Reproduced by permission. **John Morrill**: Revolt in the Provinces The People of England and the Tragedies of War, 1630-48 © John Morrill 1976, 1999. Routledge is an imprint of Taylor and Francis Books. Reproduced by permission.

We have made every effort to trace and contact all copyright holders before publication, but if notified of any errors or omissions, the publisher will be happy to rectify these at the earliest opportunity.
Brian Nugent: extract from An Creideamh published by Brian Nugent.

The publisher would like to thank the following people for offering their contribution in the development of this book: Sally Waller and Roy Whittle.

Links to third-party websites are provided by Oxford in good faith and for information only. Oxford disclaims any responsibility for the materials contained in any third-party website referenced in this work.

Contents

Introduction to features	v
AQA History specification overview	vi
Introduction to the Oxford AQA History series	viii
Timeline	x
Introduction to this book	xii

PART ONE: AS AND A LEVEL
THE ORIGINS OF THE ENGLISH CIVIL WAR, 1625–1642

SECTION 1
The emergence of conflict and the end of consensus, 1625–1629 — 1

1 The Legacy of James I — 1
- James I's management of religious issues and divisions — 2
- Relations between Crown and Parliament — 3
- Relations with foreign powers — 5
- Summary — 9

2 Monarchy and Divine Right — 10
- The character and aims of Charles I — 10
- The queen and the court — 12
- The king's advisers — 15
- Ideas of royal authority — 16
- Summary — 18

3 Challenges to the arbitrary government of Charles I — 19
- Reactions against financial policies — 19
- Reasons for and outcomes of conflict over the Church — 22
- Reactions against foreign policy and the role of Buckingham — 24
- Summary — 27

4 Parliamentary radicalism — 28
- Personalities and policies of Parliamentary opposition to the king — 28
- The Petition of Right — 31
- The Dissolution of Parliament and Charles I's commitment to Personal Rule — 32
- Summary — 35

SECTION 2
An experiment in Absolutism, 1629–1640 — 36

5 Charles I's Personal Rule — 36
- Charles I's chief ministers — 36
- Methods of government — 38
- Financial policies and reactions — 40
- Summary — 44

6 Religious issues — 45
- Laud and Arminianism — 46
- The growth of opposition from Puritans — 50
- Summary — 53

7 Political issues — 55
- The Role of Thomas Wentworth — 55
- Policies in England and Ireland — 56
- Reactions against the Crown — 60

- Demands for the recall of the English Parliament — 61
- Summary — 62

8 Radicalism, dissent and the approach of war — 63
- The spread of religious radicalism — 63
- The Scottish Covenant and the Bishops' War — 64
- The Second Bishops' War — 69
- Summary — 71

SECTION 3
The crisis of Parliament and the outbreak of the First Civil War, 1640–1642 — 72

9 The Political Nation, 1640 — 72
- The recall of Parliament — 72
- The strengths and weaknesses of Charles I — 74
- The strengths and divisions of Parliamentary opposition — 77
- Sources of division — 80
- Summary — 82

10 Pym and the development of Parliamentary radicalism — 83
- Pym's personality and aims — 83
- The Grand Remonstrance — 85
- The London Mob — 87
- Popular radicalism — 88
- Summary — 88

11 Conflicts between Crown and Parliament — 89
- Failure of negotiations between the king and the Long Parliament — 89
- The execution of Strafford and its political consequences — 91
- Summary — 94

12 The slide into war — 95
- The impact of events in Ireland — 95
- The failed arrest of the Five Members — 98
- Local grievances — 99
- The slide to war — 102
- Attempts to impose royal authority and the development of a Royalist Party — 102
- Military preparations for war — 104
- Summary — 105

PART TWO: A LEVEL
RADICALISM, REPUBLIC AND RESTORATION, 1642–1660
SECTION 4
War and radicalism, 1642–1646 — 106

13 The First Civil War: the Royalist cause — 106
- The outbreak and progression of the war — 107
- The early strengths of the Royalist cause — 107
- Decisive events in the early months of the First Civil War — 110
- How the king lost the advantage in the early months of the war — 111
- Failure of the swift, sharp blow — 113
- The consequences of Royalist failure — 114
- Summary — 115

Contents (continued)

14 The First Civil War: the Parliamentary course — 116
- The strengths and weaknesses of the Parliamentary forces — 116
- The Solemn League and Covenant — 120
- The emergence of the New Model Army — 122
- Summary — 125

15 The intensification of radicalism — 126
- Popular radicalism in London — 126
- Religious radicalism in the New Model Army — 128
- Pamphlets and propaganda — 131
- Summary — 134

16 The end of the First Civil War — 135
- Divisions among the Parliamentary leaders — 135
- Attempts at settlement — 136
- The capture of Charles I — 139
- Summary — 141

SECTION 5
The disintegration of the Political Nation, 1646–1649 — 142

17 Political and religious radicalism — 142
- The politicisation of the New Model Army — 142
- Lilburne and the Levellers — 146
- The Fifth Monarchists — 147
- Ranters and other populist groups — 148
- Summary — 149

18 Political and religious divisions — 150
- The attitude and actions of Charles I — 150
- Divisions within the opposition to the king — 151
- The failure of attempts to reach a settlement with the king — 156
- Summary — 157

19 The Second Civil War — 158
- Political causes of the Second Civil War — 158
- The Scottish invasion — 163
- The outcome of the Second Civil War — 164
- Summary — 164

20 The problem of Charles I — 165
- Divisions within the army and Parliament — 165
- The trial and execution of the king — 168
- Summary — 172

SECTION 6
Experiments in government and society 1648–1660 — 173

21 The Third Civil War — 173
- The attempted Royalist revival — 174
- Defeat and exile of Prince Charles — 180
- Summary — 183

22 Political radicalism — 184
- Failure of the Levellers and Diggers and the 'Godly Society' — 184
- Quakers, Baptists and other radical sects — 188
- The Rump Parliament as an experiment in radical republicanism — 191
- The Parliament of the Saints — 192
- Summary — 194

23 Oliver Cromwell and the Protectorate — 195
- Cromwell's personality and approach to government — 195
- The Major Generals — 196
- The limits of religious toleration — 199
- Cromwell's refusal of the Crown — 202
- The problem of the succession to Cromwell — 204
- Summary — 204

24 The monarchy restored — 205
- The political vacuum after the death of Cromwell — 205
- Negotiations for the return of the monarchy under Charles II — 210
- The legacy of the English Revolution by 1660 — 213
- Summary — 214

Conclusion — 215
Glossary — 219
Bibliography — 222
Index — 223

Introduction to features

The **Oxford AQA History** series has been developed by a team of expert history teachers and authors with examining experience. Written to match the new AQA specification, these new editions cover AS and A Level content together in each book.

How to use this book
The features in this book include:

TIMELINE
Key events are outlined at the beginning of the book to give you an overview of the chronology of this topic. Events are colour-coded so you can clearly see the categories of change.

LEARNING OBJECTIVES
At the beginning of each chapter, you will find a list of learning objectives linked to the requirements of the specification.

SOURCE   EXTRACT
Sources introduce you to material that is primary or contemporary to the period, and **Extracts** provide you with historical interpretations and the debate among historians on particular issues and developments. The accompanying activity questions support you in evaluating sources and extracts, analysing and assessing their value, and making judgements.

 PRACTICE QUESTION
Focused questions to help you practise your history skills for both AS and A Level, including evaluating sources and extracts, and essay writing.

STUDY TIP
Hints to highlight key parts of **Practice Questions** or **Activities**.

ACTIVITY
Various activity types to provide you with opportunities to demonstrate both the content and skills you are learning. Some activities are designed to aid revision or to prompt further discussion; others are to stretch and challenge both your AS and A Level studies.

CROSS-REFERENCE
Links to related content within the book to offer you more detail on the subject in question.

A CLOSER LOOK
An in-depth look at a theme, event or development to deepen your understanding, or information to put further context around the subject under discussion.

KEY CHRONOLOGY
A short list of dates identifying key events to help you understand underlying developments.

KEY PROFILE
Details of a key person to extend your understanding and awareness of the individuals that have helped shape the period in question.

KEY TERM
A term that you will need to understand. The terms appear in bold, and they are also defined in the glossary.

AQA History specification overview

AS exam

Part One content
The origins of the English Civil War, 1625–1642
1. The emergence of conflict and the end of consensus, 1625–1629
2. An experiment in Absolutism, 1629–1640
3. The crisis of Parliament and the outbreak of the First Civil War, 1640–1642

Part Two content
Radicalism, Republic and Restoration, 1642–1660
4. War and radicalism, 1642–1646
5. The disintegration of the Political Nation, 1646–1649
6. Experiments in government and society, 1648–1660

A Level exam

AS examination papers will cover content from Part One only (you will only need to know the content in the blue box). A Level examination papers will cover content from both Part One and Part Two.

The examination papers
The grade you receive at the end of your AQA AS History course is based entirely on your performance in two examination papers, covering Breadth (Paper 1) and Depth (Paper 2). For your AQA A Level History course, you will also have to complete an Historical Investigation (Non-examined assessment).

Paper 2 Depth study
This book covers the content of a Depth study (Paper 2). You are assessed on the study in depth of a period of major historical change or development, and associated primary sources or sources contemporary to the period.

Exam paper	Questions and marks	Assessment Objective (AO)*	Timing	Marks
AS Paper 2: Depth Study	**Section A: Evaluating primary sources** One compulsory question linked to two primary sources or sources contemporary to the period (25 marks) • The compulsory question will ask you: *'with reference to these sources and your understanding of the historical context, which of these sources is more valuable in explaining why…'* **Section B: Essay writing** One from a choice of two essay questions (25 marks) • The essay questions will contain a quotation advancing a judgement and will be followed by: *'explain why you agree or disagree with this view'*.	AO2 AO1	Written exam: 1 hour 30 minutes	50 marks (50% of AS)
A Level Paper 2: Depth Study	**Section A: Evaluating primary sources** One compulsory question linked to three primary sources or sources contemporary to the period. The sources will be of different types and views (30 marks) • The compulsory question will ask you: *'with reference to these sources and your understanding of the historical context, assess the value of these three sources to an historian studying…'* **Section B: Essay writing** Two from a choice of three essay questions (2 x 25 marks) • The essay questions require analysis and judgement, and <u>could</u> include: *'How successful…'* or *'To what extent…'* or *'How far…'* or a quotation offering a judgement followed by *'Assess the validity of this view'*.	AO2 AO1	Written exam: 2 hours 30 minutes	80 marks (40% of A Level)

*AQA History examinations will test your ability to:

AO1: Demonstrate, organise and communicate **knowledge and understanding** to analyse and evaluate the key features related to the periods studied, **making substantiated judgements and exploring concepts**, as relevant, of cause, consequence, change, continuity, similarity, difference and significance.

AO2: **Analyse and evaluate** appropriate source material, primary and/or contemporary to the period, within the historical context.

AO3: **Analyse and evaluate**, in relation to the historical context, different ways in which aspects of the past have been interpreted.

Visit www.aqa.org.uk to help you prepare for your examinations. The website includes specimen examination papers and mark schemes.

Introduction to the *Oxford AQA History* series

Depth studies

The exploration of a short but significant historical period provides an opportunity to develop an 'in-depth' historical awareness. This book will help you to acquire a detailed knowledge of an exciting period of historical change, enabling you to become familiar with the personalities and ideas which shaped and dominated the time. In-depth study, as presented here, allows you to develop the enthusiasm that comes from knowing something really well.

However, 'depth' is not just about knowledge. Understanding history requires the piecing together of many different strands or themes, and depth studies demand an awareness of the interrelationship of a variety of perspectives, such as the political, economic, social and religious – as well as the influence of individuals and ideas within a relatively short period of time. Through an 'in-depth' study, a strong awareness of complex historical processes is developed, permitting deeper analysis, greater perception and well-informed judgement.

Whilst this book is therefore designed to impart a full and lively awareness of a significant period in history, far more is on offer from the pages that follow. With the help of the text and activities in this book, you will be encouraged to think historically, question developments in the past and undertake 'in-depth' analysis. You will develop your conceptual understanding and build up key historical skills that will increase your curiosity and prepare you, not only for A Level History examinations, but for any future studies.

Key Term, **Key Chronology** and **Key Profile** help you to consolidate historical knowledge about dates, events, people and places

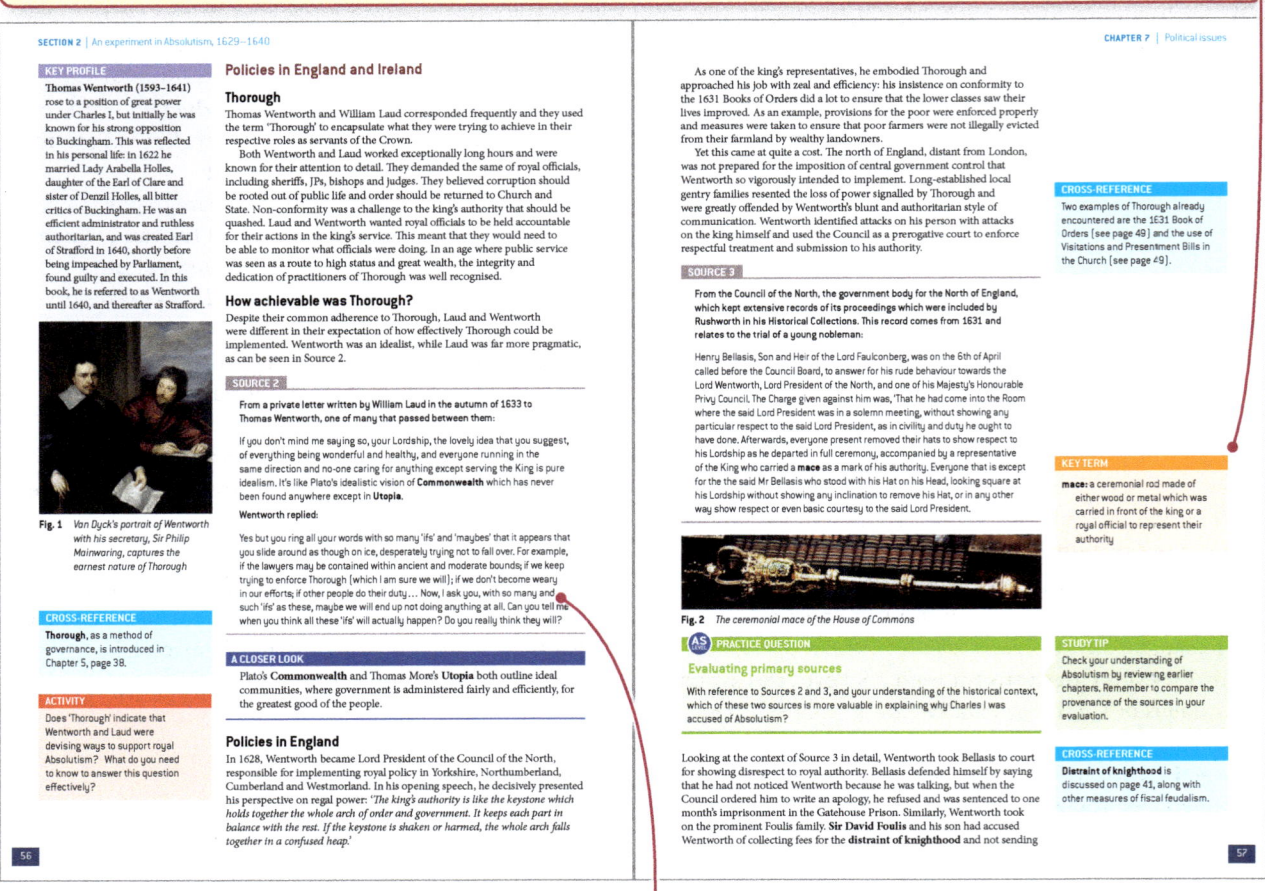

▲ The English Revolution 1625–1660

Source features support you with assessing the value of primary materials

viii

This book also incorporates primary source material in the **Source** features. Primary sources are the building blocks of history, and you will be encouraged to reflect on their value to historians in trying to recreate the past. The accompanying questions are designed to develop your own historical skills, whilst suggestions for **Activities** will help you to engage with the past in a lively and stimulating manner. Throughout the book, you are encouraged to think about the material you are studying and to research further, in order to appreciate the ways in which historians seek to understand and interpret past events.

The chapters which follow are laid out according to the content of the AQA specification in six sections. Obviously, a secure chronological awareness and understanding of each section of content will be the first step in appreciating the historical period covered in this book. However, you are also encouraged to make links and comparisons between aspects of the period studied, and the activities will help you to relate to the key focus of your study and the key concepts that apply to it. Through intelligent use of this book, a deep and rewarding appreciation of an important period of history and the many influences within it will emerge.

Developing your study skills

You will need to be equipped with a paper file or electronic means of storing notes. Organised notes help to produce organised essays and sensible filing provides for efficient use of time. This book uses **Cross-References** to indicate where material in one chapter has relevance to that in another. By employing the same technique, you should find it easier to make the final leap towards piecing together your material to produce a holistic historical picture. The individual, group and research activities in this book are intended to guide you towards making selective and relevant notes with a specific purpose. Copying out sections of the book is to be discouraged, but recording material with a particular theme or question in mind will considerably aid your understanding.

There are plenty of examples of examination-style 'depth' **Practice Questions** for both AS Level, in Part One, and A Level in Parts One and Two of this book. There are also **Study Tips** to encourage you to think about historical perspectives, individuals, groups, ideas and ideology. You should also create your own timelines, charts and diagrams, for example to illustrate causation and consequence, analyse the interrelationship of the differing perspectives, consider concepts and identify historical processes.

It is particularly important for you to have your own opinions and to be able to make informed judgements about the material you have studied. Some of the activities in this book encourage pair discussion or class debate, and you should make the most of such opportunities to voice and refine your own ideas. The beauty of history is that there is rarely a right or wrong answer, so this supplementary oral work should enable you to share your own opinions.

Writing and planning your essays

At both AS and A Level, you will be required to write essays and, although A Level questions are likely to be more complex, the basic qualities of good essay writing remain the same:

- **read the question carefully** to identify the key words and dates
- **plan out a logical and organised answer** with a clear judgement or view (several views if there are a number of issues to consider). Your essay should advance this judgement in the introduction, while also acknowledging alternative views and clarifying terms of reference, including the time span
- use the opening sentences of your paragraphs as stepping stones to take an argument forward, which allows you to **develop an evolving and balanced argument** throughout the essay and also makes for good style
- **support your comment or analysis** with precise detail; using dates, where appropriate, helps logical organisation
- **write a conclusion** which matches the view of the introduction and flows naturally from what has gone before.

Whilst these suggestions will help you develop a good style, essays should never be too rigid or mechanical.

This book will have fulfilled its purposes if it produces, as intended, students who think for themselves!

Sally Waller
Series Editor

Timeline

The colours represent different types of events, legislation and changes as follows:

- **Blue:** Ireland
- **Yellow:** Scotland
- **Red:** Political events
- **Black:** Military events
- **Green:** Religious events

1625
- Accession of King Charles I
- First Parliament
- Cadiz expedition

1626
- Second Parliament
- York House Conference

1627
- Five Knights' Case
- La Rochelle raids

1628
- Third Parliament
- Assassination of Buckingham
- Three Resolutions

1633
- Laud becomes Archbishop of Canterbury
- Reissue of *Book of Sports*
- Wentworth becomes Lord Deputy of Ireland

1634
- Thirty-Nine Articles introduced into Ireland
- Prynne's ears lopped

1635
- Ship Money extended to inland counties

1636
- Bishop Juxon becomes Lord Treasurer

1641
- The execution of Strafford
- Rebellion in Ireland
- The Grand Remonstrance

1642
- Failed arrest of the Five Members
- The Nineteen Propositions
- The outbreak of the First Civil War

1643
- The Oxford Treaty negotiations
- Royalist agreement with the Irish Confederates
- Solemn League and Covenant

1644
- Formation of the Committee of Both Kingdoms
- The Battle of Marston Moor

1649
- The trial and execution of Charles I
- The formation of the Council of State
- Cromwell's invasion of Ireland

1650
- The Treaty of Breda
- The Toleration Act
- The Battle of Dunbar

1651
- The Scots' invasion of England
- The Battle of Worcester

1652
- Petition of the army officers

1657
- Humble Petition and Advice

1658
- Dissolution of the Second Protectorate Parliament
- Death of Oliver Cromwell
- Installation of Richard Cromwell

1659
- Third Protectorate Parliament
- Reinstatement of the Rump
- Resignation of Richard Cromwell

1660
- Recall of the Long Parliament
- Convention Parliament
- Restoration of King Charles II

Timeline

1629
- Dissolution of Third Parliament
- Beginning of Personal Rule
- Peace with France

1630
- Treaty of Madrid
- Birth of future Charles II

1631
- New Book of Orders
- 'Popish Soap' monopoly granted

1632
- Publication of *Histriomastix*
- Death of Sir John Eliot

1637
- Prayer book riots in Scotland
- Ship Money trial of John Hampden
- Trial and punishment of Puritan pamphleteers

1638
- Scottish National Covenant
- Fenland riots in Norfolk

1639
- Recall of Wentworth
- Oath of Allegiance in York
- First Bishops' War

1640
- The Short Parliament
- End of the Bishops' Wars
- The Long Parliament

1645
- The *Directory of Worship* issued
- The formation of the New Model Army
- The Battle of Naseby

1646
- The surrender of the king to the Scots
- The Newcastle Propositions
- The Westminster Assembly issues its Confession of Faith

1647
- Cornet Joyce seizes the king
- The Putney Debates
- The Engagement with the Scots

1648
- The Vote of No Addresses
- The Siege of Colchester
- Pride's Purge

1653
- Dissolution of the Rump
- The Nominated Assembly
- Oliver Cromwell becomes Lord Protector

1654
- Union of England and Scotland
- The Western Design
- First Protectorate Parliament

1655
- Penruddock's Uprising
- Rule of the Major Generals
- Jews allowed back into England

1656
- Second Protectorate Parliament
- Trial of James Nayler

Introduction to this book

Fig. 1 *This woodcut image reflects the sense of disorder that gripped England in the 1640s*

A CLOSER LOOK

In the 1530s, Henry VIII declared that the Church in England should be independent of the Roman Catholic Church and that he, not the Pope, should be at its lead.

This book will take you straight to some of the most turbulent decades of British history, characterised by some as the 'English Revolution' and by others as the 'Great Rebellion'. This was a time of unparalleled debate about the nature of authority, the role of the people in government and the duties of a king. It laid the foundations for the development of the modern world, germinated a seed that would also lead to American Independence and the French Revolution, and is still of immense relevance in our world today, where freedom of speech, religious tolerance, democracy and the rule of law are values for which people fight and die.

Our story begins in 1625, when a cultured and rather shy young man, Charles I, succeeded to the thrones of England, Ireland and Scotland. His father, King James I, had been a relatively successful monarch. James had inherited a large debt (which he passed on to his son) but had generally managed to make ends meet. He had coped well with the vigorous, often acrimonious religious debate that was an ongoing legacy of the turmoil generated by Henry VIII's break with Rome, and he had escaped assassination by a group of Catholics on 5 November 1605. In foreign policy, he had tried hard to keep his kingdoms clear of the religious, dynastic and territorial war known as the 'Thirty Years' War', which broke out on the continent in 1618. He passed on a throne that was secure, and an ideology of kingship, known as the 'Divine Right of Kings', which he had not invented but which he had developed into a powerful justification for monarchical authority. In some respects, this ideology had contributed to a rocky relationship with Parliament but overall he had managed to maintain sufficient harmony with the House of Commons and the House of Lords to keep the wheels of government moving. Only in personal affairs was his reputation really tarnished, as he had indulged a preference for virile young men in his court, and had become infatuated with a dashing courtier whom he promoted to the high rank of Duke of Buckingham.

Charles I lacked experience and did not possess his father's political skills. It was unfortunate that the King of England was still supposed to be able to afford to govern the country using his own income, which had been more or less achievable for medieval monarchs but had become totally unrealistic for early modern monarchs from Henry VII onwards. Continuously running short of money, he needed Parliament to cooperate with him because they could vote him extra tax revenue. However, the House of Commons, made up of men who were elected as the people's representatives, had become stocked with lawyers, many of whom had strong religious views that – taken together – led them to challenge the king at every step, insisting that he address their complaints (known as 'grievances') before they would agree to release money to him. What is more, they began to go beyond simply arguing about specific issues and started to develop ideas about how government should be structured – ideas that posed a direct threat to the Divine Right ideology that Charles had enthusiastically adopted. Within five years of inheriting the throne, Charles I had reached such an impasse with Parliament that he decided to try to rule without it for 11 years, becoming, in the words of his critics, an 'arbitrary' ruler, accountable to no-one, and using ruthless Crown servants such as 'Black Tom Tyrant', Thomas Wentworth, to enforce his will.

He struggled and ultimately failed to keep rising religious tension under control. On the continent it appeared that Catholicism and Protestantism were locked into a battle to the death: surely, feared many English Protestants, it could be only a matter of time before the war crossed the English Channel. Many also wondered if Charles was secretly trying to emulate the great Catholic monarchs of France and Spain. He had a Catholic wife and the flourishing cultural scene of his court looked worryingly similar to that of her brother, King Louis XIII of France. Ruling without Parliament also smacked of Absolutism, where the monarch had absolute power, did not need to consult his subjects and was accountable only to God: both Louis XIII and King Philip IV of Spain were absolute monarchs. To some, evidence that Charles posed a terrible threat to the moral and spiritual safety of England was stacking up.

It was not just the Catholic–Protestant fault line that appeared dangerous. For a long time there had been a sub-set of Protestants who believed that the Church of England, which had been created by Henry VIII and established into a complete state Church by Elizabeth I, was not godly enough. These were the Puritans and they thought that good Protestants should be very prayerful, wear sober clothes and spend Sundays thinking about God and little else. A very different Protestant sub-set, the Arminians, had begun to grow in influence during the reign of James. They were Protestant, but some of their beliefs looked, to the Puritans at least, perilously close to Catholicism. Charles did not like the earnest and often argumentative Puritans. Temperamentally he much preferred Arminian practice and he promoted one of its exponents, William Laud, to the highest Church rank of Archbishop of Canterbury. By 1640, tensions were coming to boiling point.

A period known traditionally as the English Civil War followed, but in fact war broke out in all three of Charles's kingdoms in the decade between 1639 and 1649. Catastrophic mishandling of the Church in Scotland triggered a war in which the king tried to use his English kingdom – and money granted by a recalled Parliament – to subdue his Scottish realm. Then, rebellion broke out in Ireland. Finally, with Thomas Wentworth executed on Parliament's orders, and William Laud in prison, the king's authority in England began to collapse under intense pressure from the House of Commons and the wider population, especially in London. That war should break out within England in 1642 was not inevitable and there were many attempts to avert it, but, fatefully, Charles reached a point at which he felt he could no longer allow the authority of the Crown to be challenged, and he raised an army to defeat his opponents in Parliament. The First Civil War would rage for four years.

In the mid-1640s the story took another intense turn. Suddenly, with the outbreak of rebellion against the king, radical ideas that had previously been held under the surface by censorship and harsh punishments erupted into everyday life. Politically radical ideas emerged from groups such as the Levellers, who thought that all people were equal and so government should be democratic, and Diggers, who thought that property should be shared out and communal land dug for the benefit of the community. With Charles preoccupied with military matters and fearful for the safety of his family, and Laud first imprisoned and then executed, religious radicalism also surged. Presbyterians wanted to abolish the structure of Archbishops and Bishops in the Anglican Church; Quakers wanted to get rid of professional priests and worship God in communities of equals, responsive directly to the Spirit of God; Ranters believed that there was no such thing as a moral code and became notorious for their lewd behaviour. These are just a foretaste of the radical religious beliefs and sects that began to characterise the English religious landscape at this time.

This emerging radicalism meant that it became increasingly difficult to reach a settlement with the king that would bring England's turmoil to a close. Ideas about what would constitute a good relationship between monarch and subjects were rapidly changing as first one and then another proposal was made to the king, only for him to reject each in turn. While two civil wars and ongoing instability had gripped the country for nearly seven years, suddenly, in the autumn of 1648 a chain of events rapidly resulted in the trial and execution of the king for treason against his own country. There can be few more dramatic days in the history of our nation as that cold January day in 1649 when Charles stepped out of his own palace onto a hastily constructed scaffold and quietly uttered, 'I am the martyr of the people', before being beheaded.

What followed was also sensational. First a war, as the Scots supported Charles's son and unsuccessfully invaded England to help him take back his throne. Then, another war, this time an invasion of Ireland by Parliamentary forces under the command of Oliver Cromwell, and, along the way, numerous different attempts to find a governmental structure that did not rest on a monarch but could bring, in Cromwell's words, 'healing and settling' to a troubled nation. Among these innovative experiments in government were a 'Nominated Assembly', a selected group of wise men who would rule the country in a godly way; a Parliament that consisted only of a House of Commons; a period of military government, with England divided into 11 units, each governed by a Major General; and then an attempt to create what we would now consider to be a presidential-style system, with Oliver Cromwell at its head as 'Lord Protector'. Along the way, theories of government and individual rights were explored that changed the political landscape for ever.

At the heart of the matter was the relationship between the individual and people in authority: this question was played out in both political and religious spheres. In politics, the execution of the king had demonstrated that Parliament had held higher authority in the land than the monarch. This was incredibly revolutionary and it happened in a rush of events that was only gradually disentangled afterwards. Was Parliament able to take the king to court because God had unseated him? Or was it actually because individual citizens together make the nation, and they had together first given and then withdrawn their consent to be governed by a monarch? Was it this particular king who was at fault, or was the institution itself faulty? Had Parliament unlawfully stolen the king's authority? All these questions were explored either explicitly in debate or implicitly as events unfolded.

In religion, a parallel situation emerged. The question here was to do with the role of Church leadership in deciding on the faith of individuals. With so many expressions of religion suddenly appearing in daily life, questions of religious freedom and liberty of speech came to the fore. If God could speak directly to individuals, what then was the role of the priest? More to the point, what was the role of a state Church? If religious freedom was desirable, did that mean that any expression – however immoral – should be tolerated? Where should the balance of morality and freedom lie?

It was undoubtedly because these issues were so weighty that none of the governmental experiments undertaken in the 1650s were able to gain enough consensus in the country at large to provide stable government. It looked as though events had turned full-circle when, in 1658 Cromwell was asked (much to his dismay) to become England's new king.

Perhaps it was fortunate for Cromwell's peace of mind that he died shortly after being offered the throne, but it did not help bring peace to England. While his son Richard followed in his footsteps as the next Protector, the army, feeling excluded from power, toppled him, and it looked as though the country would fall back into war. Among a populace once again filled with fear of the devastation that war brings, calls emerged to offer the throne back to the Stuart dynasty so that, in 1660, Charles Stuart came into his inheritance as King Charles II in an event described as the Restoration.

This book will encourage you to grapple at first hand with a wide range of contemporary sources from a period characterised by a rush to print. With pamphlets, declarations, letters, diaries, and records of speeches, this was an age filled with words, and you will find in them concepts and emotions that resonate readily with our present times. You will be able to judge whether you think Charles I was incompetent or a victim of circumstance, and decide for yourself whether you think these years constituted an English Revolution or a Great Rebellion. You will undoubtedly find that your understanding of our world today is deepened by the events of these tumultuous years.

Part One: The origins of the English Civil War, 1625–1642

1 The emergence of conflict and the end of consensus, 1625–1629

1 The Legacy of James I

SOURCE 1

A bitter Sir John Harington, a court poet and wit under Elizabeth I but ignored by James I, describes a **masque** commissioned by the king on the occasion of the visit of his brother-in-law King Christian IV of Denmark in 1606.

One day there was a great feast and an after-dinner entertainment was planned. It was supposed to represent Solomon, his Temple and the coming of the Queen of Sheba. I say 'supposed' because while the entertainment went ahead, most of its participants went backwards or even fell over. 'Hope' tried to speak but was so drunk she had to give up. 'Charity' also gave up and joined 'Hope' and 'Faith' who were sick and spewing in the lower hall. Then 'Peace' entered and tried to approach the King but she was in a foul temper with her attendants, and despite her name, most shockingly made war with her olive branch on the heads of anyone who got in her way.

A CLOSER LOOK

A **masque** was a highly stylised courtly play. The masque in Source 1 was designed to show the great Christian virtues, Faith, Hope, Charity and Peace, commenting favourably on the Biblical meeting of King Solomon and the Queen of Sheba. It was supposed to have impressed the visiting Danish king in order to encourage him to build an informal alliance of Protestant monarchies within Europe.

James I was an experienced monarch of 37 years standing when he succeeded Elizabeth I to the English throne in 1603. Yet he displayed little of her regal poise and dignity. His court was vulgar and brash and he offended contemporary sensibilities by his pursuit of virile young men. He was mocked by Harington and other contemporaries, and perhaps the kindest epithet applied to him was that of Henry IV of France who dubbed him the 'wisest fool in Christendom'.

LEARNING OBJECTIVES

In this chapter you will learn about:

- James I's management of religious issues and divisions
- relations between Crown and Parliament
- relations with foreign powers.

KEY CHRONOLOGY

James I's legacy

1603	Accession of James I
1604–1610	First Parliament
1605	Gunpowder Plot
1606	Oath of Allegiance
1614	Second 'Addled' Parliament
1618	Outbreak of the Thirty Years' War
1621	Third Parliament
1624	Fourth Parliament
1625	Death of James I

ACTIVITY

Evaluating primary sources

Considering the provenance of Source 1 (who wrote it, when and why, for instance), how useful is it to an historian who wants to find out about the mood of James's court?

KEY PROFILE

King James VI and I (1566–1625) was the only son of Mary, Queen of Scots. As James VI (of Scotland) and I (of England), he was a flexible thinker and a generally successful ruler. He was a small and thin man but he had a firm self-confidence and saw himself as a monarch who could rise above religious, political and foreign divisions.

Fig. 1   King James I

SECTION 1 | The emergence of conflict and the end of consensus, 1625–1629

> **KEY TERM**
>
> **Scottish Kirk:** the Church in Scotland; 'kirk' is a Gaelic word
>
> **settlement:** in this sense, the resolution (or an attempt to find a resolution) of an issue of governance
>
> **Presbyterian:** a Church structure that does not have bishops
>
> **episcopal:** a Church structure that includes bishops

> **ACTIVITY**
>
> There were several significant branches of Protestantism in the seventeenth century, including Puritanism and Presbyterianism. Their different theologies and emphases are discussed on page xx. Use these terms to start your own glossary of key words, and add to your glossary as you work through this book.

James I's management of religious issues and divisions

The Church of England under James I

On Elizabeth's death, those English churchmen known as 'Puritans', who thought that Elizabeth had not taken religion seriously enough, used the opportunity to draft a list of reforms for James to consider. As the list contained over a thousand signatures, it became known as the 'Millenary Petition'. It was reasonable to think that James would look favourably on their requests because the **Scottish Kirk** was much stricter in its version of Protestantism than Elizabeth's moderate Church of England: it was hoped that he would share their enthusiasm and make a **settlement** that would establish their 'purer' form of Protestantism in England.

James rapidly convened a conference to meet in January 1604 at Hampton Court to discuss the Petition, which culminated in a debate between four puritan spokesmen and two bishops. Any hopes of a Scottish-style **Presbyterian** restructure were dashed: 'No Bishop! No King!' was James's firm response to a proposal that the Church should lose its **episcopal** structure. James encouraged argument from all sides but affirmed his independence as the Supreme Governor, above divisions and debates.

> **A CLOSER LOOK**
>
> The **Scottish Kirk** was Presbyterian in its structure. In actual fact, instead of Scottish Presbyterianism triumphing in England after James I's accession, 'No Bishop! No King!' would soon translate into the Kirk. By 1605, 10 out of 13 Scottish provinces had new bishops, and by 1606, a Scottish Parliament recognised that James was formally head of the Scottish Church: one kingdom, one religious governor.

The Gunpowder Plot

James also had to deal with the Catholics. In keeping with his personal approach to religion, James initially promised that he would not 'persecute any that will be quiet and give an outward obedience to the law'. For a very short while it appeared that England might become an unprecedented beacon for religious toleration. However, he had misjudged the English mood: public hostility to such a policy was intense and James was outmanoeuvred by his first Parliament, which forced him to reverse his tolerant approach by withholding money from him.

It was this reversal that triggered the Gunpowder Plot, an attempt by Catholic terrorists to kill the king and his government in 1605 and replace him with a Catholic monarch.

The discovery of the Gunpowder Plot had several consequences:
- **recusancy** fines increased
- Catholics were removed from government posts
- Catholics had to affirm a new Oath of Allegiance in 1606
- public fear of Catholicism grew stronger.

Interestingly, even though the Pope opposed the new Oath of Allegiance, James was able to use it to identify the moderate majority of Catholics who retained their faith while demonstrating their political loyalty, so that the Catholic question became, for a time, 'quiet'.

> **KEY TERM**
>
> **recusancy:** not attending your local parish church for services, which carried a financial penalty

Fig. 2 *The Catholic terrorist cell responsible for the Gunpowder Plot consisted of a number of English noblemen*

Defining the boundaries of the English Church

Until the outbreak of the Thirty Years' War in 1618, James was relatively successful in managing to keep the Church of England broad enough to hold moderates and Puritans in a relationship that generally worked well. In 1604, James's first appointment to the key role of Archbishop of Canterbury was the anti-Puritan Richard Bancroft. Bancroft favoured a strict approach to religious conformity, yet removed only nine Puritan clergy for non-conformity, while many more were protected by sympathetic bishops. His next appointment was **George Abbot**, who sat firmly on the Puritan side but who, in 1618, worked with James on a **Book of Sports**, which outraged Puritans by encouraging recreational activities for Sundays, which they condemned as unholy pastimes.

Similarly, James required outward conformity to the 1604 revision of the official Book of Common Prayer, which established the official liturgy (the wording of church services) in Ireland and England, but showed considerable flexibility within the Scottish Church. In Scotland, he introduced it much more slowly, revising it to include more Scottish elements, and ultimately stopping short of pushing it through Parliament in 1619 because of the resistance it was stirring up. He dearly hoped to unite England and Scotland fully under one government and one religion. This proved too difficult to achieve in his own reign, but helped to add further political and religious problems to Charles's inheritance in 1625.

> **KEY PROFILE**
>
> **George Abbot (1562–1633)**
> was Archbishop of Canterbury from 1611 to 1633. He had won favour from James I by supporting the union of the English and Scottish Churches, but he was not universally popular because he was a Puritan, which annoyed moderate Protestants. He was strongly anti-Catholic.

> **CROSS-REFERENCE**
>
> The **Book of Sports** became controversial again in 1633 which is discussed on page 50.

> **ACTIVITY**
>
> With a partner, condense James's religious strategy into 20 words. Discuss the possible strengths and pitfalls of his approach.

Relations between Crown and Parliament

The English Parliament

> **A CLOSER LOOK**
>
> #### Parliament c1603
>
> Parliament was an important part of the governmental system in England. While it was very different from our modern Parliament, it was responsible for raising and approving legislation and had to consent to certain forms of taxation which the king needed in order to raise money. The king was in charge of calling Parliament, which would trigger a general election, and dissolving it, which would bring it to a close. He could do either of these without consulting anyone else. If he wanted to temporarily suspend

Parliament, he would prorogue it. This meant that the MPs did not have to be re-elected but they would not meet until he re-called them to Westminster.

Contrary to his expectations, James inherited a very different style of Parliament in England to the one he had mastered in Scotland. The English Parliament did not function as an extension of his personal court. James found it to be argumentative, with a growing sense of its institutional independence and increasingly, manned by Members trained in law and keen to haggle over constitutional issues. He expected to be its head. Instead he found that it was a body beginning to strain towards an authority, and an existence, of its own.

> **SOURCE 2**
>
> Adapted from James's views in the House of Commons in 1614, as reported by the Spanish Ambassador. James said:
>
> The House of Commons is a body without a head. At their meetings, nothing is heard but cries, shouts and confusion. I am surprised that my ancestors should have ever permitted such an institution to come into existence. I am a stranger and found it here when I arrived, so that I am obliged to put up with what I cannot get rid of.

Table 1 *Differences between the Scottish and English Parliaments*

Scottish Parliament	English Parliament
Unicameral (one chamber)	Bicameral (two chambers: the House of Lords and the House of Commons)
King could use appointments and patronage to pack Parliament with loyal supporters, including Officers of State and bishops.	King very limited in his ability to place supporters into the Commons and had to rely on allies among the Lords (who were closer to him in rank) to try to slow or stop Commons initiatives.
King could intervene in the selection of elected members.	King very limited in ability to influence local elections – seats controlled by gentry families.
Most debate and negotiation took place in committees before coming to Parliament.	Most debate and negotiation took place within Parliament.
Sessions short.	Sessions prolonged.
Not the only legislative body in Scotland.	The only legislative body in England.

> **ACTIVITY**
>
> Write a briefing note for James to read before calling his first English Parliament, identifying the two most significant differences from its Scottish equivalent and suggesting tactics that he could use to manage its proceedings.

Financial problems

The relationship between king and Parliament was strained because James faced multiple financial problems:
- Elizabeth died with a significant debt that transferred to James.
- His household was considerably bigger than hers, with a wife and three children to provide for.
- Wars were expensive, and England was still at war with Spain when he succeeded to the throne.

- He needed to display generous **patronage** to his new subjects, particularly the nobles, to bond them to his court.
- France and Spain had glamorous, extravagant courts and James needed to maintain English prestige with an equally vibrant environment.
- He could raise a certain amount of money by **prerogative** means but needed to call Parliament for large sums. Parliament was reluctant to grant him money without getting something in return, which was known as the 'redress of grievances', whereby he would put right things they were unhappy about.
- Scotland was relatively poor and James seriously over-estimated how much money the English Crown had in contrast.
- James was extravagantly generous to a select number of courtiers and most notably to his early favourite, Robert Carr.

In 1610, one of James's officials, Robert Cecil, Earl of Salisbury, devised a fiscal measure, called the 'Great Contract', which was sensible and necessary, and would have undoubtedly revolutionised the relationship between Crown and Parliament for succeeding generations.

The Contract addressed the fact that it was an English monarch's responsibility to raise the money necessary for the safe governance, defence and expansion of the kingdom. He had a wide variety of **prerogative fiscal measures** to gather this money together, many of which originated from distant centuries and old feudal traditions. Without a professional civil service to help him, he had to rely on the honesty of his servants, often courtiers, to act as collectors. Salisbury was an expert in these prerogative rights, and had done his best to leverage them to the maximum advantage for both Elizabeth and James so that only occasionally would Parliament expect to be called on to top up the monarch's finances.

The Great Contract was intended to clear James's debts and set the Crown on a viable, professional financial footing, with an annual budget of £200,000 guaranteed by Parliament. In return, the Crown would lose many of its prerogative fiscal powers. However, the Great Contract failed for a number of reasons:

- Salisbury was in the House of Lords and could not manage the Commons as well.
- James annoyed and alarmed Parliament with long lectures about his royal authority and prerogative rights.
- Parliament worried that they would lose power if James had enough money without needing to recall them.

Parliaments had always attempted to leverage the monarch's need for money against the discussion of grievances: the fiscal chaos and increasing financial pressures surrounding King James and the failure of a sensible solution empowered Parliament to tie the grant of supply ever more closely to the redress of grievances. In financial need, James called a new Parliament in 1614, but swiftly dissolved it as it was too fractious and unyielding and gained the nickname the 'Addled Parliament' because it achieved so little. James governed without Parliament from 1614 to 1621.

Relations with foreign powers

James brought a fresh perspective on foreign affairs to England when he arrived in 1603. Scotland, a less assertive and ambitious player on the European stage, had managed to maintain reasonably good and open relationships with the great European powers throughout the sixteenth century, neither under threat of, nor threatening war with Spain or France. James consequently saw a role for himself as 'Rex Pacificus', the bringer of peace through diplomacy.

KEY TERM

patronage: the support of a wealthy or influential person for someone of lesser wealth or status; a patron might commission (and pay for) works of art, or help someone find a good job; the king acted as a patron when he gave out titles such as 'Lord' and 'Duke'

prerogative: the exclusive rights of a sovereign, which are subject to no legal restriction

A CLOSER LOOK

Prerogative fiscal measures

Until 1604, customs revenue (a tax on imports and exports) was collected in a haphazard way by Crown officials who routinely under-calculated what was owed. Salisbury replaced this system by outsourcing collection to a syndicate of merchants – 'farmers', who guaranteed a regular sum to the Crown and were financially rewarded for vigorously imposing customs dues. By bringing 'modern' efficiency to a feudal revenue stream, this 'Great Farm of the Customs' made Parliament anxious that the king would be able to streamline all his feudal dues and thus reduce his dependence on Parliament's grant of supply.

ACTIVITY

Only a few years after James moved his court to England, the Scottish Crown finances became healthy. Draw up a table to help you sort the causes of James's financial problems in England into personal and structural categories. What else do you need to know in order to be able to apportion responsibility for the Crown's weak fiscal position?

SECTION 1 | The emergence of conflict and the end of consensus, 1625–1629

A CLOSER LOOK

Succession crisis

A succession crisis occurs when there is no accepted heir to a throne. Both the Julich-Cleves Succession Crisis of 1609 and the Bohemian crisis of 1618 had a significant impact on wider European affairs. Each event saw Catholics and Protestants jockeying to get their candidates into position and thus tip the power balance in Europe to their own side.

Table 2 *James's efforts to maintain a balanced foreign policy*

	Moved closer to…
1604 Treaty of London, ended war with Spain	Spain (Catholic, anti-France)
1609 Alliance with France during Julich-Cleves Succession Crisis	France (Catholic, anti-Spain)
1612 Alliance with German Protestant Union	German Union (Protestant, anti-Catholic, anti-France, anti-Spain, anti-Hapsburg)
1613 Marriage of daughter Elizabeth to Elector Frederick V of the Palatinate (in Germany)	German Union (Protestant)
1613–18 and 1622–23, Pursuit of Spanish Princess for son, Prince Charles	Spain (Catholic)

Fig. 3 *Map showing the alliances and religious majorities that made the Thirty Years' War so complex*

A CLOSER LOOK

Marriage was still used as a powerful dynastic tool in the seventeenth century and the young Prince Charles was a high-status marital prospect, requiring an equally high-status wife. By marrying him into the top of the Spanish Royal Family, James would create a permanent diplomatic path into the Spanish court and hopefully bring greater stability to Anglo-Spanish relations, which had been very rocky in the later years of the sixteenth century.

The Thirty Years' War

In 1618, tensions in Europe that had been at simmering point for many years broke out into what became known as the Thirty Years' War, a conflict in which Catholic and Protestant power blocs fought for territorial dominance over central Europe. Despite James's preference for staying out of European squabbles, it was the actions of his Protestant son-in-law Frederick, a German prince, that sparked the war. Frederick accepted the disputed throne of Bohemia, offered to him by nobles rebelling against the Catholic King of Bohemia, who belonged to the Hapsburg dynasty which also ruled in Spain. Spanish and Bavarian troops retaliated by occupying the Palatinate, Frederick's home territory in Germany. This forced the royal family into exile, and war raged across Europe for the next 30 years.

Religious fractures appear

Archbishop George Abbot preached a sermon that recommended a decisive intervention by James, with military force in support of Frederick and in defence of Protestantism. James, on the other hand, had been strongly against Frederick's actions because he knew that it would destabilise the European situation and he saw the crisis as one primarily of political power rather than in terms of religion. As a result, his preferred response was to seek a political solution, pressing Spain to accept his mediation and maintaining his pursuit of a Spanish match for his son. If this failed, he hoped to join with the French, as, Catholic but anti-Hapsburg, he believed that they could sue for peace together. However, his policy made many English people worry that he was flirting with a return to Catholicism.

Parliament's radical involvement in foreign affairs

James recalled Parliament in 1621 in order to request money for undefined future action in the war, causing an already restive Commons to try to explain his foreign policy. Misdirected by inept signals from a small faction which centred on the **Duke of Buckingham**, they sent a petition to James in which they asked him to visibly support the Protestant cause and recommended that the Spanish match be abandoned and replaced with a Protestant marriage for Prince Charles. This was radical, because precedent did not allow Parliament to comment on foreign policy, and their intervention triggered a deeper constitutional conflict between the Crown's prerogative and Parliament's privileges. James was furious and lectured his Parliament in a lengthy statement about Parliamentary privileges and the king's authority.

SOURCE 3

The king responded to the petition by the House of Commons in a lengthy reply which was read out to the Commons and noted in the Commons Journal for December 1621.

In the Body of your Petition, you make many trespasses upon our Prerogative Royal, and meddle with things far above your reach, all the while protesting that you intend no such thing.

Treaties, wars and marriages are unfit things to be handled in Parliament, except your King should require it of you. For who can have wisdom to judge of things of that nature, but such as are daily acquainted with the particulars of Treaties, and of the variable and fixed connexion of affairs of State?

You wrote of your ancient and undoubted Right and Inheritance; but we remind you that your Privileges were derived from the grace and permission of our Ancestors and Us. Yet we are pleased to give you our Royal assurance, that as long as you contain your selves within the limits of your duty, we will be as careful to maintain and preserve your lawful Liberties and Privileges, while we also preserve our own Royal Prerogative. Do not attempt to reduce our Prerogative or we will certainly remove your privileges. But of this, we hope, there shall never be cause given.

Parliament, galvanised into action and capably staffed by proactive lawyers such as **Sir Edward Coke**, drew up a lengthy document, a 'Protestation'. This is one of the key **constitutional** documents that defined Parliament's understanding of its relationship with the Crown. James was so furious

ACTIVITY

Why was religion such a crucial issue for James to resolve? Create a mind-map that shows the different issues that had a religious connection during his reign. Branches could include domestic politics, national security and foreign affairs, as well as Church settlement.

KEY PROFILE

George Villiers, Duke of Buckingham (1592–1628), an athletic young gentleman from Lincolnshire, captivated King James when they met in 1614. As James descended into premature senility, Villiers came to completely dominate him. He swiftly began to control the court and amassed wealth and titles, culminating in becoming 1st Duke of Buckingham.

ACTIVITY

Evaluating primary sources

Read Source 4. James believed that the Protestation represented a direct challenge to his royal authority. Make a copy of the source and highlight its key words. Why was it so offensive to the king?

CROSS-REFERENCE

A Key Profile of **Sir Edward Coke** is on page 29.

KEY TERM

constitutional: refers to matters relating to a constitution, the rules that state how a country should be governed and who exercises power

with it that he tore the Protestation out of the Commons' Journal and dissolved Parliament.

> **STUDY TIP**
>
> Although in an A Level exam you will be asked to assess the value of three sources, this one asks you to assess just two. These two sources show the different perspectives of the king and the House of Commons on the crucial balance between Parliamentary privilege and Crown prerogative. You could make a copy of both sources, place them side by side, and then analyse them to look at areas of similarity and difference. Ensure you can make specific points. It will also be useful to think about provenance. What was the specific historical context that influenced James's perspective? Who were the driving forces within Parliament's opposition? Use this deeper context to add breadth to your answer.

 PRACTICE QUESTION

Evaluating primary sources

With reference to Sources 2 and 3, and your understanding of the historical context, assess the value of these two sources to an historian studying the relationship between James I and the House of Commons.

> **SOURCE 4**
>
> Adapted from the 'Protestation', which was written by MPs and approved by the House of Commons in 1621, and filed in the Commons' Journal:
>
> The Commons, now assembled in Parliament, make this Protestation. It is the ancient and undoubted birthright and inheritance of the subjects of England that Parliament holds certain freedoms, legal immunities, privileges and the right to legislate. Parliament is also responsible for conducting debates and giving advice about weighty and urgent affairs concerning the king, state, defence of the realm and the Church of England, as well as for the making and maintenance of laws and the redress of mistakes and grievances such as happen daily within this realm. In the handling of all these matters, every member of the House has a right long-established to exercise freedom of speech so that they can put forward ideas for consideration and bring such affairs to conclusion through careful thought and open discussion.

> **KEY PROFILE**
>
> **Charles I (1600–49)** Charles, the second son of James I and Queen Anne of Denmark, was born in Scotland. He became heir to the throne when his older brother Prince Henry died in 1612.
>
> **Cardinal Richelieu (1585–1642)** was a Catholic bishop who rose to political power after being appointed as chaplain to the new French queen in 1615. He became chief minister to Louis XIII thanks to his remarkable political skill and cunning. Richelieu's policies, to attack the Huguenots (Protestants), promote an absolutist French monarchy, reform the army and navy, and improve France's status in Europe, were all broadly successful.

A chaotic end

The last years of James's reign saw 'Rex Pacificus' come to nothing. His health deteriorated significantly, to the point that he lost the ability to guide his government effectively, allowing Buckingham to achieve near-total domination of public affairs. A misguided dash to Spain in 1623 by Buckingham and **Prince Charles** ended in their personal humiliation and the collapse of all hopes of a Spanish match. Buckingham next drove forward a pro-French, anti-Spanish policy, including a new marriage plan with another Catholic princess – this time, Princess Henrietta Maria of France. Within the terms of the marriage treaty that was signed in November 1624, Henrietta Maria – along with her servants and children by Charles – would be allowed to practise Catholicism in an open church, and Catholics in England and Scotland would be granted toleration. King Louis XIII's chief adviser, **Cardinal Richelieu**, offered James little in return and, specifically, no immediate commitment to a joint campaign against the Habsburgs.

James died in 1625, bequeathing Charles a very mixed legacy.

CHAPTER 1 | The Legacy of James I

ACTIVITY

Summary

In this chapter we have considered a number of aspects of **Jacobean** rule. You need to assess the significance of these years.

1. Start by making comprehensive notes. You can organise notes in different ways but a suggestion would be to use the headings *religion*, *finances*, *Parliament*, *personalities* and *foreign affairs* to provide yourself with a useful structure. Once written, read back through your notes and make sure you have identified specific dates and facts. It might help you to highlight these. Ensure you have incorporated key words into your notes so that you use effective historical terminology in extended writing.
2. Make sure you understand what you have written. If necessary, carry out further research to extend your contextual understanding. For example, look at biographies of the key personalities mentioned in the text.
3. Generate enquiry questions that will enable you to sort and deploy your factual knowledge. For example: 'to what extent was James a successful monarch?' To explore this enquiry, you could draw up a table like the one below:

Success	Failure
Examples	Examples

Once you have sorted your thoughts out in this way, form a judgement.

KEY TERM

Jacobean: a term used to describe James's rule

PRACTICE QUESTION (AS LEVEL)

'James I left his son Charles I extensive problems.'
Explain why you agree or disagree with this view.

STUDY TIP

Questions of this type expect you to explore an argument and a counter-argument. It is therefore important that you consider arguments for and against the statement. When planning your response, make sure you include solid evidence for each side of the debate. In this instance you need to identify the problems James bequeathed to his son and evaluate how significant they were. Then, you need to reflect on how James had attempted to resolve the issues so that you can consider whether these problems were still extensive or not.

2 Monarchy and Divine Right

LEARNING OBJECTIVES

In this chapter you will learn about:

- the character and aims of Charles I
- the queen and the court
- the king's advisers
- ideas of royal authority.

KEY CHRONOLOGY

1625	27 March	Death of James I and accession of Charles I
	13 June	Marriage of Charles I to Henrietta Maria
1626		Dismissal of Henrietta Maria's French courtiers
1628		Death of Buckingham
1629		First child (stillborn) of Charles and Henrietta Maria

CROSS-REFERENCE

Rubens' ceiling at Whitehall is described in more detail on page 16.

ACTIVITY

Rubens' ceiling at Whitehall is one of the most famous and impressive paintings of this time. What does this tell you about Charles I, who commissioned it?

KEY TERM

stutter: a speech disorder in which sounds, syllables, or words are repeated or prolonged, disrupting the normal flow of speech; Charles I would have found it a confidence-denting hindrance in his public role, because people tended to think that a physical problem reflected a mental problem in the seventeenth century

Fig. 1 *The impressive ceiling paintings of the Dutch painter Peter Paul Rubens were commissioned by Charles I in 1629 and installed in the Palace of Whitehall in 1636*

The character and aims of Charles I

In March 1625, King James died and the newly engaged 25-year-old Prince Charles became Charles I, King of England, Scotland, France and Ireland, Defender of the Faith. He was the fourth of seven children of King James but by the time he was 12, only he and his older sister Elizabeth were still alive. His parents left him behind in Scotland when James became King of England, because his health was so poor they feared he might not survive the journey to London. Even as an adult he found it impossible to shake off his childhood Scottish accent, which made him feel rather ill at ease among the polished Englishman of the royal court. He was very short and he had a **stutter**, which meant that he disliked the long, rambling conversations with courtiers and politicians which had been so much a part of James's effective governing style.

On his accession, Charles looked unlikely to be an energetic and bold monarch in the mould of Henry VIII or Elizabeth I, and he was not comfortable in a boisterous, argumentative court like his father had been. Charles I, in contrast to Elizabeth I or his father, did not stand out as being especially intellectual, but he was a sensitive, cultured young man. He had a passion for the visual arts and assembled a magnificent collection of artwork with an artistic judgement that is still recognised by art experts today.

A CLOSER LOOK

Many of the masterpieces Charles commissioned or bought have been on public display continuously from the seventeenth century to the present day. You can view them on the Royal Collection Trust's website: www.royalcollection.org.uk.

Because of his ongoing physical frailty, shyness and stammer, Charles undoubtedly preferred the company of a few, trusted individuals. His reign was characterised by the warm and loving relationships he had with his wife, **Henrietta Maria**, and their seven children, and the immense loyalty he showed to his trusted companions, most notably the **Duke of Buckingham**, **Archbishop William Laud**, and **Thomas Wentworth**, Earl of Strafford.

Unfortunately, perhaps, for such a reserved man as Charles, Stuart England was experiencing huge growth in the use of the printed word. The printing press had dramatically changed people's access to information, just as the invention of the internet has changed modern society. By the 1620s, there were pamphlets being printed on every subject, as well as books called 'Almanacs', which combined a diary with astrological information, local news, advertisements and religious texts. Shakespeare had blazed a trail in drama that was developed further by other playwrights, and other significant writers were at work, such as Francis Bacon, the man who turned essay-writing into a literary genre. In such a noisy environment, people thought that Charles's reticence indicated that he was cold and aloof, neither keen to talk nor (and this would prove to be a catastrophic perception) keen to listen.

The aims of Charles I

In 1625, except for the serious disquiet caused by Buckingham's continued pre-eminence, no-one would have seriously predicted the total breakdown between king and Parliament that would ensue by 1629, because there was nothing to indicate that Charles had any substantially different ideas about what a monarch should do from those before him.

Table 1 *Summary of Charles's aims*

Aim	Details
Maintain law and order within his kingdoms	Ensure effective operation of justice system.
	Support healthy management of the localities by local gentry who are in the best position to prevent local problems (e.g. famine) from triggering civil disorder.
Defend his kingdoms from external threats	Conduct effective foreign policy.
	Maintain adequate military strength in support of foreign policy.
	Promote his kingdoms as strong and efficient through careful use of public image.
Provide effective religious leadership	Maintain order in the Church of England, Scottish Kirk and the Irish Church.
	Defend true faith from heresy.
Ensure financial/economic wellbeing	Carefully manage expenditure.
	Efficiently collect income, including taxation.

New ideas of the role of Parliamentarians had developed in the reign of James I. The cost of maintaining defence had also increased, and religious differences were an ongoing problem. However, the bond between monarch and country had always proven to be strong enough to cope. In fact, the 1625 succession had been the smoothest the country had enjoyed since 1509.

With hindsight, it is easy to see how traits in Charles's personality – such as his insecurity and poor communication skills – made him particularly ill-equipped to cope with the social, religious and political turbulence unfolding across England, Scotland and Ireland. What is more, while James I had developed a powerful theory of **Divine Right** but often moderated it in practice, Charles I rigidly adhered to his perceived status as the ruler chosen by God.

CROSS-REFERENCE

Profiles for these key characters can be found as follows: **Duke of Buckingham** (page 7); **William Laud** (page 37) and **Thomas Wentworth** (page 56). **Henrietta Maria** is introduced on page 12.

ACTIVITY

Which of the aims in the table do you think Charles would find most difficult to achieve and why?

CROSS-REFERENCE

For more on the **Divine Right of Kings**, see page 17.

ACTIVITY

Who was most to blame for the English Revolution? One of the key debates in this period is whether a more politically aware monarch could have avoided the breakdown that led to the English Civil War. Did Charles I's personality drive events, or was he simply by chance the king at an unstoppable turning point in his nation's history? As you study this period, try to decide what you think about the role of individual men and women in history.

SECTION 1 | The emergence of conflict and the end of consensus, 1625–1629

KEY PROFILE

Henrietta Maria (1609–69) was the youngest daughter of Henry IV of France and the sister of his successor, Louis XIII. She was raised to enjoy the luxurious trappings of courtly life and was a committed Catholic, continuing to practise the traditions of faith despite significant criticism from the Protestant majority in England.

CROSS-REFERENCE

The **assassination of Buckingham** is covered in Chapter 4.

ACTIVITY

This chapter includes a significant amount of specialist historical vocabulary. As you read, keep a note of words that you do not yet know. Make sure that you are confident that you can use them appropriately.

ACTIVITY

Extension

The life of Wat Montagu was a colourful one. Do some research online and create your own colourful Key Profile feature of him.

KEY TERM

regent: a person who leads a state because the monarch is too young or incapable of ruling

The queen and the court

Henrietta Maria was 15 when she married Charles. As was customary at the time for royal princesses, the marriage was contracted for complex political and religious reasons. The French King Louis XIII hoped to use the match to strengthen an anti-Spanish alliance with England while at the same time preventing English sponsorship of French Protestant rebels. Henrietta Maria's formidable mother, Marie de Medici, was a fervent Catholic who hoped that her daughter would protect English Catholics and potentially even draw England back to Rome. On top of these competing ambitions, when Henrietta Maria arrived, speaking barely a word of English, the Duke of Buckingham provoked a trivial quarrel that resulted in an estrangement between king and queen (and the dismissal of her French courtiers) that lasted until **Buckingham's assassination** in 1628.

Fig. 2 In this contemporary painting of Henrietta Maria and Charles I the queen holds a laurel wreath in one hand, to commemorate her father, who was a renowned soldier, and an olive branch in the other, to represent her father-in-law James's love of peace

Growing political influence

With Buckingham dead, Charles and Henrietta Maria rapidly drew closer, which meant that she could finally begin to fulfil her principle wifely duty, producing children. This catalysed the transformation of her status and power. The arrival of a high-ranking French ambassador, the Marquis de Chateauneuf, also helped her to consolidate her position because he was a shrewd political player sent with the express aim of training her to develop political influence. He rapidly gathered a faction around her that included the Earl of Holland and Wat Montagu, and which provided a pro-French balance to the pro-Spanish faction in the court that was assembling around William Laud, **Richard Weston** and **Francis Cottington**. Marie de Medici had been one of the most powerful people in France for decades, ultimately acting as **regent** for the young Louis XIII and she orchestrated the turnaround in Henrietta Maria's position in the late 1620s and early 1630s which itself hinted at the increasingly powerful role that her daughter would play in the events of the following years.

KEY PROFILE

Francis Cottington, 1st Baron Cottington (1579–1652) rose to prominence under James I who valued him for his expertise about Spanish matters. He became secretary to Prince Charles in 1622 but his opposition to Buckingham kept him out of high office until 1629 when he replaced Weston as Chancellor of the Exchequer. He became master of the Court of Wards in 1635 where he vigorously worked to raise revenue for the king. When war broke out, he joined the king at Oxford where he took on the role of Lord Treasurer but he went into exile in Spain in 1646, openly practising Catholicism and dying there in 1653.

Richard Weston, 1st Earl of Portland (1577–1635) was a lawyer from an Essex family. He rose rapidly in royal service, becoming Chancellor of the Exchequer in 1621 and Lord Treasurer in 1628. By 1630 he had become one of the king's most valuable and influential ministers and was created 1st Earl of Portland in 1633. He was a Catholic, sympathetic to Spain and keen to avoid war, partly to reduce the likelihood that the king would need to recall Parliament. He was nonetheless a moderate man and it was after his death that Charles's difficulties began to deepen.

A CLOSER LOOK

Catholicism around the queen

Ambitious Catholic gentry who sought preferment in the 1620s and 1630s generally had to forswear (or at the very least hide) their Catholicism. To a significant extent, visible expressions of Catholicism thus rested among the women who surrounded the queen. For many Puritan onlookers, especially those of lower status, it was easy to hold the queen responsible for keeping 'Romish devilry' alive in England.

Protection for Catholics

While freedom of worship for Henrietta Maria and her attendants was written into the marriage treaty, her Catholicism posed a major obstacle to her acceptance by the country-at-large, resulting in significant slights such as the queen's exclusion from a formal coronation. However, for the one-fifth of the English gentry who had remained Catholic, the presence of a committed fellow-believer at the heart of the royal court brought about practical protection that filtered down to the lower orders. Demonstrating her growing political skill, the queen prevailed on the Protestant Earl of Holland to discreetly secure the freedom of a number of arrested priests in the early 1630s. She increasingly gathered noble Catholic women around her, prompting her godfather, Pope Urban VIII, to praise the 'amazons… who do day and night employ their utmost endeavours for the dignity of the holy see [the papacy]' (Griffey, 1909).

The development of court culture and courtly entertainment

In parallel with the growth of Henrietta Maria's political power and religious influence, so her ability to create a unique court culture also rose. Masques had been a feature of the royal court for many years but the queen was an exuberant participant during the early part of her reign, causing consternation to some of the onlookers.

A CLOSER LOOK

Henrietta Maria's growing influence was to reach its height later than the scope of this chapter; in the 1630s.

SOURCE 1

From a letter from Katherine Gorges, an English noblewoman, to her brother-in-law, Sir Hugh Symth, describing her experience of a court masque that she watched in 1625:

I was dining with my old friend and kinswoman Lady Denbeigh at Langford. She made me promise that I would go to see the Queen and the Masque in two Sundays' time which I did. I saw the Masque acted by the Queen's servants – all French – but all the English disliked it, for it was neither masque nor play but a French traditional entertainment, and the French ladies near Her Majesty were old women, rather like Nurse Ball, only Nurse is rather better-looking. Whether it was the sight of the Masque or the old French ladies I do not know but I came home the next day so sick that I stayed in bed for 3 or 4 days afterwards and am so wearied with the Court that I know I do not want to be a Courtier ever again.

ACTIVITY

Evaluating primary sources

Analyse Source 1. It reveals a lot about Katherine Gorges' attitude at the beginning of the reign of Charles. What do you think are commonly held perceptions and what do you think might be unique to Katherine Gorges? Discuss with a partner.

SECTION 1 | The emergence of conflict and the end of consensus, 1625–1629

> **KEY TERM**
>
> **Arminianism:** a denomination of Protestantism whose members did not want Puritan reformation within the Church of England;
>
> **profane:** something that is not spiritual (secular); a person or action that is disrespectful of spiritual things
>
> **Hail Mary:** a well-known prayer in the Catholic church; in Latin, it starts 'Ave, Maria' and praises Mary, the mother of Jesus, and asks for her blessing

For Puritans, objections to the queen's love of masques were much more deep seated because they felt that acting was ungodly and the participation of women particularly immoral.

A CLOSER LOOK

Their castigation was to intensify in the early 1630s when the queen performed in *The Shepherds' Paradise*, probably the first time a royal woman had acted in an English play. This prompted a fervent Puritan writer called William Prynne to attack 'women actors' (clearly meaning the queen) as 'notorious whores'.

References to the Virgin Mary

Henrietta Maria's patronage of the arts caused a flowering of works that celebrated her personality and associated her with the Virgin Mary. The famous Stuart poet **Ben Jonson**, on the occasion of one of her pregnancies, wrote in this way about her.

> **KEY PROFILE**
>
> **Ben Jonson (1572–1637)** was a playwright who once killed an actor in a duel, for which he was imprisoned. While in prison, he became a Catholic. His best-known plays are *Volpone*, *The Alchemist* and *Bartholomew Fair*. James I employed him to write and direct court masques, in collaboration with the architect Inigo Jones.

SOURCE 2

From a poem by Ben Jonson, celebrating the impending delivery of the future Charles II:

Epigram to the Queen, Then Lying In (1630)

Hail Mary, full of grace, it once was said,
And by an angel, to the blessed'st maid,
The mother of our Lord: why may not I
(Without **profaneness**) yet, a poet, cry
Hail Mary, full of honours, to my queen,
The mother of our prince? When was there seen
(Except the joy that the first Mary brought,
Whereby the safety of mankind was wrought)
So general a gladness to an isle,
To make the hearts of a whole nation smile,
As in this prince? Let it be lawful, so
To compare small with great, as still we owe
Glory to God. Then, hail to Mary! Spring
Of so much safety to the realm, and king.

A CLOSER LOOK

Ben Jonson compares the royal birth of Prince Charles to the birth of Jesus; while Jesus brought safety to mankind, the infant Charles brings safety to England.

Many court paintings from the period use Catholic iconography, such as the pearls and roses associated with the Virgin, to adorn the queen's image. It is no surprise that the atmosphere in the queen's court caused increased religious tension.

ACTIVITY

Extension

Ben Jonson's poetry is often quite straightforward and can be very humorous. His titles help put poems into their historical context, with dates and information about why he wrote them. Look up and read poems 62–68 in the *Underwood* series and think about what they can add to your understanding of this period.

> **STUDY TIP**
>
> To answer this question effectively, start by closely analysing the two sources. Make sure you understand what they mean and then draw careful inferences about what they tell you about the impact of Henrietta Maria. Next, broaden out your thinking to highlight key points about the royal court. What do you know of the royal court that is reflected in the two sources? What do the sources not tell you about the queen's impact that you have gathered from other information. Finally, conclude: what is the value of these sources?

AS LEVEL PRACTICE QUESTION

Evaluating primary sources

With reference to Sources 1 and 2, and your understanding of the historical context, which of these two sources is more valuable in explaining the impact of Henrietta Maria on the royal court of Charles I?

The king's advisers

The royal court was at the heart of Tudor and Stuart government and at the centre of the court was the inner sanctum of private rooms and personal space in which the king lived, ate, slept and consulted with his closest friends and advisers. Gaining access to this privileged world was a prize aimed at by everyone of ambition because it would bring them as close as possible to real power. The way to gain access was typically through proximity to the court, either attending every day in the hope of catching the king's ear, or by being connected to a patron who was already in place. Although such a fluid system could be frustrating, arbitrary and rather unfair, it had worked effectively throughout the Tudor period and for the first half of the reign of James because it was 'equally unfair': patrons rose and fell and clever politicking meant that people of merit and wit could find themselves elevated rapidly.

Buckingham and the inner sanctum

The trajectory of Buckingham typifies the way in which access to the person of the king was a short-cut to power. His physical attributes, charm and fluid sexuality meant that he had been able to dominate King James without having to work steadily up a more recognisable career ladder. However, by the time Charles succeeded his father, Buckingham's influence had nearly destroyed the functionality of the 'inner sanctum' because he had effectively replaced the king as the font of patronage and power and was distributing royal favour exclusively among his own faction. The court that Charles inherited was notoriously immoral, corrupted by drunkenness and sexual immorality.

The Caroline court

It was into this world that the reserved and dignified Charles stepped in 1625. His personal temperament was swiftly reflected as the court rapidly reformed and became much more moral and orderly. Buckingham initially continued to dominate patronage and, while ambitious men were unrelenting in their quest for preferment, ominously, Charles instructed the gentry to spend less time in London and more time fulfilling their duties in their regions. One member of the gentry, William Palmer, was fined £1000 in **Star Chamber** in 1632 for remaining in London without royal permission. What is more, Charles's desire for physical forms of order and decency was also a factor in cutting off access to his royal person.

> **CROSS-REFERENCE**
> Charles's main advisers after Buckingham's death are covered in Chapter 5, pages 36–37.

> **KEY TERM**
> **Caroline:** a term used to describe the period when Charles I was King of England

> **CROSS-REFERENCE**
> **Star Chamber** is introduced on page 38

SOURCE 3

A report from the Venetian Ambassador to the chief minister and ruling council of Venice about Charles I's court, April 1625.

The king has transferred himself and his household to the royal dwelling of Whitehall. His Majesty has announced his grief at the loss of his father, but he does not neglect his functions as ruler, and especially his attendance at church. He shows signs of being temperate, moderate and of exchanging all the prodigality of the past for order and profit.

Everyone observes the duke, and there are various opinions about him. The king, however, favours him completely, and while he was ill, frequently visited him in his own apartments, staying a long while and showing great confidence.

The king observes a rule of great decorum. The nobles do not enter his apartments in confusion as heretofore, but each rank has its appointed place. The king has also drawn up rules for himself, dividing the day from his very early rising, for prayers, exercises, audiences, business, eating and sleeping. It is said that he will set apart a day for public audience, and he does not wish anyone to be introduced to him unless sent for.

SECTION 1 | The emergence of conflict and the end of consensus, 1625–1629

ACTIVITY

Extension

Courtiers at the time of Charles's accession to the throne were very interested to know what Buckingham's place in the new king's court would be. Make a list of concerns or questions that a courtier might have about Charles's intentions. Try to develop your ideas to include key words and information from the previous chapter as well.

CROSS-REFERENCE

Look back to Fig. 1 in this chapter for a photo of Rubens' ceiling painting at Whitehall..

KEY TERM

apotheosis: 'to make divine', i.e. to elevate someone to the rank of a God; Rubens' work depicts James being carried towards God on the wings of a huge eagle and represents the close alliance between his royal and God's divine authority

ACTIVITY

Extension

Few things bring history to life more than seeing historical artefacts with your own eyes. Search online for heritage venues and museums where you could encounter Stuart cultural artefacts, and plan to visit one or two over the duration of this course. The websites of English Heritage, Historic Royal Palaces and the National Gallery are good places to start looking.

An unforeseen consequence of Charles's drive to bring order and decency to his court was therefore that it isolated him from those men who expected to become his natural advisers, and whose advice he would have found useful. More profoundly, even after Buckingham was assassinated, Charles failed to revert to the functionality of his father's earlier court and instead continued to prioritise order over access.

Ideas of royal authority

Demonstrations of Royal Authority

Charles was very attuned to the way that the visual arts and architecture could convey his power and authority. He made significant use of Hampton Court Palace, the impressive Tudor residence indelibly associated with the might of Henry VIII, and he invested heavily in adding to the Palace's already fine stock of paintings, furniture and tapestries with more works, not always new but often antique, of established provenance. Charles was especially keen to trace the English monarchy back to the glorious days of the Tudor monarchs, particularly Henry VIII and Elizabeth I. To help project images of power and might, he made great use of his Surveyor-General, Inigo Jones, who designed the beautiful Queen's House at Greenwich for Charles's mother Anne but completed it for Henrietta Maria, and who went on to design many other stunning buildings that captured serene grace and hinted at the might of ancient Rome, including the Banqueting House at Whitehall and the Queen's Chapel in St James's Palace.

At Whitehall, his London palace which had been extensively remodelled by Inigo Jones, he invested in a wonderful ceiling by Peter Paul Rubens which was completed in 1636. It consists of two enormous canvasses across which are painted 'The Union of the Crowns', 'The **Apotheosis** of James I' and 'The Peaceful Reign of James I'.

Fig. 3 *Hampton Court Palace was built by Cardinal Wolsey but commandeered by Henry VIII; its size and beauty demonstrated that the English Crown was rich and equally as stylish and powerful as any of its continental rivals*

The Divine Right of Kings

Charles's commission to Rubens for 'The Apotheosis of James I' reveals the depth of his convictions about royal authority and specifically the extent to which he interpreted his father's strongly held belief in the Divine Right of Kings. This was essentially the idea that the monarch was chosen by God and therefore to challenge the authority of the king was to challenge God himself.

The development of the theory of Divine Right

For centuries, Christians had believed that God chose who would be king, which is why the crucial part of the English coronation service involved a special blessing being made over the new king by the country's most senior churchman, the Archbishop of Canterbury. The Archbishop acted on behalf of the Pope, who was the leader of the Christian world and God's closest representative on earth. This service demonstrated that the Church was able to pass God's authority onto the king, giving him a Divine Right to govern. The Pope, as the head of the Church, could also 'unmake' a monarch if he identified that the king was contravening God's laws. Henry VIII's break with Rome changed this traditional doctrine because he made himself Supreme Head of the Church, no longer answerable to the Pope. Thereafter, both sacred (Church) and temporal (kingly) power resided in the one monarch, who had authority to act as God's delegated representative across all public and private spheres. Although theoretically the king was still subject to God's law, in practice there was no-one whose authority exceeded his own. Of course, it takes a long time for ideas to develop when a sudden change has occurred and although Henry practised Divine Right, the development of a theory of Divine Right was slower and took place over the century following the break with Rome. While James I was a particularly fervent proponent of Divine Right, even writing a lengthy book about it, by the seventeenth century, the idea of Divine Right was widely held. Charles built on James's theories and turned Divine Right into a new public genre of **art and architecture**.

Opposition to Divine Right

Parliament	Catholics	Puritans
Some members of the House of Lords and more in the House of Commons resisted such a view of monarchical power as it seemed to sweep all before it, removing Parliament's independent authority and subjecting Parliament to the royal will rather than on the will of the people.	Refused to accept that the Pope's authority could be displaced. This is why allegiance was such a complex issue for them, because they continued to believe that the Pope was a higher authority than the king.	Extreme Puritans believed that the king only had earthly power and should therefore not be allowed to appoint bishops and other spiritual leaders.

Fig. 4 *Opponents of Divine Right*

Charles's endorsement of Divine Right

All three 'opponents' at different times exerted intense pressure onto the Stuart monarchs, and the response of both James and Charles was to intensify their affirmations of Divine Right. Thus James hectored and

---

> **ACTIVITY**
>
> Look back at Fig. 1 at the start of this chapter. What can you see that is related to the Divine Right of Kings. Why do you think that Charles chose these themes for such prominent paintings?

> **CROSS-REFERENCE**
>
> The opposition of extreme Puritans to Divine Right explains James I's outburst 'No Bishop! No King!' because he worried that some Puritans wanted to dismantle a Church settlement with the king at the top. He knew that this would also fundamentally weaken the monarchy as a whole. See Chapter 6, page 50, for more details.

> **A CLOSER LOOK**
>
> ### Art and architecture
>
> It was only natural that a man with such a love of art and architecture as Charles should use it to demonstrate his power and authority. He employed architect Inigo Jones, painters Peter Paul Rubens and Anthony van Dyck, and other artists to create a distinctive Caroline genre. The stunning white buildings reflected purity and glory and the beautiful paintings celebrated royal dignity and honour. The court masques of the later 1630s frequently represented chaos being turned into harmony by the faithful reign of the King and Queen.

SECTION 1 | The emergence of conflict and the end of consensus, 1625–1629

lectured Parliament at great length, scolding them for their impertinent assaults on his authority. In contrast, Charles was more subtle but more inflexible. He turned the powers he possessed into tools to reinforce his royal authority and the more strident the opposition became, the more strongly he responded.

Catastrophically however, some people saw his ongoing endorsement of Divine Right as a sign that he wanted to become an absolute monarch. Absolute monarchy, where the king answered to no-one, not even a Parliament, was becoming increasingly established in Europe, particularly in the courts of France and Spain. While there is little to indicate that Charles was aiming to become an **absolute ruler** in the model of his brother-in-law, Louis XIII, his actions, and those of his wife, alarmed an increasingly anxious nation.

A CLOSER LOOK

French Absolutism

King Louis XIII, the brother of Charles's wife, was an absolute monarch. The French government was organised so that he no longer needed to call the French Parliament for money and did not have to listen to their recommendations about advisers and legislation. Louis XIII was in charge of finance, foreign affairs and domestic policy and was answerable to no-one.

ACTIVITY

Explain to your partner what historians mean by 'absolute monarchy' without using the words 'absolute' or 'monarch'!

ACTIVITY

Summary

Create a mind-map on Absolutism using these four headings as your starting point: *Charles's Character, The Queen's Court, Royal Advisers, and Divine Right*.
1. Identify key aspects that might cause an English person to fear that Charles was aiming to replicate the absolutist monarchies of France and Spain. Highlight these and add specific details, dates and facts around each one.
2. Discuss with a partner: 'Why might the theory of Divine Right have alarmed people in early Stuart England?'

STUDY TIP

You could draw up a table in which you identify similarities and differences between the two courts. When you have a simple list, think about how you can explain similarities and differences. Try to go beyond personality and think about structural changes and continuities.

 PRACTICE QUESTION

'The court of King Charles was very different from that of this father.'
Explain why you agree or disagree with this view.

Challenges to the arbitrary government of Charles I

KEY CHRONOLOGY		
1625	June	Charles I's First Parliament
	Sept	Cadiz expedition
	Sept	Treaty of Southampton between England and the Dutch Republic
1626	Feb	Charles I's Second Parliament
	Feb	York House Conference
	May	Parliament's protestation against Buckingham
1627	Oct	First expedition to La Rochelle
	Nov	Five Knights' Case
1627–29		Anglo-French War

LEARNING OBJECTIVES

In this chapter you will learn about:

- reactions and opposition to the king's financial policies
- the reasons for and outcomes of conflict over the Church
- reactions against foreign policy and the role of Buckingham.

SOURCE 1

From Charles I's speech to the House of Commons on 28 March 1626. A number of MPs were calling for the **impeachment** of the Duke of Buckingham and had criticised his foreign policy.

Now that you have all things according to your wishes and that I am so far engaged that you think there is no retreat from the war against France, now you begin to set the dice and make your own game. But I pray that you are not deceived. It is not a parliamentary way, nor is it a way to deal with a king. Remember that parliaments are altogether in my power for their calling, sitting and dissolution. Therefore, as I find the fruits of them good or evil, they are to continue or not to be. Remember that if instead of mending your errors, by delay you persist in them, you make them greater and irreconcilable.

KEY TERM

impeachment: refers to an accusation against someone in public office, claiming that they have acted unlawfully, even treacherously, in their conduct while in that office

ACTIVITY

1. How do you think an MP's opinion might have differed from Charles's view of what was a 'parliamentary way'?
2. What errors do you think Charles believed Parliament has committed?

The first four years of Charles's reign were characterised by intense disagreements between king and Parliament which centred around issues relating to the extent to which they should collaborate. Charles tended to emphasise his Divine Right and authority, wanting as little to do with Parliament as possible. Unsurprisingly, Parliament felt that this showed he wanted to establish 'arbitrary' government, which means that his will alone was executed. Conversely, Parliament emphasised its long tradition as the representative of the rights of the subjects and attempted to restrict the king's powers. Equally unsurprisingly, Charles felt that Parliament was being arrogant and innovative, demanding powers to which it was not entitled.

Reactions against financial policies

Tonnage and poundage, 1625

High on Charles's agenda in 1625 was an anti-Spanish foreign policy which put him under a lot of financial pressure because it is very expensive to equip and maintain military forces overseas. He needed about £1 million so he called Parliament, expecting that it would grant him special one-off payments known as 'subsidies' and also confirm his right to collect tonnage and poundage.

19

Tonnage and poundage was:
- a tax on imports and exports
- since 1547, used to support the navy because of their role in patrolling the English seas and ensuring that trading ships could cross the waters unimpeded
- calculated per 'ton' of wine and 'pound' of other produce
- awarded by Parliament
- normally confirmed just once, at the beginning of a new reign, allowing the monarch to collect it for the duration of the reign.

The Commons expressed its mistrust of Charles's foreign policy (particularly because they disliked the influence that Buckingham had in shaping it) by only granting him two subsidies (worth around £140,000), and one year's right to collect tonnage and poundage. This money was insufficient to give Charles freedom to conduct a foreign policy of his choice.

Tonnage and poundage was politically very sensitive. One of the key reasons why the Commons was so cautious in supplying Charles with money was because Buckingham was closely directing him and the Duke had shown himself to be not just politically over-dominant but also militarily incompetent. Even worse, one of Buckingham's many titles was Lord High Admiral, the highest naval office, so he was a direct beneficiary of the money raised by tonnage and poundage. When the Commons restricted its grant, it was striking a blow at Buckingham. The House of Lords refused to ratify this limitation as it went against tradition. To make matters even more highly charged, because Charles regarded the limited grant of tonnage and poundage as a direct attack on his own Divine Right and prerogative, he decided to ignore Parliament and ordered his tax collectors to continue collecting it beyond the first year.

A CLOSER LOOK

Forced loans

These were not demanded very often by monarchs and normally only applied to wealthy individuals. Although it was called a loan, in actuality there was little chance it would ever be repaid. In 1626 Charles ordered everyone who normally had to pay a Parliamentary subsidy to contribute to his forced loan, making it worth as much as five Parliamentary subsidies. Many were therefore concerned that Charles was using the forced loan to collect what, in effect, was taxation without Parliament's agreement.

Fig. 1 *Ships from Buckingham's fleet; one of Buckingham's many royal offices was as Lord High Admiral*

The forced loan, 1626

Without adequate Parliamentary funds, Charles resorted to asking the country at large for a benevolence, a voluntary gift of money which the king could request, through his prerogative, in times of emergency. In 1626 however, very few volunteered money for Charles. He therefore decided upon another form of prerogative income that was easier to demand, a forced loan, to help him finance war against Spain and France.

All liable were summoned to public meetings where they were individually pressed to pay. This public manner of collection made any refusal to pay a very open act of opposition, creating what was effectively a test of loyalty to the new king.

ACTIVITY

What are the advantages and disadvantages of requiring people to make public demonstrations of loyalty? Consider the Forced Loan and other examples of allegiance tests already covered.

Opposition to the Forced Loan

The forced loan was collected in the face of substantial opposition, much of which was anonymous.

> **SOURCE 2**
>
> From an anonymous pamphlet *To all English Freeholders from a Well-Wisher of Theirs*, published in late 1626. It was circulated in Lincolnshire, probably by the Earl of Lincoln who may have been its author and who was an outspoken critic of Charles I.
>
> Beware and consider what you do concerning these subsidies and loans which are now demanded of you, in case you give away not only your money but your liberty and property. For even if it is promised that it shall not set a precedent against you, yet it will lead to most dangerous consequences and that is its real aim as well as money, the gaining of a precedent to raise money without law, which will lead to the overthrow of parliament. If this happens, we shall be ourselves the instruments of our slavery and the loss of the privilege which we have enjoyed: that our goods cannot be taken from us without consent of parliament.

ACTIVITY

1. Explain the concerns of the author of the pamphlet in Source 2 with regards to the forced loan.
2. Many pamphlets were published in this period criticising the king's policies, and the majority were written anonymously. Do you think this makes them more or less reliable to an historian?

Others were more open in their opposition. In 1627 Thomas Scot, MP for Kent, attacked Buckingham in print, writing that subjects may disobey and refuse an unworthy king's command if what he wants goes beyond the normal duty owed by a subject to a king. He went on to write that faithful subjects ought to oppose a wicked ruler who failed to punish evil subjects, especially if that ruler defended their evil subjects in such a way as to cause a breach between king and Parliament, and forced him to collect loans and taxes that denied right and liberty and oppressed and exhausted the people.

Some judges refused to endorse the legality of the forced loan and one of Charles's judges, Chief Justice Carew, was dismissed as a result. George Abbot, the Archbishop of Canterbury, was suspended by Charles for refusing to license a **sermon** by Robert Sibthorpe which defended the forced loan, attempting to use the power of the Church to persuade people that it was their duty to the king to pay: 'If a prince imposes an tough – yes even an unjust – tax, the subject may not withdraw his obedience and duty; no, he is bound in conscience to submit.'

The Five Knights' Case, 1627

The king ordered the imprisonment of 76 gentry and the Earl of Lincoln who had refused to pay but he did not have them charged with any specific offence. In November 1627, five of the 76 decided to force a confrontation with the king by issuing a writ of **habeas corpus**. Under this ancient right, they had to be tried for an offence or be released. Charles therefore had no choice but to take them to trial, creating a test case which shone a spotlight on the constitutional controversy around the king's authority to raise the loan and to jail its opponents. A judgement upheld Charles's prerogative to imprison, without trial, those who refused to pay this *particular* loan.

A CLOSER LOOK

Sermons in politics

It was commonplace for sermons to be used to present political ideas and discuss current affairs. Because weekly attendance at the parish church was compulsory, there were few better ways to disseminate information to the country at large. Sometimes the king would commission a sermon and then order it to be delivered in every parish church. Ministers sometimes used the pulpit to criticise the monarch or his policies.

KEY TERM

habeas corpus: literally meaning 'you have the body' this is an ancient legal principle that prevents the punishment of anyone without making formal charges and allowing the person to defend themselves; at its heart is the presumption of innocence until proof of guilt

SECTION 1 | The emergence of conflict and the end of consensus, 1625–1629

Reasons for and outcomes of conflict over the Church

As we have seen, religion was a significant and divisive issue in early Stuart England. By the 1620s, ministers who adhered to the strand of Protestantism known as 'Arminianism' were beginning to rise into influential positions within the Church of England. Arminians were certainly Protestant but they had developed a different theology to the ideas of John Calvin which underpinned the earliest Protestant Churches. Calvin interpreted the Bible to say that God decided which people would believe in him during their earthly lives and which would reject him and end up in hell: this doctrine is called predestination. Jacobus Arminius, a Dutch minister, interpreted the Bible differently. He said that God allowed each person to make that choice freely during their earthly lives so that all *could* be saved, but not all might *choose* to be saved. This particular theological position is much closer to Catholic theology than Calvinism, which is why Puritans (who were Calvinist) attacked Arminians as being at least misguided and most likely malevolent. Some thought that Arminianism was part of a sinister plot to undermine the Church of England and return to Roman Catholicism.

ACTIVITY

Reflecting on what you know about Absolutism, for what reasons might an onlooker have been alarmed that Charles was aiming to become an absolute monarch?

Calvinism: God decided the path that humans would follow in their earthly lives: this doctrine is called predestination

Based on the ideas of John Calvin (1509–64)

Arminianism: God allowed each person to make a free choice in their earthly lives so that all *could* be saved, but not all might *choose* to be saved

Based on the ideas of Jacobus Arminius (1560–1609)

Looks similiar to

Catholicism: God has chosen everyone to be saved but people have free will and can choose not to be saved if they wish: Catholic doctrine differs substantially from Protestant doctrine in other areas such as the role of Holy Communion

Puritanism | Church of England | Laudianism

Protestantism

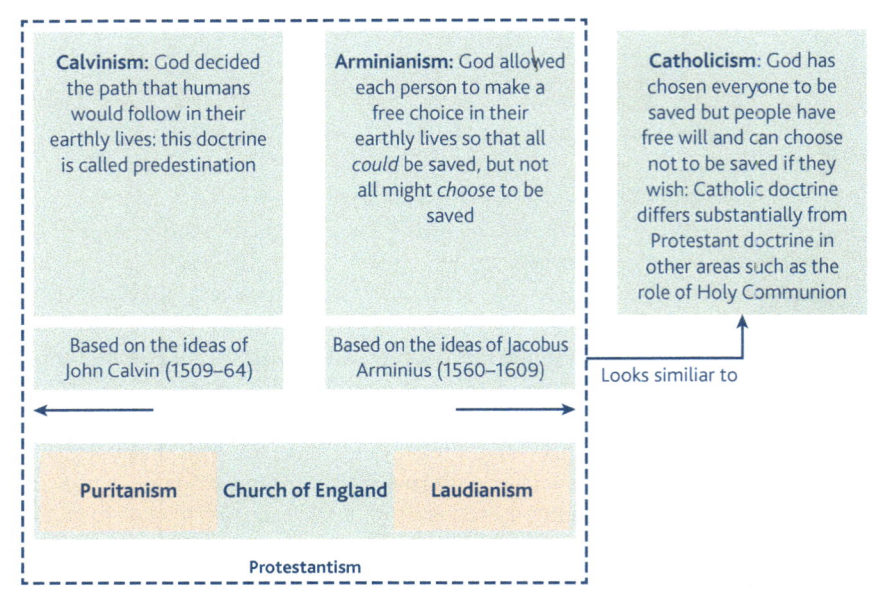

Fig. 2 *The theological differences between Puritans, Arminians and Catholics*

The overlap between the religious position of individuals and their political role is very pertinent. Parliament was made up of a significant number of Puritan members, such as John Pym, as well as more moderate Anglicans who disliked both Puritanism and Arminianism. Pym led the Calvinist grouping in Parliament which, although it is difficult to be certain, was probably the majority group throughout the Parliaments of the 1620s. **Arminian ideas appealed to Charles**, and he promoted the rise of Arminians into key Church posts. He liked the way that Arminians valued order, ceremony and hierarchy because it chimed with his ideas about Divine Right and dignity. Reflecting back to the Forced Loan, typically, Puritan Members resisted the Loan while Arminian clergymen, of whom Robert Sibthorpe was the most notable, preached in support.

CROSS-REFERENCE

The reasons why Arminian ideas appealed to Charles are explored in more detail in Chapter 6, page 46.

KEY PROFILE

Richard Rich, 2nd Earl of Warwick (1587–1658), was a staunch Puritan who took an active role in overseas affairs during the 1620s and 1630s and championed Puritan causes in the 1640s.

The York House Conference, 1626

At the request of the Puritan **Earl of Warwick,** Buckingham chaired a theological debate at his London home, York House, in February 1626. A number of prominent Puritan nobles attended, including the Earl of Pembroke who was Buckingham's chief rival at court. On the Arminian side were men such as Edmund Sheffield (who had been promoted to the Earldom of Mulgrave just the week before). Clergymen on both sides of the religious debate also attended.

Buckingham was not a particularly religious man and maintained contacts from a wide range of religious persuasions but in the heightened tensions of the mid-1620s, he was becoming increasingly vulnerable to criticism on religious grounds as his mother was Catholic and he had close links to a number of Arminian clergy. Charles had insisted that the Conference be conducted with a high degree of secrecy and no contemporary account of its proceedings was published. For Warwick, the conference was designed to persuade Charles away from the anti-Calvinism of Arminians. Buckingham acted more politically and took a stance in support of Arminianism in order to reinforce his political relationship with Charles. From the conference, it was clear that the king, who did not even consider that he should attend a discussion on his religious policy, would not be dissuaded from supporting the anti-Calvinist Arminians.

Fig. 3 York House, the venue for the Conference in 1626

The Conference initially focused on the writings of **Richard Montagu**, an Arminian clergyman who had already generated a lot of controversy during the 1610s. In 1624 he wrote a very divisive book called, *An Old Gagg for a New Goose*, in which he pointed out similarities between Catholicism and the Church of England. Montagu repeated his argument in a new work of 1625, *Appello Caesarem*. The York House Conference examined his ideas in detail to try to establish whether his doctrine was sufficiently in line with mainstream Anglicanism to allow him to continue in office but its debates then stretched beyond Montagu's work to consider the key issue of predestination. The Conference ended inconclusively but it did serve to help define a distinctive Arminian grouping within the Anglican Church.

Religious division in Parliament

The tension generated between Puritans and Arminians also erupted in Parliament. Parliament had attempted to bring Montagu to trial because of his religious writings in 1625 and renewed its attack in 1626 by passing a resolution in April that affirmed that 'Mountague is guilty of publishing

KEY PROFILE

Richard Montagu (1577–1641) was the son of an Anglican clergyman who went from Eton to Cambridge and from there into ministry, first in Somerset and then in Essex. He held a number of other Church posts, including Canon of Windsor and Archdeacon of Hereford. He was a gifted political writer and had been used by James I to draft anti-Catholic material but by the 1620s he was embroiled in numerous controversies.

A CLOSER LOOK

Royal chaplains were the private religious ministers of the monarch and Charles appointed Richard Montagu to this high-status role early in the summer of 1626. Whether this was a conscious effort to assert royal authority or evidence of Charles's political incompetence is a matter for debate.

doctrine contrary to the Articles of the Religion established in the Church of England', and which was followed by Montagu's arrest by the Commons' Serjeant at Arms, a soldier attached to Parliament who was responsible for keeping order within the Commons. Moderate non-Puritan Anglicans also resented Montagu because they felt that he characterised all his opponents as Puritans: as one MP wrote, Montagu was 'casting the odious and scandalous name of Puritans upon His Majesty's loving subjects that conform themselves to the doctrine and ceremony of the Church of England.' By pursuing Montagu, Parliament was directly challenging a clergyman and doctrine that had the support of the king and this was a key reason that Charles dissolved the Parliament in the summer.

Reactions against foreign policy and the role of Buckingham

We have seen that Parliament was very wary of Charles's active foreign policy and refused to grant him sufficient funds to pursue war with Spain without ongoing co-operation with Parliament. One of the reference points that Parliament had for believing that Charles's conduct of foreign policy was inept was the **Mansfeld expedition of 1624**. This was a military campaign that Charles and Buckingham persuaded the ageing James to support and which was intended to provide military assistance to the Elector Frederick, Charles's brother-in-law, who was trying to wrest back control of his ancestral lands in the Palatinate from its Spanish Hapsburg conquerors. They sent an army under the control of a mercenary, Count Mansfeld, which would join up with a French force to fight the Spanish in the Palatinate. It was a disaster, primarily because diplomacy broke down: the French king demanded that his allies should first help him on his own particular military mission in the Spanish Netherlands. James refused to allow them to comply and Louis XIII retaliated by refusing to guarantee safe passage for Mansfeld's men through French territory. The expedition force thus became marooned in the United Provinces, where its soldiers wasted away through starvation and sickness.

CROSS-REFERENCE

The map of Europe on page 6 will help you identify the key locations in the **Mansfeld fiasco of 1624**.

The Cádiz expedition, September 1625

Fig. 4 *A painting of the Cádiz campaign showing the Governor of Cádiz giving out instructions for the defence of the city*

Although Charles and Buckingham's anti-Spanish policy was popular in the last Parliament of James's reign, the failure of the Mansfeld expedition and the concessions to Catholics granted as part of the marriage treaty concerned and frustrated the 1625 Parliament. Charles continued to endeavour to support the Elector Frederick and next decided to send an invasion fleet to the Spanish port of Cádiz. This was financed by the queen's £120,000 **dowry**, and was intended to open a war on a second front to distract the Spanish away from the Palatinate. The Cádiz campaign, which set sail in September 1625, was a humiliating fiasco: not only did the English fail to capture the port or any of the Spanish treasure ships stationed there, but most soldiers rendered themselves useless by getting hideously drunk on Spanish wine. Parliament was understandably furious when news of the botched raid reached England, and the expensive failure was blamed on Buckingham as Lord High Admiral.

Relations with France

With the marriage of Charles to the French princess Henrietta Maria, the English expected France to cooperate with them in foreign policy to isolate their common enemy, the Spanish Habsburgs. However, Louis XIII, influenced by his chief minister, Cardinal Richelieu, was determined only to act in France's own interests. He revealed his reluctance to act against Spain in late 1625 when he refused to join an alliance agreed between the United Provinces (the Dutch Republic) and England in September. Of several other countries invited to join, only Denmark did. As a result, Charles agreed to pay the King of Denmark £30,000 to develop the Danish Army. Also in September 1625, a small number of English ships loaned to France were used by Richelieu to defeat a force of Huguenots (see 'A closer look') at La Rochelle. This was particularly embarrassing for Charles, whose attempts to recall the English ships were ignored by the French.

Furthermore, the marriage between Charles and Henrietta Maria had started very badly, with intense arguments resulting in a complete breach. It already seemed that alignment with France had proved pointless, and when the French agreed a separate peace with Spain in February 1626 it appeared positively disastrous for the Protestant cause in Europe. Buckingham – the natural focus of blame, given his role in the French negotiations – was furious, and attempted to effect the removal of Richelieu from power. He made contact with disaffected French nobles and planned an uprising supported by the Huguenots. Such an enterprise would again need to be financed, so Charles recalled Parliament in February.

The attempted impeachment of Buckingham, May 1626

While Parliament sought to place the blame for foreign policy failure on Buckingham, Charles blamed Parliament for not giving him enough money to conduct war effectively.

What made Charles even more antagonistic towards the 1626 Parliament was that despite his attempts at compromise by indicating a shift to an anti-French policy, MPs launched impeachment proceedings against Buckingham. The duke had been instrumental in reviving the practice of impeachment; now it seemed he would fall victim to his own political manoeuvres. Sir John Eliot and Sir Dudley Digges directed the attack on Buckingham in the Commons, but the testimony of the Earl of Bristol was particularly dangerous to the royal favourite: Bristol had been the ambassador to Spain when Buckingham and Charles had arrived in 1623. He therefore knew that, while in Madrid, Charles had bribed Spanish courtiers but had promised to offer concessions to English Catholics if the Spanish match was secured. Charles charged Bristol with

> **KEY TERM**
>
> **dowry:** a sum of money and other goods that a bride's family gave to her husband upon marriage

> **A CLOSER LOOK**
>
> **Religion in France**
>
> Tension between Protestants and Catholics in France was so severe it led to religious wars: in 1572 the St Bartholomew's Day Massacre saw the murder of tens of thousands of Huguenots (French Calvinists). The Edict of Nantes, signed by King Henry IV (father of Henrietta Maria) in 1598, aimed to end the turmoil but the truce was an uneasy one. By the time of Charles's reign, the Huguenots were influential in some southern French regions but Cardinal Richelieu was determined to crush them.

treason, but the earl offered evidence in the Lords that persuaded them that Buckingham should be charged with treason instead. Once the impeachment hearings were heard in May 1626, Eliot and Digges were imprisoned in the Tower of London.

ACTIVITY

1. What is Glanvile accusing Buckingham of in this speech in Source 3?
2. How does Glanvile maintain a tone of respect for the king?
3. How useful is this speech to an historian studying Buckingham's role in foreign policy at this point?

SOURCE 3

From a speech by John Glanvile, MP for Plymouth, to the House of Commons on 8 May 1626 as part of the Commons Protestation against Buckingham.

The Duke deliberately managed to make the Lords and Commons believe that English ships had not been used in 1625 and would not in the future be used against either the Huguenot Protestant inhabitants of La Rochelle or those of the Protestant religion anywhere in France. In so doing, he damaged His Majesty's reputation and was a poor servant to the King, causing our conduct of religion and foreign affairs to be seen as scandalous. What is worse, because his words were so crafty and subtle, he acted with great disrespect to both Lords and Commons and caused them to miss their opportunity to ask His Majesty to put matters right by petitioning the King. What he had said was that the English ships had not been used against the La Rochellers. What he should have said was the ships had been handed over to the French King, and he had used them against La Rochelle.

CROSS-REFERENCE

To remind yourself of Charles's **absolutist statement**, see Source 3 in Chapter 1, page 7.

To try to stop Buckingham's impeachment, Charles rather undiplomatically implied a threat to Parliament's future existence in a **statement** which smacked of Absolutism. It was easy to make a case that Charles was becoming absolutist because of his continued reliance on prerogative financial measures and the dissolution of the 1626 Parliament in order to protect Buckingham and Montagu.

The La Rochelle raids, 1627–1628

In late 1627 Buckingham launched another naval expedition in the hope of relieving the Huguenots under attack by Richelieu's forces at La Rochelle. After a series of tit-for-tat seizures of each other's shipping, England and France were now at war and the international situation was complicated further by a new alliance between France and Spain. Buckingham's force landed on the Île de Rhé, just off La Rochelle. When the French troops withdrew into the stronghold of St Martin, Buckingham laid siege. After months of deadlock, a direct assault failed because the English scaling-ladders were too short! The fleet sailed home in the aftermath of another expensive debacle.

During the years 1624 to 1628, 50,000 men had served in Buckingham's forces. It has been estimated that nearly a third of these died. Of 7833 soldiers sent to La Rochelle, only 2989 returned – and severe disappointment was expressed that Buckingham was one who survived. Charles's loyalty to the duke now appeared even more misguided and dangerous to England's interests. Worse still for Charles, all his funds had been spent and he had to recall Parliament in 1628.

STUDY TIP

Remember to consider the provenance of sources when asked to consider their value to an historian. Consider the purpose of all the sources in this chapter and the contents' reliability, which will give a good idea of what each author or speaker was trying to achieve. Consider the anonymity of source 2: could make the source more or less valuable, depending on the context.

A LEVEL PRACTICE QUESTION

With reference to Sources 1, 2 and 3, and your understanding of the historical context, assess the value of these three sources to an historian studying reasons for opposition to Charles's policies in the years 1625 to 1629.

CHAPTER 3 | Challenges to the arbitrary government of Charles I

ACTIVITY

Summary

There is a lot of overlap in the reactions to the financial, religious and foreign policies of Charles I's early reign. Choose one of the circles in the Venn diagram to remove. If this had never been an issue, how would this affect opposition to Charles's policies? Repeat this process with the other two circles.

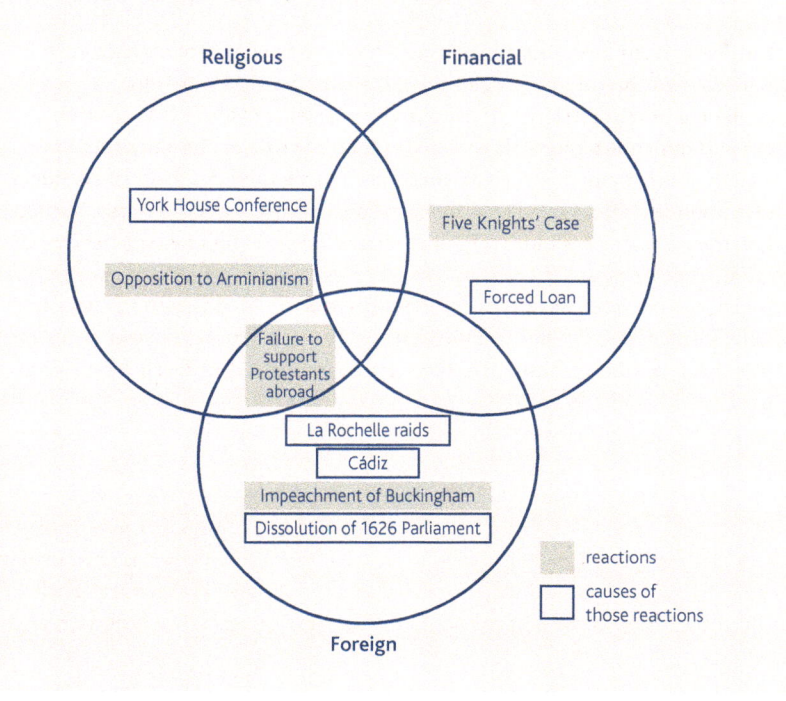

Venn diagram (Religious, Financial, Foreign):

- Religious only: York House Conference; Opposition to Arminianism
- Financial only: Five Knights' Case; Forced Loan
- Religious ∩ Foreign: Failure to support Protestants abroad
- Foreign only: La Rochelle raids; Cádiz; Impeachment of Buckingham; Dissolution of 1626 Parliament

Legend: shaded = reactions; box outline = causes of those reactions

ACTIVITY

Assume the role of an MP who wants to resume the impeachment proceedings against Buckingham. How would you report the failures of England's foreign policy to the Commons?

AS LEVEL PRACTICE QUESTION

'Most of the problems in the 1625 and 1626 Parliaments could have been avoided had Charles behaved more wisely'.
Explain why you agree or disagree with this view.

STUDY TIP

It could be useful to make a list of the key problems that arose in the Parliaments of 1625 and 1626 and analyse each one. What was at the root of each problem? In what ways did Charles's responses worsen the issues? What other factors were involved? Don't forget to look back to your notes on the reign of James: in what way did James leave a difficult legacy for his son? Try to evaluate each problem and decide which was most serious. It might be useful at the outset to define what you understand by 'wise' behaviour.

4 Parliamentary radicalism

LEARNING OBJECTIVES
In this chapter you will learn about:

- personalities and policies of Parliamentary opposition to the king
- the Petition of Right
- the Dissolution of Parliament and Charles I's commitment to Personal Rule.

KEY CHRONOLOGY

1628	Mar	Charles calls his Third Parliament
	June	Parliament issues the Petition of Right
	June	Charles prorogues the Third Parliament
	Aug	Laud and Montagu elevated to key bishoprics
	Aug	Assassination of Buckingham
1629	Jan	Recall of Third Parliament
	Mar	Three Resolutions
	Mar	Dissolution of Third Parliament

A CLOSER LOOK

Black Rod

So-called because of the long ebony staff topped with a golden lion which is the symbol of his office, Black Rod's official title is 'Gentleman Usher of the Black Rod'. He is responsible for managing the doors of Parliament, admitting only those who have a right to be there.

On 2 March 1629, in the House of Commons, the king's messenger, symbolically identified as 'Black Rod', arrived at Westminster to formally advise the House of Commons that the King had decided to dissolve Parliament. Incredibly, the door was slammed shut in his face, a devastating blow to royal authority. Aware of his duty to the King, Black Rod began to hammer on the door with his staff, demanding entrance.

Inside the Commons, the Speaker of the House, in charge of managing Parliamentary business and realising that the King wanted to dissolve the session, stood up and announced that all debates were ended. Several MPs including Denzil Holles and Benjamin Valentine grabbed at him and forced him back into his chair to keep the session open, while MP Sir John Eliot shouted out three resolutions, condemning the King's government. Members of the King's Privy Council tried to drag the Speaker back out of his chair so that business had to stop, but despite a scuffle breaking out, MPs shouted 'Aye, Aye' in support of Eliot and passed what became known as the Commons Protestation of 1629. Business complete, the shaken Speaker was released and the doors were opened to Black Rod.

It is difficult to underestimate the significance of that March day: an unparalleled affront to royal dignity and authority and a powerful demonstration of a combative spirit in the House of Commons. Two days later, Charles would dissolve Parliament and not recall it for another 11 years.

Fig. 1 *Even today 'Black Rod' makes an appearance in parliamentary proceedings*

Personalities and policies of Parliamentary opposition to the king

The Parliaments of the 1620s were packed with highly competent men, mainly lawyers, who were skilled at debating and determined to protect the rights of Parliament.

CHAPTER 4 | Parliamentary radicalism

Sir John Pym	Benjamin Rudyard	Sir John Eliot	Sir Edward Coke	Denzil Holles	Sir John Selden
(1584–1643)	(1572–1658)	(1592–1632)	(1552–1634)	(1598–1680)	(1584–1654)
'He understood the temper and affections of the kingdom as well as any man.' (Earl of Clarendon)	'A man of great learning but in debate, inept.' (Sir John Eliot)	'His vivacity was equal to his earnestness, yet never detracted from it.' (Victorian commentator)	'We shall never see his like again, praises be to be God!' (Coke's widow)	'Holles's force and reputations are the two things that give success to all his actions.' (Sir Ralph Verney)	'A man of deep knowledge but very puffed up with self confidence.' (Sir Simonds D'Ewes)
Prominent Puritan	Moved in brilliant literary circles	Left university without completing a degree	Straight-talking and afraid of no-one	A boyhood friend of King Charles	Specialist in English constitutional law
Particularly concerned about religious issues	Deployed literary skills to draft speeches and other documents	Stood up for liberties and ancient rights	Challenged prerogative powers	Zealous for the right of parliament	Most concerned about arbitrary rule

Fig. 2 *Important personalities in the parliamentary opposition to the king*

KEY PROFILE

Benjamin Rudyard (1572–1658) trained as a lawyer and travelled widely before taking up an important legal role at the Court of Wards. He became MP for Portsmouth, mainly because of the patronage of the Earl of Pembroke, and made a number of significant speeches in the Commons, most notably in 1628 when he so effectively captured the prevailing mood: 'This is the crisis of parliaments, by this we shall know whether parliaments will live or die'.

Denzil Holles (1598–1680) very nearly joined his childhood friend Prince Charles on the Madrid adventure of 1623 but instead became increasingly associated with the parliamentary opposition to the new king, especially with regard to financial matters. Holles, Valentine and Coke spent an evening together in a tavern called the Three Cranes, during which time they devised their plan to hold the speaker in his chair.

KEY PROFILE

Fig. 3 *John Pym*

Sir John Pym (1584–1643) was educated in a Puritan household and entered Parliament in 1621. He opposed Buckingham's pro-Spanish and pro-Catholic policies, attacked monopolies and supported the Protestation of 1621. He rose in prominence as an opponent of the court, helping to impeach Buckingham and supporting the Petition of Right in 1628. He worked fervently on religious committees to try to limit the king's ability to change the Elizabethan settlement. As he rose to dominate the Commons in the Long Parliament, he acquired the nickname 'King Pym'.

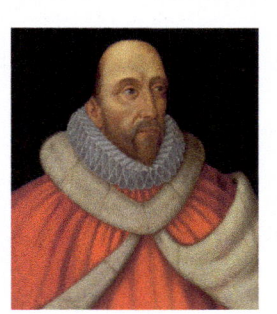

Fig. 4 *Edward Coke*

Sir Edward Coke (1552–1634) was a hugely experienced lawyer and MP who had opposed James I's articulation of Divine Right by reminding the king that the common law was superior to the king himself. He had helped draft the Protestation of 1621 which asserted that Parliament's privileges were 'the ancient… birthright and inheritance of the subjects of England'. Horrified by Charles's use of the royal prerogative in 1626–27, he drafted the 1628 Petition of Right as his last act before retiring.

> **KEY PROFILE**
>
> **Sir John Selden (1584–1654)** was the son of a minstrel who had made a very advantageous marriage to a wealthy heiress. He distinguished himself academically and became particularly focused on delving into the 'ancient constitution' of England at the expense of the Divine Right of Kings. He helped create the constitution of the colony of Virginia. He became MP for Lancaster in 1624 and rapidly became Parliament's expert on constitutional law.

> **CROSS-REFERENCE**
>
> The near-farcical conduct of Charles's foreign policy is covered in Chapter 3, as is tonnage and poundage (see page 19).

> **KEY TERM**
>
> **billeting:** the placement of soldiers into private houses where they would receive food and a bed; billeting was used to solve a logistical problem of what to do with soldiers when they were away from home

> **KEY TERM**
>
> **martial law** (or military law): this was declared by the king and overruled normal legal processes, such as trial by jury; sentences could be handed out without right of appeal

> **KEY PROFILE**
>
> **Sir John Eliot (1592–1632)** emerged as a leading critic of Buckingham, and thereby Charles, in the Parliaments of 1625 to 1629. Arrested for refusing to pay the Forced Loan, he was involved in the presentation of the Petition of Right and Three Resolutions, Eliot was regarded as too extreme by many MPs and identified as a leading 'fiery spirit' by Charles I. In 1629, he was imprisoned in the Tower of London where he died in 1632.

A crisis of Parliaments

Charles recalled Parliament in March 1628 because he was in dire need of money to fund his foreign policy but it is clear from peace-making actions on both sides that Crown and Parliament hoped to make something of a fresh start in their relationship. Charles allowed Sir John Coke, his Secretary of State, to communicate directly with MPs rather than doing so himself, which helped the Commons to feel that he was respectful of their due process. A speech by MP Sir Benjamin Rudyard urged the Commons to be co-operative in turn: 'This is the crisis of parliaments. By this we shall know whether parliaments will live or die... [we should trust the king] thereby to breed a trust in him towards us, for without a mutual confidence a good success is not to be expected.' Even Buckingham demonstrated a willingness to be flexible, reconciling himself to old political enemies such as the Earl of Arundel. The most jarring note was struck by Charles himself, informing Parliament that, unless it provided adequate funds, he would have a clear conscience in acting in whichever way he saw fit, under the authority given him by God.

As an indication of their goodwill, the Commons offered five subsidies and a grant of tonnage and poundage, rapidly addressing Charles's financial need. In return, they expected that the king should consider their grievances.

Redress of financial grievances

The Commons hoped that the king would respond to their concerns about:

- Extra-Parliamentary taxation, including tonnage and poundage and also Ship Money, an ancient tax that a king could levy on ports and coastal counties, to pay for ships to protect trade.
- **Billeting**. Troops preparing to leave for Europe were dispersed around local households who were told to billet them. Although householders were supposed to be paid expenses, this rarely happened, so billeting was also known as 'free quarter'.

Redress of legal grievances

The Commons was particularly concerned by two legal developments that they felt had far-reaching constitutional implications.

Martial Law

In order to stop the soldiers billeted in the south west from becoming out of control, **martial law** had been imposed in certain counties. Local gentry feared that the king might permanently undermine the English legal system and use martial law as a cloak for the introduction of Absolutism.

Habeas corpus

This related to those who had been imprisoned for opposing the forced loan. Although the Five Knights had been released in 1628, MPs wanted to discuss the constitutional consequences of the case in the new Parliament. In particular, they were infuriated when they found out that the Attorney General, Sir Robert Heath, who was the king's chief legal officer, had falsified the legal record of the Five Knights' Case. Whereas the judgement in the case upheld the right of the king to imprison without trial in this one *particular* instance, Heath changed the wording so that the king had the *general* right to imprison without trial. Effectively, he had attempted to create a highly significant constitutional precedent which dramatically increased the power of the king, without approval by Parliament.

A common cause

MPs across the political spectrum were horrified by Heath's action and united together in response. Some more extreme MPs, such as Sir John Selden and Sir John Eliot, recommended a radical approach: a Bill of Rights. This would be a legally binding constitutional document that would define individual rights that the king could not overrule. Demonstrating its inherent conservatism, Parliament settled on a less aggressive solution, a Petition of Right which was drafted by Sir Edward Coke.

The Petition of Right

The Petition of Right, 1628, asked the king to confirm four ancient liberties that Parliament claimed were basic precepts of English government, and that could be traced back to the **Magna Carta** of 1215.
1. Subjects could be taxed only by Parliamentary consent.
2. Subjects could be imprisoned only if just cause was demonstrated in court.
3. The imposition of billeting on the population was illegal.
4. The imposition of martial law on the **civilian** population was illegal.

During the preliminary debates about the Petition, the king's officials via the House of Lords made a case that Parliament should accept the 'word' of the king to abide by the spirit of Magna Carta. This was not enough for the Commons.

> **SOURCE 1**
>
> From an extract from the Commons Diary, of a speech given by John Pym on 6 May 1628 in which he responded to the king's suggestion that the Commons should accept the king's 'word':
>
> We would be inclined to trust **the king's word** if we actually knew what he was thinking. In any case, he made a solemn oath at his coronation to uphold our liberties. I am certain that if the king knew the law well he would know that he needs to explain himself properly. We complain of our unjust imprisonments on account of the loans. I have not heard anyone say that there will be no more such imprisonments and I have not heard anyone say that more care will be taken in the future to only call on loans in case of real emergency. As for billeting of soldiers, we say it is against the law. I daresay the Privy Council lords have their own ideas about this but I don't know what law they are using. We all rest in the king's royal word, but let us agree on principles that suit us all.

In order to be presented to the king, both the Commons and the Lords had to agree to the Petition. Some in the House of Lords tried to moderate its terms, pushing for a compromise that would not encroach on any of the king's prerogative powers. It is a mark of the extent to which Charles had alienated himself from his natural allies in the Lords that ultimately they chose not to stand up for his prerogative rights and instead gave their agreement to the Petition and passed it to the king.

Charles accepted the Petition on 7 June 1628, chiefly because Parliament threatened further proceedings against Buckingham and he was, once again, desperate for money.

> **ACTIVITY**
>
> *Habeas corpus* (see page 23) is pivotal to English law. Why might someone afraid of Absolutism be wary of changes to the tradition of habeas corpus?

> **A CLOSER LOOK**
>
> ### The Magna Carta
>
> The 'Great Charter' was forced on King John by his barons in 1215 and stated the liberties of freeborn English subjects. Successive kings reissued Magna Carta to demonstrate their willingness to rule within the law of the land.

> **KEY TERM**
>
> **civilian:** anyone who is not a member of the armed forces

> **A CLOSER LOOK**
>
> ### Ancient liberties
>
> The unwritten 'ancient' constitution of England is a mixture of Parliamentary laws, documents such as the Magna Carta, and tradition. An unwritten constitution is therefore open to interpretation, which is both an advantage and disadvantage. Where monarch and Parliament basically want to work together in order to maintain their authority over society, flexibility of interpretation is useful because it allows maximum room for compromise and negotiation.

> **KEY TERM**
>
> **the king's word:** a solemn promise, backed up by personal honour and not by legislative force

> **ACTIVITY**
>
> ### Evaluating primary sources
>
> What does John Pym in Source 1 indicate is the problem with relying on the king's word to bring harmony between Crown and Parliament?

SECTION 1 | The emergence of conflict and the end of consensus, 1625–1629

The consequences of the Petition of Right

Despite the relatively conservative nature of the Petition, any hope that it could re-establish mutual trust between Crown and Parliament swiftly evaporated. Charles initially accepted the Petition without using the specific terminology that would have made it legally binding. The Commons insisted on the correct response and, once again, used Charles's financial needs to ensure that he gave the conventional, and therefore legal, assent to the Petition.

Further deterioration in the relationship between Crown and Parliament

KEY TERM

remonstrance: a strongly worded protest

prorogue: to postpone a meeting of a parliament without dissolving it

Sir John Eliot led an attack on the Duke of Buckingham producing a **Remonstrance** condemning his military failures

Charles **prorogued** Parliament on 28 June to stop its debates.

Parliament's frustration increased

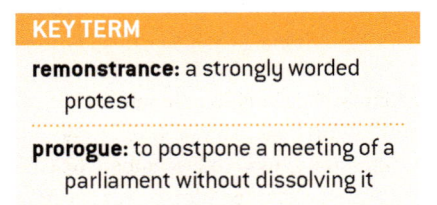

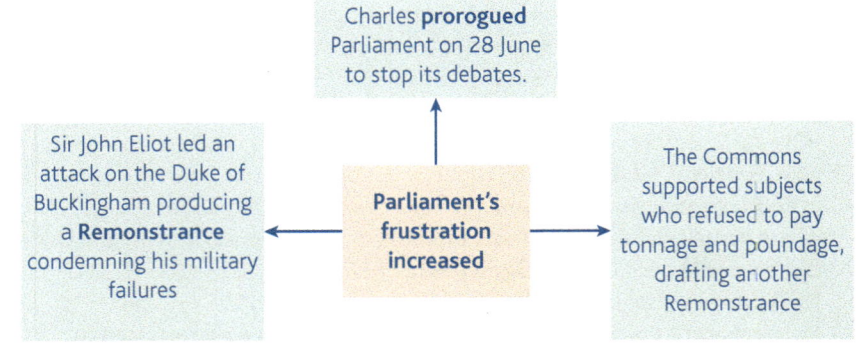

The Commons supported subjects who refused to pay tonnage and poundage, drafting another Remonstrance

Fig. 5 *Parliament became increasingly frustrated*

Impact of the Petition of Right

The Petition of Right was intended to demonstrate that king and Parliament shared a common understanding of the laws and customs of England. In fact, it had served to heighten Parliamentary fears that this particular king could not be trusted.

The Dissolution of Parliament and Charles I's commitment to Personal Rule

The assassination of Buckingham

Fig. 6 *The assassination of Buckingham was a devastating blow for the young Charles I*

On 23 August 1628, Buckingham was preparing to leave his quarters at the Greyhound Inn in Portsmouth when he was fatally stabbed in the chest. His assassin, an army lieutenant called John Felton, had fought in the catastrophic Île de Rhé expedition and had been plunged into debt by delays in pay. Spontaneous public celebrations erupted as news of the assassination spread, causing Charles to abandon any idea of a lavish funeral, even if he could have afforded it. In the end, Buckingham's coffin was carried in a torchlit procession along heavily guarded roads through London to Westminster Abbey. His body had been buried secretly the night before in case the cortège was attacked. As one man wrote:

'Here lies the best and worst of fate,
Two kings' delight, the people's hate'.

Consequences of the assassination

- Charles held Parliament responsible for the assassination because Felton said at his trial that he had been inspired to action by June's Remonstrance.
- Without Buckingham's dominant presence, Charles and his French Catholic wife Henrietta Maria fell deeply in love. Their eldest son Charles was born in 1630 and five more children followed.
- Charles was shocked by the extent of public celebration at Buckingham's death and felt personally betrayed by the apparent disloyalty of his subjects. He distanced himself further from ordinary people.
- Buckingham had amassed so many titles that his death gave Charles an opportunity to reallocate patronage to a wider circle. The team that he assembled around him, men such as **Sir Thomas Wentworth** and the Earl of Arundel, became his key advisers during the next decade.
- With Wentworth moved into the king's service and Sir Edward Coke retired, leadership in the House of Commons became more radical, centred around firebrands such as Eliot, Pym and Holles.
- Whether fair or not, Buckingham had been a convenient scapegoat for grievances over the past 10 years. Increasingly, criticism would be levelled directly at Charles.

The 1629 Parliament

Charles recalled Parliament on 20 January 1629. Two fundamental issues that had not been addressed in the Petition of Right swiftly came to dominate proceedings:

- **Tonnage and poundage:** The Petition did not explicitly mention the customs duty, impositions, or tonnage and poundage. As a result, Charles claimed he had not surrendered his rights to collect these monies and endorsed the work of customs officers, saying that 'what these men have done they have done by [the king's] command'. By removing the possibility of the Commons blaming a third party, Charles opened himself to direct censure by Parliament.
- **Religion:** During the extended recess between sessions, Charles promoted William Laud and Richard Montagu to the key bishoprics of London and Chichester. These two men were both **Arminians** and, it appeared to many that they were Catholic sympathisers which made Parliamentarians worry that the king was attracted by Catholicism and that this attraction might grow.

Trust was entirely eroded in the 1629 sessions with the shocking news that the king had instructed the royal printer to include both his non-constitutional and constitutional assents to the printed version of the Petition of Right, and to obscure the statute number so that it was not adequately visible in the printed record: taken together, the legal authority of the document became ambiguous. More radical MPs began to discuss creating a permanent means to limit his powers.

> **KEY PROFILE**
>
> **Sir Thomas Wentworth (1593–1641)** had been a key member of the Parliamentary opposition to the king in the House of Commons, as one of the 76 and a supporter of the Petition of Right. In December 1628 the king promoted him to the Crown role of 'Lord President of the Council of the North' and then sent him to Ireland in 1633, to act as the Lord Deputy, effectively a royal governor. A vigorous crown servant, he made many enemies and shortly after being recalled to England and raised to the peerage as the 1st Earl of Strafford, he was charged with crimes against the State by Parliament and executed in May 1641.

> **CROSS-REFERENCE**
>
> **Arminian** beliefs are explained on pages 22.

> **KEY TERM**
>
> **Commonwealth:** a term which contemporaries would have understood to have evolved from 'the common wealth' which signified the general wellbeing of the people in a community. When used in a political sense, as 'The Commonwealth', it meant a system of government in which the ordinary people of England were well cared for

> **ACTIVITY**
>
> Discuss in pairs: who does the Protestation threaten with death and why? What other threats can you identify in the Protestation? Why might they affect the king's ability to raise money?

> **A CLOSER LOOK**
>
> **Personal Rule**
>
> This refers to the 11 years from 1629 until 1640, during which time King Charles I ruled without calling Parliament. He deployed the personal prerogative of the sovereign to raise money and governed through royal officials such as the Leader of the Council of the North. Parliamentarians feared that the king was embarking on a deliberately absolutist policy but, with hindsight, a case can be made that he was simply trying to govern effectively in the face of specific issues with Parliamentary management.

Dissolution

It was in this feverish atmosphere that Charles sent Black Rod to suspend Parliament: recognising that he was not going to be awarded tonnage and poundage, he intended to shut proceedings down. The Speaker pinned down, Sir John Eliot called out his three resolutions which, when passed, became known as the Protestation of 1629.

> **SOURCE 2**
>
> From a record of the 1629 Protestation in the contemporary Parliamentarian Sir John Rushworth's 'Historical Collection', a compilation of notable documents, personal records and Commons diary entries, which he dedicated to Richard Cromwell:
>
> 1. Anyone who introduces innovation in religion or, whether as a favour or through personal conviction, seeks to extend or introduce Popery or Arminianism or another opinion disagreeing from the true and orthodox Church, shall be considered a traitor to this Kingdom and **Commonwealth**.
> 2. Anyone who suggests or recommends the taking and levying of subsidies of Tonnage and Poundage without approval by Parliament, or who takes part in collecting such subsidies, shall likewise be considered an innovator to our way of Government and thus a traitor to this Kingdom and Commonwealth.
> 3. If any merchant or person whatsoever shall voluntarily pay such subsidies as Tonnage and Poundage if these have not been approved by Parliament, then he shall be considered to have betrayed the liberties of England and thus counted as one of her enemies.

The beginning of Personal Rule

Charles dissolved Parliament and would not recall it until 1640: this period is known as his Personal Rule because he governed by using only his monarchical rights, without consulting Parliament.

He had eight leading opponents arrested for treason, including Sir John Eliot and Denzil Holles. Free speech was a Parliamentary privilege that should have made the MPs safe from such arrest but when the MPs issued writs of habeas corpus, the king replied that Parliamentary privileges did not extend to treason. Five of the MPs pleaded guilty and were freed; Holles paid a fine and went into exile; Eliot refused to ask for pardon and was sent to the Tower of London, where he died in 1632: Charles refused to release his body to his family for burial.

Charles issued a Declaration, explaining his response to the Resolutions.

> **SOURCE 3**
>
> From a declaration of Charles I, included in the Rushworth Collection, explaining his response to the resolutions of 1629 and justifying his decision to dissolve Parliament.
>
> We have thus declared the many and varied reasons why we had to dissolve this Parliament, in particular, how they used the demands of war to force us to agree to conditions incompatible with our kingly power. A lot of false and unfair things have been said about us so we affirm again that we will maintain the true religion and doctrine of the Church of England, firmly denying that we are backsliding into Catholicism. We also declare that we will maintain the ancient and just rights and liberties of our subjects, so honestly and fairly that they will acknowledge that under our government and gracious protection they live more happily and freely than any subjects in the Christian world. Let no-one

CHAPTER 4 | Parliamentary radicalism

though abuse that liberty nor pervert the Petition and turn it into an excuse for rebellion. In exchange for maintaining our subjects' liberties, so we expect that they will submit to our royal prerogative and be obedient to our authority and commands.

ACTIVITY

Summary

You now have sufficient evidence to form an opinion about why Charles I resorted to Personal Rule in 1629.

1. Using information from Chapters 2–4, summarise your learning by listing key factors in two categories: *structural causes* (reasons that any king and Parliament would have faced in the historical context of the 1620s), and *personal causes* (reasons that were specific to the personalities involved at the time).
2. Whose fault was the breakdown between king and Parliament? In groups of four, list reasons why the relationship broke down. Choose your top four reasons and allocate one to each person in your group. Try to persuade the others that your reason is the most significant.

ACTIVITY

Extension

One of the key reasons that Charles identified as a cause of the breakdown in relations between Crown and Parliament was the way that the war forced him to 'agree to conditions incompatible with kingly power'. Look back to the information in Chapter 1 about the 1610 Great Contract. Discuss in a group: to what extent do you think that Salisbury's failure to secure adequate financing for the Stuart monarchs led to the Personal Rule?

A LEVEL PRACTICE QUESTION

To what extent was Parliament responsible for the breakdown in relations between king and Commons in the years 1625 to 1629

STUDY TIP

To prepare for answering this question it would be useful to list specific examples of the disagreements between Crown and Commons. Analyse these closely and assess to what extent Parliament, in its efforts to limit Charles's power, may have been responsible for the breakdown of relations. Consider whether there were other factors that were equally or more responsible. Use evidence to support your answer.

AS LEVEL PRACTICE QUESTION

With reference to Sources 2 and 3, and your understanding of the historical context, which of these two sources is more valuable in explaining why the relationship between Crown and Parliament broke down in 1629?

STUDY TIP

Firstly, make sure you can are clear about the chronology and facts relating to the breakdown between Crown and Parliament. Then, analyse each source carefully to understand how its content illuminates events. Also reflect on the provenance of the sources and think critically, reflecting on your own knowledge as well.

2 An experiment in Absolutism, 1629–1640

5 Charles I's Personal Rule

LEARNING OBJECTIVES

In this chapter you will learn about:
- Charles I's chief ministers
- methods of government
- financial policies and reactions.

ACTIVITY

Paraphrase Source 1 in your own words. Find specific examples from the 1620s that are relevant to the indictment, for example, the Forced Loan was condemned by many as being against the rights and liberties of the people. Although the indictment most specifically relates to Charles's actions in the 1640s, many issues had already emerged in the 1620s.

KEY CHRONOLOGY

1629	Dissolution of Parliament
1629	Peace with France
1630	Peace with Spain
1631	Book of Orders
1635	Revised Book of Rates
1635	Ship Money levied across England
1637	Hampden Case

SOURCE 1

From the indictment against Charles I. The indictment was read on the first day of the trial in January 1649 to the court set up to try him.

The said Charles Stuart, acknowledged King of England, and therein trusted with a limited power to govern by and according to the laws of the land, and not otherwise; and by his trust, oath, and office, being obliged to use the power committed to him for the good and benefit of the people, and for the preservation of their rights and liberties; yet, nevertheless, out of a wicked design to erect and uphold in himself an unlimited and tyrannical power to rule according to his will, and to overthrow the rights and liberties of the people; he, the said Charles Stuart, for accomplishment of such his designs, and for the protecting of himself and his adherents in his and their wicked practices, to the same ends has traitorously and maliciously levied war…

In 1649, the indictment against Charles I was clear: he was on trial because he had set himself up as a tyrant – the seventeenth-century equivalent of a dictator. A key moment in the journey that led to his trial came in 1629 when Charles began to rule without Parliament. This lasted for 11 years and is known as the Personal Rule.

ACTIVITY

The extent to which Charles was aiming to introduce Absolutism into England is a topic of historiographical debate that is expressed in the terminology used to identify this period. 'Personal Rule' is a neutral term that replaced an earlier characterisation of this period as the 'Eleven Years' Tyranny'. Make sure you clearly understand 'Absolutism' and have some knowledge of the contemporary absolutist monarchies in Europe so that you can engage with the issues. While you are reading this chapter, decide for yourself what Charles was intending to achieve.

Charles I's chief ministers

With hindsight it is known that Charles governed for 11 years without Parliament but no-one in 1629 could have known or predicted that this would be the case: dissolution on its own caused no peculiar alarm. There was no precedent or legislation that governed the frequency of Parliament and only a handful of years had passed since James had ended a period of seven years without Parliament in 1621. For sure, some within the Political Nation could look overseas to the absolutist monarchies of France and Spain and be concerned about what was in Charles's mind. Parliament's developing legal sense of its privileges and rights had led MPs to press for greater involvement in government during the 1620s and they had wrung some significant concessions from the king. However, in so-doing, its leaders had pushed conventional boundaries of expectation and acceptability. Thus when Charles dissolved Parliament, he was not necessarily being innovative or radical: he was exerting his right as king to rule as he saw fit. He did not have to invent a new way of governing without Parliament because Parliament was only one of the instruments of government at his disposal. The king ruled without Parliament but not without advisors.

A Catholic faction

One of the consequences of the assassination of Buckingham was that Charles could redistribute the vast number of titles and offices that the Duke had held. These appointments, and other high royal offices, would prove to be of increasing significance as the Personal Rule evolved. By temperament, Charles preferred to deal with a few close, loyal allies and he naturally appointed staunch supporters into these key roles. Coupled with the absence of Parliament, this meant that political influence began to be concentrated within an elite group, alienating many in the broader Political Nation, and providing well-defined targets when opposition gained strength.

Table 1 *The major Privy Councillors and their role during the Personal Rule to 1640*

Richard Weston, 1st Earl of Portland	Lord Treasurer of England (1628–1635)
Francis, Lord Cottington	1628 Joined the Privy Council. Chancellor of the Exchequer (1629–1640)
	Master of the Court of Wards (1635–1640)
Henry Montagu, Earl of Manchester	Keeper of the Privy Seal (1628–1640)
Sir Thomas, Lord Coventry	Lord Keeper of the Great Seal (1625–1640)
William Juxon, Bishop of London	Lord Treasurer (1635–1640)
William Laud, Archbishop of Canterbury	First Lord of the Treasury (1635–1640)
Sir Thomas Wentworth	Lord Deputy of Ireland (1632–1640)
Sir Francis Windebank	Secretary of State (1632–1640)

The Privy Council consisted of around 35 members drawn from England's noble families and leading lawyers whose role was to support the monarch with advice through regular sessions and by enacting the royal will back in their home regions. They had a wide remit, including the development of trade to support famine-struck regions. The Privy Council should have been a source of particular strength to Charles by providing him with a broad base of advice that would help him stay in touch with the Political Nation during his Personal Rule. Two factors particularly mitigated against its effectiveness in the 1630s:

1. Charles attended the twice-weekly Council sessions on only a handful of occasions. For example, between June 1630 and June 1631, while Henry Montagu attended 89 sessions, the king attended only three times.
2. Charles allowed a group within the Council, identified by contemporaries as a 'Spanish Faction,' to gain significant influence. Cottington and Windebank were known to be Roman Catholics. Weston was suspected of sympathising and in fact, converted to Rome on his deathbed. Coupled with the Arminian Councillors Archbishop Laud and Bishop Juxon, it increasingly appeared that Charles was being steered in a pro-Catholic direction.

> **A CLOSER LOOK**
>
> Harvest failures were common in early modern England but their occurrence was increased by the steady population drift from countryside to town, which left fewer to work the land and more town dwellers to feed in an era when transport infrastructure and communications were poor. Famine was therefore a constant feature of early modern England. 1586 and 1649 were particularly bad years, but there were a significant number of smaller-scale famines in the intervening years and beyond. Times of famine tended to lead to periods of social unrest, instability and sometimes riots, especially in the West Country.

> **CROSS-REFERENCE**
>
> Additional consequences of the assassination of Buckingham are covered in Chapter 4.

Fig. 1 *Francis, Lord Cottington*, one of the most significant Privy Councillors during the Personal Rule

> **KEY PROFILE**
>
> **Henry Montagu, 1st Earl of Manchester (1563–1642)** was a successful lawyer who was appointed to lead the Privy Council as its President in 1621. He was highly valued by Charles, who made use of him as a judge in Star Chamber and created him Earl of Manchester in 1626. His son Edward became a senior parliamentary commander.
>
> **William Laud (1573–1645)** was the son of a Reading clothier, and was educated at Reading Grammar School and Oxford. A controversial figure, his rise to power began when he entered Buckingham's faction in the 1620s, becoming his religious adviser in 1624. His humble background made him an easy target for critics who felt he did not understand the culture and traditions of the gentry.

> **CROSS-REFERENCE**
>
> A Key Profile of Sir Thomas Wentworth is in Chapter 4, page 33.
>
> A Key Profile of Francis Cottington is on page 13.

KEY PROFILE

Sir Thomas Roe (1581–1644) was one of the best-travelled English men of the century. He searched for the legendary 'City of Gold' in South America; became Ambassador to the court at Agra, India, and Ambassador to the Ottoman Empire; concluded a treaty with Algiers; was friends with the Patriarch of Constantinople (the equivalent of the Pope in the Greek Orthodox Church); through diplomacy, enabled Sweden to intervene in the Thirty Years' War; negotiated treaties with Denmark and Danzig, and sponsored an exploration of the Arctic. A lifelong supporter of Charles's sister Elizabeth and a fervent Protestant, he used his influence to secure the return of the Palatinate from the Emperor. He joined the Privy Council in 1640.

A CLOSER LOOK

Prerogative courts were established under the early Tudor monarchs in order to help govern the country more efficiently in an age when government was becoming increasingly centralised. Prerogative courts did not become contentious until the 1630s when they began to be seen as tools that gave the monarch too much power without accountability.

KEY TERM

Canon Law: the laws that apply within the Church

the king's peace: refers to peace and order being maintained in the kingdom, because of the correct application of law and justice, which has the king at its head

CROSS-REFERENCE

More on the policy of **Thorough** and the application of it is in Chapter 7, page 56.

ACTIVITY

Sir Thomas Roe wrote about how, instead of there being healthy political debate, one faction dominated everything and no-one outside the faction had any influence. With your partner, discuss what he meant and why such a perspective might present a problem to Charles.

Methods of government

Interpreting the law

In the absence of Parliament, Charles could not enact any new laws but he did have considerable influence over how existing laws would be interpreted through a number of powerful **prerogative courts** and so he relied on these to secure law and order during the Personal Rule.

Star Chamber

The Court of Star Chamber was made up of Privy Councillors selected by the monarch. The king could remove cases from the common-law courts and bring them to Star Chamber where defendants could be questioned in private and fined, imprisoned or forced to undergo corporal punishment. It was especially useful to attack those who disagreed with government policy, and had been used extensively by Henry VII to establish his authority as England came out of a prolonged period of dynastic war. It could not hand down a death penalty but it could impose huge fines.

The Court of High Commission

This was technically the chief court of the Church, designed to enforce conformity to **canon law**. In practice, the monarch could convene it to discuss civil as well as religious cases, and its judgements could be passed on to Star Chamber for sentencing.

Regional Councils

The Council of the North, situated in York, and the Council of the Welsh Marches, administered from Ludlow Castle, could function as prerogative courts to impose royal control far away from Westminster. The leader of each Council, known as the 'Lord President,' acted as a regional governor, ensuring local officials carried out royal requirements effectively. The Council used imprisonment and fines as its primary punishments.

Privy Council

Although chiefly an advisory body, the Privy Council could function as a prerogative court.

The administration of government

The aim of local government in Stuart England was to ensure that **the king's peace** was maintained, so that communities could enjoy stability and order. The entire infrastructure of local government rested on cooperation between local families and the king because there were no professional, salaried royal jobs. Communication was vital, as was goodwill.

Thorough

William Laud and Thomas Wentworth together used their authority as Privy Councillors to govern by imposing strict standards upon royal officials including sheriffs, JPs, bishops and judges. They referred to their rigorous policy as '**Thorough**'.

The Book of Orders, January 1631

Books of Orders were a long-established means of communication between Crown and local government. First issued in 1578, the twelfth revision of the Book of Orders was published in 1631 in response to chronic poverty caused by harvest failures in 1629 and 1630. The 1631 Book of Orders set out a significant reform of local government, which was the brainchild of Privy Councillor Henry Montagu, Earl of Manchester, and his brother, who was a JP. It consisted of eight Orders and twelve Directions. The Directions were conventional: instructions for preventing **vagrancy**; allocating poor children to apprenticeships; employing the idle; repairing the roads. What was innovatory was the nature of the Orders, because they outlined new, more professional working practices for the JPs:

- JPs to convene a monthly meeting of enforcement officials at **hundred** level. This would include constables, petty constables, churchwardens and overseers of the poor.
- JPs to send monthly reports about their meetings to the sheriff.
- Sheriffs to report from the JPs to the Circuit Judges.
- Circuit Judges to report upwards to the Privy Council.

A penalty was added for non-compliance: punishment by Star Chamber.

Fig. 2 *Counties were divided into hundreds and parishes*

KEY TERM

vagrancy: the state of being a vagrant, which means a homeless person who survives by begging and often travels from place to place looking for shelter and food

hundreds: administrative units made up of a number of parishes within a county; a parish is the smallest administrative unit of local government and is formed of the dwellings that are serviced by a particular church

A CLOSER LOOK

The Stuart Court System

Just as today, there was a hierarchy of courts in which judges sat to hear civil or criminal trials. In London, High Court Judges sat in the Court of King's Bench, Court of Exchequer and Court of Chancery. In the counties, Circuit Judges sat in the Assize Courts which convened twice a year. Assize Courts were essential for law and order and they also provided an important contact point between Crown and County, where the king's wishes and in particular, his legislative requirements, could be communicated.

ACTIVITY

Historians debate whether the 1631 Book of Orders was an attempt by the king to bring local government to heel – and possibly therefore a step towards Absolutism – or an attempt by a king to remind local gentry of their God-given duty to protect the weak and vulnerable in their communities. Perhaps they were nothing more than an attempt to address a specific crisis. In threes, debate the argument. What do you need to know to be sure?

ACTIVITY

Put yourself in the position of a gentry family from a county such as Yorkshire or Devon and think through the different aspects of Stuart government that intersect with your life. You will need to think about the king's royal court in London as well as regional government. Which type of government has most impact on your life?

Lord Lieutenant of the County	Deputy Lieutenants	Justices of the Peace (JPs)	County Sheriff	Constables
Responsible for ensuring local defence and, if required, mobilising the county militia into the national army. Appointed by the Crown.	Appointed by the Crown on the advice of the Lord Lieutenant.	About 50 per county. Appointed by the Crown judged lesser criminal cases and escalated more serious cases to higher courts. Enforced including poor relief, road maintenance and alcohol licensing.	Appointed by the Crown. Traditionally responsible for the administration of justice. In the 1630s also responsible for collecting taxes.	Responsible for policing the 'hundreds' – several parishes, grouped together. Unpaid, they served for one year. Reported to the Sheriff.

Fig. 3 *Overview of aspects of the local government system (hierarchy of positions from right to left)*

A CLOSER LOOK

Ordinary or extraordinary taxation?

Stuart (and earlier) England made a distinction between the ordinary, private income of the Crown and its extraordinary, tax-based, income. Article 12 of Magna Carta in 1215 said: 'No scutage [taxes] or aid shall be imposed in our kingdom unless by common counsel [agreement of the people] of our kingdom', and this formed the basis of the precedent that extraordinary income could only be granted by Parliament.

CROSS-REFERENCE

Implications of the peace treaties for Charles's religious policy are covered in Chapter 6.

A CLOSER LOOK

Access to credit

The strength of the Crown meant that monarchs could normally borrow money from the City of London and other financiers in anticipation of future income. However, the Crown Jewels were pawned in the Netherlands in the 1620s, and in 1633, Charles's failure to meet his loan repayments caused a credit crunch that destroyed his chief financier, Philip Burlamachi and his network of investors. As a result, Charles's ability to access credit was very limited.

Financial policies and reactions

Charles had called Parliaments in 1625, 1626 and 1628 because he needed money. He dissolved Parliament in 1629 because Parliament was exploiting his need for financial help to impose what he felt to be unacceptable limitations on kingly power. Of course, Parliament's counter-argument was that they were trying to maintain their traditional rights and privileges against an innovative king. Ultimately, Charles's only remaining option was to find an alternative way to fund Crown expenditure so that he could become financially independent of Parliament. This meant replacing his reliance on extraordinary taxation granted by Parliament by exploiting the ordinary, private income of the Crown, while making savings.

Prudence

In 1629, Charles had a debt of £2m, far exceeding his income. To put that into context, King James inherited a debt of £300,000 in 1603, which had risen to £600,000 by 1607, and £726,000 by 1617. In 1621 it was estimated that the cost of a German military campaign would be £500,000 and the highly controversial 1627 Forced Loan brought in £240,000. Lord Treasurer Weston and Chancellor Cottington therefore counselled Charles to cut expenditure:

1. Reduce spending on foreign affairs by concluding peace with France (1629 Treaty of Susa) and Spain (1630 Treaty of Madrid).
2. Reform of Charles's household, to dramatically reduce its share of royal expenditure. In 1628, the royal household cost 40% of Charles's ordinary income, dropping dramatically in 1629–30 (only to double in 1630–31).

Sources of revenue during the Personal Rule

In 1635 William Laud commissioned a report into Weston's management of the Crown finances. He discovered that, while the debt had not been substantially reduced, Crown income was beginning to run ahead of Crown expenditure, an undeniable success and the first time this had been accomplished in decades. The collective term which describes these non-Parliamentary methods for raising finances is 'fiscal feudalism' and two of the most efficient revenue sources were customs duty and monopoly grants.

Customs Duty

Products that incurred Customs Duty were listed in an official Book of Rates which also indicated the value of each product and the amount of tax levied on it. The amount of tax was either a fixed rate or a percentage of the listed value of the item, so it did not change if the price at which the product was bought or sold went up or down. The price of goods rose significantly (inflation) in the early modern period but the Book of Rates had only been infrequently updated (in 1558 and 1608) so when Charles ordered the Book to be revalued in 1635, he was able to immediately and dramatically increase the revenue he would receive from Customs.

Monopolies

Huge profits could be made by being the sole producer or merchant of a particular product and so the sale of monopolies was a ripe avenue for corruption. Parliament had vigorously attacked monopolies in the early 1620s and the use of monopolies in the 1630s led to charges of corruption at court. Sir Richard Weston was a particular target because he procured a monopoly of soap for a consortium of his friends. The product was satirised as 'Popish Soap' because it was rumoured to have been financed by Catholic friends of the queen. Many Protestant households refused to buy the soap and so a black-market trade sprang up.

Table 2 *Overview of different fiscal measures applied by King Charles*

Source	Definition	Enforcement	Impact
Customs Duty	Including tonnage and poundage, this was a tax on imports and exports.	Granted to Charles for only one year in 1625, he continued to collect it throughout the Personal Rule. In 1635, a new Book of Rates updated official valuations.	Trade improved once England was no longer at war with France and Spain so customs revenue increased. 1631–1635: £270,000 pa. Increased again post-1635 to £425,000 pa.
Recusancy fines	Fines on those who refused to attend compulsory Church of England Sunday services.	Enforcement was tightened up to maximise income.	1620s' revenue: £5,300 pa 1634: £26,866
Distraint of knighthood	Anyone holding land worth £40 pa or more had to attend the coronation of a new monarch and to be knighted, or incur a fine.	Not applied since Tudor times but revived in the Personal Rule.	By 1635, revenue of £175,000 had been raised from gentlemen including Oliver Cromwell.
Monopolies	Buying a monopoly gave a corporation the sole right to produce, import or sell a product.	Holding a monopoly by an individual had been made illegal in the 1624 Monopolies Act but a loophole meant that Charles could sell monopolies to corporations.	The most notorious monopoly, for 'Popish Soap' earned Charles £33,000.
Wardships	The Crown could administer the estate of an heir who inherited under the age of 21.	Grants of wardships were exploited by loyal officials to maximise Crown income.	Wardships raised £45,000 revenue at the beginning of the Personal Rule. Cottington became Master of the Court of Wards in 1635 and by 1640 annual revenues were £84,000, collected very efficiently.
Forest fines	Fines for any land owner who had extended their boundaries into land belonging to the royal forests.	William Noy scoured ancient maps and documents to identify encroachments and many landed families could not produce centuries-old documentation to disprove his claims.	£38,667 raised (£20,000 from the Earl of Salisbury) at the cost of significantly angering rich and powerful landowners.
Building fines	Fines for building beyond the chartered boundaries of a town.	Rediscovered ancient charters against which new buildings could be assessed.	Burden particularly fell on builders working around London where over 60,000 new homes had been built since 1603.
Enclosure fines	Fines on landowners for illegally enclosing (fencing, for use as fields) common land.	Not new, but vigorously enforced.	Seen as a fine on landowners wanting to improve their estates.

KEY PROFILE

Willam Noy (1577–1634) was a Cornish lawyer who first entered Parliament in 1603. He led an attack on monopolies in the 1621 Parliament. In 1631, he became Attorney General and applied himself vigorously to the task of locating forgotten soures of prerogative income. He recorded these in a small book, known as 'Noy's Report'.

SECTION 2 | An experiment in Absolutism, 1629–1640

A CLOSER LOOK

Since Norman times, all subjects owed allegiance and service to the king and, in return, the king granted land to his subjects. While initially, 'service' particularly meant the provision of equipped and fed soldiers to join a royal army, over time, 'service' increasingly meant the provision of money, hence '**fiscal feudalism**'.

KEY TERM

Ship Money: a prerogative form of income that a monarch could levy on coastal towns to provide emergency funds in time of conflict or threat, in order to defend coastal regions and equip the fleet

ACTIVITY

Look at the list of revenue sources shown in Table 2 on page 41.
1. Which are 'ordinary' examples of fiscal feudalism? Are there any that could be attacked as 'extraordinary' in the context of the seventeenth century? To do this, you will need to consider whether an existing method was tightened up or extended (ordinary) or whether a lapsed method or innovative method was used (extraordinary).
2. With a partner, make a list of the different types of people who might be alienated by the fiscal measures of the Personal Rule.

Ship Money

Despite the broad efficiency of Weston and Cottington's efforts, Charles still needed more money and he turned to **Ship Money** to raise it.

He had previously tried to levy Ship Money in 1628, when he issued writs to coastal counties, which would have brought in £170,000. He quickly cancelled the writs because of opposition by local collectors who refused to collect a tax that Parliament, recently prorogued, had not endorsed. As a Yorkshire commissioner said, 'having no legal power to levy the same upon the subject we dare not presume to do it'.

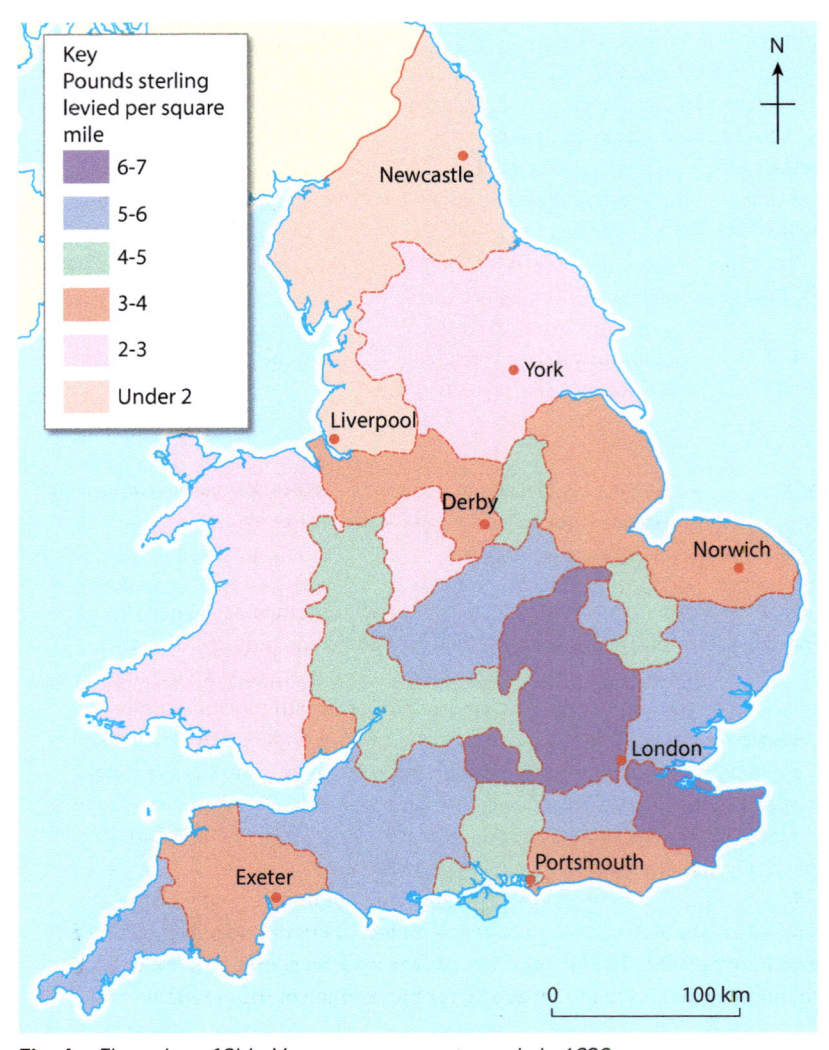

Fig. 4 The value of Ship Money assessments made in 1636

In October 1634, Charles levied Ship Money on coastal towns and cities, but he extended it to the whole of England in 1635. As a result, he raised approximately £300,000 pa, the equivalent of three Parliamentary subsidies, with initially at least **90 per cent compliance**. Guidance to the Sheriffs who were responsible for enforcing collection was confusing and many applied Ship Money to more people than would have been reached by a Parliamentary subsidy.

The Hampden Case

In November 1637, Sir John Hampden, a prominent Puritan MP, was taken to court for failing to pay his Ship Money dues. The case became a test case for the king's prerogative and Hampden's cause was championed by some of the finest legal minds in the country at the time.

> **SOURCE 2**
>
> From the records of the Court of the Exchequer, 1637. The Puritan lawyer, **Oliver St John**, defends **John Hampden**, a prominent Puritan from Buckinghamshire, for refusing to pay Ship Money:
>
> His Majesty applies the law and justice to his subjects with the assistance of his Judges, his established legal advisers. So likewise, in other cases, he needs the assistance of his great Council in Parliament My Lords, the Parliament is best qualified and ready to levy Ship Money among all ranks of people and across all parts of the kingdom. His Majesty declares the danger; Parliament, because it best knows of the wealth of all men within the realm, is best placed to compare the danger and men's wealth, so that it can proportion aid accordingly.
>
> Parliament is appointed by the law as the ordinary means for supply upon extraordinary occasions, when the ordinary supplies will not do it: My Lords, the writs for Ship Money do not identify any war at all has been proclaimed against our State, so the case is, whether in times of peace His Majesty may, without consent in Parliament, alter the property of the subject's goods for the defence of the realm.

The verdict in the Hampden case was close, with five judges out of twelve agreeing with him that Ship Money was unlawful.

> **SOURCE 3**
>
> From the summing up of the chief judge, Sir Robert Berkeley, Justice of the King's Bench, explaining the decision in the case of John Hampden who refused to pay Ship Money:
>
> I agree the Parliament is the most ancient and supreme court where Peers and Commons may make known their grievances and petition him for redress But the law knows no king-yoking policy. There are two maxims of the law of England 'The King is a person trusted with the state of the Commonwealth' and 'the King cannot do wrong'. Upon these two maxims the highest rights of majesty are grounded with which none but the King himself has to meddle, as, namely, war and peace, value of coin, Parliament at pleasure regal powers to command provision (in case of necessity) of means from the subjects to be adjoined to the King's own means for the defence of the Commonwealth. Otherwise I do not understand how the King's Majesty may be said to have the majestical right and power of a free monarch the King of mere right out to have, and the people of mere duty are bound to yield unto the King, supply for the defence of the kingdom.

A CLOSER LOOK

90 per cent compliance

This suggests that Ship Money was widely accepted and caused little unrest. However, the only safe and culturally acceptable way to oppose the king at this time was through Parliament, which was not in session. Individual criticism might have incurred royal anger; gathering opposition outside Parliament would have felt dangerously radical in such a conservative, hierarchical society.

KEY PROFILE

Sir Oliver St John (1598–1673) trained as a lawyer. He defended John Hampden in the Ship Money case and became an MP for the first time in 1640, representing Totnes. He was related to Oliver Cromwell through marriage.

Sir John Hampden (1593–1643) met Sir John Eliot while in jail. Certainly, this period of imprisonment marks the beginning of his activities as a vigorous Parliamentarian. He was a close confidante of Viscount Saye and Sele. Hampden died from wounds received in battle in 1643.

ACTIVITY

Evaluating primary sources

Oliver St John's speech in Source 2 builds the case against Ship Money with a series of statements that lead up to his final argument. Create a flow diagram to identify the different steps in his case. What is at the heart of the defence?

SECTION 2 | An experiment in Absolutism, 1629–1640

SOURCE 4

From the Venetian Ambassador in London, reporting back to Venice, 27 February 1637. The Ambassador gives his perspective on the case of John Hampden:

Your Excellencies [the Venetian government] can easily understand the great consequences in this decision, as at one stroke it roots out for ever the meeting of Parliament and renders the King absolute and sovereign. It has created such consternation and disorder that one cannot judge what the outcome will be. If the people submit to this present prejudice, they are submitting to an eternal yoke, thus finally the goal will be reached for which the King has been labouring so long.

STUDY TIP

First try to ensure you have a good understanding of the constitutional issues raised by the Ship Money case. You should also aim to review your learning about foreign policy, particularly relating to war with France and Spain. It would be useful to consider why this particular case became so noteworthy when there were lots of other innovative fiscal measures in the 1630s. Remember to comment on the provenance as well as the context of the extracts.

A LEVEL PRACTICE QUESTION

With reference to Sources 2, 3 and 4, and your understanding of the historical context, assess the value of these three sources to an historian studying the significance of the Hampden case.

The Hampden Case reduced the speed of collection of Ship Money but the most significant impact of the case was that it raised the debate of wider constitutional issues as the opinions of the judges were widely circulated.

Table 3 The collection of Ship Money, 1635–39

Year	Value of Ship Money levy	Actual amount collected	% compliance
1635	£218,500	£213,964	98
1636	£196,400	£189,493	96
1637	£196,413	£178,566	91
1638	£69,750*	£55,690	80
1639	£210,400	£53,000	25

*In 1638, war broke out in Scotland and the king was able to levy different charges, including 'Coat and Conduct', which meant that he could reduce the Ship Money levy.

ACTIVITY

Summary

In this chapter you have learned about two aspects of Charles's Personal Rule: methods of government and financial policies. You now need to consider whether they reveal legitimate behaviour (Charles's perspective) and whether they could be criticised as potentially absolutist or Catholic innovations (a Puritan perspective).

Make a table that will help you analyse the key events and features of his Personal Rule.

STUDY TIP

You will not only need to examine how successful Charles I was in increasing his income and balance this against any failures, you will also need to reflect on the 'cost' of his actions in order to address his overall success.

AS LEVEL PRACTICE QUESTION

'Charles I increased his royal finances successfully in the years 1629 and 1640.' Explain why you agree or disagree with this view.

6 Religious issues

SOURCE 1

From the Rushworth Collection, containing an account of the sentence meted out to three Puritan pamphleteers in 1637, who had published criticisms of the Archbishop of Canterbury:

Mr Burton spoke much while in the pillory to the people. The executioner cut off his ears deep and close, in a cruel manner, with much flowing of blood, an artery being cut, as there was likewise of Dr Bastwick. Then Mr Prynne's cheeks were seared with an iron made exceeding hot which done, the executioner cut off one of his ears and a piece of his cheek with it; then hacking the other ear almost off, he left it hanging and went down; but being called up again he cut it quite off.

Fig. 1 This Victorian engraving of the trial of Prynne, Bastwick and Burton shows the pillory in action; pillories were used for public punishment in order to humiliate offenders and give the community an opportunity to express their disapproval of the crime by pelting the offender with rotten food and even excrement

LEARNING OBJECTIVES

In this chapter you will learn about:

- Laud and Arminianism in England and Scotland
- the growth of opposition from Puritans.

KEY CHRONOLOGY

1629	Bishops ordered back to their dioceses
1629	Scottish Protestants ordered to kneel for communion annually
1633	William Laud becomes Archbishop of Canterbury
1633	Re-issue of Jacobean *Book of Sports*
1633	Abolition of Feoffees for Impropriations
1634	All Scottish Bishops are made Justices of the Peace
1635	Archbishop Spottiswoode becomes Lord Chancellor of Scotland
1636	Bishop William Juxon of London becomes Lord Treasurer of England
1637	Trial and punishment of **Prynne, Bastwick and Burton**

CROSS-REFERENCE

Find out more about Prynne, Bastwick and Burton later in this chapter, page 52.

ACTIVITY

Pair discussion

Using your knowledge of the period so far, do you think the punishments meted out to Burton, Bastwick and Prynne were reasonable? Discuss with a partner.

SECTION 2 | An experiment in Absolutism, 1629–1640

> **KEY TERM**
>
> **libel:** the offence of writing something that harms someone's reputation
>
> **sedition:** the offence of stirring up a rebellion against the established order; so, seditious libel means writings that threaten governmental order
>
> **Mount Calvary:** the location in Jerusalem where Christians believe that Jesus was crucified, on a cross alongside two thieves
>
> **stigmata:** meaning 'sign'; mystical markings on the skin, in the same location as where nails were struck in the hands and feet of Jesus on the cross; medieval Christianity in particular believed that stigmata were a special sign of God's favour

Three men, their heads and arms fixed in pillories, stood in the yard in Westminster: a doctor, a clergyman and a lawyer. Star Chamber had found them guilty of seditious libel because they had written pamphlets attacking the policies of Archbishop William Laud. The lawyer, William Prynne, had already had the tops of his ears chopped off in 1634 as punishment for writing a book that attacked Henrietta Maria's court. Now he lost his ears entirely and had the letters 'SL' for '**seditious libel**' burned onto his cheeks. Each of the men called out defiantly from the pillory: 'Me thinks I see **Mount Calvary** where the three Crosses … were pitched' was Burton's evocative cry. The quip swiftly went round that SL actually stood for '**Stigmata** Laudis,' a pun meaning either 'sign of praise' or 'sign of Laud'. What was particularly shocking about the use of the pillory for Prynne, Bastwick and Burton was that it was not traditionally a punishment for gentlemen. It seemed to suggest that William Laud, who pushed for their trial, was not respectful of society's hierarchies and traditions. In 1644, Prynne avenged himself by leading the trial of William Laud that resulted in the Archbishop's execution for treason.

Laud and Arminianism

> **A CLOSER LOOK**
>
> ### Bishops and Archbishops
>
> Bishops are senior clergy in the Anglican Church, reporting to either the Archbishop of Canterbury or York. A bishop is responsible for all the parishes and priests in his diocese, which is an administrative and pastoral district connected to a cathedral. Bishops are assisted by a small number of Archdeacons. Synonyms for diocese are bishopric and see, while things connected to the bishops are called 'episcopal', and the system of government by bishop is known as 'episcopacy'. The Archbishopric of Canterbury is senior to that of York, and in the same way, there is an implicit hierarchy of bishops, headed by the Bishop of London.

James I had found William Laud too divisive a character but Charles I, influenced by Buckingham, felt quite differently about him. He admired Laud's desire for order and ceremonial in the Church, partly because it reflected Charles's own love of hierarchy and authority and promoted him rapidly: Dean of the Chapel Royal in 1626, Bishop of London in 1628 and Archbishop of Canterbury in 1633.

Theologically, Laud was an **Arminian**. Yet to describe what he set about to achieve in the Anglican Church of the 1630s as an 'Arminian agenda' is imprecise. He developed and executed his own particular vision of Anglican churchmanship and therefore the term 'Laudian' is more appropriate than 'Arminian' because it expresses the unique nature of his reforms.

Laudianism

At the beginning of the 1630s, an observer might be able to associate certain developments within the Anglican Church with Laud. By the end of the decade, most Protestants were able to unite against Laudianism as a common enemy, identifying its key themes and seeing them expressed in different ways across the whole Church.

Fig. 2 *When Laud became Bishop of London in 1628, he was in fact becoming the most powerful clergyman in England because Archbishop Abbot was ineffectual; Laud became Archbishop of Canterbury in 1633*

> **CROSS-REFERENCE**
>
> The difference between **Arminianism** and Calvinism is explained on page 22.

CHAPTER 6 | Religious issues

Table 1 *Distinctive features of Laudianism*

Key emphasis of Laudianism	Key terms	Impact
The physical setting of the church as the holy house of God.	Beauty of Holiness	Decoration of churches lay the Church open to charges of churches being Catholic in appearance.
The status and role of ministers.	Priests	Emphasis on the sacred status of clergy, more like Catholic priests (with special powers to mediate between God and man) than Puritan brothers.
The set prayers and rituals increased in priority and enforced more rigidly.	Liturgy (the standard words and actions used in public worship), order, decency	Emphasis on conformity posed a challenge to the broad tolerance of the Jacobean Church, where the whole spectrum of Protestant practice was tolerated as long as it did not try to impose itself elsewhere.
Priority on prayer rather than on preaching, especially public prayers through liturgy.	Public prayer	A direct challenge to the Puritan emphasis on preaching as the main purpose of church services.
Renewed emphasis on the sacraments, especially communion (eucharist).	Altar	Generated significant controversy over the physical location of the altar. Open to charges of being Catholic because Catholicism also put a very high value on sacraments.
Activity on Sundays a matter for the Church to decide; not a scriptural imperative. Sunday just one of many holy days in the annual life of the Church.	Anti-sabbatarianism (against the principle that only religious activities were acceptable on Sundays)	Direct challenge to central Puritan theology of the Sabbath, heightened by the revised *Book of Sports*.

Altar controversy

Laud rigorously pursued decency and order in church practice. The earliest Reformation churches had downgraded the status of the altar, turning it from a sacred, quasi-magical shrine into a plain table, and moving it into the central body of the church. Laud reversed this policy, in part in response to reports such as the following witnessed in a London church: '[I saw] a woman dandling and dancing her child upon the Lord's holy table; when she was gone I saw a great deal of water upon the table; I verily think they were not tears of devotion, it was well it was no worse.'

Laud instead insisted on a new altar policy:
- North-South alignment of the communion table (altar) against the easternmost wall of the church, where the Catholic altar would have been
- Chancel, where the altar stands, raised by steps and separated by a rail from the rest of the church
- Covered with a decorated embroidered cloth
- Enforcement checked by annual '**visitations**'.

Consequences of Laud's altar policy

- Some contemporaries thought this might presage a return to the Catholic mass: as a writer in 1633 declared, 'It is generally thought that the times will every day grow better and better for Catholics.'
- Many felt alarmed at such a dramatic break with tradition, particularly because churchgoers sat in the same place in church each week, with the people of higher status sitting in the same pews, towards the front, as their ancestors had occupied for many generations. It was often necessary to remove these family pews to accommodate the new location of the altar, implying a dangerous innovation and a lack of respect for tradition and the social status quo.
- Strict enforcement narrowed the broad tolerance that was essential for religious stability.

CROSS-REFERENCE

See pages 49–50 for more on The Beauty of Holiness.

A CLOSER LOOK

In 1637, Bishop John Williams was imprisoned because he published a pamphlet entitled *The Holy Table, Name and Thing*, which attacked the altar policy and specifically the use of the word 'altar' which smacked of Popery, rather than the puritan term 'table'.

KEY TERM

visitations: made by bishops to each of the parishes in their diocese on a regular basis; bishops had to check that the churches were in good order, well maintained and with the altars in the right place

SECTION 2 | An experiment in Absolutism, 1629–1640

Fig. 3 *A Laudian church*

Fig. 4 *A Puritan church*

Politicisation of the clergy

The Laudian emphasis on the status of the clergy was matched by the way Charles promoted many of them into other areas of public life.
- All Scottish Bishops were made Justices of the Peace (1634), an innovation swiftly extended into England and Ireland.
- Archbishop Spottiswoode became Lord Chancellor of Scotland (1635)
- Bishop William Juxon of London became Lord Treasurer of England (1636) – the first cleric to hold this role since the fifteenth century
- Laud himself became Chancellor of Oxford University (1630), served as a Treasury Commissioner and joined a Privy Council committee on foreign affairs.

By allowing such an overlap between religious and political spheres, Charles allowed his circle of advisers to narrow further and made his clergy vulnerable to political assault. As clerical confidence grew, and churchmen began to feel more powerful, they began to be perceived as a threat to the power and influence of the gentry.

Laudianism and Absolutism

Laudianism appeared to threaten religious expression in England and Scotland but its significance was heightened because, to many, it suggested that the drive for conformity in the Church was evidence that Charles was absolutist at heart. Laudian expressions in favour of authority and order connected the religious and political spheres together.

ACTIVITY

Evaluating primary sources

1. In pairs, summarise Manwaring's argument in Source 2.
2. The Parliament of 1628 tried to impeach Manwaring for this sermon. What did the House of Commons find so offensive? Consider both the religious and political aspects in your answer.
3. To what extent does Manwaring's sermon represent a radical perspective on royal power?

SOURCE 2

From a sermon by the Arminian Roger Manwaring in the 1620s, preaching in front of King Charles and demonstrating the Laudian conception of monarchical power:

Among all the powers that are delegated by God, the kingly power is most high, strong and large: kings are above all, inferior to none, to no multitudes of men, to no Angels. When a royal command is given, all loyal subjects should entirely respect its Godly origin and authority. In fact, though any king in the world should command flatly against the law of God, yet his power should not be resisted or rebelled against because that is clearly unlawful. Instead, they should endure with patience, no matter what pain his pleasure should inflict upon them. By their patient and humble suffering of their sovereign's will they become glorious martyrs, whereas by resisting of his will they should for ever endure the pain and stain of hideous traitors and unholy evildoers.

Establishing conformity

In much the same way as the 1631 Book of Orders was intended to tighten up local government, Laud set about enforcing greater discipline and conformity within the Church. For Charles, who had so struggled with unruly subjects in the Parliaments of the 1620s, anyone aiming at order and obedience was a true supporter.

- **Asserting conformity.** Laud tightened up on the use of liturgy as a way of creating uniformity in church services. Clergy were given renewed instructions about the format and words to use in each service. Church canons (rules) were revised to include the new altar policy. Proclamations requiring churches to attend to maintenance and repairs were issued at frequent intervals.
- **Auditing conformity.** In 1629, Laud ordered all the bishops to return to their dioceses and take responsibility for ensuring that their parish priests were obeying instructions. Visitations and **Presentment Bills** were used to report on conformity to Laud.
- **Enforcing conformity**. Star Chamber and the Court of High Commission were used with much greater frequency and punishments were harsher. In 1634, Laud orchestrated the removal of Robert Heath, Chief Justice of the Common Pleas, because he thought that Heath would decide against him in court cases relating to religious uniformity.

> **KEY TERM**
>
> **Presentment Bills:** reported directly to the Archdeacon and listed failings in church buildings, conduct of clergy or behaviour of parishioners

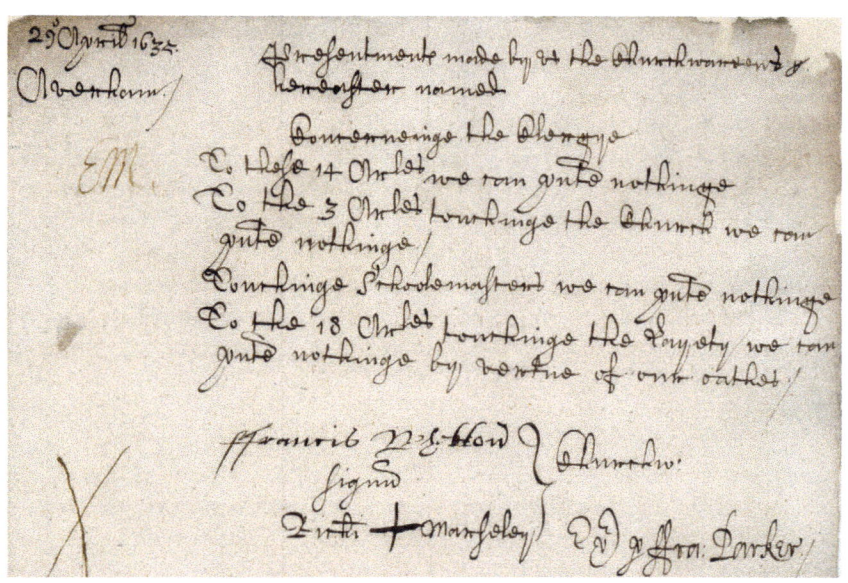

Fig. 5 *This example of a Presentment Bill comes from Nottinghamshire in 1635; Presentment Bills demonstrated a new efficiency in the Laudian Church that some interpreted as indicative that the king was tightening his control over religious affairs*

> **CROSS-REFERENCE**
>
> Aiming for discipline and conformity became a characteristic of the Personal Rule and began to be bracketed under the word 'Thorough'. Wentworth was the other key proponent of Thorough, as discussed in Chapter 7, page 56.

> **KEY TERM**
>
> **vestments:** the special clothes worn by clergymen; under Laud, use of vestments became more ornate than the Puritans felt was appropriate, increasing fears of insidious Catholicism

Laudianism in Scotland

One of the main differences between the Churches of England and Scotland at this time is demonstrated by King James's funeral in 1625. Archbishop Spottiswood of St Andrews was careful not to look as though he was less important than Archbishop Abbot. He refused to wear the same funeral **vestments** that the English clergy wore, preferring instead a sober, plain black robe that was much more in keeping with the Scottish Presbyterian tradition. When Charles I became King of Scotland he showed a terrible lack of awareness of the delicate balance that needed to be maintained between the Churches of Scotland and England and the distinctive nature of Scottish Protestantism.

The Beauty of Holiness

Shortly after becoming king, Charles attempted to take back old Church lands that had been given or sold to the Scottish gentry since 1540, in order to

SECTION 2 | An experiment in Absolutism, 1629–1640

> **ACTIVITY**
>
> In 1604, King James shouted 'No Bishop! No King!', but, in 1633, Charles absolutely aligned the status of the bishops in Scotland with the monarchy. Refresh your memory about Presbyterianism in Scotland. Do you think it was wise of Charles to put such a focus on Scottish episcopacy?

> **KEY TERM**
>
> **canons:** rules that apply within the Church (see Canon Law, page 44) and are made up of a number of articles, which each cover a specific topic
>
> **excommunication:** a well-established religious punishment which meant that a person was excluded from attendance in church and would automatically go to hell when they died

> **KEY TERM**
>
> **dogma:** the set of religious beliefs that inform one's religious practice; to become more **dogmatic** means that you insist on being able to pursue your beliefs to the full, which in 1630s' England meant that religious divisions began to sharpen in focus

bring wealth back into the Scottish Church. In particular, he wanted St Giles' Cathedral in Edinburgh to be refurbished. His efforts were met with anger, even panic, among the gentry, and resulted in widespread disobedience, while at the same time raising public fears that bishops would become over-mighty.

When he finally travelled to Scotland to be crowned in 1633, he arranged for a ceremony that sent further shockwaves around the Church. A railed-off, raised altar decorated with candles and a crucifix representing the cross of Christ, was built for the occasion in the Holyrood Kirk, and six Scottish bishops, including Spottiswoode, wore ornate golden vestments as they helped William Laud officiate. Charles swore a new Coronation Oath that promised to defend the bishops and preserve the privileges of the Church.

Conformity

In 1629, all Scottish subjects were told that they had to kneel to take communion in their parish church, at least once a year. To a Scottish Protestant, kneeling carried dangerous connotations of Catholicism and it indicated that Charles was ensuring that his royal authority extended across the Church. In 1636 however, he raised the bar for conformity to a new height by publishing a new set of Scottish **canons**, a revision of Church law as it applied in Scotland. For the first time, the Scottish canons were based on the English canons, not on traditional Scottish **articles**, and they were dramatically different in several important respects:

- These new canons were to be imposed on the Church without needing to be ratified by the Scottish General Assembly.
- Bishops were given their authority by a formal ceremony of consecration, not by election by other ministers, which would have been a compromise with the Presbyterian tradition.
- There was no mention of the traditional institutions of Scottish Church government such as the General Assembly, presbyteries or kirk sessions.
- There would be a new Prayer Book which everyone, clergy or laity, had to use. Dissenters would be **excommunicated**.

The growth of opposition from Puritans

There were two major reasons for the growth of opposition to Laudianism.
1. Laudianism specifically challenged beliefs and practices central to Puritanism. Sensing an increasing threat, many Puritans began to become more radical and **dogmatic**.
2. Laudianism looked perilously close to Catholicism and raised fears that Charles was steering towards Rome. It united the majority of Protestants against the spectre of a Popish plot.

In summary, not only were Laudians being promoted to high office within the Anglican Church, tipping the governance of the Church away from Puritanism, but Laudianism increasingly defined a narrow range of acceptable practice within the Church of England and thus broke the broad consensus that was the basis of the Elizabethan and Jacobean settlement.

Direct assaults on Puritanism

Not only were many Laudian practices distasteful to Puritans but some of his policies appeared to directly attack Puritan beliefs.

1633 *Book of Sports*

Laud re-issued the 1618 *Book of Sports*, which outlined a range of sports and activities – including morris dancing – that people could do after attending the compulsory Sunday morning service. This directly challenged the Puritan idea of the purpose of Sundays, which they believed to be prayerfulness and Bible reading. As in 1618, priests were directed to read from the Book or be expelled from their parishes but in 1633, enforcement was administered more effectively through visitations and Presentment Bills.

1633 Abolition of the Feoffees for Impropriations

An old Church law stated that a member of the laity could buy ('impropriate') the right to collect the **tithe** of a parish, provided that they arranged and paid for a suitable minister for that parish. In the past it had been used as a way for a rich person to gain control of their local church so it was quite open to corruption and had fallen into disuse. In the 1620s however a group of Puritan merchants and landowners based in and around London began to buy up the right to collect tithes so that they could put well-trained and vigorous Puritan ministers into parishes. This group were known as Feoffees, which is another word for trustee – someone who has a weighty responsibility.

In 1633, Laud used Star Chamber to abolish the Feoffees for Impropriations.

> **KEY TERM**
>
> **tithe:** the tax that everyone in the parish had to pay in order to finance their minister; tithes were generally collected by the clergy

Fears of Catholicism

Throughout the 1630s, fears rose that there was a co-ordinated attempt from within the Catholic world to overthrow England's Protestant Church. It is clear that many strands could be linked together to support such a perspective.

ACTIVITY

Extension

Complete the following table with evidence from this and the previous chapter, and add an alternative view. Some entries have been completed for you.

Theme	Evidence of Popery	Alternative view
Catholicism of Henrietta Maria	In 1632, a new Catholic chapel commissioned by Charles for his queen and built within Somerset House was consecrated in front of a congregation of 2000.	
Preferment of Catholics and Catholic sympathisers during Charles's Personal Rule		Charles had to find men to govern for him but many of the most capable men he could have chosen were too associated with the Puritan Parliamentary opposition of the 1620s for him to want to deploy them.
Diplomatic initiatives	Charles I was the first monarch since the Reformation to welcome a Papal Emissary, Gregorio Panzani, at court in 1634. He was a poor choice for the role but his successor, George Con, was more effective.	
Laudianism		Temperamentally, Charles appreciated order, hierarchy and ceremonial. Laud's rise reflects only this, not a move to Catholicism.
Add your own categories…		

SECTION 2 | An experiment in Absolutism, 1629–1640

KEY PROFILE

John Lilburne (1614–57) was a Durham gentleman. He served an apprenticeship to a master who introduced him to Bastwick's network. He became involved in printing unlicensed pamphlets such as Prynne's *News from Ipswich* and Bastwick's *The Letany*. Lilburne was arrested for importing *The Letany* from the Dutch presses into London and was fined, pilloried, imprisoned and tortured. From prison, he began to write and smuggle out his own pamphlets, including *A Worke of the Beast*.

John Bastwick (1593–1654) was a good example of how moderate Puritans could become radicalised in the Laudian climate of the Personal Rule. Bastwick was a doctor who published a couple of anti-Catholic pamphlets in the early 1630s, but by 1637 he had extended his opposition to bishops within the English Church. Bastwick's attacks on Laudianism were often earthy and vulgar. According to his *Letany*, 'The Church is now as full of ceremonies as a dog is full of fleas.'

Growth of a Puritan Opposition

Puritans expressed their opposition to Laudianism in a number of different ways.

Emigration

Some Puritans emigrated, particularly to the American colonies, to escape Laudianism and establish a new life in a new society. The 1630s saw a particular upsurge in emigration, including the departure of one of the Feoffees who emigrated to the new Puritan colony in Pennsylvania, in New England.

A CLOSER LOOK

Puritan emigrants

'New England' is the name that was used in the seventeenth century to describe the group of colonies that were being established on the East Coast of America for a variety of reasons. As religion caused increasing strife in the 1620s and 1630s, new colonies took on distinctively religious complexions. Maryland derives its name from Queen Henrietta Maria and became a refuge for Catholics. The colony of Massachusetts was founded in the late 1620s: within a decade, over 20,000, primarily Puritan, migrants had made their home there.

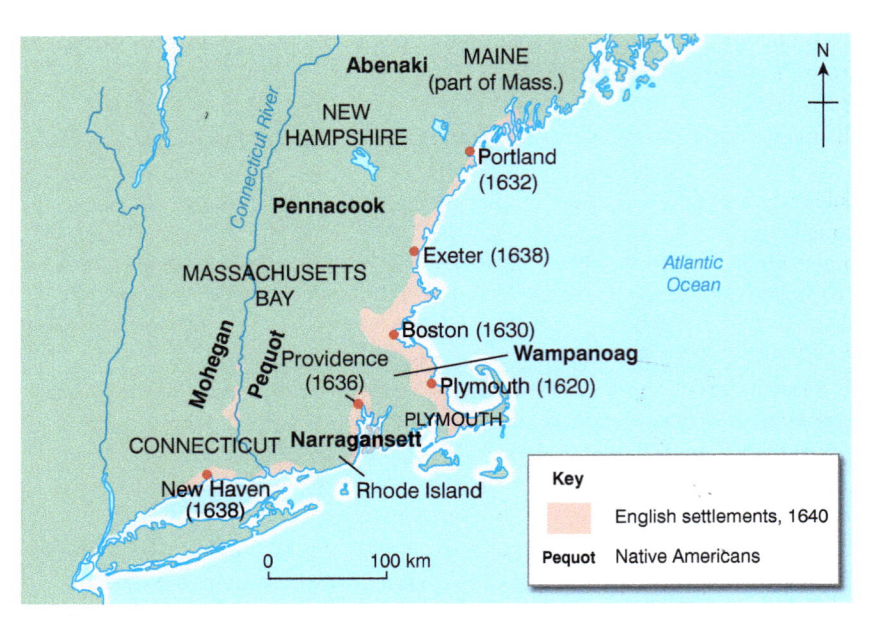

Fig. 6 *Migration to the new colonies in America surged in the 1630s for a number of reasons, of which a desire for a more Puritan culture was often the most significant*

Pamphlets

Bolder Puritans committed their opposition to Laudianism in print, with pamphlets describing bishops as 'tigers', 'vipers', 'bloodsuckers' and 'cruel stepfathers of the Church'. Many pamphlets were anonymous, but prominent pamphleteers included **John Bastwick**, Henry Burton, William Prynne and **John Lilburne**.

A CLOSER LOOK

On the other hand, men such as Peter Heylyn argued directly against the likes of Bastwick and Burton. A prominent churchman who rose to become Chaplain to the king, Heylyn preached sermons attacking the Feoffees for Impropriations, and in 1637 published *A brief and moderate answer to the seditious and scandalous Challenge of H. Burton*, among other tracts and pamphlets.

Examples of the works of the Puritan pamphleteers

Title	Author	Publication Date	Synopsis
Histriomastix, or Actor's Tragedy	William Prynne	1632	An attack on the theatre in which Prynne described actresses as 'notorious whores,' which was immediately understood to be targeted at Henrietta Maria, who commissioned and acted in plays and masques.
For God and the King	Henry Burton	1636	A collection of sermons, in which he accused bishops and priests of Catholicism.
The Letany	John Bastwick	1637	An attack on the office of Bishop, denouncing them as devilish enemies of God.
A Worke of the Beast	John Lilburne	1638	A graphic account of his trial and the tortures he suffered, the 'Beast' of the title is a reference to the Devil, credited by Lilburne with dominating the 1630s' Church.

Resistance

Some opponents of Laudianism simply attempted to refuse to conform. Parishioners of **St Gregory's Church** in London resisted the required move of their communion table, but Charles brought them to account in front of the Privy Council in 1633, enforcing conformity.

Some ministers continued to espouse Puritan doctrine and were dismissed from their posts. Nathaniel Ward (1578–1652) was one such: as a leading Puritan minister in Essex, he was censured by William Laud in 1631 and dismissed from his post in 1633. He emigrated to Massachusetts.

Others took a firmer line: in 1633, Henry Sherfield, a clergyman from Salisbury, was prosecuted for destroying a stained glass window that he considered to be idolatrous. He felt it was so beautiful that it inspired such praise for its creator that it eclipsed its purpose as inspiring praise for God. Fortunately for him, his case was heard by a Puritan.

Emerging Puritan groupings

The Hampden Circle: John Hampden, a Puritan, was defended in the **Ship Money** trial by a team of Puritan lawyers from his friendship circle, including Oliver St John and Robert Holborne. While the trial did not have any direct religious import, it is not surprising that enemies of Laudianism would stand up against absolutist tendencies in their monarch.

The Puritan pamphleteers: As has been seen, there is evidence of a functional network around Prynne, Bastwick and Burton. However, there are other examples of pamphleteers operating independently.

The Providence Island Company: In 1629, following the discovery of Providence Island, which is off the coast of modern Nicaragua, a group of 20 investors formed a business that would run plantations of tobacco, cotton and sugar cane on the island. Again, although the Providence Island Company had no involvement in direct opposition to Laudianism, it consisted mainly of Puritans, many of whom would become pivotal in the Puritan Parliamentary opposition to Charles which emerged in the 1640s. The Company provided a meeting point for men such as John Pym, Oliver St John, **William Fiennes**, 1st Viscount Saye and Sele, and Gregory Gawsell, later treasurer for the Eastern Association, a Parliamentary military unit in the Civil War.

Summary

In the climate of the Church in the 1630s, conflict between Puritans and Laudians began to focus on the issue of 'innovation' – the question of whether it was Puritanism or Laudianism which was new and antagonistic to the ethos of the tradition and practice of the Anglican Church. Laudianism was divisive

A CLOSER LOOK

The church of St Gregory, by St Paul's in London, was the scene of another controversy in the 1630s, when the king's favourite architect, Inigo Jones, began to knock it down in order to extend nearby St Paul's. In 1641, the House of Commons took up the parishioners' complaint and persuaded the House of Lords to force Jones to rebuild it.

CROSS-REFERENCE

The Ship Money trial is covered in the previous chapter (see pages 42–43). The Puritan connection to the trial demonstrates the extent to which Charles's opponents were connected together in multiple ways.

KEY PROFILE

William Fiennes, 1st Viscount Saye and Sele (1582–1662) was a leading opponent of James I and Charles I although his friendship with Buckingham led to him being made Viscount in 1624. In 1637, Charles had his letters searched for evidence of treason but found nothing. He corresponded with the Covenanters and refused to swear the Oath of Allegiance to the king in 1639. He later raised a Parliamentary regiment against Charles.

SECTION 2 | An experiment in Absolutism, 1629–1640

and propelled both sides to greater extremes, so with hindsight it is possible to detect 'innovation' in both Puritan and Laudian camps. It is a charge Laud addressed comprehensively in front of Star Chamber at the end of the 1637 trial of Prynne, Bastwick and Burton (see Source 3).

SOURCE 3

From a speech delivered in Star Chamber at the trial of Prynne, Bastwick and Burton, by William Laud on 14 June 1637, which was published with a dedication to the king on its front page:

I can say it clearly and truly, as in the presence of God, everything I have done, as a senior churchman, to the uttermost of what I am conscious, has come out of an honest heart, and with a sincere intention for the good Government and Honour of the Church; and the maintenance of the Orthodox Truth and Religion of Christ expressed, established, and maintained in this Church of England.

In my care of this Church, I have brought it back into Order. I have brought back respectful patterns of Worship into it. I have returned it to the correct rules that were created when it was first created. This malicious storm is a response to my actions and has put a terrible cloud upon Me & some of my Brethren. And in the meantime, my attackers accuse us of Innovation, when in fact they are the chief Innovators of the Christian world. I say it again: they themselves and their accomplices are the greatest Innovators that the Christian world hath almost ever known. I will agree that others have spread more dangerous Errors in the Church of Christ; but no men, in any age of it, have been more guilty of Innovation than they.

ACTIVITY

Summary

To consolidate your learning from this chapter, make a list of the developments that took place in the Church of England and Scotland in the 1630s. In groups, discuss whether the changes are genuinely innovative or a renewal of earlier emphases in the Church. Then as a class, divide into Puritan and Laudian, and debate which was the more innovatory.

STUDY TIP

It may be helpful to prepare for your answer by making a list of Laud's reforms of the Church of England in the 1630s. Use this, and your contextual knowledge of the period, to give a balanced assessment and also to support your own argument.

A LEVEL PRACTICE QUESTION

'To what extent did Laud's reforms of the Church of England in the 1630s, undermine the compromise that had been established by Elizabeth I and continued by James I?'

STUDY TIP

You should aim to comment on provenance and content. Identify how the two sources are similar and different in their emphasis and understanding. Why might someone who heard either of these sources be able to construe them as hinting at Absolutism? Which source contains most that could alarm?

AS LEVEL PRACTICE QUESTION

Evaluating primary sources

Using Sources 2 and 3, and your understanding of the historical context, which of these two sources is more valuable in explaining the fear of Absolutism in the 1620s and 1630s.

7 Political issues

SOURCE 1

From a letter to Thomas Wentworth from his steward, which was found by a Victorian historian and included in a *Life of Sir Thomas Wentworth*, published in 1874. It refers to the progress of Wentworth's home building project. 'Mr William' was about four, and his sister, 'Mrs Ann', two or three:

At our arrival in York we found your lordship's family, including Mr William and Mrs Ann, to be all very well. Your children were delighted with your gifts and yet they said that they would be even happier if you and their worthy mother had been with them in person. Everyone entirely agreed with this sentiment and wished that your lordship could visit as often as their thoughts and hearts turned to you.

Your lordship's children are all very well and your lordship need not fear about how your building works are progressing when you have such a careful **steward** as Mrs Ann. She complained to me very much of two rainy days, which, as she said, prevented her from coming down and the building from going up because she was enforced to stay indoors and therefore could not supervise the workmen!

Sir Thomas Wentworth, 'Black Tom Tyrant', executed for high treason in 1641, was a loving husband and devoted father. Frequently absent from home on the king's business, he made every effort to keep in touch with domestic matters. Not only is he a key figure in the downfall of Charles I, but his life reveals the **vicissitudes** of early Stuart England.

The Role of Thomas Wentworth

Thomas Wentworth came from a Yorkshire gentry family and attended Cambridge University. At the age of 21, he sat in the 'Addled Parliament' as MP for Yorkshire. In the next three Parliaments he was a vocal critic of Crown policy and a fierce opponent of Buckingham and his pro-Spanish policy, to such an extent that Charles manoeuvred him out of the 1626 Parliament by appointing him Sheriff of Yorkshire. In 1627 he was imprisoned for refusing to pay the Forced Loan, and in 1628, he was one of the MPs who devised the Petition of Right. However, later in that same year, Wentworth was given a key royal appointment – the presidency of the Council of the North – and thereafter he was a fervent servant of the king, rising to be one of Charles's most trusted and influential advisers. This dramatic shift alienated his previous allies among Parliamentarians, for which he was given the nickname 'The Grand **Apostate**'.

- Wentworth identified Buckingham as the instigator of the foreign policy that he loathed and which drove him to oppose Charles's requests for money in Parliament and to attack Buckingham at every opportunity. In 1628, Buckingham was assassinated and, without his leadership, war with France and Spain was no longer pursued vigorously: a cause for Wentworth's opposition was removed.
- Wentworth was Protestant but not Puritan. He did not share the anxieties about Charles's religious ideas that galvanised men such as Pym.
- Although Wentworth is identified with the Petition of Right, he had championed an earlier, more moderate version, which was less directly critical of the king and less radical in its ambitions. After putting his name to the Petition, he gave a speech that stressed his belief in a traditional understanding of the role of the king.

LEARNING OBJECTIVES

In this chapter you will learn about:
- the role of Thomas Wentworth
- policies in England and Ireland
- reactions against the Crown
- demands for the recall of Parliament.

KEY CHRONOLOGY

1628	Wentworth becomes Lord President of the Council of the North
1631	New Book of Orders issued
1633	Wentworth becomes Lord Deputy of Ireland
	New Book of Rates issued in Ireland
1634	Anglican Thirty-Nine Articles introduced into Ireland
	Irish Parliament grants six subsidies
1639	Wentworth recalled to England

KEY TERM

steward: a servant (who may be nonetheless of a high status) who is given responsibility for looking after an absent master's affairs

vicissitudes: changes in life and fortune; it tends to have a negative connotation – unwelcome moments; ups and downs

apostate: a person who abandons a religious or political belief

ACTIVITY

Extension

As you learn more about Thomas Wentworth, create a timeline that reflects the changing fortunes of his life. You will need to refer to earlier chapters. Discuss: What are the turning points in his life? What was his moment of greatest triumph? Was his demise inevitable?

SECTION 2 | An experiment in Absolutism, 1629–1640

KEY PROFILE

Thomas Wentworth (1593–1641) rose to a position of great power under Charles I, but initially he was known for his strong opposition to Buckingham. This was reflected in his personal life: in 1622 he married Lady Arabella Holles, daughter of the Earl of Clare and sister of Denzil Holles, all bitter critics of Buckingham. He was an efficient administrator and ruthless authoritarian, and was created Earl of Strafford in 1640, shortly before being impeached by Parliament, found guilty and executed. In this book, he is referred to as Wentworth until 1640, and thereafter as Strafford.

Fig. 1 *Van Dyck's portrait of Wentworth with his secretary, Sir Philip Mainwaring, captures the earnest nature of Thorough*

CROSS-REFERENCE

Thorough, as a method of governance, is introduced in Chapter 5, page 38.

ACTIVITY

Does 'Thorough' indicate that Wentworth and Laud were devising ways to support royal Absolutism? What do you need to know to answer this question effectively?

Policies in England and Ireland

Thorough

Thomas Wentworth and William Laud corresponded frequently and they used the term 'Thorough' to encapsulate what they were trying to achieve in their respective roles as servants of the Crown.

Both Wentworth and Laud worked exceptionally long hours and were known for their attention to detail. They demanded the same of royal officials, including sheriffs, JPs, bishops and judges. They believed corruption should be rooted out of public life and order should be returned to Church and State. Non-conformity was a challenge to the king's authority that should be quashed. Laud and Wentworth wanted royal officials to be held accountable for their actions in the king's service. This meant that they would need to be able to monitor what officials were doing. In an age where public service was seen as a route to high status and great wealth, the integrity and dedication of practitioners of Thorough was well recognised.

How achievable was Thorough?

Despite their common adherence to Thorough, Laud and Wentworth were different in their expectation of how effectively Thorough could be implemented. Wentworth was an idealist, while Laud was far more pragmatic, as can be seen in Source 2.

SOURCE 2

From a private letter written by William Laud in the autumn of 1633 to Thomas Wentworth, one of many that passed between them:

If you don't mind me saying so, your Lordship, the lovely idea that you suggest, of everything being wonderful and healthy, and everyone running in the same direction and no-one caring for anything except serving the King is pure idealism. It's like Plato's idealistic vision of **Commonwealth** which has never been found anywhere except in **Utopia**.

Wentworth replied:

Yes but you ring all your words with so many 'ifs' and 'maybes' that it appears that you slide around as though on ice, desperately trying not to fall over. For example, if the lawyers may be contained within ancient and moderate bounds; if we keep trying to enforce Thorough (which I am sure we will); if we don't become weary in our efforts; if other people do their duty… Now, I ask you, with so many and such 'ifs' as these, maybe we will end up not doing anything at all. Can you tell me when you think all these 'ifs' will actually happen? Do you really think they will?

A CLOSER LOOK

Plato's **Commonwealth** and Thomas More's **Utopia** both outline ideal communities, where government is administered fairly and efficiently, for the greatest good of the people.

Policies in England

In 1628, Wentworth became Lord President of the Council of the North, responsible for implementing royal policy in Yorkshire, Northumberland, Cumberland and Westmorland. In his opening speech, he decisively presented his perspective on regal power: *'The king's authority is like the keystone which holds together the whole arch of order and government. It keeps each part in balance with the rest. If the keystone is shaken or harmed, the whole arch falls together in a confused heap.'*

As one of the king's representatives, he embodied Thorough and approached his job with zeal and efficiency: his insistence on conformity to the 1631 Books of Orders did a lot to ensure that the lower classes saw their lives improved. As an example, provisions for the poor were enforced properly and measures were taken to ensure that poor farmers were not illegally evicted from their farmland by wealthy landowners.

Yet this came at quite a cost. The north of England, distant from London, was not prepared for the imposition of central government control that Wentworth so vigorously intended to implement. Long-established local gentry families resented the loss of power signalled by Thorough and were greatly offended by Wentworth's blunt and authoritarian style of communication. Wentworth identified attacks on his person with attacks on the king himself and used the Council as a prerogative court to enforce respectful treatment and submission to his authority.

SOURCE 3

From the Council of the North, the government body for the North of England, which kept extensive records of its proceedings which were included by Rushworth in his Historical Collections. This record comes from 1631 and relates to the trial of a young nobleman:

Henry Bellasis, Son and Heir of the Lord Faulconberg, was on the 6th of April called before the Council Board, to answer for his rude behaviour towards the Lord Wentworth, Lord President of the North, and one of his Majesty's Honourable Privy Council. The Charge given against him was, 'That he had come into the Room where the said Lord President was in a solemn meeting, without showing any particular respect to the said Lord President, as in civility and duty he ought to have done. Afterwards, everyone present removed their hats to show respect to his Lordship as he departed in full ceremony, accompanied by a representative of the King who carried a **mace** as a mark of his authority. Everyone that is except for the the said Mr Bellasis who stood with his Hat on his Head, looking square at his Lordship without showing any inclination to remove his Hat, or in any other way show respect or even basic courtesy to the said Lord President.

Fig. 2 *The ceremonial mace of the House of Commons*

CROSS-REFERENCE
Two examples of Thorough already encountered are the 1631 Book of Orders (see page 49) and the use of Visitations and Presentment Bills in the Church (see page 49).

KEY TERM
mace: a ceremonial rod made of either wood or metal which was carried in front of the king or a royal official to represent their authority

AS LEVEL PRACTICE QUESTION

Evaluating primary sources

With reference to Sources 2 and 3, and your understanding of the historical context, which of these two sources is more valuable in explaining why Wentworth was accused of Absolutism?

STUDY TIP
Check your understanding of Absolutism by reviewing earlier chapters. Remember to compare the provenance of the sources in your evaluation.

Looking at the context of Source 3 in detail, Wentworth took Bellasis to court for showing disrespect to royal authority. Bellasis defended himself by saying that he had not noticed Wentworth because he was talking, but when the Council ordered him to write an apology, he refused and was sentenced to one month's imprisonment in the Gatehouse Prison. Similarly, Wentworth took on the prominent Foulis family. **Sir David Foulis** and his son had accused Wentworth of collecting fees for the **distraint of knighthood** and not sending

CROSS-REFERENCE
Distraint of knighthood is discussed on page 41, along with other measures of fiscal feudalism.

KEY PROFILE

Sir David Foulis (unknown–1642) hated the authoritarian rule of Wentworth as Lord President of the Council of the North. After being found guilty of slander in 1632, despite appealing to the king, he was fined £8000. Being unable to afford this, he was imprisoned in the Fleet Prison in London and only released in 1641. He was a prosecution witness in Wentworth's trial.

them onwards to the king, which would have been an act of **embezzlement**. In retaliation, Wentworth had them charged with **slander**. During the Council's deliberations, Wentworth made explicit the connection between himself and the king: '*[I am] Chief Governor under his Majesty, his Lieutenant and President of his Council, which makes this a direct mutiny and stirring up a sedition against the royal authority as well as me.*'

ACTIVITY

1. Discuss in pairs the role of Thorough in contributing to the breaking down of traditional bonds between king and country.
2. To what extent do you think that Thorough was an instrument of royal Absolutism? How could it have been interpreted as such? What other explanation can you give for Thorough?

KEY TERM

embezzlement: the theft of money that belongs to one's employer

slander: when someone makes a false verbal statement that damages another person's reputation

Policies in Ireland

In July 1633, Thomas Wentworth was promoted to the role of Lord Deputy of Ireland, the highest royal office in that kingdom. In part, this was due to the reputation for loyal and efficient service that he had gained in the North, but it also reflects the fact that although Charles greatly appreciated Wentworth's talents and loyalty, he did not personally warm to him and, as a result, kept him at a distance. Previous Lord Deputies had been drawn from within Ireland's elite families: Wentworth, as an outsider, saw his role as bringing royal authority to bear on the whole of Irish society, showing favouritism to none.

ULSTER PLANTATION
Mainly English Puritans and Scottish Presbyterians
Deliberately settled to extend royal influence from 1609 onwards

Land held by native Irish Catholics and old English settlers (Catholic) who had migrated to Ireland since Medieval times

Other areas (shaded pink) settled by English and Scottish Protestant migrants from Tudor times onwards

Fig. 3 *A map of Ireland in the 1630s showing ethnic and religious diversity*

Wentworth had three overarching goals for Ireland:
1. To impose the authority of the English Crown
2. To impose religious uniformity and conformity, in a Laudian style, on the Irish Church
3. To make Ireland profitable for the king

In keeping with Thorough, he quickly applied himself to the task in hand.

SOURCE 4

From a personal letter from the diplomat **Sir Thomas Roe** to his personal friend, Elizabeth of Bohemia, who was the older sister of Charles I:

The Lord Deputy of Ireland does great wonders, and governs like a king. He has taught that kingdom to behave so well that we should be jealous of it. It both has parliaments and knows how to use them wisely, for they have given the King six subsidies. This is a great service. To tell you about the character of the man: in business and when out and about he looks fierce but he is gentle in private conversation; he keeps his friendships private, but he is very loyal; he is a ruthless judge, and a strong enemy; a servant violently zealous in his master's ends and not neglectful of his own; one that will have what he will, and when his will coincides with his master's business he can become even more determined to succeed. He manages to achieve glory while looking as though he does not want fame. He's the sort of person that cannot just coast along being moderately successful; being so energetic, he will either be the greatest man in England or the least.

CROSS-REFERENCE
There is a Key Profile of **Thomas Roe** on page 38.

The impact of Thorough in Ireland

Supporters say	Issue	Critics say
Impose political authority on the Irish Council	Deployment of trusted advisers, brought in from England. Included George Radcliffe, former secretary; Christopher Wandesford, cousin; **Philip Mainwaring**, appointed as secretary.	Alienated political elites who found their influence reduced.
	Ruthless suppression of critics. Careful selection of high-profile targets such as Sir Piers Crosby, a Privy Councillor, and Lord Mountnorris, who organised opposition to Wentworth's management of the customs system. Mountnorris was court-martialled for treason and sentenced to death in 1635.	Destabilised the balance that factional politics brought to Ireland and united all parties against the Crown. Particularly damaging to relationships with the New English elite, which included Crosby, Mountnorris and the Earl of Cork.
Impose religious (Laudian) authority on the Irish Church	In 1634, the Anglican (Laudian) 39 Articles were introduced into the Irish Church. John Bramhall, Wentworth's former chaplain and a Laudian, appointed to the key bishopric of Derry / Londonderry. New Irish Court of High Commission established to enforce Laudianism.	Antagonised Protestant Irish who saw Laudianism as quasi-Catholicism. Particularly offensive to the Scottish Presbyterian settlers on the Plantations, who were most strongly Calvinist. Irish Catholics and Old English Catholics also increasingly isolated as conformity to Laudian Anglican Church enforced more strictly than previously.
	Juries in courts such as the Commission for Defective Titles and the Court of Castle Chamber were pressurised into agreeing with what the Crown wanted in church land disputes. For example, the Earl of Cork, Ireland's leading Protestant landowner, was forced to return land that he had taken from the Irish Church.	Alienated landowners, particularly among the New English who had benefitted most from the change in land ownership brought about by the Reformation.

SECTION 2 | An experiment in Absolutism, 1629–1640

Supporters say	Issue	Critics say
Restore Ireland to profitability and make it contribute to the English Crown finances	The Book of Rates was re-issued so that Crown income from customs doubled between 1633 and 1640.	Impacted on merchants and traders who had to pay significantly more in customs.
	1634 Irish Parliament manoeuvred into voting six subsidies.	Particularly offended the Old English and Irish Catholics because of the Graces (see below), but also led to a general feeling of disempowerment in the Irish Parliament.
	Revival of measures of fiscal feudalism that had fallen out of use. 1634 Statute of Uses enacted and enforced, which stopped heirs from being able to avoid paying a form of inheritance tax payable on land transfers. Court of Wards and Liveries revitalised. Sale of monopolies used as fiscal expedient.	Increased financial burden on wealthy elites and laid the Crown open to accusation of corruption and unfair practice (see Chapter 6).

ACTIVITY

Create a table that compares Thorough in England and Ireland, and use your findings to summarise the key features of Thorough in 100 words.

The 'Graces'

In 1628, the previous Lord Deputy and representatives of the Catholic Old English and Irish Catholics had reached an agreement to smooth Parliamentary business. In return for a Parliamentary grant of three subsidies of £120,000 over three years, the Deputy would agree to grant the following concessions:
- Recusancy fines would not be collected
- Relaxation of requirement for Catholics in public office to take the Oath of Supremacy
- Guarantee of land titles over 60 years old.

The expectation was that Wentworth would honour this agreement. It appeared that he would because he suggested that the Parliament should have two sessions: the first would deal with finance, and the second would address grievances, to include the Graces. In fact, once the subsidies were voted, the Graces were not addressed.

KEY PROFILE

Philip Mainwaring (1589–1661) led a life that demonstrates the vicissitude of Stuart England. He was Member of Parliament for Boroughbridge (1625 and 1626) and Derby (1628) and became Wentworth's Principal Secretary in 1634 and Member of the Irish Parliament for Clonakilty (1634) and Carysfort (1640). Also in 1640, he became MP for Morpeth, was imprisoned in 1650 and in 1660, became a member of the Irish Privy Council.

Reactions against the Crown

Reactions in Ireland

In 1639, Charles summoned Wentworth to England. On his departure, Ireland was profitable, more efficiently administered, with a reformed Church but at a cost for the future. Every group in Irish society had been negatively impacted in multiple ways by his policies but there was not yet an organised opposition to Wentworth or the Crown:
- The factional basis of Irish politics before Wentworth, and the complex ethnicities of Ireland would take time to unite into concerted opposition. Initially, all factions aimed to exert particular influence over Wentworth and it only gradually became clear that he was resolutely able to stand outside factional politics.
- Wentworth's ruthless suppression of critics and his iron grip over the tools of law and order allowed him to act swiftly when opposition began to emerge, frightening all but the most determined opponents into submission.
- The Irish Privy Council was traditionally more subservient than its English equivalent and therefore posed less of a challenge to Wentworth's rule.

Within two years, the tensions that had developed during his tenure would erupt into rebellion for two main reasons:
1. The settlement policies begun in Tudor times and accelerated under James I exacerbated existing ethnic and religious fault lines, which became unbridgeable in the crises of the late 1630s.

2. Wentworth's efficiency and grip on political matters meant that he had forced change onto the existing political factions and structures in Ireland. His departure created a significant vacuum that generated a factional struggle for dominance.

Reactions in England

In summary therefore, by the late 1630s, opposition to the king's Personal Rule was becoming more visible and sustained:

- The Hampden Ship Money case had directly mobilised a significant network of Puritan gentleman and was the main reason why general Ship Money receipts dropped at the end of the 1630s (see page 66).
- The trial and punishment of Prynne, Bastwick and Burton was widely known and discussed, casting a light on both the severity of the king's repression of critics and also on the presence of dissenting voices.
- The king's circle of advisers continued to shrink into a ruling clique, creating increasing alienation and therefore discontentment among his natural supporters in the gentry.
- The very efficiency of Thorough provoked opposition because it meant that the king's authority reached further into the localities than had previously been possible. While this was sometimes good, in instances such as the better deployment of measures against poverty, it also provoked anger when it disrupted local communities and individuals who had benefitted from a lack of efficiency from government, particularly in relation to financial matters.

On the other hand, the Earl of Clarendon identified quite the reverse in his *History of the Great Rebellion* (see Source 5).

SOURCE 5

From the *History of the Great Rebellion*, which was written between 1649 and 1660 by **Edward Hyde** — a strong supporter of monarchy and a close adviser to Charles II:

This kingdom and all his Majesty's dominions enjoyed the greatest calm and the fullest measure of good luck that any people in any age for so long a time together have been blessed with, to the wonder and envy of all the parts of Christendom… his three kingdoms flourishing in entire peace and universal plenty, in danger of nothing but their own surplus, and his dominions every day enlarged, by sending out colonies upon large and fruitful plantations; his strong fleets commanding all seas; and the numerous shipping of the nation bringing the trade of the world into his ports; in fact, trade between his lands was safer than anywhere else in the world; and all these blessings enjoyed under a prince of the greatest mercy and justice, and of the greatest piety and devotion, and the most indulgent to his subjects and most concerned for their happiness and prosperity.

Demands for the recall of the English Parliament

Clearly, the growing swell of opposition voices demonstrated that tension was building across Charles's kingdoms. The problem would rapidly become acute in England because he had reduced the ways in which pressure could be vented:

- The absence of Parliament prevented the Political Nation from debating and expressing its collected will to the king.
- Thorough's control of the regions meant that those who would normally have had their voices heard at Westminster were also experiencing a clampdown on their ability to dissent in the home localities as well. They were also being brought into greater conformity and accountability with central directives through the reforms aimed at improving the JPs' system.

CROSS-REFERENCE

The Irish rebellion is covered in more detail in Chapter 12.

ACTIVITY

Consider the impact of Thorough on the North and Ireland. Was Charles wise to try to bring such close control to his kingdoms? Discuss this with your partner and create a mind-map around the theme 'Was Thorough a wise policy?'

ACTIVITY

Develop your vocabulary and check your factual recall. First, use a dictionary to help you understand Clarendon's words. Then, pick out three key phrases from the source and briefly explain them. Make sure you include specific facts and detail. Next, collect five more key phrases from others in your class.

KEY PROFILE

Edward Hyde, 1st Earl of Clarendon (1609–74) was a lawyer who became an MP. Although he was slightly critical of Charles I, he was a Royalist and became a strong opponent of the Parliamentarian cause. He accompanied Charles Stuart, son of Charles I, while he was in exile on the continent after his father's execution and he was a leading figure in bringing about the restoration of Charles II.

SECTION 2 | An experiment in Absolutism, 1629–1640

- The increasingly narrow court circle around Charles, which reflected his distaste for factional politics at court and his preference for supportive, loyal voices, meant that the nobility lost their personal access to the monarch as well as their institutional access via Parliament.

However, in 1637, despite much individual disquiet and some organised groupings, there were no assembled voices demanding that Parliament should be recalled or the king's powers limited. It was events in Scotland that would bring about the seismic shift that led to war.

Fig. 4 *The king loved hunting and commissioned court artist Van Dyck to paint him in a pose that makes him look totally at ease in his surroundings*

ACTIVITY

Summary

1. Create a detailed response to the question of whether Charles I was trying establish royal Absolutism. Start by making notes about key aspects of Charles's Personal Rule covered so far, around the following sub-headings:
   - The Caroline Court of the 1630s
   - Prerogative Justice
   - Feudal Fiscalism
   - Thorough
   - Laudianism
   - The breakdown of relationship between king and gentry
2. Divide the class in half and prepare to debate whether Charles was aiming to become an absolute monarch during his Personal Rule. To create a well-developed case, consider different facets, including the king's court; the legal system; Thomas Wentworth and Thorough; William Laud and the Laudian Church.

STUDY TIP

Define the term 'the fundamental principles of government'. Use your definition to shape your answer so that you stay very focused on the question. Try to ensure you include specific details to support your ideas.

PRACTICE QUESTION (A LEVEL)

To what extent was Parliament correct in describing Charles's government in the 1630s as contrary to 'the fundamental principles of government'?

8 Radicalism, dissent and the approach of war

In 1638, William Laud wrote to Thomas Wentworth: *'It is not the Scottish business alone that I look upon, but the whole frame of things at home and abroad, with vast expenses out of little treasure, and my misgiving soul is deeply apprehensive of no small evils coming on. God in heaven avert them; but I can see no cure without a miracle, and I fear that will not be showed.'*

The 'Scottish business' had leapt to centre stage in July 1637, when the Dean of St Giles' Cathedral in Edinburgh attempted to use the new Scottish Prayer Book for the first time. Demonstrators had organised themselves in advance, packing out the area in front of the pulpit, armed with a range of projectiles including tools and sticks. Legend has it that the first to throw was a local cabbage seller called Janet (or Jenny) Geddes, who bellowed 'Will you say a mass in my ear, Popish fool?'

LEARNING OBJECTIVES

In this chapter you will learn about:

- the spread of religious radicalism
- the Scottish Covenant and the Bishops' War
- the Pacification of Berwick
- the Second Bishops' War.

KEY CHRONOLOGY

1637		Book of Common Prayer introduced in Scotland
	23 July	Prayer Book riot in St Giles' Cathedral
	Nov	Formation of The Tables
1638	Feb	Non-conformity is made treasonous
	Feb	Scottish National Covenant
	Nov	General Assembly and Parliament suspend the Prayer Book, Canons and Episcopacy
1639	April	Oath of Allegiance in York
	18 June	Pacification of Berwick
	Sept	Wentworth recalled from Ireland
1640	April–May	English 'Short' Parliament
	July	Covenanters launch pre-emptive attack on England
	Sept	Treaty of Ripon

ACTIVITY

Extension

1. Using the key chronology from this and previous chapters as a starting point, create a timeline from 1625 to 1640 that focuses on religious affairs in England and Ireland. What are the most significant events on the timeline? Explain your ideas to your partner.
2. Some historians use the term 'War of the Three Kingdoms' to refer to the Civil War period. You will be assembling evidence to support and challenge this perspective over the next few chapters. Create three sub-headings, 'War with Scotland', 'War with Ireland' and 'War with England', and begin to collect bullet-point notes of key dates and events. Look for similarities and differences between events and ideas.

The spread of religious radicalism

Religious radicalism is an umbrella phrase that holds diverse facets together. Connected with personal faith, religious radicalism in this period is characterised by a shift onwards from puritanism. Radical believers, with a focus on an individual's connection to God, expected to hear from God for themselves and looked for evidence of the working of his Holy Spirit in the world around them. Connected with the public sphere, religious radicalism is characterised by a drive for tolerance, the relaxation of conformity regulations and the mobilisation of ordinary people, inspired by God, into changing the political landscape for the better.

For reasons that will be explored later, religious radicalism surged between 1640 and 1660, revealed in multiple ways and in many theological directions, with sects such as the Quakers, Seekers, Ranters and Muggletonians expressing unique perspectives on faith and religious practice.

However, it was in the 1630s that the seeds of this radicalism were sown. For the main part, the radical sects of the future would be led by educated men, such as Richard Overton, who were at university during the 1630s. Typically, they had arrived at university, as their fathers had done before them, to undertake a conventional education, which would generally lead to a career in the law or the Church. When they arrived at university, those who were planning to enter the Church would have found themselves in an atmosphere of noisy religious debate, as the Church struggled to cope with the profound impact that Laudianism was making. What is more, the academic environment stimulated them to think more critically about the world they

SECTION 2 | An experiment in Absolutism, 1629–1640

CROSS-REFERENCE

Religious radicalism 1640–1660 is covered in Chapter 17 and 22.

lived in and they were also exposed to a rise in satirical writings that posed a challenged to accepted, traditional ways of thinking.

Early radical practice

In Chapter 6, we saw how Archbishop Laud's drive for conformity around Arminian practice polarised the Church in the 1630s, leading to some Puritans choosing to emigrate to the New World and others to attack Laud in print. By the later 1630s, opposition to the Laudian Church also began to result in an increasing number of congregations splintering out of the Anglican Church, forming their own 'Independent' communities of faith.

Independent communities of faith

The idea that churches could be 'independent' from the Anglican Church was in itself radical in the context of Stuart England. Elizabeth I and James I had both endeavoured to keep the Church of England broad enough to be able to hold most believers and practice within its boundaries, enabling those outside – known as 'dissenters' – to be easily identifiable as too extreme for stability, or even heretical. The existence of functional churches, outside the boundaries of Anglicanism, had been a facet of the English Church landscape since the Reformation, but they had been small in number and low in influence, marginalised by the breadth of the Anglican Church.

A CLOSER LOOK

Congregational churches place a low emphasis on the special role of the priest and instead believe that everyone in the church should be able to understand the Bible for themselves and pray directly to God without intermediary. Congregational church structure allows each church to operate separately, with the minister appointed by the congregation and without formal oversight or a requirement to adhere to a particular set of canons.

One such 'Independent' church was founded by William Wroth. Until the 1620s, Wroth was a good example of a classic middle-of-the-road Anglican clergyman with a parish in Wales, but he became one of the 'hotter sort' when a parishioner dropped dead on his way to a party. Wroth saw this as divine punishment for a frivolous attitude and became a committed Puritan. In 1633, he refused to read the *Book of Sports* from his pulpit, for which he was reported to the Court of High Commission by his bishop. Under continued pressure to conform, he resigned in 1638 but continued to preach, to growing crowds of people. In 1639, he set up the first Independent church in Wales, in the small town of Llanvaches. All churches need some sort of structure and Wroth copied the model of the New England non-conformist 'Congregational' churches.

Wroth's church joined a small tradition of Independent churches and he was helped at Llanvaches by a leading figure in the dissenting movement called Henry Jessey. Until the later 1630s however, the number of independent congregations was relatively small, with a minimal impact on the religious scene. Wroth's church was part of a growing tide that would swell into a significant proliferation of many more such churches in the 1640s.

ACTIVITY

Considering the perspective of a proponent of Thorough, what objections can you envisage to Independent church practice?

The Scottish Covenant and the Bishops' War

It was mismanagement by Charles and his Archbishop that sparked the chain of events that would lead to the king's first internal war and ultimately to the English Civil War itself.

Reaction in Scotland to the Prayer Book

The kirk was ordered to use the new prayer book from July 1637 onwards. Knowing the strength of popular opposition, some priests took pistols with them to church in case they needed to defend themselves. The riot in St Giles' was swiftly followed by a similar uprising in Glasgow. In this instance, a leading Presbyterian, Robert Baillie, was supposed to have led the crucial service but managed to persuade a colleague, William Annan to take his place. As Baillie later recounted, Annan was lucky to escape with his life (see Source 1).

Fig. 1 *Riots broke out all across Scotland*

SOURCE 1

From a description of the Glasgow uprising from the contemporary notes of **Robert Baillie**, a leading Scottish Presbyterian academic and diplomat:

As he left the church, about 30 or 40 of our most forthright women, as though with one voice, criticised, cursed and scolded Mr William Annan with loud shouting in front of the Bishops and town magistrates. All day long, wherever he would go he was threatened with words and looks. After supper, in the mirky night he went out with three or four Ministers but some hundreds of enraged women from all social classes swarmed around him with sticks and clods of earth (but no stones). They got the better of him, tearing his cloak, ruff and hat. He shouted so much that candles appeared in many windows as people peered out. He escaped with bloody wounds but he was in great danger. So many people were involved that the town leaders though it best not to investigate too far, either for plotters or participants, because they worried that important townsfolk of high status were likely to be among the perpetrators.

Resistance grew and petitions against the policy began to proliferate as an opposition movement developed. Further riots broke out, causing the Scottish Privy Council to abandon Edinburgh in October. However, leaning on Laud and Wentworth, Charles refused to yield. Convinced that the authority of the Crown would prevail, in February 1638, he issued a new proclamation that made it treason to protest against the Prayer Book.

King or Covenant?

In response to Charles's proclamation and led by the nobility, the Scots took decisive action. A small group from within the Scottish Parliament formed. Known as 'The Tables', it drew up a 'National Covenant' in February 1638. It was a solemn promise made by the people of Scotland to the king that they would not comply with his requirement that the kirk be transformed.

The Covenant was entirely in keeping with Scottish tradition because, in the absence of a genuinely independent and representative national Parliament, Scottish noblemen had always been able to express concerted resistance to royal policy by collective refusal. Thorough had not extended into Scotland, so regional government was still functioning in its traditional way and therefore the 'Covenant' was a final remaining avenue for opposing the king. There is no evidence that the Scottish nobility expected the Covenant to lead to war: there was no precedent that suggested that their king would not yield to such a concerted move.

Fig. 2 *This picture from the eighteenth century shows the National Covenant being signed in the grounds of Greyfriars Kirk, Edinburgh*

ACTIVITY

Evaluating primary sources

Read Source 1.
1. Why do you think Baillie declined to lead the service?
2. The rioters were not punished for taking part. Why not? Look carefully at the text and also draw your own conclusions.

KEY PROFILE

Robert Baillie (1602–62) was born in Glasgow. He studied Divinity (theology) at Glasgow University and was ordained into the Church of Scotland in 1630. A Presbyterian at heart, Baillie was a member of the 1638 Glasgow Assembly which abolished episcopacy and the Prayer Book and he accompanied the Convenanter Army as chaplain to their commander, Alexander Leslie. In 1640, the Convenanters sent him to London to represent their case Against William Laud.

ACTIVITY

To what extent do you think that Charles was aiming to introduce Absolutism into Scotland?

A CLOSER LOOK

The National Covenant consisted of two key Scottish doctrinal documents: the 1580 Confession of Faith (an outline of Calvinist theology), and the Negative Confession of 1581, which was a condemnation of Catholicism that was used as an oath of allegiance for holders of public office. It also renounced the 1633 Canons and the Prayer Book.

Hundreds of thousands of Scots put their names to the Covenant and thus became known as Covenanters. Charles only had two choices: to back down, or use the resources of his other kingdoms to enforce his will. Catastrophically, Charles persisted in his inflexibility, explaining to his trusted Scottish adviser the Marquess of Hamilton, 'I will rather die than yield to these impertinent and damnable demands (as you rightly call them), for it is all one, as to yield to be no king in a very short time… I intend not to yield to those traitors, the Covenanters'.

The Bishops' War

The scene was set for armed conflict and both sides began to mobilise. To buy himself time, Charles allowed the Scots to call a religious General Assembly at Glasgow in November 1638, which immediately voted to remove the episcopacy and abolish the Prayer Book. By April 1639 however, war was imminent and, when it began, it became known as the Bishops' War, as the struggle over episcopacy was so central.

	Covenanters	King's army
Speed of mobilisation	Rapid (a miscalculation by Charles who had not realised that the Scots nobility could so swiftly raise an army).	Patchy and slower
Resources	The Covenanters made use of their good relationship with the Protestant powers of Northern Europe to buy weapons and equipment in Holland and the Baltic. Support for the Covenant was so strong that local committees were able to raise hugely increased taxes in order to fund the mobilisation.	Accessing only non-Parliamentary finance such as feudal revenues, personal loans and private gifts, Charles struggled to fund his army. Many deserted because they were not paid. Ship Money receipts dropped, partly in response to the Hampden Case and partly because many in England sympathised with the Covenanters. Collection fell from 90% to 20%. Charles endeavoured to raise 'Coat and Conduct' money, a prerogative levy to support militia fighting outside their own county. He met with widespread opposition and non-compliance.
Composition of forces	A large number of Scottish soldiers, both nobility and common folk, returned from Europe where they had been fighting in the Thirty Years' War. Battle-hardened and professional, they were used to train less experienced recruits. The Scottish nobility also mobilised local soldiers using a militia system of military districts pioneered in Protestant Sweden. The Covenanters also asked the King of France for help.	Wentworth's Protestant Irish Army Loyalist Scottish highland nobility English nobility were summoned to York in April 1639, ordered to take an oath of allegiance and commanded to put men and money at the king's disposal. Charles forced men into the army rather than using the established local militia, possibly because he did not trust their political loyalty. In a politically inept move, Charles let it be known that he was planning to bring in Catholic troops from Ireland and Spain to fight alongside him, and he reinforced the impression by allowing a Spanish Army to march across southern England to avoid the Dutch fleet who were lying in wait for them.

	Covenanters	**King's army**
Size and Leadership	Around 12,000 men led by General Alexander Leslie, veteran of the Thirty Years' War. Regimental commanders were drawn from the nobility, but all other key leadership positions were reserved for professional soldiers who were able to direct the army efficiently. The political leadership of the Covenanters was also strong, with men such as the **Earl of Argyll** effective at maintaining political momentum and support for their cause.	Around 15,000 men led by the Earl of Arundel, supported by the Earl of Essex. Charles then annoyed both by putting Lord Holland in independent command of the horses and soldiers of the cavalry.
Discipline and order	Well disciplined, highly motivated and expertly commanded, the smaller Scottish forces were ready to fight.	Disorderly and ill-prepared, the English Army committed robberies, riots and murder as they were marched up to the north.

SOURCE 2

From an open letter written by Henrietta Maria to English Catholics in 1638, encouraging them to support Charles I's cause in Scotland with financial aid, and saved by John Rushworth:

We are so certain of the Loyalty and Love of his Majesty's Catholic subjects that we are certain that they will agree that they are fully supportive of their King as he ventures into the Northern Parts for the defence of his Honour and Dominions. The nobility, judges, gentry and others among his English subjects have offered service in person and material aid to the King's service and we have willingly confirmed that his Catholic subjects will particularly show their support to the King as part of their pious devotion, showing how grateful they are for all his kindnesses. We know that we have already expressed our earnest desire that our Catholic subjects will assist his Majesty with a considerable amount of money, freely and cheerfully given. Now, to make this all much more public and authoritative, we give you a definite instruction to do so.

In contrast, Pope Urban VIII (from whom Charles hoped to receive financial assistance) sent quite a different message for his representative in England to share with the Catholic community (see Source 3).

SOURCE 3

Messages sent between the Pope and his Nuncio in England, from John Rushworth's Historical Collections. This extract comes from Volume 2 which was published in 1721 and notes a communication from Pope Urban VIII in 1638:

You are to command the Catholics in England that they immediately stop offering to send men as soldiers for this Northern Expedition which we hear they have all-too-willingly been doing already. Likewise, it is crucial that they don't offer too much money, certainly no more than the Law and Duty requires them to pay. They should definitely not offer anything new or anything that might weaken their position in the kingdom. Tell the Peers and Gentlemen, in person or by letter, that they should not make themselves objectionable in any way in case Parliament, the highest court, should be called. Tell them not to complain about any Acts of Parliament as long as these do not directly challenge anything to do with Religion.

KEY PROFILE

Fig. 3 *Archibald Campbell, head of the powerful Campbell clan*

Archibald Campbell, 1st Marquess of Argyll, 8th Earl of Argyll (1607–61) was a Presbyterian and head of the Campbell clan. He was a Gaelic Highland chief whose power spread across the western Highlands. Argyll was driven into opposition by a variety of reasons, including Charles's vocal support of his clan's arch-rivals, the MacDonald and MacDonnell clans, led by the Catholic Earl of Antrim.

KEY PROFILE

John Rushworth (1612–1690) was a lawyer who worked in the administrative department of the House of Commons as a clerk where he sympathised with the views of John Pym. He acted as a war correspondent for the early battles of the First Civil War, sending news back to Westminster, and then became private secretary for first Thomas Fairfax and then Oliver Cromwell. From 1657 onwards he was MP for Berwick.

SECTION 2 | An experiment in Absolutism, 1629–1640

STUDY TIP
This question allows you to tackle the crucial issue of ultimate allegiance that was so significant for Catholics living in Protestant England. You could use the mind-map you created in the Activity to help ensure that your answer is as deep as possible. Engaging with issues of provenance, particularly authorship, will help you shape your argument.

ACTIVITY
Create a spider diagram with 'Fear of Catholicism' in the centre and then add as many relevant branches as you can so that you build up a deep picture of Catholicism in the 1630s. Remember to consider aspects of religion, economics (remember Popish Soap), foreign policy and domestic politics. Then, review the two sources and connect them to as many aspects of the mind-map as possible.

AS LEVEL PRACTICE QUESTION

Evaluating primary sources

With reference Sources 2 and 3, and your understanding of the historical context, which of these two sources is more valuable in explaining Catholic reaction to the Bishops' War?

A CLOSER LOOK
By 1639, Lord Brooke and Viscount Saye and Sele (see page 58) were in secret contact with the covenanting leaders because of their shared hostility to Laudianism. Both men refused to swear the oath in front of the king at York and were briefly imprisoned.

Charles expected that his forces would prove so intimidating that the Scots would choose not to fight, and was certainly confident that his army would have the upper hand in any skirmishes.

English military strategy
1. York 1639: Charles musters noblemen and their militia
2. English muster at Berwick-upon-Tweed April 1639
3. Hamilton leads a naval assault
4. Lord Huntley leads army to rendezvous with Hamilton
5. Naval blockade
6. Huntly and Hamilton's combined forces march on Edinburgh
7. Reinforcements from Ulster under the Earl of Antrim
8. More Ulster troops sent to garrison at Carlisle
9. English Army invades from Berwick-upon-Tweed

Edinburgh, 1637: Prayer Book riots

Covenanters request help from France

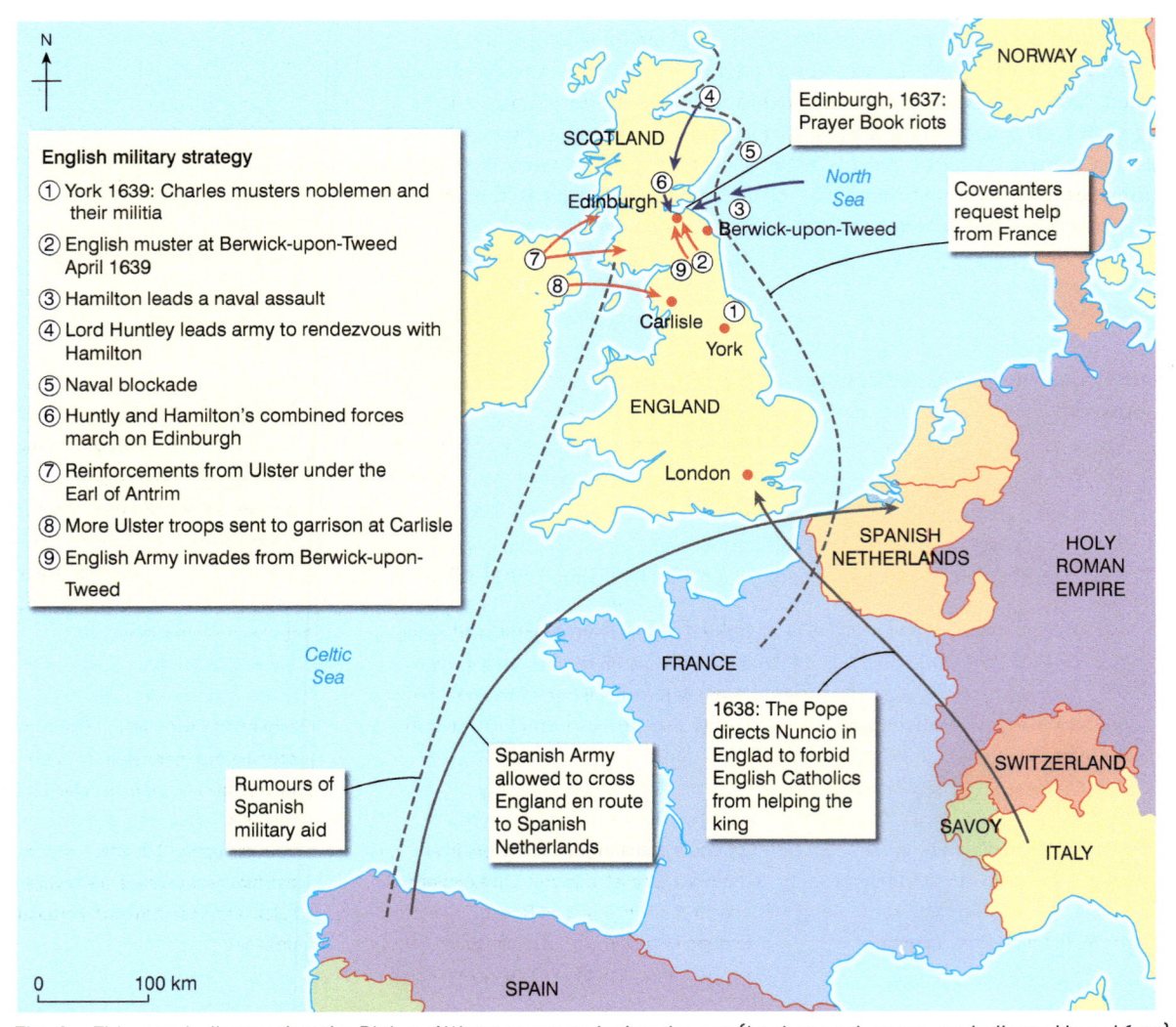

1638: The Pope directs Nuncio in Englad to forbid English Catholics from helping the king

Rumours of Spanish military aid

Spanish Army allowed to cross England en route to Spanish Netherlands

Fig. 4 This map indicates that the Bishops' War was not an isolated event (background events are indicated in red font)

CHAPTER 8 | Radicalism, dissent and the approach of war

Outline of Charles's strategy
- Hamilton would lead an assault by boat on the north-east coast of Scotland with 5000 men.
- From northern Scotland, a loyal nobleman would lead a **Royalist** force to join up with Hamilton.
- Both forces would move south towards Edinburgh.
- Naval forces would blockade the Scottish coasts.
- Troops would be transported from Ulster in northern Ireland to western Scotland, led by the Earl of Antrim, Randall McDonald.
- More forces from Ireland would be brought in to strengthen the garrison at Carlisle.
- The main English Army would assemble at Berwick-upon-Tweed, near Newcastle and move north.

The Pacification of Berwick

The English Army **mustered** at Berwick-upon-Tweed and prepared to enter Scotland while the Scottish Army under Leslie were assembled 12 miles away in Duns. Charles gave the order to advance into Scotland and Lord Holland unprofessionally allowed his cavalry to run too far ahead of the **infantry**, into the Scottish Army. Leslie had distributed his forces cleverly to make them look much stronger than they were; Holland's cavalry turned back and spread exaggerated stories of Scottish strength among the English Army.

Running out of money, having failed to intimidate the Scots into submission, with a chaotic and poor quality army and with reports of a well-armed, well-organised Scottish fighting force ahead of him, King Charles negotiated the Pacification of Berwick on 18 June 1639. This Pacification (also described as the Truce or Treaty) of Berwick contained an agreement from both sides to disband their armies; Charles also agreed to recall the Scottish General Assembly and Scottish Parliament.

> **KEY TERM**
>
> **Royalist:** supporters of the king during the Civil War period

> **ACTIVITY**
>
> Consider with a partner the likely consequences of this confrontation. Consider consequences in England as well as Scotland.

> **KEY TERM**
>
> **infantry:** soldiers who fight on foot, as opposed to cavalry – soldiers on horseback
>
> **muster:** when troops gather together for inspection or to go into battle; it is expensive to muster troops because you have to pay for them and their food; musters normally lead swiftly to battle

The Second Bishops' War

Table 2 *Options available to Charles at the end of the Bishops' War*

Option	Detail	Impact
Strengthen his circle of advisers	Thomas Wentworth was recalled from Ireland in September 1639 and elevated to become Earl of Strafford.	In his absence, order in Ireland began to unravel. Irish Protestants began to offer help to the Covenanters. Strafford advised Charles to continue to be strong and unyielding.
Rethink his Scottish Policy	Charles could abandon his Scottish policy, remodel the Scottish Privy Council to make it more broadly representative and allow Scottish governing bodies such as the Assembly to work in their traditional ways.	Not attempted. Charles did not believe that he should bend his will to accommodate the 'rebels', as he called them.
Raise more money to launch a proper military campaign	Call the English Parliament for a subsidy.	Parliament was recalled in 1640 and started in a conciliatory manner, but Charles resented having had to call it and dissolved it after three weeks.
Negotiate with European powers	Negotiate with King Philip IV of Spain and Pope Urban VIII for cash and credit in exchange for concessions for Irish and British Catholics.	His preferred option, but little financial aid reached him as quite separate revolts broke out in Catalonia (northern Spain), Portugal and Italy.
Surrender to the Scottish demands	Scotland would have been allowed to continue dismantling royal power and govern itself.	Unthinkable.

SECTION 2 | An experiment in Absolutism, 1629–1640

> **A CLOSER LOOK**
>
> **The Treaty of Ripon** was an agreement between king and Covenanters to reach a permanent settlement. While that was underway, the king agreed the following:
> - The Scottish Army could remain in Northumberland and County Durham, with headquarters in Newcastle.
> - They would be paid £850/day for the duration.
> - The English Parliament would be recalled and could not be dissolved until the Scots had been paid and had returned to Scotland.

> **ACTIVITY**
>
> Discuss the terms of the Treaty of Ripon. What do you think the most significant condition is and why? Make sure you reflect on the nature of the Council of Peers to develop your ideas.

> **KEY PROFILE**
>
> Fig. 5 Lady Brilliana Harley
>
> **Lady Brilliana Harley (1598–1643)** was a well-educated English gentlewoman with strong Puritan views. She corresponded regularly with her husband, the MP Sir Robert Harley, while he was in Westminster and her letters show her mastery of the local political situation as well as her personal bravery as she went on to defend their family home from Royalist assaults during what became known as the siege of Brampton Bryan in the First Civil War.

Despite the Pacification, neither king nor Covenant disbanded their armies. Charles showed himself to have been insincere in his agreement to recall Parliament and Assembly by asserting that, just because he had reached a compromise on this occasion, this should not be taken as a precedent. The new General Assembly met in Edinburgh and confirmed the decisions made by the Glasgow Assembly of 1638. The Scottish Parliament met, confirmed that episcopacy was abolished and set about dismantling royal power in Scotland. The situation was still aflame and in need of resolution.

Having taken the decision to renew the war against Scotland, Charles, remaining in London, ordered a muster of his troops at York. Amid reports of unrest in the country, with no money and little popular support for the English Army, the Scottish Army launched a pre-emptive attack on Northumberland in July 1640. The English Army was effectively leaderless as the Earl of Northumberland withdrew from command under cover of illness and the Earl of Strafford (Thomas Wentworth) was genuinely ill with gout. Following a brief skirmish at the Battle of Newburn, the Covenanters took Newcastle and began to advance on York. To make matters even worse, leading Covenanters were now in regular communication with English opponents of the king.

With no options remaining, Charles called together an ancient institution, a Council of Peers which met in York in September 1640. The Council of Peers was a meeting of nobles and senior churchmen that dated back to Norman times. Henry VII was the last king to have made use of the Council because it had become redundant with the presence of the House of Lords. Charles revived the Council; they advised making peace swiftly so in October, the king signed the **Treaty of Ripon** with the Covenanters.

The impact of the Scottish Wars

Impact in England

Opinion in England was very mixed in response to the Scottish Wars.

Anxiety:
William Laud wrote to Thomas Wentworth, 'It is not the Scottish business alone that I look upon, but the whole frame of things at home and abroad, with vast expenses out of little treasure, and my misgiving soul is deeply apprehensive of no small evils coming on. God in heaven avert them; but I can see no cure without a miracle, and I fear that will not be showed.

Faith:
Lady Brilliana Harley, a staunch Puritan, wrote to her son Ned: the 'cause is the Lord's and He will work for his own glory,' – a perspective echoed by a number of significant Puritan leaders with government such as Lord Saye and Sele.

Enmity:
Thomas Windebank (son of Sir Francis Windebank, cross reference Ch x) joined the English Army in the First Bishops' War and wrote of the Scots, 'those scurvy, filthy, dirty, nasty, lousy, itchy, scaby, shitten, stinking, slovenly, snotty-nosed, insolent, barbarous, bestial, false, roguish, devilish, atheistical, puritanical crew of the Scottish Covenant.'

Optimism:
Some hoped that the Bishops' Wars would force Charles to recall Parliament, re-opening communication and allowing discussion of grievances which had been so stifled during the Personal Rule.

Impact in Scotland

In August 1640, a group of eighteen Scottish nobles, led by the Earl of Montrose, signed an agreement, the 'Cumbernauld Band' which expressed their loyalty to the king and a desire to defend his authority. They had been alarmed by the development of radicalism within the ranks of the Covenanters because they felt that they were being pushed too far, from voicing grievances (albeit forcibly), into outright rebellion against the monarch.

SOURCE 4

From a letter written to the Earl of Suffolk in February 1639 by Charles, mindful of the significance of events in Scotland:

Great and considerable forces have recently been raised in Scotland without order or approval from us but instead through the instigation of some divisive people who are hostile to monarchical government. They seek to cloak their obviously rebellious plans under pretence of religion, despite the fact that we have often given them good assurances of our resolution to steadily maintain the religion established by the laws of our Scottish kingdom. As a result, we have been pushed into a position whereby we need to take steps to safeguard our kingdom of England, which is our royal duty, because it is now at risk. We must ensure its preservation and ongoing safety because the chaotic upheavals caused by these divisive spirits threaten a spread of turmoil or even invasion.

ACTIVITY

Summary

One valid interpretation of these turbulent years identifies the early autumn of 1640 as the turning point at which Charles lost his control over his kingdoms. Using the evidence in this chapter, construct a chart detailing how each aspect of Charles's rule suggests that a continuation of the Personal Rule was viable and how it suggests it was not.

Aspect of rule	Evidence Personal Rule was viable	Evidence Personal Rule was problematic
Control over the Church	Anglican Church well established and broad…	William Laud deeply unpopular…

ACTIVITY

Extension

Charles's attempt at Personal Rule failed for many reasons. One reason is that he tried for too long to suppress differences of opinion. Using Chapters 4-8, identify three specific examples of this. What common elements do each of your case studies share and how do they differ?

PRACTICE QUESTION

'Before 1637, the Personal Rule was a triumph for Charles I.'
Assess the validity of this view.

STUDY TIP

An important part of answering such questions is structuring your ideas effectively. Plan your answer before you begin to write it. Make sure that you show your understanding of the key words and themes involved in answering the question and indicate the general direction that your argument will take so that your introduction is effective.

3 The crisis of Parliament and the outbreak of the First Civil War, 1640–1642

9 The Political Nation, 1640

LEARNING OBJECTIVES

In this chapter you will learn about:

- the recall of Parliament
- the strengths and weaknesses of Charles I
- the strengths and divisions of Parliamentary opposition.

KEY CHRONOLOGY

1640	13 Apr	Opening of the Short Parliament
	5 May	Dissolution of the Short Parliament
	Aug	Petition of the Twelve Peers
	3 Nov	Opening of the Long Parliament
	Nov	Impeachment of Strafford
	Dec	Root and Branch Petition, impeachment of Laud
1641	15 Feb	Triennial Act
	May	Act against Dissolution

ACTIVITY

The chapters within this section overlap in chronology because so much happened in such a short space of time. Use a large piece of paper to create a timeline from April 1640 to August 1642 which you can then annotate. Once complete, colour code your notes to reflect different categories of information on the timeline.

The recall of Parliament

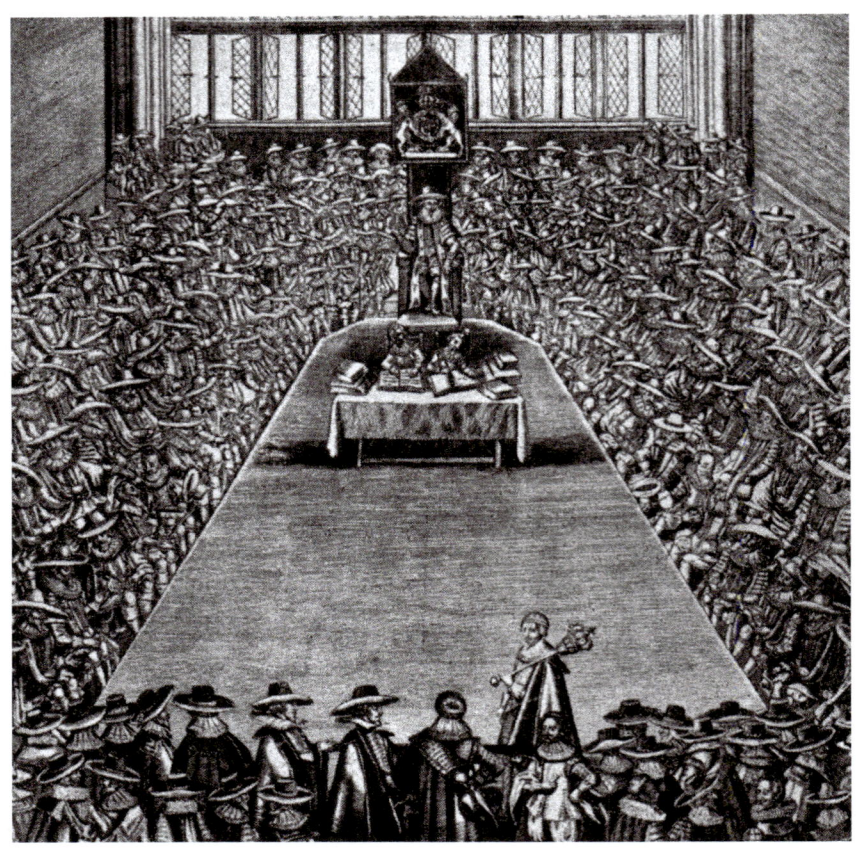

Fig. 1 *The Short Parliament*

SOURCE 1

From the speech of Sir John Finch, Lord Keeper, at the opening of Parliament in April 1640, from Rushworth's Historical Collections:

You are assembled here today because of His Majesty's Will and Royal Command to hold a Parliament. I am sure you rejoice to be here today and with all humbleness of Heart acknowledge the great Goodness of his Majesty, who has forgotten all about the discouragements he experienced in preceding Assemblies. He has the affection of a Father to his People and a Confidence that they will not fail in their duty to him.

His Majesty wants you — at least for a while — to lay aside all other debates and concentrate instead on hurrying through an Act of as many Subsidies as you think your loyal love for him would suggest.

And his Majesty is graciously pleased to give you his Royal Word that once you have done this, he will give you time to consider matters you think will be good for the Common-Wealth. He is graciously pleased to wait to hear your just Grievances and bring redress to them, to bring this Parliament to a happy conclusion with the promise of many more meetings with you.

Thus began the Short Parliament of 1640.

The Short Parliament

Without access to enough money to fight the Scottish Covenanters, Thomas Wentworth, now Earl of Strafford, advised the king to recall Parliament. The session began on 13 April 1640, with a clear outline of the king's expectation: Parliament needed to grant subsidies and then he would listen to grievances. What is more, the king possessed an intercepted letter from the Covenanters to the king of France, seeking help. The prospect of French forces helping the Scots would, he quite reasonably surmised, push Parliament to support him. By tradition, Convocation, which is the Church's equivalent of Parliament, was recalled at the same time and met at St Paul's Cathedral.

SOURCE 2

From a letter from the Covenanters to the king of France, read by Sir John Finch in the House of Commons, 13 April 1640. The letter was read in French as that was the original language of the letter and this extract comes from the translation in the Commons Journal:

Your Majesty being the refuge and sanctuary of afflicted Princes and States, we have found it necessary to send this Gentleman, Mr Colvil, to tell Your Majesty about our honesty and straightforwardness and to tell you what we have done and what we intend to do. We are not ashamed of our actions and are happy for them to be known in the bright light of day as well as for them to be shared with Your Majesty. We most humbly plead with you to trust him and believe he represents us faithfully, knowing that we have given him leave to negotiate with you on our behalf in all matters that concern us.
Your Majesty's most humble, obedient and affectionate Servants

- Rothes
- Montross
- Lesley
- Marre
- Montgomery
- Loudon
- Forester

Despite the urgency of the king's need and the prospect of foreign armies on British soil, the Parliament was dissolved on 5 May with neither subsidies granted nor grievances discussed. It was dissolved because:
- Charles still had some expectation that he might get money from the Spanish king or the Pope.
- In a recent Privy Council meeting, Stafford had suggested using the Irish Army (which he had overhauled while Lord Deputy) to help put down the Covenanters.
- Strafford himself was ill and therefore unable to help the king with political management.
- Some in Parliament sympathised with the Covenanters and did not want them to be crushed.
- Many in Parliament were desperate to discuss grievances and did not trust the king to keep his word once subsidies had been granted.

The Long Parliament

It was events in Scotland that again provided the reason for the recall of Parliament in November 1640. As has been seen in Chapter 8, the Truce of Ripon which ended the Second Bishops' War contained two specific clauses that were of great significance:
- the king had to recall Parliament, and
- the king could not dissolve Parliament until it had voted the subsidies that would enable the Scottish Army to be paid off, which would trigger its withdrawal from the north of England back into Scotland.

ACTIVITY

The Lord Keeper was a royal officer and the speech in Source 1 (on page 72) was therefore drafted in close collaboration with the king. In what ways does Charles use the occasion to assert his royal authority? Identify keywords and discuss with a partner.

A CLOSER LOOK

William Colvil (sometimes written Colville) was the Covenanters' liaison man with the French Court. A connection between Protestant Covenanters and the French Catholic Court is initially difficult to understand, but both shared an enmity of Charles I and many Scots had fought alongside the French Army against another shared enemy, Hapsburg Spain. Cardinal Richlieu, Louis XIII's chief minister, discussed Colvil's request with King Louis XIII, partly through anxiety about what Colvil might reveal about French agents while under arrest.

A CLOSER LOOK

Laud used this session to issue a new set of canons which put the religious settlement under even more pressure because they contained a new, compulsory oath of allegiance, nicknamed the 'Et Cetera Oath', through which adherents pledged to follow 'the discipline, or government… archbishops, bishops, deans and archdeacons etc as it now stands established in the Church of England'. This was a further blow to the Puritan wing because it put the emphasis onto the Church, particularly the bishops, as the interpreters of God's will, (echoing the way that the Catholic Church placed its emphasis on the Pope and Church Fathers), rather than on the Bible. The 'et cetera' (meaning 'and others') seemed to open a door to any kind of innovation.

Charles was politically, financially and militarily so weak that he could not defy the terms of the Truce. Parliament was recalled and began its first session on 3 November 1640. It earned its nickname 'Long' because it was not formally dissolved until 1660, although in those chaotic years, other Parliaments and assemblies gathered and dissolved. Certainly, Charles was trapped and had little choice but to recall Parliament because he had reached the end of his ability to raise money by prerogative means, though he was realistic enough to understand that Parliament would perhaps not grant subsidies until their grievances were heard.

The strengths and weaknesses of Charles I

King Charles was strong in 1640 because he was the king, with the same power and authority claimed by monarchs since ages past. As John Finch described to the Commons in the same speech referenced in Source 1:

His Majesty's Kingly Resolutions are seated in the Ark of his sacred Breast… let us ever remember, that though the King sometimes sets aside the Beams and Rays of Majesty, he never sets aside Majesty itself.

England in 1640 was still a very traditional, conservative country (as witnessed by the fact that both sides in the religious debate levelled the accusation 'innovators' against each as an insult). Order, hierarchy and Divine Right were all accepted, respected, even welcomed. There were no public voices of any significance advocating the overthrow of the monarchy.

Sources of the king's strength

Support in the House of Lords

In 1640, the weight of power lay within the Lords and not the Commons. Despite their frustrations, the natural allegiance of the majority of the Lords rested with the king as the cornerstone on which their own status and wealth rested and he could generally still rely on a majority of them finding for his side in debates.

Supremacy in the legal system

Charles sat at the pinnacle of the justice system and was able to use it for his own ends. After the dissolution of the Short Parliament for example, he arrested the three Lords he regarded as his leading critics, Warwick, Brooke and Saye and Sele, and the two Commons members causing him most problems, Sir **John Pym** and John Hampden. Soldiers searched their homes to find evidence that they had been conspiring with the Scots, but failed to locate anything which would enable the king to take them to court so the men were released.

Command of the army

The king had the authority to call the militia in England and Strafford had revitalised the Irish Army and put it at the king's disposal. Charles could deploy the army at will and, as the Lord Holland fiasco showed, his authority was not challenged from among his commanders.

Censorship of the press

Although the king's hold over the press was about to collapse, in early 1640, he still retained command over what could be published and was able to exert pressure, even extreme punishment, on those who offended him or challenged his authority.

> **CROSS-REFERENCE**
>
> **John Pym** is profiled in Chapter 4, page 29.

Authority over foreign policy

There were no legislative or functional restraints on the king's pursuit of foreign policy. He was at liberty to approach foreign powers such as the King of Spain and the Pope for aid, despite the fury and fear that such a course might arouse.

Determined and effective ministers

As the Scottish crisis deepened, Charles was able to rely on support from his two most committed servants, William Laud and Thomas Wentworth, Earl of Strafford. Laud backed him up with the 1640 Canons and Strafford's return from Ireland, now profitable and well managed, meant that he had his most ruthless and efficient adviser at hand.

Resources of the three kingdoms

As King of Ireland, King of England and King of Scotland, Charles had access to resources, (fiscal, military, religious and political), from three sovereign states. He had already used Strafford in Ireland and he had deployed Laud's episcopacy in Scotland. Ireland was profitable; England should be able to finance war with Scotland. Strafford might well be able to bring the English Parliament firmly into line as he had already achieved in Ireland.

Fatal Weaknesses?

Most of Charles's strengths could be described as structural, relating to his position as monarch. His weaknesses broadly came from his words and actions. Disquiet was interpreted as outright criticism.

We have already seen how Charles's style of government and the absence of Parliament during the Personal Rule, combined with Laud and Strafford's drives for centralisation, had caused those not in his inner circle, and especially gentry in the regions, to feel alienated. Unlike his father, Charles was unable to handle debate and dispute without seeing it as dangerous disloyalty and increasingly, rebellion.

> **SOURCE 3**
>
> From a letter from the Earl of Northumberland, Lord General of Charles's army to his brother-in-law the Earl of Leicester, dated May 1640. Robert Sidney, Earl of Leicester kept going a family tradition of archiving huge volumes of records which are collectively known as the Sidney Papers:
>
> Not deterred by the dissolution, the king intends to vigorously pursue his earlier plans and raise the same army of 30,000 foot soldiers and 3000 cavalry. He wants them to assemble in about three weeks' time but as yet I have not been able to establish how on earth we are going to be paid even one shilling towards the massive expense of raising these troops. What will the world think of us when they see us undertake such an action as this when it is quite clear that we have no idea how we can afford it to maintain it for even one month? It grieves my soul to be involved in such an enterprise and to make matters worse, some people interpret my forebodings of misery as disloyalty.

Effective government relied on consensus and good will. Despite attempts to bring greater efficiency to government administration through the policy of Thorough, in most parts of his kingdoms, Charles was still reliant on the voluntary goodwill of the officers of local government to enforce his commands. We have already seen how Ship Money collection rates dropped dramatically during the Scottish crisis, which is attributable directly to the lack of enthusiasm for the Bishops' War. Likewise, a group of 12 leading peers,

> **A CLOSER LOOK**
>
> Charles had tried, albeit with limited success, to overhaul the militia during the 1630s, increasing the accountability of the counties for maintaining equipment and training soldiers on the Muster Rolls but, as he experienced to his cost in the First Bishops' War, his militia reforms had not gone far enough, nor had he the finances to maintain militia in the field.

including the Earls of Bedford and Warwick, petitioned Charles in August 1640 and asserted that they would not cooperate with him unless he called a new Parliament.

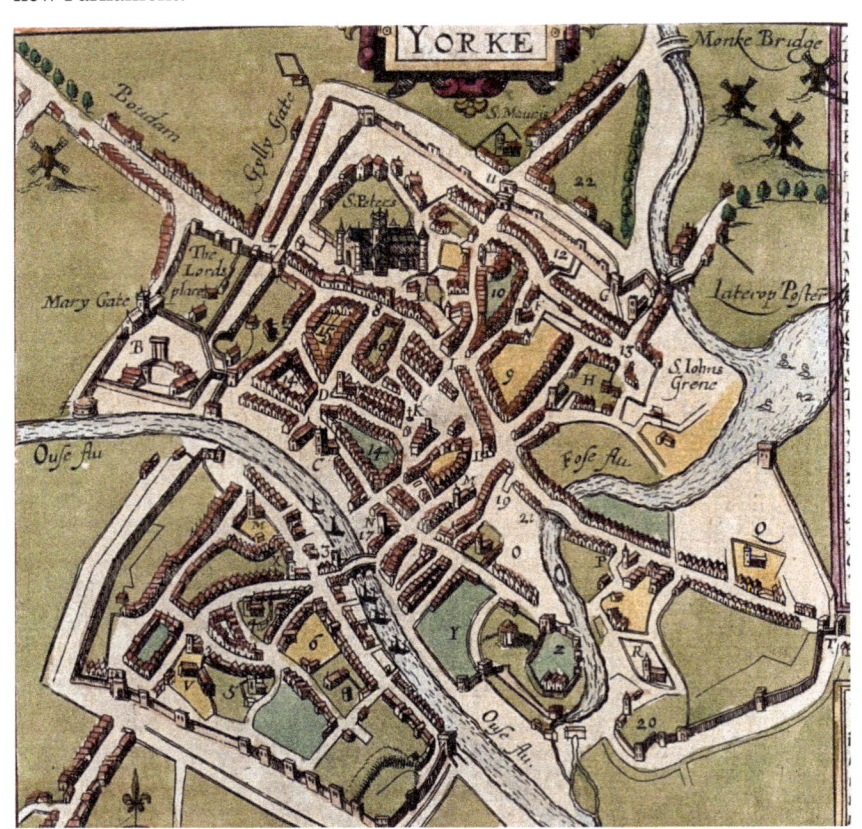

Fig. 2 *York was a thriving and significant city in the seventeenth century, not least because of its geographical location*

SOURCE 4

From the Petition of Twelve Peers, presented to the king at York on 12 September 1640. This copy of the Petition was added to the personal library of Robert Harley, 1st Earl of Oxford (1661–1724) whose grandmother, Lady Brilliana Harley, took a leading role in resisting Royalist forces during the Civil War:

The sense of that duty we owe to God's sacred Majesty and our affection to the welfare of this your realm of England have moved us to tell you, wise prince, about the apprehension which we have of the great danger threatening this Church and state. Your Majesty's sacred person is exposed to hazard and danger in the present expedition against the Scottish Army, and by occasion of this war your revenue is much wasted, your subjects burdened with additional taxes, billeting of soldiers, and other military charges. There have been many assaults on property and disorders committed in several parts of this your realm, by the soldiers raised for that service, and your whole kingdom has become full of fear and discontented people.

We are concerned about much more, including your numerous innovations in matters of religion; the oath of canons; the great increase of popery and the employing of popish recusants, especially in commanding of men and arms... We are worried about the great mischief that may fall if the bringing in of Irish and foreign forces should take effect; the heavy charge of merchants; the multitude of monopoloies; the long intermission of parliaments... We believe that there is a remedy, which is why, in humility, we beseech your majesty to summon a parliament.

CHAPTER 9 | The Political Nation, 1640

AS LEVEL PRACTICE QUESTION

Evaluating primary sources

With reference to Sources 3 and 4, and your understanding of the historical context, which of these two sources is more valuable in explaining the impact of the Scottish Wars on England?

STUDY TIP

Using the provenance of each of these sources to guide your thinking, you will be able to identify the differing perspectives of the king and noblemen on the events within this chapter. As you prepare this question, focus carefully on the purpose of the sources as well as the political context. You could look back to Chapter 8 to help you.

ACTIVITY

1. Itemise the different complaints within Source 4. Where you can, link them with your prior learning. For example, billeting of soldiers had been an issue earlier in Charles's reign – when and why?
2. Consider Charles's position in 1640. Copy this diagram and bullet-point your ideas according to 'strength' 'weakness' 'opportunity' and 'threat'.

| Strength | Weakness |
| Opportunity | Threat |

3. How would you advise Charles to proceed in November 1640? Suggest three strategies to pursue and one to avoid, then compare your ideas with a partner.

The strengths and divisions of Parliamentary opposition

In his 'History of the Great Rebellion', Edward Hyde identified a 'governing party' across the Lords and Commons. His use of the word 'party' needs further explanation because he applied the term using hindsight, as the great division into Royalists and Parliamentarians had not yet occurred. Nonetheless, the key actors that he assigned to the grouping who drove forward the legislation of the early Long Parliament did form a relatively stable opposition to the king.

Table 1 The key actors across the Lords and Commons

Lords	Commons
Robert Devereux, 3rd Earl of Essex	John Hampden
William Fiennes, Viscount Saye and Sele	Nathaniel Fiennes
Robert Greville, 2nd Lord Brooke	Denzil Holles
Edward Montagu, Viscount Mandeville	John Pym
Francis Russell, 4th Earl of Bedford	Oliver St John
Robert Rich, 2nd Earl of Warwick	William Strode
Philip Warton, 4th Lord Wharton	Sir Henry Vane, Jnr

A CLOSER LOOK

Party politics

Edward Hyde spoke of a governing party but he used the word 'party' in its archaic sense, as a group of people who took the same 'part' in an argument, or who were 'party' to the same opinion. Be careful to keep this use of the word distinct from our modern understanding of political parties, where a 'party' is an organised political grouping with a defined ideological programme and a distinctive structure.

Sources of strength

Unity of purpose

Broadly speaking, in the Short Parliament (April–May 1640) and the first session of the Long Parliament (November 1640–September 1641), the majority of the Commons and Lords were united in the goals they shared in opposition to the king:
1. To remedy the abuses of the Personal Rule.
2. To revive the relationship between the king and the country, represented in Parliament.

This unity made it possible for them to pass measures swiftly in order to redress these two issues.

CROSS-REFERENCE

The role of **Robert Devereux, 3rd Earl of Essex**, in the Bishops' War is covered in Chapter 8.

SECTION 3 | The crisis of Parliament and the outbreak of the First Civil War, 1640–1642

CROSS-REFERENCE

See page 19 for a definition of **impeachment**.

Table 2 *Overview of measures taken to remedy grievances issuing from the Personal Rule*

Goal	Action
Dismantle the prerogative courts of Star Chamber and High Commission	Star Chamber abolished by Habeas Corpus Act: 1640 and confirmed in July 1641
	High Commission abolished by Triennial Act: Feb 1641
Abolish the fiscal feudalism of Ship Money and tonnage and poundage	Ship Money repealed by Ship Money Act: 1640
	Tonnage and poundage regulated by the Tonnage and Poundage Act: June 1641
Remove the king's 'evil counsellors'	Strafford **impeached**: Nov 1640
	Laud impeached: Dec 1640
	Both men were accused of treason and imprisoned in the Tower of London to await trial.
Remove Laudian excesses from the Anglican Church	Prynne, Bastwick and Burton were released from prison.
	Root and Branch petition presented to Commons: Dec 1640
Ensure regular Parliaments	Triennial Act: 15 Feb 1641
Prevent dissolution without consent	Act against Dissolution: May 1641

KEY TERM

Root and Branch petition: called for the abolition of the episcopacy from the 'roots' and in all its 'branches', and was signed by 15,000 Londoners; it led to the Root and Branch Bill

The broadly united Parliament took a significant step towards constitutional change intended to bring stability in February 1641 with the passage of the Triennial Act, 15 February 1641.

SOURCE 5

The opening statement of the Triennial Act of 1641. As with all Parliamentary records, this is filed in the Commons Journal and maintained as a public record:

By the Laws and Statutes of this Realm, Parliament ought to be held at least once every year for the redress of grievances with the date and time for this meeting decided by the will of His Majesty and his Royal Offspring. Experience shows that the lack of Parliaments causes many and great problems and inconveniences to the King's Royal Person, the Church and the Commonwealth. To prevent such problems and inconveniences in the future:

If no Parliament has been summoned before 16th September in the 3rd Year after the last Day of the last Sitting, then Parliament will automatically assemble at Westminster. The Lord Chancellor and Commissioners will take an Oath to confirm that they shall be responsible for calling this Parliament and setting the date for its recall and they will issue Writs for elections.

ACTIVITY

The opening statements of an Act of Parliament outline the purpose and key points of the new law. Create a flow diagram to help you deconstruct the text of Source 5 so that you can identify its terms and extract Parliament's explanation of why the Act was necessary.

Interconnections

There were many interconnections between key individuals in the Parliamentary opposition to the king in the early Long Parliament, which suggest the existence of an opposition network that coalesced in the 1620s, simmered in the 1630s, and exploded in the 1640s. Certainly, the period of Personal Rule had not prevented leading figures in the political nation from communicating together, despite the absence of Parliaments.

CHAPTER 9 | The Political Nation, 1640

Providence Island Company

Earl of Warwick
Lord Brooke
Viscount Saye and Sele
Oliver St John
John Hampden
John Pym

(Sir Henry Vane Jnr was Governor of Massachusetts Colony in the 1630s)

Petition of Twelve Peers

Drafted by John Hampden, John Pym

Signed by Earl of Bedford, Earl of Warwick, Viscount Saye and Sele, Lord Brooke, Viscount Mandeville

Hampden Case

Oliver St John
John Hampden

Also Refusers:
Denzil Holles

Family Connections

Edward Montagu was married to Warwick's daughter Anne

Nathaniel Fiennes was William Fiennes' son

Lord Brooke was married to the Earl of Bedford's daughter Catherine

Oliver St John was Saye and Sele's family lawyer

Prosecuted in Star Chamber

Denzil Holles, William Strode (for Protestation)

Earl of Bedford (case dropped)

John Hampden (Ship Money)

Drafted Petition of Right 1628

Viscount Saye and Sele
Earl of Warwick

Drafted Resolutions 1629

Denzil Holles,
John Hampden,
John Pym

Fig. 3 Some of the important connections within the Parliamentary opposition

ACTIVITY

Be aware that the connections represented do not tell the full story. The Earl of Strafford, for example, was married to Arabella Holles, sister of Denzil Holles until her death in 1631 and the Earl of Bedford had an amicable relationship with William Laud. What do you think some of the issues are when considering the English political landscape of 1640?

Quality of intellect

The men who formed the opposition to the king, most particularly those in the Commons, were well-educated, intelligent and professional men who brought their talents into politics.

Table 3 Resumes of key figures in the Commons opposition grouping

		Constituency in 1640	Background	Beliefs
John Hampden	1595–1643	Buckinghamshire	Lawyer; at centre of Ship Money test case	Moderate
Nathaniel Fiennes	1608–1669	Banbury	Wealthy son of Viscount Saye and Sele; travelled around Europe then returned in 1639.	Puritan
Denzil Holles	1599–1680	Dorchester	Very active in the Parliaments of 1625–1629.	Moderate
John Pym	1584–1643	Tavistock	Active in the Parliaments of 1625–1629.	Puritan
Oliver St John	1598–1673	Totnes	Lawyer for Hampden in the Ship Money case.	Moderate
William Strode	1598–1645	Bere Alston	Very active in the Parliaments of 1625–1629.	Moderate
Sir Henry Vane Jnr	1613–1662	Hull	Spent 1630s in America, as Governor of the Massachusetts Bay Colony	Puritan, with extreme tendencies

Political support from Londoners

The 15,000 signatures appended to the Root and Branch Petition give some indication of the extent to which Londoners were vocal in their demands that Parliament should push through significant reforms. There were numerous demonstrations and pamphlets supporting widespread changes.

CROSS-REFERENCE

Londoners' demonstrations and demands for reform will be covered in more detail on page 107.

Sources of division

While it was easy for Parliament to agree on the abuses of the Personal Rule and to work together to disassemble them, deciding what to put in their place was much more complex, bringing in interwoven questions of culture, background, social status and, not least, religious persuasion.

Some agreed with Pym that the king would not willingly reach a negotiated settlement and therefore felt that they had no choice but to push forward a radical agenda that would force a settlement onto him. Others could not bring themselves to abandon their conservatism and wanted to continue to pursue a negotiated settlement. Some genuinely felt that the king was in the right.

During the spring of 1641 two issues stand out as being of particular significance: how to work effectively with the king and how to administer the Church.

Initiatives intended to restore a good working relationship with the king

Because there was no single solution that all agreed upon, initiatives came independently from the Lords and the Commons, which made it easier for Charles to resist pressure to change.

Initiative from the House of Lords: Bridge Appointments

The Earl of Bedford was fundamentally a moderate man who did not share the strong Puritan theology of men like Viscount Saye and Sele and John Pym. He proposed a scheme known as Bridge Appointments which would provide Charles with a workable financial settlement while in return, Charles would agree to hold regular Parliaments and abolish the most hated tools of his Personal Rule. To ensure good co-operation in the future, Laud and Strafford would lose their pre-eminence and be replaced by men such as Bedford who would become Lord Treasurer and Pym, who would take on the role of Chancellor of the Exchequer. In this way, Parliament would be closely involved with the king's finances.

Charles went some way towards adopting the spirit, if not the letter, of this plan. On 19 February 1641, Bedford, Saye and Sele, Essex and Mandeville were appointed to the Privy Council, and Oliver St John became Solicitor-General.

However, the scheme collapsed because Bedford and his allies were collaborating with the Scottish Covenanters so that they could work together to broker an agreement that would be acceptable to both Scots and king. On 21 February, the Covenanters sent a note demanding that the episcopacy be abolished and Strafford executed or they would not work with the Bedford plan. While Warwick wanted Strafford dead, Bedford feared that the Covenanters' demands would make it impossible for the king to agree to his scheme. The plan began to unravel and Bedford's death from **smallpox** in May 1641 brought it to a decisive end.

A CLOSER LOOK

Historiography

Historians disagree over Bedford's intentions. Conrad Russell argued that Bedford's ideas were 'not an opposition programme, but an attempt, with backing from inside the heart of government, to drag the king kicking and screaming into the real world, and thereby to reunite the country'. Conversely, John Adamson suggests that Bedford led a group of peers who were vigorously pursuing a new and highly calculated policy of constitutional reform that would reduce the king's authority and power to that of the **Venetian doges**.

ACTIVITY

Pair discussion

Discuss the Bridge Appointments scheme with your partner. What were its strengths and weaknesses? What do you think motivated Bedford to suggest it? Would you have counselled Charles to accept his recommendation?

KEY TERM

smallpox: a viral disease with a mortality rate of between 30 to 90 per cent; depending on precise variation, smallpox symptoms (like severe chicken pox) emerge after about 12 days, and most deaths occur within 16 days from infection, it was common during the sixteenth and seventeenth centuries

KEY TERM

Venetian doges: the Venetian Republic was famous for its system of government, where a group of wealthy, powerful citizens known as oligarchs elected a leader from among their ranks whose title was the Doge

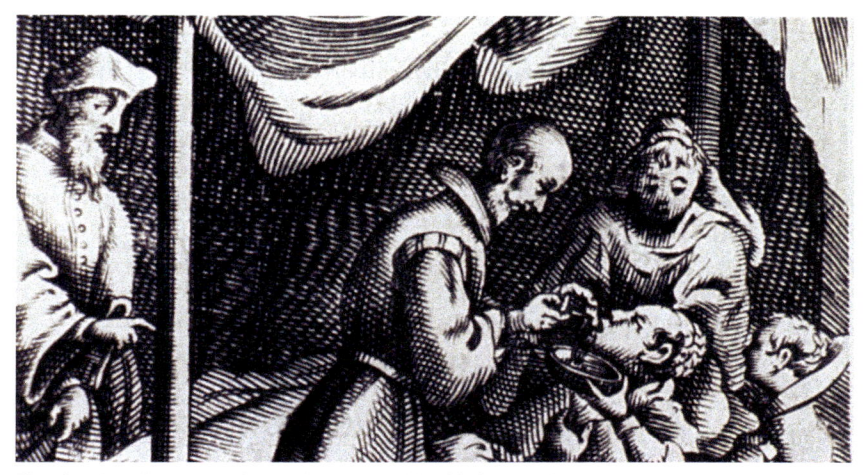

Fig. 4 *Smallpox was feared because of its high mortality rate*

Initiative in the Commons

What is certain is that, following the collapse of Bedford's scheme, the impetus for reform shifted firmly into the Commons, and it was now that attention really began to focus directly onto Pym as the leader of a significant group within Parliament. The epithet 'King Pym' was intended to be derogatory; others identified 'Pym's **Junto**'. The Venetian Ambassador wrote that Pym was 'the director of the whole machine', while Hyde described him as being 'able to do most hurt'. Applauded by many, he was also reviled by some: in a particularly nasty letter he was accused of corruption and treachery and a dirty cloth, apparently dragged through a plague sore, was enclosed.

The Ten Propositions

A 'confused and rambling' document, as the great Stuart historian JP Kenyon described it, the Ten Propositions were a list of suggestions, brought by Pym before Parliament on 24 June, which outlined how a settlement might be made with the king. In part the Propositions were very general, 'The Eighth Head [point]: That his Majesty be pleased to give directions to his learned counsel to prepare a general pardon in such a large manner as may be, for the relief of His Majesty's subjects' and elsewhere, very specific, 'The Fourth Head: … that the College of Capuchins [Catholic monks] at Somerset House may be dissolved and sent out of the Kingdom.'

All things considered, the key terms would have dramatically limited the king's powers:
- The disbandment of the army in the north
- Parliamentary input into who would be in the Privy Council
- Oversight of the queen's household (particularly in relation to the number of Catholics in her circle)
- Parliamentary control over the education of the royal children.

Parliament took the Propositions seriously and established a series of Committees to cover each of its points but events moved on before the Committees could report back. The significance of the Propositions lay more in the radical nature of their terms, introducing dramatic constitutional innovations, rather than in their outcome.

The Root and Branch debates

The Root and Branch Petition of December 1640 opened up an intense debate into how the Church should be administered now that Parliament was able once again to have a voice in its direction. Oliver St John redrafted the Londoners' Petition into a Root and Branch Bill which was presented to the Commons by Henry Vane Jnr and Oliver Cromwell in May 1641.

> **KEY TERM**
>
> **Junto:** a political grouping and a precursor to our modern idea of political parties

> **ACTIVITY**
>
> Why do you think the Propositions were 'confused and rambling'? What do they reveal to you about attitudes in the Long Parliament?

Context of the Bill

The Long Parliament quickly set about reforming the Church of England and specifically, putting right 'Laudian' excesses. In the space of just three days in November 1641, Pym presented a petition from Mrs Burton and Mrs Bastwick which sought the release of their husbands from prison; introduced a measure intended to have Catholics removed from London; and sought the right to appoint the next Dean of Durham Cathedral, traditionally a Crown appointment. These were just three of a long series of measures of varying significance which collectively represented an unprecedented involvement by Parliament in the day-to-day governance of the Church of England.

Content of the Bill

Of all these reforming measures, the Root and Branch Bill was the most significant. It was intended to 'root out episcopacy, root and branch' by abolishing the offices of archbishop and bishop. This would dismantle the structure of the Church of England and substantially alter the composition of the House of Lords. Politically it would reduce the king's power, because he appointed bishops, and thus could ensure that he had loyal supporters in the Lords.

Arguments over the Bill

The difficulty presented by the Bill was that it exposed divisions within Parliament that centred around the different attitudes individual MPs had towards the Church. A significant group of MPs wanted to remove Laud's influence from the Church because they felt that he had tried to rise higher than the king's own authority. As Pym put it, he had 'made the king's throne a footstall for his own, and his bishops', pride'. Within this group were those who simply wanted to restore the Church to its pre-Laudian state, returning it to what they described as the 'true reformed Protestant religion' under the king's authority. The Root and Branch Bill was a drastic way to remove Laud and the Arminian bishops he had promoted and some felt that it went too far. A smaller number wanted to fundamentally alter the structure of the Church to bring it more into line with the Puritan Congregational churches that were springing up in the New England colonies and elsewhere. For them, the Root and Branch Bill was a great step towards what they described as a new 'godly reformation' of the Church. The involvement of personal faith often meant that debates over religious issues were contentious, as opposed to attempts to negotiate a political compromise. This was certainly the case in the debates over the Bill. Ultimately, the Bill proved so divisive (at the second reading, it was passed by just 139 to 108) that it was shelved in August 1641.

> **ACTIVITY**
>
> Now construct a SWOT (strengths, weaknesses, opportunities and threats) chart for the Parliamentary opposition. Did Charles or Parliament have the upper hand at the beginning of 1640? What about by the summer of 1641?

> **ACTIVITY**
>
> **Summary**
>
> The personalities referred to in this chapter played a key role in the events of the early 1640s. Use the information in this and preceding chapters, supplemented by your own research, to create profiles of a selection of characters, starting with their first appearance on the political scene. Reflect on their age and relative experience at key points.

> **STUDY TIP**
>
> To plan an effective answer to this question, make a note of the different groups in England and compare each of their overall aims. Consider their similarities and differences and take these into account when preparing your answer. Use examples to strengthen your argument.

> **A LEVEL PRACTICE QUESTION**
>
> 'The grievances expressed in the Short Parliament and the early months of the Long Parliament indicated a united reaction to the Personal Rule of Charles I'. Assess the validity of this view.

10 Pym and the development of Parliamentary radicalism

SOURCE 1

From the Commons Journal, December 1640. Documentation required to impeach William Laud was prepared by the House of commons and sent, in John Pym's Hands, along to the House of Lords. The text is found in the Commons Journal:

My Lords, there is an expression in the Scripture which is too weighty for me to presume to understand or interpret. However, to an untutored eye, it seems to have some relevance to the person and cause before you. It is a description of the work of evil spirits, which appears in a passage about 'spiritual wickedness in high places'. We can see the work of evil spirits when we look at such men as this, who are malevolently influenced in their soul, will and understanding to think about spiritual matters such as God's worship and man's salvation. When their evil thoughts are turned into action by power, authority, education and other advantages, then they become crimes, committed by men who can quite fairly be condemned for 'spiritual wickednesses in high places'.

You will find in this man pride, malice, injustice. In fact you will find the accused to be a traitor against his majesty's crown; one who starts a fire against the peace of the state; the highest, boldest, most impudent oppressor that ever was, and moreover an oppressor of king as well as people.

It is impossible to understand John Pym without recognising the religious faith that linked together all his actions. He was certain that Charles had been deceived by the malicious lies of those who threatened true religion and therefore he insisted that any political settlement had to contain a religious settlement as well.

Pym's personality and aims

Pym's personality

Opinions vary about Pym's personality. Clarendon said he had 'a very appropriate and serious way of expressing himself, with a wonderful vocabulary, straightforward and respectful and that he understood the temper and affections of the kingdom as well as any man.' More recent historians have developed different interpretations of the man. John Morrill has challenged the extent to which his speechmaking was effective, attributing his political success to skill behind the scenes rather than in set-piece speeches. Conrad Russell highlighted his lack of humour and poor people skills. Wherever the exact truth rests, Pym, more than anyone else, shaped the work of the Commons in the crucial years between 1640 and his death from cancer in 1643.

Pym's aims

Although Pym was an active Parliamentarian, he was not inherently revolutionary. In the 1620s he had recognised the need to sort out the king's finances and this he now picked up again in the Long Parliament. As a lawyer, he feared that the king, especially through Thorough, was trying to undermine the English legal system. He was Puritan and anti-Catholic but he did not want to create a separate, Puritan Church: he felt simply that Laudianism had led the Anglican Church astray and his goal was to restore it to how it was during the early reign of James I. While Pym was at the forefront of Parliamentary affairs in the early months of the Long Parliament, we have seen that there was great

LEARNING OBJECTIVES

In this chapter you will learn about:

- Pym's personality and aims
- the Grand Remonstrance
- the London Mob
- popular radicalism.

KEY CHRONOLOGY

1641	19 Apr	Charles orders army officers to return to their troops
	3 May	News breaks of the Army Plot
	6 May	Protestation Oath presented to Parliament
	10 May	Death of the Earl of Bedford
	10 May	Act against Dissolution
	Sept–Oct	Parliamentary recess
	Nov	Grand Remonstrance

ACTIVITY

Using earlier chapters and your own research, create a detailed timeline of Pym's life from the 1620s onwards. Ensure you cover such key features as the attempted impeachment of Buckingham, the Petition of Right and the Providence Island Company. Your goal is to provide a context for Pym's role in the Long Parliament so that you see him holistically and stay alert to the danger of stereotyping historical personalities.

consensus across both houses. Until the spring of 1641, it could be argued that Pym administered Parliament's will rather than proactively shaped it.

The Army Plot

Although it appeared that Parliament had the upper hand in 1640–1, no-one forgot that the king was still the king, with all the powers that office conferred. Mistrusted and feared, rumours spread that Charles was planning to use force to make Parliament reverse its legislation.

On 19 April 1641, news emerged that Charles had ordered all his army officers to return to their commands with the English Army in the north. Pym officially broke this information to Parliament in early May, triggering intense debate that reflected the high tension felt by many Parliamentarians. Rumours quickly abounded that Charles's order was the opening gambit of a more elaborate plot. Once reunited with its officers, the army would march from the north of England down to London where it would free Strafford from the Tower of the London and enable the king to forcibly dissolve Parliament. Although much of this plot was hearsay, the king did send a troop of loyal soldiers to the Tower, which suggested there was truth to the rumours.

In actuality, the Tower was well fortified by soldiers loyal to Parliament; Strafford remained incarcerated and the plot, whatever its precise details, was exposed. Crowds gathered around Whitehall Palace, the London home of the royal family, because further rumours indicated that the queen had been in negotiation with Catholic powers to bring foreign troops over to help Charles. This marked the beginning of a new level of scrutiny of the actions of the queen and her Court.

The significance of May 1641

Pym was able to use the Army Plot to push the Commons into a new burst of activity:

1. A 'Protestation Oath' was issued on 6 May.
2. The Act against the dissolution of Parliament without its own consent was passed on 10 May.
3. Parliament stepped up its efforts against Strafford, leading to his execution on 12 May.

Also, significantly, the Earl of Bedford died in early May, finally ending the 'bridge appointments' scheme.

The Protestation Oath

Under intense pressure, not least because of the threat to his wife and family, in July 1641, Charles gave his royal assent to the Oath: responsibility for enforcing it fell to the Justices of the Peace. Initially intended only for office holders including magistrates, in 1642, the scope of the Oath was extended to encompass all adult males in England and Wales.

The Protestation Oath was despatched to each parish in England and a list of subscribers was sent back to Parliament.

> **ACTIVITY**
>
> Why were these rumours considered plausible? Use these words in your answer: Absolutism, Popery, Thorough, Berwick, Ireland.

> **CROSS-REFERENCE**
>
> Bedford's bridge appointments scheme is covered on in Chapter 11, page 89.
>
> The execution of Strafford is covered in Chapter 11, page 91.

SOURCE 2

From the text of the Protestation Oath from the Commons Journal, May 1641:

I do in the presence of Almighty God, promise, vow and protest to maintain and defend, as far as lawfully I may, with my Life, Power and Estate, the true reformed Protestant Religion, Expressed in the Doctrines of the Church of England, against all Popery and Popish Innovations, within this Realm, contrary to the same Doctrines, and according to the Duty of my Allegiance, His Majesties Royal Person, Honour and Estate, as also the Power and Privileges of Parliaments, the Lawful Rights and Liberties of the Subjects. As far as lawfully I may, I will oppose and by all good ways and means endeavour to bring to punishment all such as shall, either by Force, Practice, Counsels, Plots, Conspiracies, or otherwise, do any Thing to the contrary of any Thing in this present Protestation contained; and further, that I shall in all just and honourable ways, endeavour to preserve the Union and Peace between the three Kingdoms of England, Scotland and Ireland; and neither for Hope, Fear nor any other Respect shall relinquish this Promise, Vow and Protestation.

In many communities, congregations assembled to make the Oath together in their church. These occasions were not always peaceful. In fact, because all adult males across England and Wales had to swear the Oath, it played a crucial role in spreading the debates raging in London across the whole country. Every parish, church and county assembly now had the opportunity to identify some of the key issues that were passing through Parliament and discuss them at length.

Fig. 1 *What might appear to us to be vandalism was saluted by Puritans who were glad that churches were being stripped of Popish furniture*

A CLOSER LOOK

Concurrent events

Pressure was also building up in the autumn of 1641 as a result of the Cumbernauld Band and the 'Incident' in Scotland and the outbreak of rebellion in Ireland. The Irish Rebellion posed a military threat to England and therefore raised the issue of how the king could be trusted to raise an English Army in defence of the kingdom.

The Grand Remonstrance

In November 1641, Pym introduced a 'Grand Remonstrance' into the Commons. The divisions that had begun to emerge in the spring now opened up into significant fissures.

The content of the Grand Remonstrance

In the Parliamentary recess from 9 September to 20 October, Pym took command of the Recess Committee that worked on shaping policy to introduce in the autumn session. This Committee, which included John Hampden among its membership, worked on a Grand Remonstrance.

A CLOSER LOOK

Making the oath at the London church of St Thomas the Apostle

Most of the congregation swore the Oath and headed home but a leading parishioner, John Blackwell used the opportunity to attempt to break down the altar rails, claiming that they were popish innovations, against the spirit of the Oath. One of the churchwardens began wrestling with him over the rails and soon more parishioners joined in. The churchwarden later filed a petition for the arrest of Blackwell, because not only had he violently pulled the rails down but he threatened to burn the vicar and his priestly robes as well.

ACTIVITY

1. Make a copy of the Protestation Oath and annotate it so that you draw out three aspects of the historical context behind its key phrases. Take time to use specific facts and details. Swap your copy with others in your group so that you develop an in-depth understanding of the meaning and significance of the Oath.

2. Historians debate whether the Protestation Oath had the impact that was intended. Anthony Fletcher, for example, writes, 'the Protestation arose from a yearning for unity, yet paradoxically, it was immediately divisive'. With this in mind, what might a Laudian priest say about the Oath? With hindsight, do you think that Oath was a wrong move by Pym? To develop your answer, consider other oaths from earlier chapters.

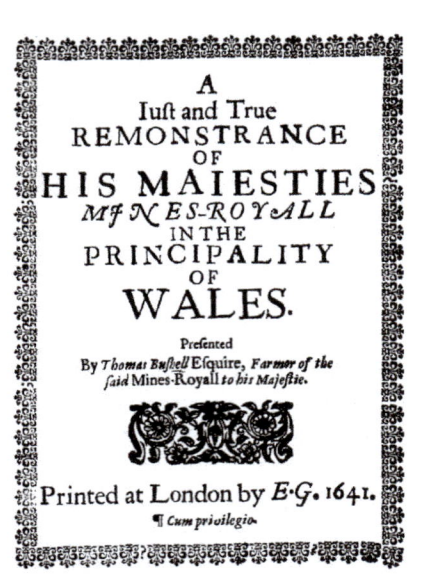

SECTION 3 | The crisis of Parliament and the outbreak of the First Civil War, 1640–1642

Fig. 2 *The front page of the published version of the Grand Remonstrance*

The Grand Remonstrance contained an overview of Charles's reign. It blamed evil advisers, corrupt bishops and papists for the present troubles in the kingdom and it presented a list of demands for constitutional change. Parliament was to have more influence over the selection of royal officers; the House of Lords was to be cleared of Bishops and Catholic peers; the Church was to be reformed under the watchful eye of an Assembly. Underneath the hyperbole, the Grand Remonstrance actually began to shift the focus from removing sources of 'mischief' to a proactive programme of limiting the king's own power and reforming the Church.

SOURCE 3

From the text of the Grand Remonstrance of November 1641, found in the Rushworth Collection:

The root of all this mischief we find to be a malignant and wicked design of subverting the fundamental laws and principles of government, upon which the religion and justice of this kingdom are firmly established. The actors and promoters hereof have been:

1. The zealous Papists, who hate the laws, who get in the way of reform and try to bring about the subversion of religion which they so much long for.
2. The Bishops, and the corrupt part of the Clergy, who cherish formality and superstition as the natural consequences and natural pillars of their own ecclesiastical tyranny and unwarranted authority.
3. Such Councillors and Courtiers as for private ends have engaged themselves to further the interests of some foreign princes or states to the prejudice of His Majesty and the State at home.

[The Remonstrance continued with an itemised list of particular abuses of the Personal Rule, for example]

27. The monopolies of soap, salt, wine, leather, sea-coal, and in a manner of all things of most common and necessary use.

STUDY TIP

To answer this question effectively, it could be useful to use learning from Chapters 9–11 and a timeline of the events of the Long Parliament.

A LEVEL PRACTICE QUESTION

Evaluating primary sources

Using Sources 1, 2 and 3, and your understanding of the historical context, assess the value of these three sources to an historian studying the development of divisions within the Long Parliament in 1641.

A CLOSER LOOK

Royalist grouping

Edward Hyde and Viscount Falkland were two of the Members who opposed the Remonstrance: they both took the king's side in the Civil War.

KEY TERM

pyrrhic victory: a victory that is so devastating for its victor that it is, in a way, a defeat

Pym's miscalculation?

The Recess Committee put forward the Grand Remonstrance as a whole; MPs were given only the options of supporting it or rejecting it. Supporting it meant accepting its most radical clauses; rejecting it implied a rejection of its critique of the Personal Rule and therefore a demonstration of significant support for the king.

The Remonstrance was passed by only 159 votes to 148, a close margin that indicated real division within the Commons. Pym, sensing a **pyrrhic victory**, decided not to push it onwards to the House of Lords. A huge debate then exploded in the Commons over whether to publish the Remonstrance. Those in favour of publication hoped that it would force the king, who had been prevaricating, to respond. Swords were drawn within the Commons for the only time in Parliamentary history. The Commons went ahead with publication but the issue had been fraught and the arguments over the

Remonstrance mark the beginning of a move towards the coalescence of a Royalist grouping, loyal to the king

The decision whether or not to publish the Remonstrance was particularly highly charged because of two factors:
- tradition – fear of disorder
- a new force in politics – the London Mob.

Tradition

Open criticism of the king was seen as dangerous, tending to sedition, likely to stir up rebellion and therefore to be avoided. Publishing the Remonstrance would destabilise the political order of the country. As Sir Edward Dering commented, 'When I first heard of a Remonstrance, I presently imagined that like faithful counsellors we should hold up a glass to His Majesty… I did not dream that we should remonstrate downwards and tell stories to the people.'

A new force in politics

At the same time, there was a growing awareness of the potential power of the London Mob to push through a more radical agenda.

The London Mob

Fig. 3 *London in the 1640s was a bustling city with a rapidly growing population*

The connection between the Mob and Parliament

In the immediate aftermath of the Reformation, Protestantism (especially Calvinism) spread through Europe along trade routes. Calvinism endorsed a strong work ethic and connected with the developing commercial economy of the early modern era. Historians trace connections between Calvinist Protestantism – in England this was most closely associated with Puritanism – and capitalist commercialism. This explains for example the link between Puritanism and the Providence Island Company. As the financial and commercial centre of England, London had become a key point of contact for Puritan merchants who spread their influence further into the city through their links with manufacturers, artisans, consumers and fellow church-goers.

Puritan sentiment in London had already begun radicalising under the pressure of Laudianism. It was to radicalise further in the 1640s as Charles lost control over censorship and the press. Pamphlets flooded the streets, stimulating political conversation as never before.

Parliament began to actively harness the Mob to increase pressure on the king. They were most readily mobilised in support of religious reform: the

A CLOSER LOOK

The London Mob

The phrases 'London Mob' and 'London Crowd' are typically used in a derogatory way to describe the population of London who participated in politics. The term is tied up with a snobbish perception that the Mob was made up of the 'lower sort' of people and is tinged with anxiety about what might happen if the social order should be destabilised by the Mob rising to be too strong. Be careful not to over-emphasise the extent to which the 'Mob' was a cohesive movement: the term suggests a form of membership and structure that did not exist. It is nonetheless a convenient way to group the political actors operating beyond the halls of Westminster.

CROSS-REFERENCE

The role of London in the politics of the 1640s is discussed in greater detail on page 126.

A CLOSER LOOK

Newspapers and Tracts

In the 1630s, about 7700 titles were published in England and Wales. This number tripled in the 1640s. The first-ever weekly newspapers commented on key developments. Major speeches by leading members of Parliament were copied and sold for pennies. Satires such as *The Wren's Nest Defiled,* an attack on the Laudian Bishop Matthew Wren, and other anti-episcopal tracts of 1641 did much to spread and endorse radical ideas, connecting people together, not least by helping them see that they were not alone in their opinions.

SECTION 3 | The crisis of Parliament and the outbreak of the First Civil War, 1640–1642

ACTIVITY

1. Review your learning so far to create a map of the involvement of the London Mob in events up to November 1641. How does the concept of the Mob change your perspective on the causes of Civil War? What challenges does the Mob present to historians?
2. Draw a table to sort reasons for and against the publication of the Grand Remonstrance. Do you think the Commons was right to publish it?

Root and Branch Petition of December 1640, for example, was signed by 15,000 Londoners, but they also turned out in force at other points too.

Popular radicalism

It was religious radicalism that most significantly rose to the fore in the early 1640s, fed by a number of factors shown in Fig. 4.

Evidence of popular radicalism

The riot that broke out in St Thomas the Apostle after the Protestation Oath was by no means the only such incident. Similar fracas were seen elsewhere, such as at St Olave's in Southwark and St Magnus the Martyr. Rails were pulled down and burned; priests threatened with bodily harm. Reports came in across the country of services being interrupted by protesters finally able to vent their fury about the Laudian Prayer Book: it 'doth stink in the nostrils of God and hath been the means of sending many souls into hell' was the reported diatribe of a Puritan minister from Cheshire.

Books written, but that had been formerly censored, finally reached their intended audiences. Samuel How, a cobbler by trade and the pastor of a separatist church in London, had a book published posthumously in 1640. Its title alone: *Sufficiencie of the Spirits Teaching without Humane Learning*, would have shocked many a moderate churchman in its incredibly radical conception of religion. It meant that neither priests nor education were necessary to understand the ways of God.

It is no wonder that the momentum that popular radicalism was picking up should be deeply unsettling to more conservative Englishmen. 'Freedom of their consciences and person is not enough, but they must have their purses and estates free too. Nay they go higher, even to the denial of the right to property in our estates' was the verdict of Sir Thomas Aston, who presented to Parliament his own petition, *Remonstrance against Presbytery*, in February 1641.

ACTIVITY

What did Aston specifically fear? Can you trace his anxiety back to the concept 'No Bishop! No King!'?

ACTIVITY

Summary

So much happened in 1640 to 1641 that it can be difficult to maintain a chronologically accurate, narrative framework while, at the same time, tracing through the key themes. Continue to add to your in-depth timeline covering the content of Chapters 9–11.

Neutralising of William Laud
In December 1640, Laud was impeached and imprisoned to await trial for treason.

Abolition of Prerogative Courts
With Star Chamber and High Commission removed, radical ideas and practice were no longer so dangerous.

The collapse of censorship
Pamphlets and newsletters, spreading radical ideas, surged after 1640.

Religious radicalism 1640–42

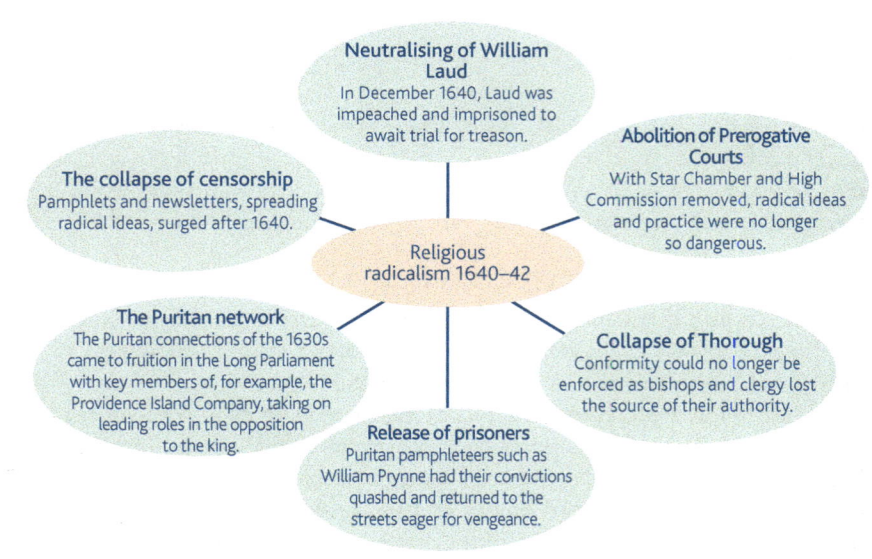

The Puritan network
The Puritan connections of the 1630s came to fruition in the Long Parliament with key members of, for example, the Providence Island Company, taking on leading roles in the opposition to the king.

Collapse of Thorough
Conformity could no longer be enforced as bishops and clergy lost the source of their authority.

Release of prisoners
Puritan pamphleteers such as William Prynne had their convictions quashed and returned to the streets eager for vengeance.

Fig. 4 *Factors feeding religious radicalism, 1640–42*

STUDY TIP

To answer this question effectively you need to use language and chronology precisely. How you define 'radicalism' and 'emerged' will determine how you structure your answer. The two-year timeframe in the question enables you to isolate radicalism within and beyond 1640–41 so that you can look for change and continuity.

A LEVEL PRACTICE QUESTION

'Radicalism emerged as a new force in England between 1640 and 1641.' To what extent do you agree with this view?

11 Conflicts between Crown and Parliament

Fig. 1 *Charles was entitled to address the House of Lords*

The year 1641 was an '**annus horribilis**' for Charles. Pressed on every side, from every kingdom, over religion, politics, even the education of his children, Charles was a king under pressure. Temperamentally, he had nonetheless shown great resilience, many would say obstinacy, in previous crises. Could he restore his authority and force Parliament back into submission?

Failure of negotiations between the king and the Long Parliament

By September 1641, Charles had not refused any of Parliament's demands and yet Pym and Parliament felt a strong need to press on and insist on greater control over the king. To a large extent, this was the result of Charles's own actions as he tried to deploy those powers he still retained in order to win back those powers he had lost. While appearing to concede and address grievances, he regularly managed simultaneously to alarm and alienate.

Bedford's 'Bridge Appointments' scheme

We have already considered this scheme from the perspective of opposition. For Charles, it was the only form of settlement that was presented to him in 1640–41 that appeared to fit satisfactorily with his own view of kingship because it represented no fundamental change to the system of government. Instead it was simply creative in its conception of a 'bridge' between Crown and Parliament. Although Charles hated the personal implications of potentially losing Laud and Wentworth from his side, to sacrifice unpopular ministers in order to restore royal authority had strong precedent and had been seen to work in the past. What is more, Bedford's scheme would have substantially resolved Charles's financial predicament, reducing his vulnerability to the intense 'grievances before supply' debates that had dogged him in all his Parliaments.

That the Bedford scheme collapsed was not the result of direct mismanagement by Charles: with Bedford dead from smallpox, it had lost its champion. However, Bedford's death did mean that another opportunity for settlement had been lost. What is more, with Warwick's call for the execution

LEARNING OBJECTIVES

In this chapter you will learn about:

- the failure of negotiations between the king and the Long Parliament
- the execution of Strafford and its political consequences.

KEY CHRONOLOGY

1641	Mar	Trial of Strafford opens
	April	Impeachment abandoned
	May	Death of Bedford
		The Army Plot
		Strafford executed under Act of Attainder
	Aug	Charles travels to Scotland
	Oct	The 'Incident'
	Nov	The Grand Remonstrance
	Dec	The king's answer to the Petition

KEY TERM

annus horribilis: first used by Queen Elizabeth II, the term means a 'horrible year' and has entered our vernacular to describe a period dominated by one catastrophe after another

of Strafford no longer being moderated by Bedford, the situation began to deteriorate even more rapidly.

The Army Plot

As we have seen, the Army Plot of April–May 1641 was a catastrophically misguided move by the king. It is worth a second look because it is very revealing of the difficulty that Charles was in. To choose not to deploy the army, one of his key strengths, would have taken a great deal of confidence in his own ability to handle negotiations with Bedford and, more widely, Parliament, as well as a great deal of faith that his opponents would also choose not to press home their advantage.

Charles's attempt to keep two plates spinning in the hope that one would not smash is a common feature of his style of government, most recently seen when he was simultaneously seeking money from Spain, Rome and the Short Parliament.

Critics accused him of being insincere and deceitful. With hindsight, he appears to have been wavering, indecisive and lacking in confidence.

Settlement in Scotland

With the collapse of the Bedford Scheme and the disaster of the Army Plot, Charles needed to settle the situation in Scotland, which was providing such momentum to events in England.

The Cumbernauld Band

To step back in time to August 1640, a group of 18 Scottish nobles, led by the **Earl of Montrose**, signed an agreement, the 'Cumbernauld Band' which expressed their loyalty to the king and a desire to defend his authority. They had been alarmed by the development of radicalism within the ranks of the Covenanters because they felt that they were being pushed too far – from voicing grievances (albeit forcibly), into outright rebellion against the monarch.

Connections between Scotland and England

In the aftermath of the Bishops' Wars, the Scottish Parliament had sent representatives ('Commissioners') down to Westminster to liaise with the English Parliament over matters of concern to both kingdoms. In fact, the Long Parliament drew a lot of inspiration from how Scotland had managed to dismantle the excesses of the king's power, not least in the area of Church governance. Robert Baillie and two other clergymen had accompanied the Commissioners specifically in order to answer any questions that arose about the Presbyterian Church government established by the 1638 Glasgow Assembly. On arrival, he felt encouraged to find that episcopacy was already under assault and Parliament appeared keen to negotiate with the Covenanters. 'We are very welcome here', he wrote, 'Episcopacy itself is beginning to be cried down and a Covenant cried up and the Liturgy to be scorned.'

By the spring of 1641, the Long Parliament was in full flow and as a result was becoming less reliant on political and military support from Scotland. The cost of paying for Scottish soldiers to be billeted in the north of England was beginning to outweigh the need to keep such pressure on the king because, while the king had agreed that the Scottish soldiers should be paid, the bill had fallen on Parliament and the local communities. Moreover, Scotland itself was beginning to stabilise as it became apparent that Charles could not any longer take military action, which in turn meant that the settlement between king and Assembly made between 1638 and 1640 looked increasingly permanent. By the summer of 1641, Scottish troops were beginning to drift home.

> **KEY PROFILE**
>
> **James Graham, 1st Marquis and 5th Earl of Montrose (1612–50)** was a leading member of the Scottish nobility and passionate in his opposition to the Laudian reforms of the Kirk. He signed the National Covenant and fought in the Bishops' Wars. But, he had become alarmed that religious radicals in the Covenanting movement, such as the Earl of Argyll, were endangering the natural order of society. So, to preserve order, he threw himself back in with the king.

> **ACTIVITY**
>
> Refresh your memory about the contextual background to the Covenant by reviewing Chapter 8. Why might Montrose have felt that the Covenant had become too radical for him?

The 'Incident' of October 1641

During August, the king travelled up to Scotland, a visit that had been agreed in the Truce of Ripon. He hoped to win political support and gain agreement to remove the rest of the army from England and he started well, making concessions to the Covenanters, meeting the Scottish Parliament, holding talks with General Leslie, and appointing moderate Covenanters, such as Montrose and Rothes, into key roles.

The Commons were understandably anxious about what Charles might achieve, so the Parliamentary Committee of Defence decided to send their own commissioners, one of whom was Hampden, to keep an eye on him.

In any event, Charles once again wrecked his own strategy because he was simultaneously plotting to remove the most radical Covenanters, particularly Argyll and Hamilton, through military action led by the Earls of Crawford and Montrose. The 'Incident', as it became known, came to a head when Charles attended the Edinburgh Parliament on 12 October accompanied by an armed force, but the plot had been leaked by one of the conspirators and its targets had escaped.

The 'Incident' was significant because it proved again that Charles could not be trusted, it brought to an abrupt end the rapprochement that had been developing and it crystallised divisions within the Scottish nobility, particularly between **Argyll** and Montrose, which would harden into the two sides of the Civil War.

CROSS-REFERENCE

A Key Profile for the **Earl of Argyll** can be found on page 67.

The execution of Strafford and its political consequences

Fig. 2 *The execution of Strafford*

Strafford and Laud had both been impeached by December 1640 and imprisoned in the Tower to await trial. There was significant consensus that they had been 'evil counsellors' to the king; that their pursuit of 'Thorough' had very nearly succeeded in creating an absolutist state and that they needed to be removed from the political scene in order to rebuild the relationship between king and country and restore balance to the Commonwealth.

However, while Laud was left languishing in the Tower until his execution in 1645, Strafford swiftly became the hook onto which all the hostility to the Personal Rule was hung, becoming a symbol for all abuses and frustrations, not just those of his own direct making. More than that, he was feared for what he might do now he was back in England.

- As President of the Council of the North, and particularly as Lord Deputy of Ireland, Strafford had shown considerable skill in managing government assemblies. Through threat and political skill, he had browbeaten both the

A CLOSER LOOK

The execution of Strafford was a turning point in relations between King and Parliament. The king bitterly regretted signing the death warrant and never forgave the Commons for pushing him to that point. Compromise became an impossibility from that point onwards. In Ireland, where Strafford had ruled so vigorously, news of his death lifted the possibility that he might return and by the autumn, full, bloody rebellion had broken out. Among more moderate members of Parliament, the execution of a peer, even such a divisive man, on unconvincing charges caused disquiet. This gradually contributed to the emergence of the Royalist party.

Council and the Irish Parliament into submission. Back in England, would he not be more than a match for the Parliamentary opposition?
- He had reformed and revived the Irish Army. Not only had he offered it to Charles in May 1640 for use 'in this kingdom', but could he not also push through a reformation of the English Army that had been so shabby when mustered in Berwick? And with a powerful, well-organised army to face, who could stand against the king? Was it beyond him to bring over the Irish Army, rally the English, defeat the Scots and march down to London?

The Trial of Strafford

Strafford's trial was held before Parliament and began in March 1641. The prosecution's case was that Strafford had tried to establish 'arbitrary government' in England in a number of ways that collectively amounted to treason.

The prosecution case was very weak:

- Strafford was able to defend himself effectively against the individual charges that were being used to establish an overall case of treason because he had been following the king's commands. Such acts as bringing the JPs into line and tackling lax and corrupt practice was easily portrayed as good, not treacherous, service. In fact, he said, in attacking the king's loyal servant, it was his prosecutors who were treacherous: 'These gentlemen tell me they speak in defence of the commonwealth against my arbitrary laws. I speak in defence of the commonwealth against their arbitrary treason.'
- Some charges were seriously flawed. A key prosecution point was that Strafford intended to commit treason in the future by bringing the Irish Army to England for Charles to use to restore order by force. It hinged around Sir Henry Vane Jnr's copy of his father's minutes of the Privy Council meeting of May 1640 where Wentworth said, 'You have an army in Ireland you may employ here to reduce this kingdom.' If 'this kingdom' meant England, then the charge could stick; if Scotland, then it did not. The case was unprovable.
- The quality of prosecution witnesses was poor: Sir Pierce Crosby, for example, was accused by Strafford of bearing an unjustified grudge.

On 12 April, first Strafford and then Pym, representing the House of Commons, made their closing statements. Strafford summed up his defence ably: a long list of small and controvertible charges could not be added up to the immense charge of treason.

A CLOSER LOOK

Crosby as a witness

It would appear that Strafford had good reason to identify Crosby as a malicious witness. A William Fitzharris had given evidence against Crosby in 1639, confessing that he had helped Crosby bring a false charge against Stafford while he was Lord Deputy, arranging to pay £1000 to one Margery Esmond if she would bring false testimony – a role for which Fitzharris lost his ears in pillory as well as £1000 in fines.

SOURCE 1

An excerpt from the record of Strafford's own defence at his trial in 1641, from *A Collection of the most Remarkable and Interesting Trials to Point out the Crimes of the Great*, which was published in 1775:

To make a case of constructive treason, or treason by collecting together many small instances, you have brought lots of fragments of evidence against me as though, by creating a compost heap of petty crimes and misdemeanours you will find a tiny seed which could perhaps sprout into treason.

Here I am charged with having plotted the ruin and overthrow of religion and State. Perhaps you have strongly disagreed with my actions but that does not amount to guilt. There is not the least proof that I have schemed with the Popish faction, nor could there be any ever found. No servant in authority under the King my master was ever more hated and more maliciously attacked by my accusers than me, while all I have ever done has been to accurately and impartially carry out the law.

Pym's response reflected the problematic nature of the charge and the effectiveness of Strafford's skilful defence. He was not able to make an attack on Strafford's specific actions that would stick, so the trial shifted to consider the theoretical issues of whether Strafford had distorted the constitutional balance of law and prerogative.

SOURCE 2

Pym's summing-up of the case against Strafford in the trial of the Earl of Strafford is included in the Rushworth Collection, dated 12 April 1641:

The Earl of Strafford has endeavoured by his words, actions and counsels to subvert the fundamental law of England and Ireland to introduce an arbitrary and tyrannical government.

Law entitles a king to the allegiance and service of his people; it entitles the people to the protection and justice of the king. The law is the boundary between the king's prerogative and the people's liberty. But if the prerogative of the king overwhelms the liberty of the people it will be turned into tyranny; if liberty undermines the prerogative, it will grow into anarchy.

It cannot be for the honour of the king that his sacred authority should be used in the practice of injustice and oppression, that his name should be applied to patronise such horrid crimes as have been represented in evidence against the Earl of Strafford.

AS LEVEL PRACTICE QUESTION

Evaluating primary sources

With reference to Sources 1 and 2, and your understanding of the historical context, which of these two sources is more valuable in explaining the significance of the trial of Strafford.

STUDY TIP

This question hinges on the extent to which Strafford was pursued to trial on the basis of his implementation of Thorough, rather than for the wider constitutional issues that were at stake. You could think back to your learning about the difficulty of criticising the monarch directly to help shape your answer.

Strafford's defence was effective. As the Attorney-General said, 'not being Convict of the Letter [the details] thereof, he could not be Convict of Treason'. It looked quite possible that the trial would collapse, with potentially terrifying consequences for those who would then face a vengeful Strafford.

The Bill of Attainder

Pym changed tactics. He brought the impeachment to a halt and instead drew up a Bill of Attainder to use against Strafford.

Table 1 *The differences between impeachment and attainder*

	Impeachment	Bill of Attainder
Role of Commons	Case brought by the Commons.	Introduced into the Commons, voted on and passed to the Lords.
Role of Lords	Prosecution must prove guilt of accused according to full court process. Lords are the judges.	Lords can agree that accused is traitor without needing legal proof.
Role of monarch	Not directly involved.	Monarch has to give assent to turn the Bill into an Act.

Using a Bill of Attainder meant that it was much easier to act against Strafford. It also brought the king into direct involvement in the case, turning it into a test of his goodwill towards Parliament.

SECTION 3 | The crisis of Parliament and the outbreak of the First Civil War, 1640–1642

A CLOSER LOOK

Stone dead hath no fellow

The Earl of Essex was so aware of Strafford's devastating efficiency that he could not contemplate his being left alive. 'Stone dead hath no fellow' was his maxim, because only when dead could Strafford have no further influence.

ACTIVITY

Why do you think that Laud was left in prison but Strafford was vigorously pursued? Make a list of all the ideas that occur to you and then, through discussion, put them into order of importance.

Pym whipped up the London Mob to demand that Parliament should pass the Bill, and it went through the Commons with 204 votes in favour and 59 against. Nearly half of the Commons MPs stayed away. When it reached the Lords, there were even fewer members present. Viscount Saye and Sele claimed illness and went home. The Earl of Bedford, and even Denzil Holles, now 1st Baron Holles, were reluctant to agree. Edward Hyde reported Bedford having said that the trial was a 'rock upon which we should all split' because Parliament seemed so determined to pursue Strafford for reasons far deeper than his actions perhaps deserved.

Despite pressure from enemies such as the Earl of Essex, it still looked as though the attempt to remove Strafford might fail until the Army Plot broke. Spurred on by the anxiety generated by the Plot, the Lords passed the Bill, and despite agonising over the betrayal of his promise to keep Strafford safe, Charles gave his assent. 'Put not your trust in princes' was Strafford's wry comment. Pleading unsuccessfully with the House of Lords for the sentence to be commuted to life imprisonment, Charles could do nothing but watch as the Earl was executed on 12 May 1641 in front of a crowd of about 100,000. Signing the death warrant was his greatest regret and marked the end of any possibility of compromise based on trust and goodwill between king and Parliament.

ACTIVITY

Summary

By December 1641, Charles could have been quite justified in feeling that his position at least with regard to Parliament was stronger than it had been in January. To draw together your learning, create a timeline of events in 1641. Use a Y axis to plot whether they strengthened or weakened Charles. What was the highest moment of his power? What was the lowest?

STUDY TIP

At first glance it appears obvious that Strafford's execution was a reason for Charles's weakness, so you will need to think carefully if you wish to build a counter-argument. You could also consider other reasons behind the king's weakness.

AS LEVEL PRACTICE QUESTION

'The main reason for Charles I's weakness in 1641 was the execution of Strafford.' Explain why you agree or disagree with this view.

12 The slide into war

The impact of events in Ireland

Because Ireland was a strongly Catholic nation, it was a source of anxiety for the Tudors and early Stuarts, who feared that it might be used as part of an invasion plan to overthrow their rule and install a Catholic monarchy instead. As a result, Elizabeth I began a policy that involved sending Protestants to settle in the north of Ireland, in Ulster. The plan accelerated under James I, who encouraged Scottish settlers to move to Ireland as well. These settlers were intended to provide a political balance to the Catholics in the Irish Parliament and a military counterbalance to the Catholics in the Irish Army, and they were given lands, 'plantations' that had been taken from Catholic landowners.

A small but powerful group of Irish Catholic nobleman including men such as **Phelim O'Neill** had been watching events in Scotland with interest and, from about February 1641, rumours of plotting and conspiracy began to emerge. These rumours aimed at overthrowing the Protestant Ulster Plantation and re-asserting the power of the Catholic nobility within the king's Irish realm. The date set was 22 October, and the rebels swiftly took control of the key strongholds of Charlemont, Mount Joy Castle, Tandargee and Newry. Their action coincided with a massive popular uprising against the Protestant settlers in Ulster, resulting in a bloodbath that would spread across the entire country by 1642. Conflict gripped Ireland for nearly a decade.

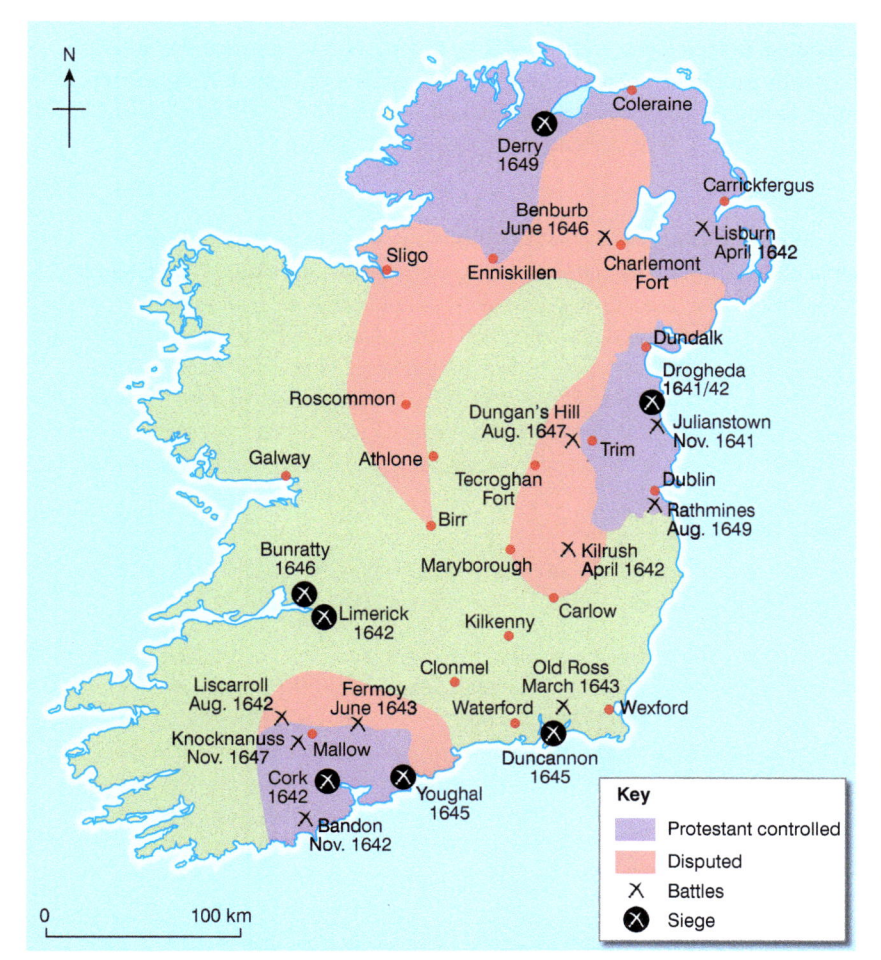

LEARNING OBJECTIVES

In this chapter you will learn about:

- the impact of events in Ireland
- the failed arrest of the Five Members
- local grievances
- the slide to war
- attempts to impose royal authority and the development of a Royalist Party
- military preparations for war.

CROSS-REFERENCE

Review your learning about Ireland in the 1630s on page 58.

1646–47	Parliamentary regiments sent to Ireland to prevent Irish Royalists from helping Charles.
1649 Mid–Aug	Dublin Garrison commander launch surprise attack and defeat the combined Royalist/Confederate armies at their rendezvous point in Rathmines (south of Dublin) where they had been preparing to attack Dublin.
1649 3–11 Sept	Cromwell besieges and storms Drogheda, and massacres its inhabitants.
1649 Oct–Nov	Siege and storm of Wexford, followed by further sieges in south-east Ireland, including Waterford and Duncannon. A mutiny in the Irish army at Cork leads to most of south-east being handed to Cromwell
1650 May	Cromwell leaves and Ireton takes command
1650 June	Ulster Irish forces defeated by combined army of New Model soldiers and British settlers.
1650 Oct	Sieges of Limerick and Galway.
1650 Nov	Ireton dies of plague
1652	Surrender negotiated

Fig. 1 *Major events in the Irish Rebellion, 1641*

SECTION 3 | The crisis of Parliament and the outbreak of the First Civil War, 1640–1642

KEY PROFILE

Phelim O'Neill (1603–53) was a powerful Irish Catholic landowner who had spent his childhood under the legal guardianship of King James I after his father and grandfather were killed fighting for the king during a rebellion in 1608. He became an opponent of Charles I while Strafford was Lord Deputy because of the policy of sending Protestant settlers from England and Scotland into Ireland.

KEY CHRONOLOGY

1641	Oct	Outbreak of Irish Rebellion
	Nov	The 'Additional Instruction'
		Charles returns from Scotland
	Dec	The Militia Bill
1642	Jan	Failed Arrest of the Five Members
	Feb	Exclusion Bill
	Mar	Militia Ordinance
	July	The Nineteen Propositions
		Parliament raises an army
	Aug	Charles raised his standard

Reasons for the Irish Rebellion

Constitutional reform

Thomas Wentworth's recall to England in 1639 created a power vacuum in Irish government. The Catholic noblemen behind the October plot of 1641 wanted to lead a programme of constitutional reform that would give them a similar settlement to that achieved by the Scots in 1638–1641, but with a strong Catholic flavour. Simultaneously the Long Parliament had begun to put together a plan to manage Ireland from Westminster, to enforce strengthened anti-Catholic legislation and to renew and extend the plantation policy that Wentworth had begun to revive. Inspired by Scotland, and fearful of the growing strength of Presbyterian and Puritan elements in politics, the plotters turned to action.

Vengeance

The initial popular uprising was not directly connected to the noble plotters but happened somewhat autonomously. Catholics whose families had been evicted by Ulster Plantation settlers decided to take revenge and rose up, given additional military muscle by soldiers returning from fighting in the Thirty Years' War. Because of the chaos that broke out, the number of Protestant settlers who were massacred has never been definitively established, with estimates ranging from 2000 to 200,000, (Clarendon reckoned that 40,000 were murdered). What is not in doubt is that the Catholic rebels committed horrendous war crimes.

ACTIVITY

Extension

Witness statements were taken in the wake of the Rebellion and are being turned into a searchable database by Trinity College Dublin. The archive (found at http://1641.tcd.ie) provides a unique source of information for the causes and events surrounding the 1641 rebellion and for the social, economic, cultural, religious, and political history of seventeenth-century Ireland, England and Scotland. You can use this site to find out whether the experiences recounted by Partington in Source 1 were accurate and typical.

SOURCE 1

From a letter sent by Thomas Partington, a Protestant settler in Ireland, to a friend in England, read out to the Commons in 1641:

The rebels daily increase in number, exercising all manner of cruelties and striving to see who can be most barbarously elegant in tormenting the poor Protestants where ever they come from, cutting off their private parts, ears, fingers and hands, plucking out their eyes, boiling the head of little children before their Mothers' faces and then ripping up their Mothers' bowels; stripping women naked, killing the children as soon as they are born, and ripping up their Mothers' bellies as soon as they are delivered; driving men, women and children by hundreds upon Bridges and from thence cast down into Rivers.

Fig. 2 *This illustration captures the chilling nature of the barbarity meted out to the Protestant settlers*

Significance of the Irish Rebellion

Reports from the Irish Rebellion radicalised the Long Parliament because they elided with the intense fear of Catholicism that was such a pervasive strand in the cultural mindset of Stuart England. The extent to which accounts were distorted and exaggerated is debated – multiple witnesses confirmed an atrocity at the Bridge of Portadown which matches Partington's account – without doubt, the news from Ireland created profound anxiety in Westminster.

What is more, Parliament next faced a difficult issue: obviously an army should be sent to Ireland to quash the violence but could the king be trusted to lead it? This issue was greatly complicated by the fact that Phelim O'Neill claimed that the king had ordered him to rebel in order to strike a blow at the Westminster Parliament. When a forged order to this effect emerged in November 1641, divisions deepened further.

In early November, Pym introduced an 'additional instruction' to be sent to the Commissioners in Scotland, which was considered in the Commons. It stated that the Commons would help raise an army to subdue Ireland if the king agreed that he should appoint only councillors approved by Parliament, or that Parliament 'should take such a course for the securing of Ireland as might likewise secure ourselves'. The vote was close, at 151 for and 110 against.

The Militia Bill

On 7 December 1641, **Sir Arthur Haselrig** introduced the Militia Bill. This was a radical step forward because it removed the king's power to summon the militia and gave Parliament the power to appoint army commanders. Charles was clear about how presumptuous Parliament had become, criticising 'the strange exorbitant power which the two Houses at this time, misled by a few factious, malicious spirits, pretend to transfer to themselves and by which the Militia is put in execution; it being so supreme and absolute, that our consent is not thought necessary for the execution of anything they judge to be convenient for the welfare of the kingdom.'

Debates over the Bill were so heated and extensive that they dragged on into February, by which time events had intensified further.

> **KEY PROFILE**
>
> **Sir Arthur Haselrig (1601–61)** was MP for Leicestershire in the Short and Long Parliaments, supported the Attainder of Strafford, and was one of the Five Members who managed to escape Charles's arrest attempt (see below). He was a fervent Puritan.

SECTION 3 | The crisis of Parliament and the outbreak of the First Civil War, 1640–1642

ACTIVITY

1. Who do you think Charles meant by 'a few factious, malicious spirits'?
2. By autumn 1641, Royalist sympathisers were beginning to identify a trend towards 'Parliamentary Absolutism' in the work of the Long Parliament. Write an explanation of Parliamentary Absolutism, using the Militia Bill as a specific case study.

KEY TERM

aldermen: high-ranking members of a city or borough council, next in status to the Mayor

The failed arrest of the Five Members

By the end of 1641, the king felt that he was strong enough to try to reassert his royal authority.

- Welcoming crowds and the City **aldermen** greeted him when he returned to London from Scotland in November 1641.
- The close nature of recent votes and debates in Parliament revealed a strong degree of support for the king in Parliament.
- Petitions in support of the episcopacy were coming in from the counties.
- He had assured command of the Tower of London by managing to place a hardline Royalist, Colonel Thomas Lunsford, in charge.

Fig. 3 *This painting of the failed arrest of the Five Members is by the Victorian artist Charles West Cope and hangs in the Houses of Parliament; the Victorians were particularly proud of English democracy and approved of Parliament standing up to the king in the 1640s*

Impeachment proceedings

On 29 December, the Lords accepted a Commons vote of impeachment against the bishops. This would lead to their exclusion from the House of Lords, which in turn would weaken a source of support for Charles in the upper chamber. Parliament had been galvanised into action by a petitioning campaign, which resulted in 30,000 signatures being presented in support of exclusion. The king's response was rapid and decisive.

On 3 January 1642, Charles issued his own impeachment proceedings for treason against six 'factious spirits':

Commons members:
- John Pym
- John Hampden
- Denzil Holles
- Sir Arthur Haselrig
- William Strode

From the House of Lords:
- Edward Montagu, Viscount Mandeville

These impeached members sat in Parliament on 4 January. Hearing that they were there, Charles assembled 500 soldiers and, accompanied by his brother-in-law, the Elector Frederick of the Palatine, marched from Whitehall to Westminster. He left his armed guard at the door but, in shocking defiance of Parliamentary privilege, entered the Commons chamber. Apologising for his unconventional presence, he ordered the Speaker, William Lenthall, to point out the five Commons MPs. Lenthall's response was significant because he put the privilege of Parliament above the orders of the monarch: '*May it please your majesty, I have neither eyes to see nor tongue to speak in this place but as this house is pleased to direct me whose servant I am here; and humbly beg your majesty's pardon that I cannot give any other answer than this is to what your majesty is pleased to demand of me.*'

The Five Members of the Commons had been forewarned and had fled by boat to safety in the City of London. 'I see that the birds have all flown' was Charles's response.

Aftermath

The London Mob surged onto the streets in protest against the king's action. Charles was escorted to safety by the Lord Mayor and other civic dignitaries but they themselves were attacked on their way home,.' The next night a false rumour spread that the king was advancing on the city with 1500 cavalrymen. Within an hour, the city was ready to defend itself. Gates were shut, portcullises lowered; women built barricades across the streets with stools and tubs, and boiled water to throw on the cavalry; thousands of well-armed men got ready to repel the king's troops. Offers of support poured in from the outskirts of London and from over 1000 sailors, both merchant seamen and men from the king's fleet. Several thousand men assembled in Buckinghamshire, ready to march to London in support of John Hampden who was their MP.

Terribly worried, Charles took the momentous decision to move his family from Whitehall out to Hampton Court Palace, which was then still a country retreat. From there, he despatched his family to Europe and took his court up to York. The failed arrest was disastrous. By showing that he was prepared to use force and disregard Parliament's legitimate privilege, Charles once again demonstrated absolutist tendencies. By leaving London (and he did not return until 1649), he lost physical connection with the capital, making negotiation with Parliament and key ministers much more difficult, and allowing the Mob to radicalise even further in his absence.

A flood of petitions arrived in the capital from the counties, probably organised centrally by the Commons and particularly focused on redressing religious grievances. Even moderate Royalists were shaken and a new flurry of legislation followed, including the Exclusion Bill of 5 February 1642, which removed bishops from the House of Lords, and the **Militia Ordinance**, which was put before Parliament on 15 February.

Local grievances

The Buckinghamshire rising in support of Hampden opens the window onto the wider phenomenon of the 1640s: the split of the country at large into Parliamentary and Royalist divisions. This issue itself exposes particular historiographical problems. The Westminster-centred narrative of 'King against Parliament' holds together quite cohesively and is supported by a lot of evidence including voting records, official Parliamentary documentation and royal archives. Looking across the English nation as a whole, the picture is much more complex and by no means so easy to categorise. A multiplicity of interests affected each individual decision, as seen by the fact that many families split into two and supported different sides in the war. As the contemporary writer **Lucy Hutchinson** explained: '*Before the flame of the war broke out in the top of the chimneys, the smoke ascended in every country [county]… in many places there were fierce contests and disputes (almost to blood) even at the first; for in the progress every county had the civil war (more or less) within itself.*'

It is possible to draw out trends and themes, but great care must be taken to avoid facile stereotyping.

ACTIVITY

1. Turn the events in this chapter into a diagram, including numbers of participants and clearly showing chronology to help you visualise the speed and scale of the changing circumstances of late 1641/early 1642.
2. What advice would you give to the king from his new location in York?

Fig. 4 *Entrance into London could be blocked by shutting the many city gates such as this one at St Bartholomew the Great*

A CLOSER LOOK

Militia Ordinance

Haselrig's Militia Bill was replaced in February 1642 by a Militia Ordinance, which transferred the authority to appoint Lord Lieutenants and their deputies from the king to Parliament, which meant that Parliament put itself in command of the militia. Turning this legislation from a Bill to an Ordinance meant that Parliament could make it law without needing Charles's royal assent: the Ordinance was enacted on 5 March 1642. Ironically, Parliament proposed raising £400,000 in support of the militia by the old Ship Money mechanism.

SECTION 3 | The crisis of Parliament and the outbreak of the First Civil War, 1640–1642

A CLOSER LOOK

Lucy Hutchinson is famous for the history book that she wrote about her husband's role in the Civil War, entitled *The Life of Colonel Hutchinson*. However she was a polymath and also produced one of the first translations of a poem *De Rerum Natura*, by the Roman atheist Lucretius.

Indicators of local allegiances

Religion

Definitely the easiest predictor of someone's allegiance was their religion. As the leading Civil War historian Lawrence Stone identified in Yorkshire, all the Parliamentary leaders and half of the Parliamentarians were strong Puritans, while one third of the Royalist gentry were Catholics.

What was true in Yorkshire provides a general guide to the rest of the country. Catholics would only support the king, Puritans would support Parliament, while those of more moderate Protestant persuasion are more difficult to readily categorise.

Geography

Connected with religious faith, different regions were more likely to support one side or the other. Puritanism was typically strongest in the South and East of England, particularly in London, but also in the bigger regional cities such as Manchester and Bolton. While overall the Lancashire gentry tended towards moderation in religion and royalism in politics, efforts to conscript Bolton men into the Royalist forces foundered as Puritans from the outskirts headed into the city to help their brethren.

The king based his court in York and, generally speaking, the North and West tended towards royalism. That said, relative proximity to Ireland could merge with fear of an invading Irish Catholic Army to provide local circumstances in which this geographical trend was bucked. Joseph Lister of Bradford, in the West Riding of Yorkshire (with its easy access to Liverpool and North Wales and therefore the closest sea crossing to Ireland), wrote: 'I well remember what sad discourses I heard about this time, the papists being desperate bloody men… [with] hundreds of Protestants… daily murdered in Ireland and fearing the same tragedy would be acted in England…'

Employment

In some contexts, people's employment decided their allegiance. In Gloucester, for example, the city corporation agreed to support Parliament on behalf of all its members. Elsewhere, local gentry insisted that their tenant farmers fought in Royalist militia under threat of eviction. By and large, independent traders, artisans and the emerging professional classes had more freedom to decide who to support while those tied into local employment networks had to follow the lead of others.

Fig. 5 *Independent tradesmen had more freedom to choose their allegiance; on the whole they tended to support Parliament*

Individual rivalries

Sometimes, individuals took sides with much less reference to the constitutional or religious issues being raised in Westminster than to particular circumstances. **Sir John Hotham** was a Yorkshireman who had been pushed out of local power by the rise of the Wentworth family and aligned himself with the Parliamentarians in response. With the subsequent rise of the Parliamentarian Fairfax family in Yorkshire, he found himself again out of contention and switched sides to become a Royalist in 1643. For this, both he and his son were executed for treason on the orders of Parliament.

Leadership

Some regions were mobilised for one or other sides by the force of character and skill of key local figures. In the East Anglian counties, the predominantly Royalist gentry proved unable to resist the mobilisation of the ordinary people by their MP, **Oliver Cromwell** of Huntingdon.

Neutralism

Neutralism, choosing to take neither side, also rose as a growing force during 1642 and was probably the natural choice of the majority of ordinary Englishmen. It is often the case that those on the extremes make most noise but most people found themselves forced to make a decision for king or Parliament that they did not want to make.

> **CROSS-REFERENCE**
> More on **Hotham's** treason can be found on page 104–05.

> **CROSS-REFERENCE**
> A Key Profile for **Oliver Cromwell** can be found on page 118.

SOURCE 2

From a letter from Sir Thomas Knyvett to his wife in May 1642, waiting of his dilemma in siding with king or Parliament:

Oh sweetheart, I am now in a very tricky situation and do not know what to do. I was walking in Westminster when Sir John Potts, with Commissary Muttford, saluted me and gave me orders from the Lord of Warwick, to raise our local militia and command them again, by Ordinance of Parliament. I was surprised and did not know whether to agree or refuse but it was tricky to argue, so I agreed. I hoped to have some time to think further but only a few hours later I was given an opposite order from the King. I now think it is wisest and most safe to keep as quiet as I can in these dangerous times. I am going to try to keep out of everyone's way and see who raises which troops before I decide what to do.

> **ACTIVITY**
> What are some of the difficulties a historian might face when trying to study questions of allegiance in the English Civil War? Discuss your ideas with a partner.

That Knyvett's dilemma was typical was borne out by John Morrill's seminal work 'The Revolt of the Provinces' in which he uncovered evidence that at least 22 counties attempted to make neutrality pacts. Despite the pressing constitutional crisis being played out in Westminster, reports of the devastating effect of the Thirty Years' War on western Europe, and a fear that war would unleash catastrophic social collapse were the typical drivers of neutralism.

In some counties such as Cheshire and Yorkshire, the Royalist Commissioners of Array and the Parliamentary Militia Commissioners agreed together not to raise forces but to move on elsewhere. In other counties such as Lincolnshire and Leicester, local gentry put aside their individual preferences and raised county militia to repel incursions from either Parliamentarian or Royalist forces. An attempt by the Earl of Bath to raise Royalist militia was repelled by the men of South Molton in Devon who attacked his commissioners 'with loaded muskets, spears and axes, some with clubs… [while] the women had filled all the steps of the [market] cross with great stones and got up and sat on them, swearing if they did come there they would brain them.'

A CLOSER LOOK

The **royal standard** is the name given to the particular flag that is flown when the monarch is present. By unveiling his standard in Nottingham, the king was summoning those loyal to him to join him, ready to fight.

A CLOSER LOOK

Popular disorder

In the first half of the 1640s, at least 26 English counties saw riots against enclosure, where landowners turned common land into their own farmland by enclosing fields with fences. Enclosure riots were not new but the scale and scope of the riots was unnerving.

The slide to war

From January 1642 onwards, the prospect of conflict looked increasingly likely, not least because it takes time to prepare for war but the very act of preparation generates its own momentum. Within the political sphere, king and Parliament failed to reach a settlement. The concept of a drift to war is supported by the fact that, in the country at large, efforts to gain control of the militia caused sporadic conflicts to break out in the early summer while the king only declared war by unveiling his **standard** in Nottingham in August and it was another three months before the first pitched battle of the war took place in November at Edgehill.

Attempts to impose royal authority and the development of a Royalist Party

We saw in Chapter 11 that the king endeavoured to gain control of London in May 1641 by force in the Army Plot. During these crucial months of 1641, the general population of England began to divide into the sides that they would take in the Civil War.

Reasons to support the king
Fear of disorder

For some, the prospect of civic, religious or political disorder was entirely terrifying and triggered a reaction for the king as the pinnacle of order and stability. For a number of reasons there was a slight peak of **popular disorder** in the early 1640s that looked to some as though ordered society was disintegrating.

Constitutional royalism

The breakdown of unity revealed by the fierce debate over the Grand Remonstrance is a good indicator of how Parliamentary consensus was stable while attacking abuses of the Personal Rule but crumbled as radical ideas about what should come next began to predominate. The narrow margin of Commons vote on the Remonstrance (159 to 148) definitively exposed the scale and membership of this group and its general position was defined by the king's response to the Grand Remonstrance.

SOURCE 3

From *The King's Answer to the Petition*, drafted by the king with the help of Edward Hyde, published on 23 December, and included in the Rushworth Collection:

Considering your first point, preserving this kingdom from the Popish party. We follow the will of the people expressed in parliament. When you say you want to deprive Bishops of their votes in Parliament, we remind you that their right to vote is built into the fundamental law of the kingdom and the constitution of Parliament.

Our conscience is clear: no Church in the world professes true religion with more purity of doctrine than the Church of England. It has been established by law and, with God's help, we will maintain it not only against all invasions of Popery but also from the unholy ideas of those who would like to break the Church apart.

As to your second point, no-one is beyond the reach of the law, no matter how close they are to us, but you need to bring a definite charge and sufficient proof against him.

You have promised to support our royal office with honour and plenty, power and reputation and we have promised the same to you. In fact, this is what we have always done and will always do, for the happiness of our people.

This emergent ideology is known as constitutional royalism, reflecting support for the institution of the monarchy providing that it stayed within the bounds of tradition and common practice. Constitutional royalism gathered greater momentum as opposition groups in Parliament became increasingly radical.

Religious moderation

There was considerably greater uniformity among religious faith and practice on the Parliamentarian than the Royalist side. Catholics as well as Laudians would naturally find themselves on the king's side but many more moderate Anglicans did as well. It is because religion was so divisive that Pym delayed debate over the Root and Branch Bill in August 1641 and it explains why Charles was so keen to emphasise the conservative nature of his religious policy against the 'the unholy ideas of those who would like to break the Church apart'.

The failure of negotiations between king and Parliament

Parliament's last effort to contain the king came in the form of the Nineteen Propositions of June 1642. Radical, confrontational and impossible for the king to approve, the Propositions began effusively:

> **SOURCE 4**
>
> From the Nineteen Propositions, from the Journal of the House of Lords, the official record of proceedings in the Upper House, from 1 June 1642:
>
> Your Majesty's most humble and faithful servants, the Lords and Commons in Parliament, consider the just and faithful performance of their duty to your Majesty and this kingdom to be a thing most precious and a weighty responsibility. In fact, it is only secondary to their duty of honour and service to God. In this spirit, they do in all humility and sincerity present this petition and advice to your Majesty, in fulfilment of this duty. Through your princely wisdom you strive to establish your royal honour and safety and protect with gracious tenderness the welfare and security of your subjects and dominions. They hope that you will be pleased to grant and accept these their humble desires and propositions, as the most necessary means – through God's blessing – of removing those jealousies and differences which have unhappily fallen between you and your people. In this way, they hope that a steady path of honour, peace and happiness may be found for both your Majesty and your people.

The conciliatory, even affectionate, tone was not sustained, as 19 conditions were laid out for the king, including that:
- Parliament should have to give its assent to all the key royal appointments
- Parliament would take on responsibility for educating the royal children and arranging their marriages
- New, stronger anti-Catholic legislation should be enacted
- The Anglican Church should be reformed according to Parliament's direction
- The Five Members should be cleared of all charges
- The king should approve the Militia Ordinance and drop his use of Commissions

Entirely predictably, the king rejected the Propositions:

> **SOURCE 5**
>
> From a statement drafted by Viscount Falkland and Lord Culpepper, published on 18 June 1642, in which the king rejected the Nineteen Propositions of Parliament:
>
> We call God to witness that for our Subjects' sake we have these rights in our person. We are resolved not to let go of them, nor to undermine (even in a

A CLOSER LOOK

Another war of religion?

Religious persuasion provides a clear indication as to whether someone would support the Royalist or Parliamentarian cause, a factor that has led some historians to characterise the English Civil War as a continuation of the religious wars being fought on mainland Europe which are grouped together as the 'Thirty Years' War'. While this is a useful hypothesis, it does not explain the peculiar circumstances of the context of the 1640s, although it does shed some light on them.

ACTIVITY

How effective do you think Charles was as a king by the end of 1641? You will need to analyse his strengths and weaknesses and take into account the actions of others to help you decide. What do you think was his greatest weakness?

ACTIVITY

Thinking point

Why was it unthinkable that the king would approve of the Propositions? What do you think he would object to most?

Parliamentary way) the ancient, equal, happy, well-balanced and entirely commendable Constitution of the Government of this Kingdom. The power legally placed in both Houses is more than sufficient to prevent and restrain the power of Tyranny even without the power which is now asked from us. We shall not be able to do our duty, for which we have been appointed King if we give up the power that is being demanded from us and to do so would be a total subversion of the fundamental laws and excellent Constitution of this Kingdom and would end in a dark chaos of confusion and rebellion. For all these reasons, to all these demands our answer is 'We are unwilling to change the laws of England.'

The king's defence was supported by a petition that swiftly followed from Hertford, warning Parliament against its 'new, unheard of state-in-law and logic, to style and believe that a Parliament which is divided in itself and severed from the King, the head thereof.' Parliament declared the Hertford petition to be a scandalous libel.

SOURCE 6

From a speech by Sir Benjamin Rudeyard to Parliament in July 1642, published in *A Parliamentary History of England* in 1775, demonstrating the fact that there was significant disquiet, even among Parliamentarians:

Let us set ourselves three years back. If any man had told us that within three years the Queen shall be gone out of England in to the Low Countries, the King shall remove from his Parliament from London to York, declaring himself not to be safe here, that there shall be a total rebellion in Ireland, such discords both in Church and state here as now we find; we should have trembled at the thought of it. On the other side, if any man had told us, that within three years you shall have a Parliament, it would have been good news; that Ship Money shall be taken away by an Act of Parliament, the reasons and justification of it so rooted out, as that neither it, nor anything like it, can ever grow up again; that monopolies, the High Commission Court, the Star Chamber, the bishops' votes shall be taken away; that you shall have a triennial parliament, we should have thought this a dream of happiness. Yet now we are in the real possession of it, we do not enjoy it.

STUDY TIP

To answer this question effectively you will need to ensure that you use specific examples rather than generalisations. You could consider how each of the key Parliamentarians were related to one another and how complex the situation was in 1642.

A LEVEL PRACTICE QUESTION

Evaluating primary sources

With reference to Sources 2, 3 and 4 and your understanding of the historical context, assess the value of these three sources to an historian studying the reasons why England divided into two sides in 1642.

Military preparations for war

The passage of the Militia Ordinance in March opened up a period of five months in which Parliament and the king struggled together over military command.

Since February, the queen had been in The Hague, the capital of the Dutch Republic, where she tried to pawn or sell off Crown Jewels and to persuade European royalty, particularly Frederick Henry, Prince of Orange and the Danish King Christian IV, to support Charles. She was not terribly successful, not least because potential buyers were concerned that any jewels they bought might be subsequently claimed back by Parliament or the king once the crisis had passed.

CHAPTER 12 | The slide into war

In April, the king went to Hull to requisition the arms and ammunition that were in storage following the Bishops' Wars. Sir John Hotham had been appointed to be the new Governor of Hull by Parliament in January 1642. He refused to let the king enter the city without a warrant from Parliament to set alongside the king's own royal order. A propaganda struggle ensued with both king and Parliament seeking to turn the Hull incident to their own advantage. Later in the summer, the Royalist Lord Strange tried to seize arms and weapons from the **arsenal** at Manchester: a skirmish ensued, and Strange left empty-handed.

By May, both sides began to issue orders for local gentry to raise the militia.

In June, Parliament issued a formal order to raise the militia, which the king countermanded by invoking a different, prerogative means of raising an army, called the Commissions of Array. Commissions had last been used in the early 1500s; leading figures in the counties were given particular authority to raise forces for the Crown.

On 12 July, Parliament passed a resolution to raise a full army under the command of the **Earl of Essex**.

KEY PROFILE

Robert Devereux, 3rd Earl of Essex (1591–1646) was a leading Puritan nobleman who worked in close alliance with John Pym. He was one of the most fervent prosecutors of Strafford and forewarned the Five Members of their impending arrest. He was relatively well equipped for his role as Lieutenant-General of the Parliamentary army, having seen military service in Europe during the Thirty Years' War.

On 22 August, the king raised his standard in Nottingham, summoning all loyal English men and women to his cause. The war was underway.

Fig. 6 *While the queen had her own personal jewellery, she endeavoured to raise money from state jewels, which were passed down the line of monarchs*

ACTIVITY

Summary

The events leading up to the outbreak of Civil War intertwine considerably. Complete your timeline from the recall of the Short Parliament in 1640 to the outbreak of war in 1642. Then, identify what you think are the key events on your timeline according to themes such as:

- Charles's political ineptitude
- the impact of fear and anxiety
- the role of anti-Catholicism
- Pym's role.

KEY TERM

arsenal: a large store of weapons; in the 1640s there were significant arsenals in London, Hull, Oxford and Bristol

AS LEVEL PRACTICE QUESTION

'The failed arrest of the Five Members was the key event in the outbreak of the Civil War in the years 1640 to 1642.'
Explain why you agree or disagree with this statement.

STUDY TIP

This question is asking you to identify the causes of the Civil War. You will need to be clear in your mind about causation, so that you can evaluate possible explanations for the War since 1641, before reaching your final decision.

Part Two Radicalism, republic and Restoration, 1642–1660

4 War and radicalism, 1642–1646

13 The First Civil War: the Royalist cause

LEARNING OBJECTIVES

In this chapter you will learn about:

- the strengths and weaknesses of the political and military leadership of the Royalist cause.

KEY CHRONOLOGY

1642	Aug	Charles raises standard at Nottingham
	23 Oct	Battle of Edgehill
	13 Nov	Standoff at Turnham Green
	Nov	Charles retreats to Oxford
1643	Jan–April	Oxford Treaty negotiations
	30 June	Battle of Admalton
	13 July	Battle of Roundway Hill
	Aug–Sept	Siege of Gloucester
	20 Sept	First Battle of Newbury

A CLOSER LOOK

Roundheads versus Cavaliers

Cromwell wore his hair short (for the time), in common with many other Parliamentarians, which is what earned them the contemporary derogatory nickname 'Roundheads', as they looked as though they had cut their hair using a round bowl as a template. Supporters of the king were known as Cavaliers, which contemporaries understood to mean a courtly, high-class gentleman rather too interested in his own appearance and arrogantly demanding admiration from others. While Parliamentarians embodied the Puritan values of simplicity and piety in their battlefield dress, the Royalists wore contrastingly fashionable battlefield dress, embodying dashing glamour.

Fig. 1 'Roundhead' and 'Cavalier' were used as derogatory terms in contemporary cartoons

ACTIVITY

Create a table under the heading 'strengths and weaknesses of the political and military leadership of the Royalist cause', and add to it as you work through this chapter.

Royalist strengths	Royalist weaknesses

It might help if you start by filling out the table with relevant information, then at the end categorise according to whether you each item is a political or military weakness.

The outbreak and progression of the war

The First Civil War broke out because of a political problem; this was the need to find an up-to-date answer to the age-old question: 'What should be the constitutional balance between the power of the king and the rights of his subjects?' Attempts to settle this question within the traditional framework of court and Parliament had repeatedly failed throughout the first half of the seventeenth century, so that by 1642 a storm had developed that pushed the dispute out of the confines of Westminster and Whitehall. This created or exacerbated divisions across the Political Nation, and led to increasingly charged public demonstrations followed by military skirmishes and the raising of armies by the summer of 1642.

Because the Civil War was therefore fundamentally a political struggle turned martial, it could only be resolved once either king or Parliament had either been able to negotiate a mutually acceptable settlement, or when one side had been able to force absolute military victory, leading to an imposed settlement, onto the other.

A broad chronology helps define the course of the English Civil Wars:
1. The failure of both sides to reach a settlement that would have averted war in the summer of 1642.
2. The failure of the king to achieve absolute military victory in the summer of 1643.
3. The failure of both sides to negotiate a settlement in the winter of 1645.
4. Parliament's successful achievement of military victory in June 1645.
5. Parliament's imposition of a settlement in January 1649.

The situation in England had deteriorated by 1642 because it had become evident that there was no prospect of both sides reaching a mutually agreed settlement that might have averted war. This realisation was what propelled Parliament to begin getting ready for war during the spring and Charles to summon his army on 22 August in Nottingham.

The early strengths of the Royalist cause

Loyalty and tradition

In the conservative culture of Stuart England, natural allegiance fell towards the king, and as the Political Nation polarised in the early summer of 1642, support for the Royalist cause began to rise.

Just as the king's response to the Nineteen Propositions was designed to foster the support of moderates, so his rallying call in Nottingham in August 1642 and the declaration in Source 1 were calculated to reach out to his natural supporters with arguments emphasising the radical nature of Parliament's actions and the steady traditionalism of the king's.

> **ACTIVITY**
>
> Defining civil war and deciding what constitutes a victory provide an interesting conceptual exercise. With a partner, consider the concept of 'war'. What is it? It might help you to brainstorm all the different terms that you can think of that are connected to war, such as conflict, terrorism, battle. More importantly, how are wars won? Is the end of hostilities the same thing as a victory?

> **ACTIVITY**
>
> Create a flow chart of the five events listed here and add detail as you read this chapter.

SOURCE 1

From the king's declaration of 27 September 1642, 'to all his loving subjects', in which he put the blame for the war firmly onto the shoulders of select Members of Parliament for refusing to reach an agreement with him that would have preserved peace. A copy of this declaration was preserved in John Rushworth's collection:

We all know that the House of Commons contains nearly 500 members and yet only 300 members currently attend. The rest have been driven away from fear of tumults and threats or have from conscience withdrawn themselves from participating in the desperate machinations of that House. Furthermore, out of 100 Peers of the Realm, there are no more than 16 who concur in their miserable Resolutions. Many of these peers have been driven to this point by their own personal poverty and are grateful for the money that they are earning as Commanders in this war. These men have dominated the nobility, gentry and

SECTION 4 | War and radicalism, 1642–1646

> **ACTIVITY**
>
> In Source 1, why do you think Charles included numbers to help make his case?

Commons of England and they are encouraging our subjects to rebel against us. We draw back from accusing all those opposing us because we know many have been misled by cunning and malice or frightened by the power of the men who lead the attack. It is these leaders who I accuse and I have enough evidence to prove that the law of this land would find them guilty of High Treason.

Access to resources

Men and money

The Royalist armies typically came better equipped than their Parliamentarian counterparts because of the individual wealth of the Royalist commanders. While some key nobles such as the Earl of Essex mobilised in defence of Parliament, a greater number deployed their troops for the king and some of these, such as the Earl of Worcester, who donated over £300,000 to the war effort, and the Earl of Newcastle had huge resources of money and manpower. Some Royalists were directly involved in industries that produced military equipment, such as the **Evelyn family** of Surrey who owned a substantial gunpowder manufacturing business centred around the village of Chilworth.

> **CROSS-REFERENCE**
>
> An extract from John Evelyn's diary can be found on page 208.

On the other hand, in terms of the types of industrial resources that were available to the king, regional factors also came into play, as Figure 4 shows.

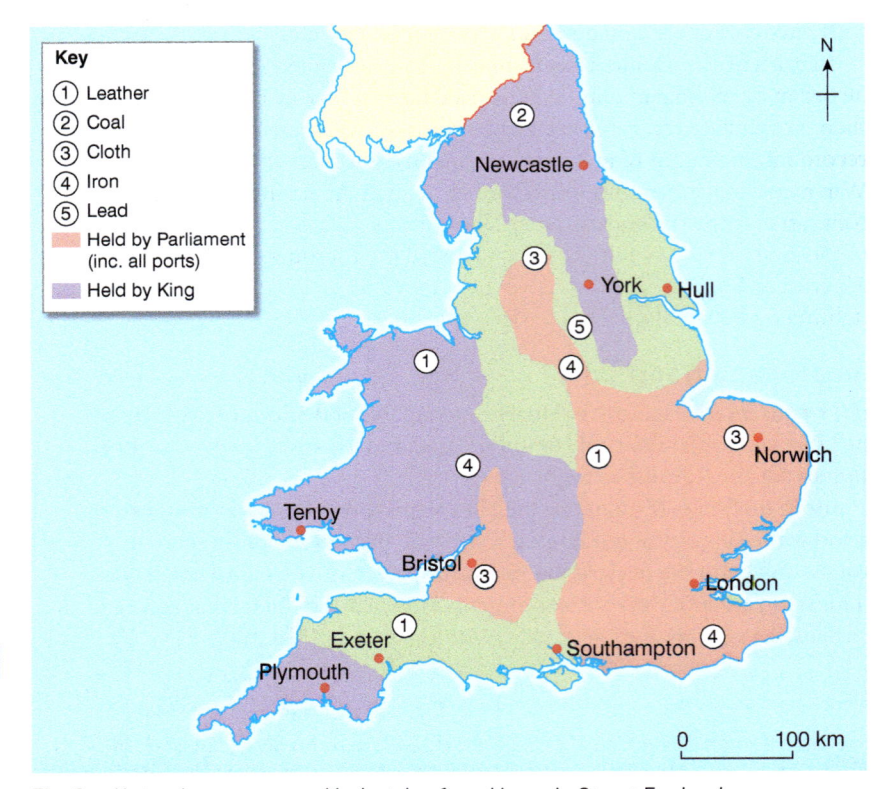

Key
(1) Leather
(2) Coal
(3) Cloth
(4) Iron
(5) Lead
— Held by Parliament (inc. all ports)
— Held by King

Fig. 2 *Natural resources and industries found in early Stuart England*

> **KEY PROFILE**
>
> **William Cavendish, Earl of Newcastle (1593–1676)** raised 8,000 men from his estates when the Civil War broke out, including a famous fighting force known as the Whitecoats, or 'Newcastle's Lambs'. In June 1642, Charles put him in command of all the Royalist forces in the North. He secured York, Pontefract and Newark for the king, and swiftly dominated the whole of Yorkshire except Hull.

Access to tax revenues

In 1642, local Royalist county committees had begun to form, to manage the Commissions of Array and marshal resources to the king. Charles increasingly tried to supplement the gifts and loans of the loyal nobility with local taxes, raised using the traditional tax structures and collected by local men. Theoretically at least, his requests for money fitted the old constitutional pathways and had his authority to back them up. In practice, he faced the same problems in funnelling money from the localities to the centre that had been such a problem for him throughout his reign. Not only was he reliant on the energy and commitment of the local JPs and collectors, but neutralism and local anxieties put pressure on local officials to keep the money for use within the county itself.

By 1643, the relatively informal nature of the County Committees was replaced by a more overtly militaristic structure in those areas of the country wholly controlled by Charles. Six military districts were formed by grouping counties under the command of his leading noblemen, designated 'Lords Lieutenant': the Earls of **Newcastle**, Derby and Carbery, the Marquess of Hertford and Lords Herbert and Capel. Nonetheless, the process of effectively mobilising men and money from the localities proved tough to master.

Unified command

One of Charles's greatest potential strengths was that he was king and therefore at the top of the military command structure. In leading his army out against an enemy, Charles fell back into the traditional role he had only recently assumed during the Bishops' War – the monarch as commander-in-chief. Because his leadership structure was unified with everyone under his authority, no-one challenged his right or capacity to command. In comparison, the Parliamentary forces marched out under a radical and embryonic constitutional command structure: old-style noble leaders such as the Earl of Essex, in service to a new form of democracy. While the Parliamentary army had to organise itself from a standing start, Charles had all the tools of a functional military to deploy immediately.

In practice Charles had a very uneven record as a man-manager. Although he began by making appointments based more on social and political status than on competence, he increasingly promoted nobles with a good track record into positions of authority and he brought them into a Council of War, based in Oxford, from which to co-ordinate their efforts. The Earl of Newcastle is one such appointment and was followed by the summoning of the king's nephews Rupert (who replaced the Marquess of Hertford) and Maurice to England from Europe where they had gained invaluable experience fighting on behalf of the Dutch Republic.

> **CROSS-REFERENCE**
> Refer to page 117 to see how Parliament created Associations as an alternative military structure to the Lords Lieutenant.

> **CROSS-REFERENCE**
> The passage of the Militia Ordinance can be found on page 99.

Fig. 3 *Landseer's eighteenth-century painting of King Charles on the eve of the Battle of Edgehill*

However, Charles continued to make woeful personnel decisions that annoyed or alienated even his most loyal supporters. Thus on the night before the Battle of Edgehill in October 1642, **Prince Rupert** argued openly with the General-in-Chief, the Earl of Lindsey, about the best way to deploy the cavalry. The king sided with his 23-year-old nephew against the 60-year-old war veteran and gave him independent command of the

SECTION 4 | War and radicalism, 1642–1646

CROSS-REFERENCE

For more information about what happened at **Duns**, see Chapter 8, page 69.

KEY PROFILE

Fig. 4 *Prince Rupert*

Prince Rupert (1619–82) was the son of Charles's sister Elizabeth and her husband, the Elector Frederick of the Palatinate. He was only 14 when he became a soldier, fighting alongside Frederick Henry, Prince of Orange where he achieved some notable successes as a cavalry commander. In August 1642 he travelled to England with his brother Maurice and a troop of professional soldiers. He embodied the 'Cavalier' ideal of courtly, glamorous swagger and martial skill.

Sir Faithful 'Faskie' Fortescue (1581–1666) spent the early part of his life in Ireland where his uncle was Lord Deputy from 1604 to 1616 and he was given lands in the Ulster Plantation, becoming Governor of Drogheda. Fleeing from the Irish rebels, his troop of cavalry and infantrymen were commandeered by the Earl of Essex to be used for the Parliamentarians at Edgehill. Before the battle, Fortescue met with Prince Rupert and promised to desert with his men once the fighting was underway.

ACTIVITY

In pairs, discuss why it should have been such an advantage for Charles to have a clear strategic goal.

cavalry: Lindsey resigned his post. In an uncanny echo of Lord Holland's lack of control at **Duns**, Rupert's horsemen ran ahead too far, lost discipline in the field and left the Royalist infantry undefended at a crucial point in the fighting.

A CLOSER LOOK

Prince Rupert was both a liability and an asset to Charles at Edgehill. He was a liability because he provoked the resignation of the General-in-Chief but he was an asset because he secured the desertion of a troop of Parliament's cavalry under the leadership of **Sir Faithful Fortescue**.

Charles also failed to capitalise on the opportunity that unity of command should have given him. In 1643 he set up a second headquarters, under his son Prince Charles, with its own War Council in Bristol and sent some of his best advisers, including the Earl of Clarendon along there. His intention was to ensure that king and heir could not be captured at the same time, but it meant that strategic unity was lost.

Strategy

Charles should also have benefitted from the fact that he had a clear strategic goal: to restore his monarchical authority by defeating the Parliamentarian armies so that he could return in power to London which he had abandoned in 1642. This was a tangible war aim that could be planned for, whereas the Parliamentarian war aim was less defined being simply to do enough to force the king to accept negotiation terms.

Decisive events in the early months of the First Civil War

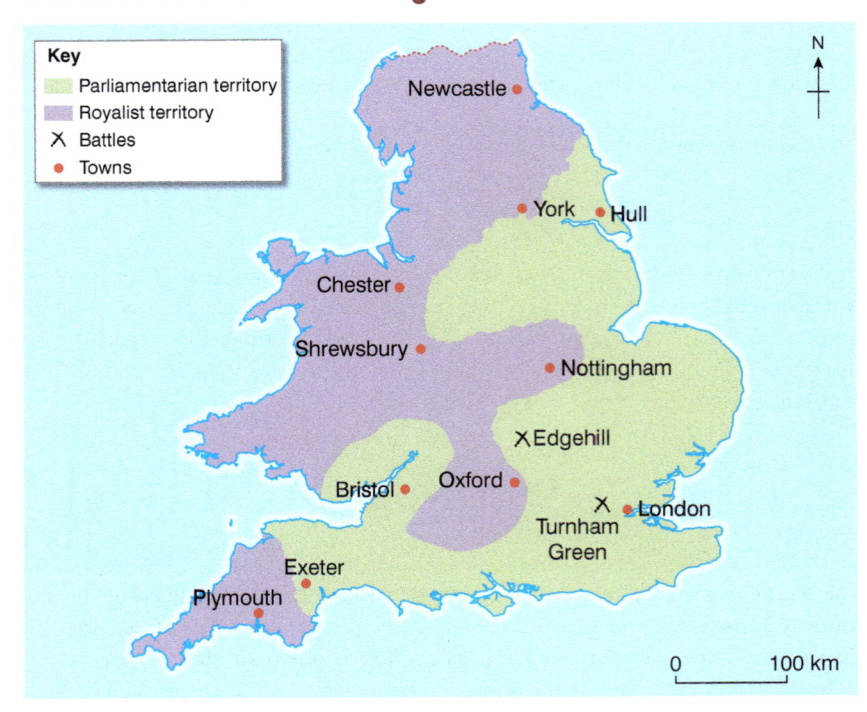

Fig. 5 *This map shows the major events of 1642*

Once Charles had raised his standard in Nottingham, he set up headquarters in Shrewsbury and from there set out with his troops to march down to London. At Edgehill, Warwickshire, they came into contact with a large

Parliamentary army under the Earl of Essex, which they met in battle on 23 October 1642. As night fell, over 3000 soldiers lay dead on the battlefield with neither side able to claim a victory. Charles's commanders regrouped their troops and prepared to continue their march towards London the next day. By the time they had reached Reading, having taken Banbury, Abingdon, Aylesbury and Maidenhead, there was pressure from among the officers to open negotiations with Parliament. Charles paused to consider whether to try to reach a peace but was persuaded against it by Prince Rupert who advocated continued military action. The delay, while Charles considered which course to follow, allowed time for the Earl of Essex to collect together his troops from Edgehill and, circling around the Royalist armies, reach London in time to head off Rupert's advancing force at Turnham Green on 13 November 1642.

> **SOURCE 2**
>
> From an account of the standoff at Turnham Green by John Rushworth; this account featured in a collection of private papers that was first published in 1721:
>
> There were about 3000 soldiers from the Earl of Essex's army stationed at Kingston. They were directed to march to the flank side of the King's army at Hounslow while the 24,000 well-equipped and highly motivated men in Essex's main army, joined by the London Trained Bands and ordinary citizens, would advance directly against the King so his army would be surrounded. This plan was put in motion with the addition that John Hampden's regiment were ordered to march round the back of the King's army to await a sign to attack from that direction as well. However, when Hampden's men had only marched about a mile, this order was rescinded and so they marched back to Turnham Green where both armies stood facing one another for several hours. The officers from Parliament and the counties wanted to engage but the officers who had been brought in as professionals advised against it. While they were still debating, the King drew back his gun carriages and retreated. Then there was another debate: should the Parliamentary army pursue them, but again, the veteran soldiers opposed this plan. So the King marched away and back to Oxford via Reading, and the Trained Bands and London citizens marched back to London.

While a number of Royalist actions in the opening months were successful, there were several opportunities that Charles missed in the early years of the war, where he could perhaps have pressed ahead to a decisive military victory. The first of these was that it was probably a miscalculation to turn back after the standoff at Turnham Green when he still had the advantage in terms of size, equipment and support from the regions.

How the king lost the advantage in the early months of the war

The failure of the king to achieve a political settlement during the early months of the Civil War while the balance of equipment and resources was tipped to his side was arguably the greater catastrophe than the military setbacks he suffered later in the war.

Political division in the Royalist leadership

Whereas the military understanding of what would constitute a victory was straightforward, two political factions had emerged with different views on what would constitute a victorious settlement.

KEY CHRONOLOGY

Events of the First Civil War, 1642

Aug	King raises Standard at Nottingham
	King makes headquarters at Shrewsbury
23 Oct	Battle of Edgehill
Nov	Battle of Turnham Green
	King retreats to set up headquarters at Oxford

	'War' faction	'Peace' faction
Key members	Henrietta Maria	Earl of Clarendon
	Prince Rupert	Viscount Falkland
	(Later) George, Lord Digby, Earl of Bristol	
Views	Demand significant submission from Parliament, achieved through all-out victory	Welcome a moderate settlement in the hope that the country can be extricated from war

The competing influence of the war and peace parties caused problems for Charles, leading him to prevaricate in negotiation and be indecisive in military command.

The Oxford Treaty

The Battle of Edgehill and the Turnham standoff in the autumn of 1642 clearly demonstrated that the war could not be swiftly fought and won, by one side or the other, not least because neither side had actually wanted to fight at Turnham Green. It was generally understood that Charles was in a better position than the Parliamentary forces and so the House of Lords, in liaison with the moderate Royalist Lord Falkland, who was with the king in Oxford, put pressure onto the Commons to try to reach an agreement with the king. Led by Pym, they debated and drew up what was essentially a slightly softened revision of the Nineteen Propositions. The king granted safe passage to Parliament's commissioners and they brought the terms to the king at Oxford in January 1643.

SOURCE 3

The king confirmed to the House of Lords that he would attend negotiations with Parliament, by sending this response, noted in the Rushworth Collection, on 6 February 1642:

Were it not that His Majesty was entirely committed to bringing about peace and reconciliation with his people, he would have every cause to resent the serious allegations made against him in the opening lines of these propositions. These presume to tell his subjects that this war began in order to defend religion, law, liberty and the privileges of Parliament from his royal person. The truth is the exact opposite. His Majesty was born into the true Protestant religion and has sworn to faithfully live and even die in defence of this religions. His Majesty has also sworn to defend the laws, liberties and privileges of Parliament which were well-established long before any army was raised against him. In truth, he has raised an army for his Defence. However, despite these scurrilous attacks, his Majesty is pleased to support a speedy decision on when and where he should meet with both Houses to discuss these propositions and his Majesty's own terms.

ACTIVITY

What might be the consequences of Charles's apparent willingness to embrace martyrdom? Add your ideas to your strength/weakness table.

Edward Hyde, bitterly, reckoned that the king had entered the negotiations with no intention of reaching a settlement and his opinion is supported by the fact that Charles caused the preliminary discussions to drag on until March before destroying the Treaty absolutely by requiring Parliament to restore its expelled members and leave Westminster for Oxford before he would continue to negotiate. Parliament's commissioners left Oxford in April.

Charles did not pursue negotiations because:
- Royalist armies were prevailing in the north and west. Prince Rupert, brimming with military optimism and having achieved notable successes, gave the king confidence he could succeed absolutely.
- Charles was developing a mindset in which he could embrace his own death in the cause of the kingship. In December 1642 he had written to the Duke of Hamilton, 'I shall either be a glorious king or a patient martyr.'
- Henrietta Maria, greatly influential, returned in the spring of 1643, bringing with her money and weapons (including cannons) sent by King Christian IV of Denmark and Prince Frederick Henry of Orange and a promise of troops from France. She continuously advised him to stand firm on his prerogative and power.
- The king was so attached to the ideology of Divine Right that it was deeply distasteful for him to have to negotiate with Parliament.

Consequences of the Oxford Treaty

While the war faction triumphed over the Oxford Treaty, it is said that Lord Falkland was so devastated that the peace negotiations had failed that he deliberately threw away his life at the First Battle of Newbury. Falkland's death left Clarendon increasingly isolated and even more so as Lord Digby replaced Falkland as Charles's Secretary of State.

Failure of the swift, sharp blow

By the summer of 1643 it looked as though the king, sweeping all before him, would be able to achieve all-out victory.

Fig. 6 *The major events of 1643*

KEY CHRONOLOGY	
Events of the First Civil War, 1643	
Jan	Oxford Treaty negotiations begin
March	Scarborough Castle declared for the king
April	Oxford treaty negotiations collapse
May	Battle of Stratton
30 June	Battle of Adwalton: defeat of Parliamentary army under Fairfax
July	Royalists take Bristol and Exeter
5 July	Battle of Lansdowne Hill
13 July	Battle of Roundway Down
Aug–Sept	Siege of Gloucester
20 Sept	First battle of Newbury

Charles's army had remained relatively intact after the Battle of Edgehill and progressively took control of the region around Banbury and Oxford where they remained without significant challenge throughout the summer of 1643.

SECTION 4 | War and radicalism, 1642–1646

KEY PROFILE

Sir Hugh Cholmeley (1600–57) was MP for Scarborough in all Charles's Parliaments. Alongside Sir John Hotham, he resisted Wentworth's application of Thorough in Yorkshire and refused to pay Ship Money. He fought for Essex at the Battle of Edgehill, but in the spring of 1643 he switched allegiance to the king.

Sir Thomas Fairfax (1612–71) was born into a Yorkshire gentry family and briefly fought for the Prince of Orange's Protestant cause in the Dutch Republic wars which were a campaign in the Thirty Years' War. In 1639 he fought alongside the king in the Bishops' Wars and advocated Parliamentary moderation in the Long Parliament. Ultimately though, he and his father fought for Parliament in the Civil Wars.

CROSS-REFERENCE

The progress of the First Civil War after the Royalist high point of 1643 is covered in depth in Chapter 14.

A CLOSER LOOK

Developments after 1643

Parliament began to organise its army more effectively. It secured an alliance with the Scottish Covenanter Army that proved decisive at the Battle of Marston Moor in July 1644. This opened the way for Parliament to crush the Royalist army in the north of England. A brief Royalist resurgence followed in the south-west of England but Parliament asserted final military dominance having created the New Model Army in the winter of 1645. This was a vastly superior fighting force, in equipment, leadership and military discipline. At the Battle of Naseby in June 1645, the King's entire army of 7,500 was outnumbered by 14,000 New Model soldiers. It was a devastating defeat which effectively signalled the end of the war.

In March 1643, Scarborough Castle, with its arms and armaments, was turned over to the king by its former Parliamentarian keeper, **Sir Hugh Cholmeley**. The Royalist Earl of Newcastle had fortified Newark and, at the Battle of Adwalton on 30 June decisively defeated the Parliamentary army in Yorkshire which had been under the command of the Fairfax family.

Only Hull still held out for Parliament, and both Lord Fairfax and his son **Sir Thomas** were holed up there hoping for relief. By July, the Earl of Newcastle was readying his troops to march on down towards London.

In the west, Royalist control had spread eastwards from its Cornish heartland. Sir Ralph Hopton brought forces through Devon, defeating a Parliament force at Stratton in May, to meet up with Prince Maurice's army in Somerset: together they beat a Parliament army at Roundway Down on 13 July 1643 and went on to take Exeter. Only Plymouth held out for Parliament in the south west.

To the dismay of Parliament, in July, Prince Rupert led a force from Oxford to besiege and then successfully storm the crucial city of Bristol, England's second port and location of a significant arsenal.

The king next led an army to besiege Gloucester. It was now the single major city that would prevent all the Royalist armies from linking up and advancing together towards London, which Charles intended to eventually blockade, besieging it into surrender rather than taking on the London trained bands again. The Royalists looked unstoppable but within a few short months, Charles's fortunes had taken a bad turn. His failure to force the surrender of Gloucester in August 1643 by opting instead for the much longer process of a siege was the second of his significant tactical blunders because it allowed time for Parliament to organise its army to come to Gloucester's relief.

Reversal of fortune

The summer of 1643 was the high point of Royalist strength and yet Charles was unable to push through to conclude the war and assert his authority. Parliament's fortunes began to shift. The increasing likelihood that the Scottish Army might yet again take up arms against the king meant that the Earl of Newcastle wavered about leaving the North undefended if that second front opened up. In the south-west, the siege of Plymouth did not collapse in the same manner as that of Bristol and the Royalist armies became bogged down with autumn approaching. The Earl of Essex brought a Parliamentary army to relieve Gloucester and struck a decisive blow against the king's army at the First Battle of Newbury, 20 September 1643. The king's cause never recovered and the war dragged on for three long years, robbing him of his short-term advantages and allowing Parliament to deploy its long-term strengths.

The consequences of Royalist failure

Charles failed to win a decisive victory in the early years of the First Civil War and he also failed to leverage the ascendancy of the Royalist forces in 1643 to bring about a favourable settlement. By terminating the Oxford Treaty negotiations, despite a process lasting five months, he convinced the Parliamentarian leadership that they had no choice but to pursue outright military victory. As a consequence he gave Parliament the motivation it needed to reshape itself into a sophisticated military command structure, effectively marshalling its resources and creating a professional army that would eventually prove to be an unstoppable force.

ACTIVITY

Summary

1. Complete your table showing the strengths and weakness of the king.
2. Using the notes from your table, prepare two SWOT analyses for the Royalist cause, one dated to August 1642 and one dated to August 1643. Identify the most significant strengths and weaknesses to add to these analyses.

Strengths	Weaknesses
Opportunities	Threats

3. If you were a trusted adviser, how would you brief the king to proceed in August 1643?

A LEVEL PRACTICE QUESTION

Evaluating primary sources

Using Sources 1, 2 and 3, and your own knowledge of the historical context, assess the value of these sources for a historian studying the reasons why people supported the Royalist cause in the First Civil War.

STUDY TIP

Refresh your knowledge about who tended to support the Royalist and Parliamentary parties and try to add data from your own research to provide some statistical analysis in your answer. Be aware of generalisations. Consider the case of those for whom neither side was appealing. Reflect also on the provenance of sources.

A LEVEL PRACTICE QUESTION

'At the beginning of the war, the king was in a much stronger position than Parliament.'
Assess the validity of this view.

STUDY TIP

You could use your table of strengths and weaknesses to help create a balanced answer to this question. Try to go beyond simply blaming the king for incompetence and consider the undercurrents that made his job difficult. To answer the question fully it will be useful to work through Chapter 14.

14 The First Civil War: the Parliamentarian cause

LEARNING OBJECTIVES

In this chapter you will learn about:

- the strengths and weaknesses of the political and military leadership of the Parliamentary forces
- the Solemn League and Covenant
- emergence of the New Model Army
- the Self-Denying Ordinance.

KEY CHRONOLOGY

1642	20 Dec	Formation of the Eastern Association
1643	15 Sept	Cessation Treaty
	23 Sept	Solemn League and Covenant
1644	July	Battle of Marston Moor
	Dec	Introduction of Self-Denying Ordinance
1645	Jan	Execution of William Laud
	Feb	New Model Ordinance
	June	Battle of Naseby

KEY TERM

Parliamentarian army: the army raised by the Parliamentary opposition to the king

CROSS-REFERENCE

The flight of Charles from London is discussed on page 99.

The strengths and weaknesses of the Parliamentary forces

Because the balance of power broadly rested with the king in the early months of the war, the initial goal of the **Parliamentarian army** was to survive rather more than to conquer. The most significant issue relating to survival was that the Long Parliament was the first (and only) English Parliament to have put an army into the field against the monarch which presented unique issues to resolve. In this respect, control of London (and more widely, the south-east) was a great asset.

ACTIVITY

Create a table under the heading 'strengths and weaknesses of the political and military leadership of the Parliamentarian cause', and add to it as you work through this chapter.

Parliamentarian strengths	Parliamentarian weaknesses

It might help if you start by filling out the table with relevant information, then at the end categorise according to whether you each item is a political or military weakness.

The importance of London

- **Political:** Westminster was at the heart of the Political Nation and in order to re-assert political dominance, Charles would have to physically dominate Westminster.
- **Financial:** London was the wealthiest city in England because of its place at the heart of national and international trade. London's wealth brought power, so Charles would need to control London's wealth in order to fully undermine the resources which sustained Parliament militarily.
- **Demographic:** Events such as the demonstrations of the London Mob against the Failed Arrest of the Five Members showed that London's sizeable population and particularly its trained bands were a military force in their own right. They would need to be defeated if the king was going to establish total victory.

Finance and funding

It is extremely expensive to maintain an army in the field and a poorly financed army generates significant problems, not least that:

- without money, soldiers are poorly equipped, cannot fight effectively and are inclined to desert
- inadequate or erratic pay generates ill-discipline, which rapidly tips into disorder, with soldiers looting local communities in order to remunerate themselves directly. Disorder alienates local communities who then want nothing more than to get rid of the soldiers and so will either fight alongside their enemy, fight directly against them or entirely stop paying anything towards the war effort.

A significant part of Parliamentary business in the early months of the war was therefore intended to create adequate funding to sustain the Parliamentary war effort. Initially these tended to be ad hoc measures, for example:
- June 1642: An ordinance for the securing of £100,000 to be lent to Parliament by several companies and citizens of London for the use of the kingdom.
- August 1642: An ordinance for raising money in London.
- November 1642: An ordinance for the better provision of food and other necessities for the army and for payment to be made for such provisions.

Gradually however, financial ordinances in the Commons record reveal the emergence of an increasingly sophisticated taxation system.

Table 1 *Ordinances and their significance, 1643*

Date	Measure	Significance
February 1643	Ordinance for raising money for the maintenance of the army by a Weekly Assessment	Weekly assessments used the formula applied by Ship Money and required each county to provide money on a weekly basis, changing to monthly later. Assessments were foundational to Parliamentary finance and raised considerably more money than Parliamentary subsidies.
March 1643	Ordinance for sequestering notorious Delinquents' Estates	In the wake of the Oxford Treaty, local commissioners were given permission to confiscate ('sequester') the estates of Royalists which they would then manage, sending profits to Parliament's coffers.
May 1643	An Order, engaging the public faith, to secure repayment of money, etc., advanced for the support of the army…	Reminiscent of the Forced Loans of the 1620s, all those worth over £10 a year from land or £100 a year for goods had to make a loan of 20% of their annual revenue from land, or £50 from goods, to Parliament, to be repaid 'upon the public faith.'
July 1643	Ordinance for the speedy raising and levying of moneys by way of charge or impost upon several commodities.	A purchase tax on a very wide range of goods which affected everyone and was very unpopular.

To enforce these ordinances, Parliament used the county committees but (in an uncanny echo of Thorough) made them accountable to central committees in London.

Leadership and command
Shortcomings of the County Militia

From the moment that Haselrig's Militia Ordinance became law in March 1642, Parliament and the king both scrambled to mobilise soldiers into their own armies. Initially, both sides tried to make the traditional militia infrastructure work. In August, for example, Parliament despatched officers to co-ordinate county defences through County Committees. It quickly became apparent that the county militia were reluctant to fight outside their own counties because they saw their role as being primarily defensive but the demands of the Civil War meant that it was necessary for them to travel well beyond their county boundaries

> **CROSS-REFERENCE**
>
> The passage of the Militia Ordinance can be found on page 99.

Associations

By the late autumn of 1642, in order to overcome this problem, Parliament began to group counties together to form Associations. The Eastern Association would become the most significant of these. Founded on 20 December it consisted of the county militia of Norfolk, Suffolk, Essex, Cambridgeshire and Hertfordshire, under the leadership of Lord Grey of Warke. The idea behind the Associations was that they would create meaningful military units which would remain connected to their localities

> **CROSS-REFERENCE**
>
> Refer to page 109 to see how the king used Lords Lieutenant to organise provincial armies.

> **KEY PROFILE**
>
> Fig. 1 Oliver Cromwell
>
> **Oliver Cromwell (1599–1658)** was born into a gentry family in the Cambridgeshire town of Huntington, becoming the town's MP in 1628. He subsequently had a profound spiritual awakening which led to him develop strong Puritan ideals. When he entered the Short and Long Parliaments as MP for Cambridge he became allied with the Puritan faction. On the outbreak of the Civil War he began to create a cavalry regiment from within Cambridgeshire which was brought into the Eastern Association.

> **CROSS-REFERENCE**
>
> The progress of the First Civil War up to the Royalist high point of 1643 is covered in depth in Chapter 13.

> **KEY TERM**
>
> **conscript:** to enlist someone into an army by law rather than by their own decision

through their provincial origins and local commanders and could, if necessary, be sent out of their region. They did not fully achieve this goal. A gentleman from Huntingdon, **Oliver Cromwell**, complained of the 'wrong opinion of our unexperienced country soldiers that they ought not to be deployed beyond the bounds of the five counties'.

> **ACTIVITY**
>
> Compare the king's use of Lords Lieutenant with the Parliamentarian Associations. Which structure was stronger, in your opinion?

Early engagements of the First Civil War

The king possessed the early advantage because his own wealth and that of his noble supporters meant his army was better equipped than its parliamentarian equivalent. His leaders tended to have more experience in the field. Early indecision on both sides at the Battle of Edgehill in October 1642 and the Standoff at Turnham Green during November 1642 were perhaps caused by a residual unwillingness to commit to full scale war. However by the summer of 1643, Royalist forces had progressed swiftly through the south-west of England and were amassing, ready to advance on London.

The likelihood of defeat

The Royalist surge in the spring and summer of 1643 led to a sense of impending crisis in the Eastern Association as the Royalist Earl of Newcastle brought his immense army southwards, occupying Stamford and threatening Peterborough. By mid-August he controlled almost all of Lincolnshire and appeared ready to sweep all before him. The Cambridge Committee wrote to the Essex Deputy-Lieutenants: 'the whole association will be exposed to the fury and cruelty of the Popish army. If you desert us, we fear we shall never be in a position to trouble you with letters any more.' Cromwell expressed the same desperation in his letters to his commanding officers: 'There's no argument left: we need every soldier we can find. Raise all your militia men. Find what volunteers you can. Hurry your horses. Cautious advice and indecisive actions put everything at risk. Send help at once or all will be lost unless God steps in.'

Panic in East Anglia led to calls in some newspapers for the creation of a 'flying army', a centrally commanded force that could be deployed anywhere. In an effort to put the Associations on a stronger footing and with a focus initially on the Eastern Association, progressive measures were introduced:

- August 1643: **Impressment Ordinance** this Parliamentary measure created a legal right to **conscript** soldiers into the Parliamentarian army.
- August 1643: Appointment of the Earl of Manchester, a more capable commander, to lead the Eastern Association with authority to conscript 20,000 men, the Earl set about removing weak officers and promoting skilful soldiers (as long as they 'love Christ in sincerity').
- January 1644: Financial restructure monthly assessments increased revenue by 50% and the money was put into the Earl of Manchester's direct control.

Political issues within the Parliamentary leadership

There were divisions within the Parliamentary leadership that reflected those among the Royalists. The leading Stuart historian Barry Coward categorised MPs into 'peace', 'war' and 'middle' groups, allowing of course for the fact that political alliances shift and flex.

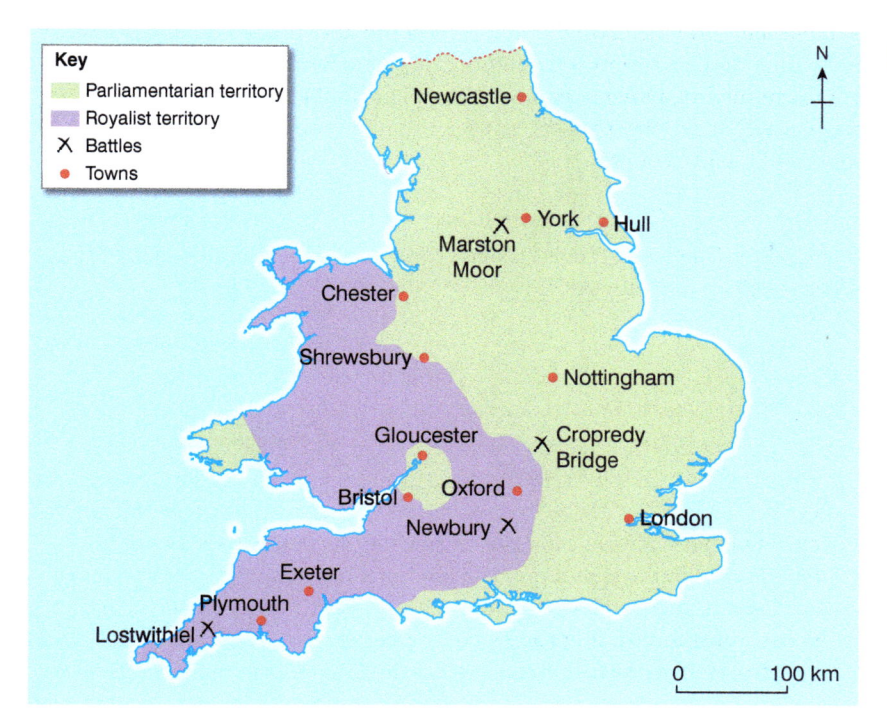

CHAPTER 14 | The First Civil War: the Parliamentarian cause

Fig. 2 *Major events in 1644*

KEY CHRONOLOGY

Events of the First Civil War, 1644

April–July	Siege of York
29 June	Battle of Copredy Bridge
2 July	Battle of Marston Moor
Aug–Sept	Lostwithiel Campaign
27 Oct	Second battle of Newbury

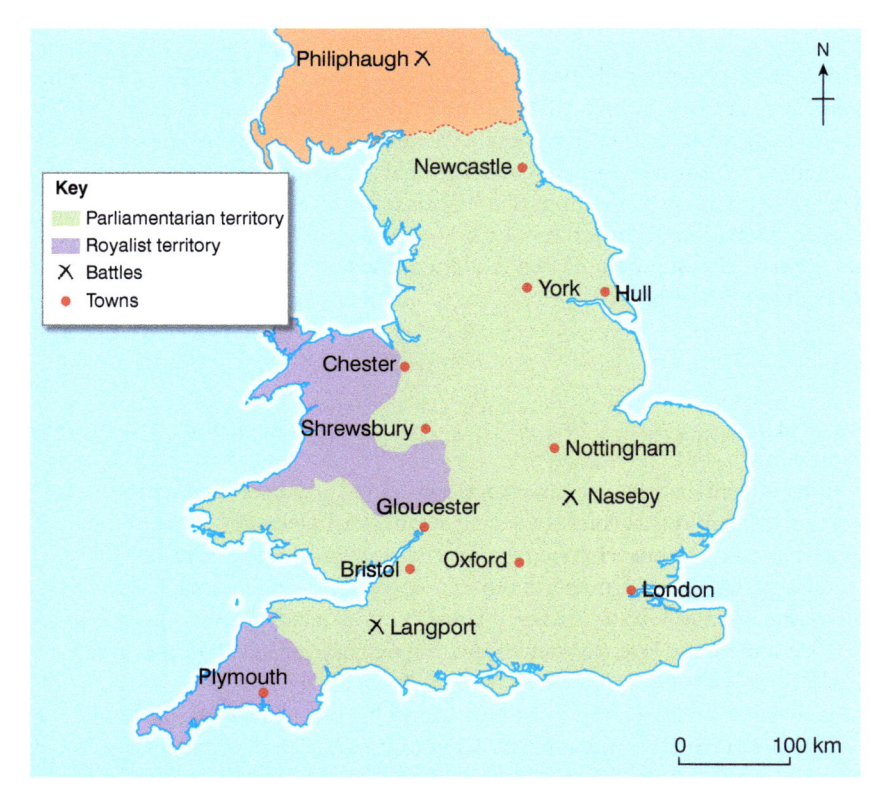

Fig. 3 *Major events in 1645*

KEY CHRONOLOGY

Events of the First Civil War, 1645

14 June	Battle of Naseby
10 July	Battle of Langport
23 Aug–10 Sept	Siege of Bristol
13 Sept	Battle of Philiphaugh

119

SECTION 4 | War and radicalism, 1642–1646

Table 2 Members, aims and motivations of the three groups

	The peace group	The middle group	The war group
Leading members	Denzil Holles, Sir Simmonds D'Ewes	John Pym, Oliver St John, Viscount Saye and Sele	Arthur Haselrig, Henry Vane Jnr, Henry Marten
War aim	Purely defensive	Offensive strategy	Offensive strategy, if necessary carried out by new generals
Settlement aim	Reach settlement with the king at any price; they were happy to accept the king's word that he would not reverse the legislation of 1641.	Negotiation of a traditional constitutional settlement with the measures of 1641 included	No negotiation with king; imposition of settlement to (in Clarendon's words) 'change the whole frame of the government in State as well as Church.'
Motivation	Fear of the disorder and chaos unleashed by war	Effective prosecution of the war is essential because the king cannot be trusted so duress needs to be applied.	Radically change the constitutional balance, possibly even become a republic

ACTIVITY

When you add the strengths and weaknesses of political leadership into your table, ensure you include the individual political ability of John Pym. While it is easy to identify ways in which division weakened leadership in Parliament, can you think of any ways in which division might bring strength?

That Parliamentary divisions did not cripple the efficiency of its armies is very much down to the skilful political ability of John Pym. In particular, he managed to maintain the Earl of Essex in his role as Commander-in-Chief during the spring and summer of 1643, despite pressure from the Peace Group to negotiate a settlement and pressure from the War Group to replace him with a more militaristic leader. By retaining Essex, Pym smoothed relations with the House of Lords and reassured county gentry that the war would not tip the country into outright chaos.

The Solemn League and Covenant

In August 1643 Parliament sent Commissioners to Scotland to negotiate an alliance. The Scots were keen to sign because they knew that the king would waste no time in reversing their constitutional gains of 1638–40 if he managed to defeat the English Parliament. The Westminster Commissioners and the Scottish Parliament together devised a 'Solemn League and Covenant' which they signed on 7 August 1643. All that remained was for it be ratified by the Westminster Parliament.

SOURCE 1

From the Solemn League and Covenant, signed between the Scottish Covenanters and the Commissioners of the English Parliament, 7 August 1643:

We have resolved to enter into a mutual and solemn league and covenant to which we shall all subscribe in the sight of the Most High God.

Whatever our status and job, we shall endeavour to preserve the Protestant religion in the Church of Scotland in doctrine, worship, discipline and government, against our common enemies.

We shall endeavour to wipe out Popery, episcopacy, superstition and heresy.

We shall endeavour with our money and our lives to preserve the rights and privileges of the Parliaments and the liberties of the kingdoms and to preserve and defend the King's person and authority as he seeks to preserve and defend the true religion and liberties of the kingdoms so that the world may bear witness of our loyalty. We have no thoughts or intentions to diminish His Majesty's rightful power and greatness.

We shall also assist and defend all those that enter into this league and covenant.

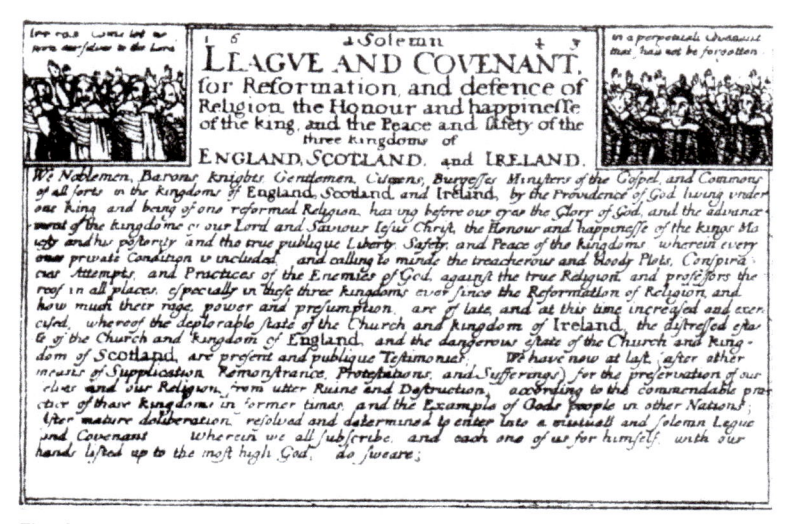

Fig. 4 *Cover of the Solemn League and Covenant*

A CLOSER LOOK

Terms of the Solemn League and Covenant

- Scotland would send an army of 22,000 soldiers to England to fight alongside Parliamentary forces.
- A 'Committee of Both Kingdoms' would provide joint command over the combined armies.
- The English Parliament would commit to a Presbyterian settlement for the Anglican Church.

Although the Solemn League and Covenant would strengthen the Parliamentarian cause, it provoked furious debate when it was presented to the English Parliament to be ratified. Partly this reflected historical tensions. Anglo-Scottish relations had been littered for centuries with tension and rivalry; the English tended to look down on the Scots and the Scots tended to think that the English were obnoxiously patronising. What was more problematic than this was the notion of a Presbyterian settlement that was necessary in order to 'wipe out... episcopacy'. The English Parliament felt that they should decide England's religious settlement, not be forced to accept one from the Scots. Furthermore, peace group MPs were very anxious that the king would never be brought to a settlement if the Covenant was signed.

John Pym came to the rescue with a politically skilful resolution. He split the religious component out from the rest of the Covenant terms and recommended that it should be sent to a joint 'Assembly of Divines' made up of representatives from Scotland and England which became known as the Westminster Assembly. This would naturally slow the process of decision making down because there was little prospect of a swift agreement on anything relating to religion. Presbyterianism was a strong priority for the Scots but military survival was the crucial point for the English. As one of the Scots Commissioners observed, 'The English want a civil League, we want a religious Covenant.' Finally, to reassure the peace group, Pym managed to have **Henry Marten**, one of the most radical Parliamentarians, removed from Parliament and imprisoned for suggesting that the monarchy should be abolished.

ACTIVITY

Why would Pym's plan slow down religious debate, and why do you think this is what he wanted to do?

KEY PROFILE

Henry Marten (1602–80) was a lawyer who represented Berkshire in the Short and Long Parliaments. He joined the attack on Strafford and expressed republican views that put him on the extreme wing of the war party.

The Irish Cessation

Ultimately, it was a tactical blunder by the king that pushed the Solemn League and Covenant into being. In September 1643, he signed a 'Cessation Treaty' with the Irish Catholic Rebels. It was probably simply intended as a ceasefire, so that the king could stop fighting on a second **front** and use all his troops in England. However, rumour spread that the king was intending to bring over a Catholic Irish Army; fear of popery exploded again and Parliament pressed ahead with the Covenanters: the Solemn League and Covenant was signed by both parties on 23 September 1643.

The Battle of Marston Moor

The military impact of the Solemn League and Covenant was fully realised in July 1644 at the decisive Parliamentary victory at the Battle of Marston Moor, which was followed by the seizure of the York. The combined armies

KEY TERM

front: the point at which one army engages with another; fighting on more than one front at a time puts enormous pressure onto an army because it effectively means that two or more complete armies, with equipment, food and manpower, have to be created out of one

SECTION 4 | War and radicalism, 1642–1646

> **ACTIVITY**
>
> Carry out some independent research into the military campaigns of General Fairfax and add information about him to your table.

of Fairfax, Manchester and the Scottish Covenanters effectively destroyed the Royalist army in the North.

Setback for the Parliamentarians

Parliament was not able to follow Marston Moor with other significant victories in the ensuing months. Quite the reverse was true: the Earl of Essex took his army down into the south-west, where it became trapped and the Covenanters became distracted by a front that opened against them in the Scottish Highlands, led by the Earl of Montrose.

The emergence of the New Model Army

The Self-Denying Ordinance

In December 1644 the War Party introduced a measure into Parliament called the 'Self-Denying Ordinance'. It separated political leadership in Parliament from military command in the field because it said that no MPs (from either the Lords or the Commons) could be in positions of command in the army or navy.

> **ACTIVITY**
>
> **Pair discussion**
>
> Before reading on, discuss with a partner what sort of debates you think this Ordinance might generate.

The main reason that the Self-Denying Ordinance was introduced was that political unity was breaking down in Parliament. Because leadership of the military forces was substantially being carried out by men who were also members of Parliament, this political disunity was threatening the military integrity of the Parliamentarian armies because what might be desirable politically might not be the best militarily.

Fig. 5 *Uniform of a New Model Army soldier*

Reasons for disunity

Military setbacks: The Earl of Essex, bogged down in the south-west, was becoming demoralised because it was so difficult to win and his army was weary. He began to align himself with the peace party's calls to make a settlement with the king, while the war party began to press for his removal.

Religious tensions: The boost to religious debate caused by the Covenant, coupled with a massive upsurge of radical religious pamphlets triggered by the collapse of censorship meant that religious issues were becoming of rising importance both within and beyond Westminster and in the army itself. This religious disunity was already beginning to cause problems within the army.

As an example, Major General Lawrence Crawford, a Presbyterian Scottish Commander within the Eastern Association tried to clamp down on religious radicalism that was beginning to surge among his soldiers by removing officers he judged to be too radical and disciplining soldiers caught in radical religious practices, such as preaching without a licence. Cromwell, also an officer in the Eastern Association, strongly criticised Crawford for trying to impose his Presbyterianism onto the army. The impact of this and other similar instances was that divisions were opening up between commanders that bore no relation to military decision-making.

Fear of disorder: We have seen how religious debate caused social tensions to rise. As the war progressed, a new element of social tension was introduced as ordinary soldiers from the rank-and-file who distinguished themselves in battle began to be promoted into positions traditionally reserved for the higher social classes. This alarmed moderates such as Denzil Holles, who criticised the nature of such appointees, complaining that 'most of the colonels are tradesmen, brewers, tailors, goldsmiths, shoemakers and the like'. Behind his snobbish comment lies a widely shared anxiety that the war was beginning to change the nature of English society.

Impact of religious zeal among soldiers: What is more, typically, these lower-status soldiers who were rising through the ranks brought with them a religious zeal that accounted for their immense motivation and energy: they were among the most efficient and effective of the Parliamentarian officers. Cromwell was such a man; a Puritan **zealot**, the cavalry regiment that he commanded at Marston Moor, known as the 'Ironsides' decisively outperformed Prince Rupert's Royalist cavalry. Particularly in the Eastern Association, a sub-set of officers was beginning to form, those of strong religious zeal; in terms of military capability they were beginning to overshadow the rest and they were promoting other men of zeal. Altogether, this meant that the prevailing culture within the army was changing.

Anxiety about the future: As the enormity of what Parliament had undertaken in fighting the king continued to sink in, some began to fear that there was little prospect of a good ending. The Earl of Manchester declared for the peace party, saying despondently, 'Gentlemen, I beseech you let's consider what we do; the king need not care how he fights but it concerns us to be wary, for in fighting we venture all to nothing. If we fight a hundred times and beat him ninety and nine times, he will be king still… but if he beat us but once, or the last time, we shall be hanged, we shall lose our estates and our posterities be undone.'

Introduction of the Ordinance

For all these reasons, momentum was growing in Parliament among the members of the peace party against the war party. The introduction of the Self-Denying Ordinance into Parliament in December 1644 by Cromwell and his allies was a decisive attempt to regain the political initiative for the War party.

> **CROSS-REFERENCE**
>
> Religious radicalism in the army is discussed in depth in Chapter 15, page 128.

> **KEY TERM**
>
> **zealot:** someone with a powerful enthusiasm in pursuit of a cause or an objective

> **ACTIVITY**
>
> Consider motivation as a source of both strength and weakness to add to your table.

SOURCE 2

From a speech made by Oliver Cromwell to the House of Commons on 9 December 1644 in his preamble to the Self-Denying Ordinance:

We must save our Nation which is now bleeding, no, dying because this war has so dragged on. Unless we speed things up by being more vigorous and effective, we shall make the Kingdom weary of us and hate the name of a Parliament. What does our enemy say? Even worse, what do many now say who were our friends at the beginning of Parliament? They say that Members of both Houses have given themselves high status and important commands and have armed themselves and now that they have both power in Parliament and power in the army, will perpetually continue themselves in such grandeur and actively work against ending this war lest their power ends with it. I am saying this openly because others say it behind our backs. I personally do not agree; I know the worth of those Commanders who are also MPs but it is my honest opinion that

SECTION 4 | War and radicalism, 1642–1646

A CLOSER LOOK

Failed agreement at Uxbridge, February 1645

The abortive Treaty of Uxbridge demanded that the king himself subscribe to the Solemn League and Covenant and thereafter allow his prerogative to be limited by the joint agreement of both English and Scottish Parliaments. With Montrose enjoying some success in Scotland, evidence of disunity among the Parliamentarian forces and his personal commitment to episcopacy, there was no way that Charles would agree to its terms.

---

unless we reorganise the army and boost our military effectiveness the People will turn against the War and will press you into a dishonourable Peace.

The terms of the Ordinance included:
- Acknowledgement that Parliament had become divided and needed to reunite
- A separation of political and military functions
- Military men, barred from becoming MPs, would create and lead a new, central army
- Veteran gentry generals would lose their command but stay in the Lords.

Initially, the Ordinance was held up by the Lords but impetus to pass it came with the failure in February 1645 of a renewed attempt to reach a settlement with the king through negotiations at Uxbridge which this time involved not just Parliamentary but also Scottish Commissioners. It was finally passed on 3 April.

The debate over the Self-Denying Ordinance was a significant step in the formation of Parliament's professional military force, the New Model Army, established by the New Model Ordinance of February 1645. The armies of the Earls of Essex and Manchester and Sir William Waller were merged into a single fighting force under a unified command. This new fighting force was not linked to localities: its soldiers would be trained and equipped to fight wherever they were needed. Two units of the old Parliamentary army remained outside the New Model Army, the Northern Association and the Western Association.

Leadership

Two of the three key appointments in the New Model Army were uncontroversial choices:

- **Lieutenant-General:** Thomas Fairfax, moderate Puritan and proven military commander.
- **Major General of the Infantry:** Sir Philip Skippon, moderate Puritan and leader of the Trained Bands at Turnham Green in 1642.

No generally acceptable candidate for the role of Lieutenant General of the Horse could be found, so in June 1645, Fairfax secured Parliamentary agreement to approve of a temporary commission for Oliver Cromwell, renewable every three months.

Organisation

KEY TERM

dragoons: infantrymen who rode to battle on horses but then left their horses behind the front line to fire their muskets

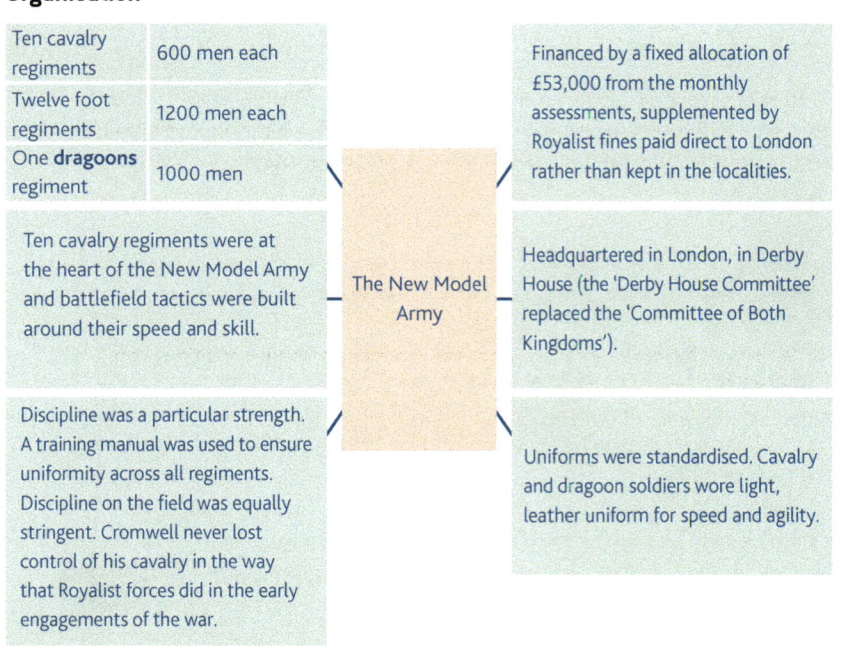

The New Model Army	
Ten cavalry regiments — 600 men each; Twelve foot regiments — 1200 men each; One dragoons regiment — 1000 men	Financed by a fixed allocation of £53,000 from the monthly assessments, supplemented by Royalist fines paid direct to London rather than kept in the localities.
Ten cavalry regiments were at the heart of the New Model Army and battlefield tactics were built around their speed and skill.	Headquartered in London, in Derby House (the 'Derby House Committee' replaced the 'Committee of Both Kingdoms').
Discipline was a particular strength. A training manual was used to ensure uniformity across all regiments. Discipline on the field was equally stringent. Cromwell never lost control of his cavalry in the way that Royalist forces did in the early engagements of the war.	Uniforms were standardised. Cavalry and dragoon soldiers wore light, leather uniform for speed and agility.

Fig. 6 Summary of the New Model Army

Impact

Financial Impact: The New Model Army was put on what should have been a secure financial footing as it was financed by the use of assessments, a form of taxation, which was governed by Parliamentary legislation. This is what ultimately made it a professional army rather than an enhanced county militia because wages were managed from central government. The impact of this change was that the New Model Army would now need to negotiate with Parliament over pay and conditions, creating a new political relationship between Westminster and its soldiers.

Military Impact: The New Model Army proved an unstoppable force at the decisive Battle of Naseby in June 1645 where it outmanned the Royalist army by 14,000 to 7,500 despite the king having brought together his entire strength. By the end of the battle, the king's military forces were destroyed, with the Earl of Newcastle's 'Whitecoats' slaughtered in a courageous last stand.

ACTIVITY

Add the finance of the New Model Army into your table of strengths and weaknesses. You will need to think about the potential weaknesses of this arrangement.

A CLOSER LOOK

Disastrous advice from Lord Digby at Naseby

Prince Rupert advised the king not to fight at Naseby but instead to settle with Parliament because it seemed to him so apparent that the Parliamentarian army would win. George Digby counselled exactly the opposite and managed to convince Charles that Rupert was unreliable. Rivalry between the two men accelerated but it was Digby who persuaded Charles to remove Rupert from command.

With such a demonstration of military might, the tide of the war had visibly turned against the king.

CROSS-REFERENCE

A Key Profile of **Lord Digby** can be found on page 139.

ACTIVITY

Summary

1. Complete your table of strengths and weakness of the Parliament's political and military leadership during the First Civil War.
2. Imagine you are Oliver Cromwell and write a letter to your constituents in Huntingdon after the Battle of Naseby.
3. Explain to them how the New Model Army led to the triumph at Naseby.
4. Compare and contrast your two tables. Overall, which side was best placed to win the war? How did their relative positions change over time?

A LEVEL PRACTICE QUESTION

Evaluating primary sources

With reference to Source 1 in Chapter 13 and Sources 1 and 2 in this chapter, assess the value of these three sources to an historian studying the impact of divisions within the Westminster Parliament between 1643 and 1645.

STUDY TIP

Don't forget to stay within the chronology specified in the question and evaluate both provenance and content in your answer. Support your comments with specific source references.

A LEVEL PRACTICE QUESTION

'At the beginning of the war, the king was in a much stronger position than Parliament.'
Assess the validity of this view.

STUDY TIP

You could use the table of strengths and weaknesses that you began in Chapter 13 to help create a balanced answer to this question.

15 The intensification of radicalism

LEARNING OBJECTIVES

In this chapter you will learn about:

- popular radicalism in London
- religious radicalism in the New Model Army
- pamphlets and propaganda.

KEY CHRONOLOGY

1643	May	An Humble Proposal of Safety
	June	Licensing Act
1645	July	The Kings Cabinet Opened
1646		Publication of Gangraena

ACTIVITY

What can you infer about Marvell's religious views from Source 1? Check your deductions by carrying out further research.

KEY TERM

polemicist: someone who makes powerful attacks on ideas or people in a carefully constructed format filled with argument and counter-argument

KEY PROFILE

Andrew Marvell (1621–78) worked as a tutor for Mary Fairfax, daughter of Sir Thomas Fairfax and became an MP in the 1659 Parliament. Although he had close links with Cromwell and leading Parliamentarians, he managed to navigate a political career throughout the 1660s and 70s. His poetry is beautiful, but to contemporaries he was best known for the sharp satire of his political writings, attacking folly and corruption wherever he saw it.

SOURCE 1

From a 1672 satire, *The Rehearsal Transpos'd*, in which the poet and **polemicist Andrew Marvell** looked back on the Civil Wars:

It's not worth spending much time wondering whether it was a war of religion or a war of liberty. Whichever you decide, the other is true as well. My opinion is that religion and liberty are so important that war was not the right response. Men ought to have trusted God and they should have trusted the king. The weapons of the Church are prayers and tears. The weapons of the subjects are patience and petitions. This Rebellion had numerous fatal consequences. Now, we have Sibthorps' Church and Manwarings' Church, and Montagues' Church and a whole raft more who, for decencies' sake, I will not name. Every man can now invent a new opinion, or a new ceremony, or a new tax, or a new Church of England.

The concept of 'radicalism' is central to an understanding of what was revolutionary about the English Revolution and two definitions of the term are particularly relevant:

- **A departure from tradition.** There is much evidence of the early Stuart Political Nation being 'radical' in the sense of 'departure from tradition', particularly during the consensus-based reforms of the early months of the Long Parliament in legislation such as the Triennial Act. Crucially, we have also seen how both king and Parliament claimed that the other was being radical through their innovations, used in a critical way to identify an *unwanted* departure from tradition.
- **Support for complete political or social reform.** As the 1640s unfold, we begin to see the world being 'turned upside down,' driven by enthusiastic forerunners who *intended* to generate a different, genuinely revolutionary, society. New conceptions of culture and community arose, with a proliferation of ideologies and beliefs as different individuals and groups gained their own momentum for change.

With the long view from the twenty-first century, we can see our modern political, social and religious world in its embryonic phase during the crisis of the seventeenth century with the formation of the modern idea of 'liberty' as in the rights of an individual to act freely across all spheres of life *and* an ideology of religious liberty which is a forerunner of modern conceptions of religious tolerance.

Popular radicalism in London

The turbulence of the Civil War was vigorously expressed among the citizens of London and some writers claimed that London had itself caused the war. A pamphlet of August 1643, with the helpful title *Lord Have Mercy Upon Us: or a Plaine Discourse Declaring that the Plague of Warre Took its Beginning in and from the Citie of London*, blamed London for the 'whole course of this Rebellion, which it first bred and doth still nourish at her breasts… all the misery of war, blood and destruction of property which do now overflow the Kingdom, come from no other fountain than the City of London.' These sentiments were shared by the Royalist writer John Berkenhead in his pamphlet *A Letter from Mercurius Civicus to Mercurius Rusticus*, also dating from August 1643: '…the proud, unthankful, Schismatical, Rebellious, Bloody City of London broke down the bounds… dissolved Monarchy, enslaved the Laws and ruined their Country.'

On the side of Parliament, the pamphlet *Londons New Colours Displaid*, of July 1648, endorsed London's credentials as 'the first in opposition to oppression; the first leader and example towards freedom.'

Fig. 1 *New Palace Yard in Westminster was the scene of many petitions and demonstrations*

Londoners' readiness to take direct action was ahead of its time. It was the mobilisation of the London Crowd in January 1642 that caused the king to rapidly leave the city. In November 1642, Lord Brooke called on each London merchant to 'shut up his shop… arm himself and arm his apprentices and come forth with boldness and with great courage', resulting in the massed ranks of Londoners who persuaded the king to withdraw to Oxford from **Turnham Green**.

On one occasion, the militant wives of Billingsgate fishmongers marched in army fashion behind a symbol of the goddess of war in support of Parliament. Parliamentary records from the summer of 1642 onwards are filled with detailed Ordinances connected with the many and various ways that Londoners and their businesses would support the Parliamentary war effort. Indeed, a plan was mooted in the spring of 1643 to create a standing army of Londoners on rotation, who would be accommodated in tents or temporary wooden huts. *An Humble Proposal of Safety* (May 1643) further recommended shutting all shops in London and the suburbs so that the men who would form this new standing army would have no excuse for failing to turn up at these new camps.

> **CROSS-REFERENCE**
> The Standoff at **Turnham Green** is discussed on page 111.

An example of freedom?

In the upheavals of the 1640s, distinctly innovative governing bodies were discussed and in some instances, brought into being in London. Control of the London Militia became the focal point for political radicalism during the war as City committees experimented with entirely new governance. In 1643, and again in 1644, the Salters Hall Committee pushed to create its own private army (entirely separate from the standing army) for the City of London, which would be managed by the Committee itself, without reference to Parliament, king or corporation.

In similar vein, there is evidence that suggests the awakening of a sense of the capacity of the ordinary people to make decisions that would in earlier years have been taken by established authorities. The historian Robert Brenner cites the example of the church of St Dunstan's-in-the-East whose Vestry Book (containing notes about church business) includes an incident from late 1642 in which: *'The Vestry Men chose Mr William Browne and Mr Bernard Hide to be churchwardens of the parish for the following year. That same day, most of the parishioners met in the church. They agreed that although it was traditional for the Vestry Men to appoint the churchwardens, that process should now be changed so that the parishioners also had to give their consent to the appointment.'*

Londoners also took a lead in shaping radical ideology. Sometimes ideology leads and practice follows. To a very great degree, the Long Parliament

enacted practice, out of necessity and in a hurry, which the people then had to comprehend with ideology. The issues that arose included:
- What consent means in terms of the king and the people.
- The use of debate to discern the will of the common folk.
- The place of authority and reason in society.
- The shift from secrecy to openness in governmental affairs, particularly in respect of the king's advisers.
- The extension of political discourse from the governing elite 'down' to the people.
- How to manage a politicised general population, using them to push policy through but controlling them to prevent social breakdown.

In 1643, the City Council, dominated by radicals, presented a 'Petition and Remonstrance' into Parliament, which placed the people, not the king, at the heart of the political process, explaining that sovereign authority came from the will of the people and that thus Parliament was supreme over the king. Political leaders within London, such as Randall Mainwaring, Stephen Estwicke and Samuel Warner, sat both in Parliament and on key London governmental committees including the most radical, the Militia Committees. They acted as a bridge between London radicalism and Parliamentary debate, creating the conditions in which the truly radical developments of the later 1640s and early 1650s could take place.

> **ACTIVITY**
>
> Using your knowledge of the context of the early Stuart period, what would have been the reaction to radicalism in London from (i) individuals (such as the king), and (ii) groups of people (such a regional gentry)? Add other groups that are likely to have held distinct opinions.

Religious radicalism in the New Model Army

The divisions that arose between Parliamentarians, both political and military, in the latter part of 1643, and which culminated in the formation of the New Model Army, can be interpreted using a sliding scale from pragmatism to radicalism. Parliament had been radical in its decision to raise arms against the king but by 1643/44, commanders such as Essex and Manchester, and MPs including Denzil Holles increasingly signalled that their radicalism was reaching its limit. Theirs had been a radicalism born out of a pragmatic need to provide effective opposition to a king who they felt had become unconstitutional. As the war progressed, they began to push more forcefully for a settlement with the king that might restore good order. In addition, by aligning with the Presbyterian agenda for the Church, they clearly indicated the limits of their religious radicalism.

By contrast, the New Model Army had a distinctive Puritan zeal that propelled it into genuinely new, progressive, and ideologically radical territory.

The religious character of the New Model Army

> **KEY PROFILE**
>
> **Richard Baxter (1615–91)** was a Puritan minister and theological writer. He refused to swear to the 'et cetera oath' and became attached to the garrison at Coventry where he ministered to the troops. Although he was a strong Puritan he firmly believed that the Church should stay unified.

Contemporaries were very clear about the zealotry of the New Model Army. In 1645, a moderate Presbyterian minister, **Richard Baxter**, visited the army at Naseby and described what he felt to be a concerning development. Whereas he understood the war was being fought in part to maintain the Anglican Church against a papist onslaught, he believed that the New Model Army was aiming at a revolution within the Church, attempting to 'subvert the Church' by introducing democracy into Church governance, which he understood to be a dreadful development.

Baxter's observations were backed up by those of Thomas Edwards, who was a specialist in matters relating to heresy. He was primarily concerned with categorising the many and varied beliefs and practices that were proliferating in the 1640s so that faithful Christians could distinguish between orthodox and heretical practice. Although his writings were sensational and rarely objective, his works provide a useful view on religion in the 1640s.

CHAPTER 15 | The intensification of radicalism

Fig. 2 *Identifying radical practices generated a huge flurry of pamphlets*

SOURCE 2

From a highly controversial pamphlet in 1646: *Gangraena, or A Catalogue and Discovery of Many of the Errours, Heresies, Blasphemies and Pernicious Practices of the Sectaries of this Time*. This listed a significant number of beliefs felt to be dangerous or heretical, while endorsing the pure theology of 'Independents':

Many people say, in news books, pulpits and meetings that the army is Independent in religion (although I think only about one in six soldiers are really Independent), yet of those, I do not think that there are more than 50 genuine Independents. All the rest are assortments of Anabaptism, Antinomianism, Enthusiasm, Arminianism, Familism, all these errors and more too sometimes meeting in the same persons, strange monsters, having heads of Enthusiasm, their bodies of Antinomianism, their thighs of Familism, their legs and feet of Anabaptism, their hands of Arminianism, and Libertinism, as the great vein going through the whole; in one word, Religion of that sort of men in the army, is liberty of conscience and liberty of preaching.

Consequences of the religious nature of the New Model Army

Soldiers who fought for the New Model Army entered an organisation that was engaged in two related but distinctive battles. On the one hand, the New Model Army was fighting to win the struggle for constitutional settlement between king and Parliament. On the other hand, some felt that it was engaged in an apocalyptic struggle in which the godly soldiers of the true Church fought against the Antichrist (located on earth in the Papacy) for the soul of England.

SOURCE 3

From *The Souldiers Catechism*, a pamphlet published in 1644 that explained the purpose and morality of the cause:

Question: What profession are you of?
Answer: I am a Christian and a soldier.
Question: What side are you of, and for whom do you fight?
Answer: I am for King and Parliament…

A CLOSER LOOK

The execution of William Laud

Archbishop William Laud had been languishing in the Tower of London since his arrest in 1641. A trial in 1644 failed to end in a conviction and he was returned to imprisonment. Just as with Strafford, it was difficult to find a charge that could be proven. Also like Strafford, he was finally condemned by a Bill of Attainder and despite the fact that Charles issued a royal pardon, he was executed on 10 January 1645.

A CLOSER LOOK

Religious sects in the 1640s

Anabaptists believed that baptismal vows could only be made by adults, not on behalf of babies as was the existing Protestant practice. **Antinomians** believed that nothing was sinful for Christians although they should still act in moral ways. Doctrinally, **Arminians** believed that everyone could be saved, in a renunciation of Calvinist predestination theology. **Familists** saw God at work through natural law, not through direct action in the world. **Libertinism** was a pejorative term, meaning unbounded by morality.

CROSS-REFERENCE

The beliefs of the religious sects that arose in this period will be explained in detail in Chapter 17, page 149.

KEY TERM

catechism: a summary of the principles of Christian religion in the form of questions and answers used for religious instruction

SECTION 4 | War and radicalism, 1642–1646

1. I fight to recover the King out of the hands of a Popish Malignant Company…
2. I fight for the Laws and Liberties of this Country, now in danger…
3. I fight for the preservation of our Parliament…
4. I fight in the defence and maintenance of the true Protestant Religion…

Question: But is it not against the King that you fight?

Answer: No, yet if the King will join himself with them that seek the ruin of his people and the overthrow of Religion, surely, both we and all good Subjects may lawfully stand in the defence of both.

Question: But is it not lamentable that Christians of the same Nation, should thus stain their hands in one another's blood?

Answer: I confess it is, but there is an inevitable and absolute necessity of fighting laid upon the good people of the Land.

STUDY TIP

In an exam you will be given three sources to assess, but this question gives you to two to practice your skills of assessment. This question requires you to have a solid understanding of the place of religious radicalism in the Civil War period but more importantly, an appreciation of the provenance of these sources. You will need to consider reliability before you can evaluate utility. Do not forget that something can be unreliable but still extremely useful.

CROSS-REFERENCE

Cromwell's defence of religious toleration in the army is considered from a leadership perspective on page 200.

PRACTICE QUESTION (A LEVEL)

Evaluating primary sources

With reference to Sources 2 and 3, and your understanding of the historical context, assess the value of these two sources to an historian studying the New Model Army.

The religious radicalism of the New Model Army had various impacts:

- Proportionately, only a small number of New Model officers and soldiers were truly extreme, most were simply Puritan. However, the radical nature of the extremists in the army was so alarming that contemporaries tended to see them as more numerous and more influential than they were, and to respond out of fear as a result. In December 1646, for example, a petition from the City of London demanded that the New Model Army should be disbanded because it was a heretical body.
- In some instances, the New Model Army actively brought about civilian religious separatism. For example, the Congregational Church at Dagger Lane in Hull was founded through the support of the local garrison chaplain, John Canne.
- New Model commanders, including Cromwell, defended the religious freedom of their soldiers especially against crackdown attempts by Presbyterian commanders, which began to create an ideology of religious toleration in its modern form. Cromwell's view, that religious practice was a private matter, carried both an echo of the discretion required by the Jacobean Settlement and a genuinely radical concept of the rights of men to hold private opinions that the public sphere had to respect.

A CLOSER LOOK

The development of ideas of tolerance

An examination of the correspondence that passed from Cromwell to Major General Crawford in defence of an Anabaptist soldier illuminates contemporary ideas about toleration:

Ay, but the man is an Anabaptist… Shall that render him incapable to serve the public? …bear with men of different minds from yourself… take heed of being sharp, or too easily sharpened by others against those to whom you can object little but that they square not with you in every opinion concerning matters of religion.

Oliver Cromwell, through his military prowess, found himself at the head of an effective and religiously zealous fighting force, which meant that his religious radicalism could combine with military strength to create political influence and power. Early signs of his growing political power can be seen in Source 4.

SOURCE 4

From one of Oliver Cromwell's regular updates from the battlefield to Parliament throughout the Civil Wars. This extract comes from a letter written from Cromwell after the Battle of Naseby in June 1645:

'Sir… O that men would… praise the Lord and declare the wonders that He does for the children of men!…this is none other but the hand of God; and to Him alone belongs the glory, wherein none are to share with him. …The General [Fairfax] served you with all faithfulness and honour; and the best commendations I can give him is, that I dare say he attributes all to God and would rather perish than assume to himself. Which is an honest and thriving way, and yet as much for bravery may be given to him, in this action, as to a man. Honest men served you faithfully in this action. Sir, they are trusty; I beseech you in the name of God, not to discourage them. I wish this action may beget thankfulness and humility in all that are concerned in it He that ventures his life for the liberty of his country, I wish he trust God for the liberty of his conscience, and you for the liberty he fights for. Your most humble servant, OLIVER CROMWELL

Pamphlets and propaganda

The collapse of censorship and the resultant explosion of the press in the early 1640s was absolutely central to the spread of political and religious radicalism. While pamphlets and tracts were well-established, cheap to produce, cheap to buy and consumed voraciously by the common folk, the 1640s saw significant developments in journalism and other forms of public discourse.

Newspapers

Newspapers were effectively invented in the early years of the Civil War and by the end of the 1640s there were more than 10 titles to choose from on a weekly basis, including *Mercurius Civicus: Londons Intelligencer*, and the Oxford-based *Mercurius Rusticus; or the Countries Complaint of the Barbarous Outrages committed by the Sectaries of this late flourishing Kingdom*.

Typical content included battlefield news, reports of speeches by the king and accounts of debates in Parliament, often accompanied by opinionated commentary and satirical cartoons. On the whole, pro-Parliament titles tended to be more accurate and the pro-Royalist news tended to be more humorous but less truthful.

The emergence of propaganda

Public opinion was such a rising force in politics that both sides recognised how valuable the press could be for forming popular perception.

The king fled the field at Naseby in June 1645, leaving behind most of his possessions, including a cabinet filled with personal correspondence from the previous two years. Within a month, pro-Parliament printers had published selected letters in a pamphlet entitled *The Kings Cabinet Opened*. Although touching, with the king professing immense affection for his 'Dear Hart', the content was devastating. As the introduction explained, 'The king's counsels are wholly managed by the queen; though she be of the weaker sex, born an alien, bred up in a contrary religion, yet nothing great or small is transacted without her knowledge and consent.'

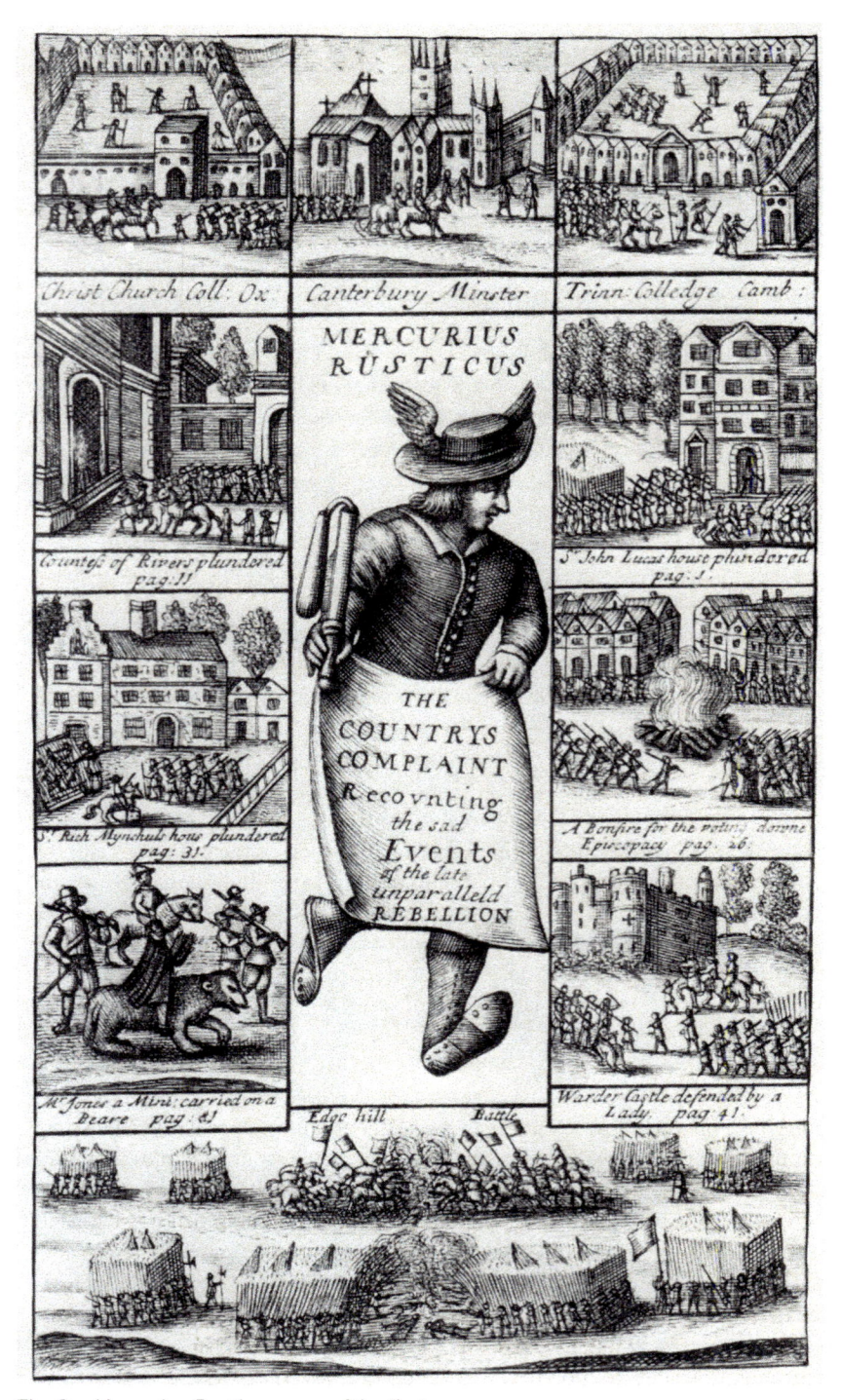

Fig. 3 Mercurius Rusticus, *one of the first newspapers*

The correspondence included private letters from the king to the Marquis of Ormond, encouraging him to suspend anti-Catholic legislation and bring a Catholic army over to fight for the king in England as well as numerous urgings from the queen to resist all overtures from Parliament for a settlement and go on fighting until God restore him to full authority.

Even within the Parliamentary cause, pamphlets were used for **propaganda** as we have seen with Thomas Edward's attack on the religious radicalism of the New Model Army.

KEY TERM

propaganda: information, often misleading or biased, that is used to promote a particular cause

Fig. 4 The Kings Cabinet Opened *struck a devastating blow against the king's public image*

The spread of public debate

Pamphlets brought debate out of Westminster and Oxford and onto the streets among the general population, widening the spread of radicalism dramatically. Argument and counter-argument were common, resulting in trails of pamphlets on particular themes, especially relating to that most divisive of all issues, religion. Across all the pamphlets, deeper trends can be seen to emerge.

John Morrill conducted a study of pamphlets, which demonstrated how debate changed over time. He identified that between 1640 and 1643 over 400 pamphlets emerged in London, mainly concerned with defending the 'true reformed Protestant religion by law established' and written by assorted clergy, lawyers and laymen. By 1643, the content of pamphlets begins to show a new strand emerging in the religious discourse, as the Presbyterian puritans argued against advocates of a form of Congregationalism imported from the New World as the best model of Church governance. From 1647 onwards, the debate moved again, reflecting divisions between those who preferred compulsory membership of a reformed state Church and those who wanted complete religious liberty.

Freedom of expression

In another uncanny echo of Charles's policies of the 1630s, the Long Parliament was spurred on by the developments into attempting its own form of print regulation. Essentially, censorship structures that had been used by Star Chamber were revised and reintroduced by the Licensing Act of 1643. The preamble to the Act explains why it was felt necessary, explaining that: 'very many Stationers and Printers have taken upon them to set up sundry private Printing Presses in corners, and to print, vend, publish, and disperse books, pamphlets and papers, in such multitudes, that no industry could be sufficient to discover or bring to punishment all the several abounding Delinquents'.

John Milton, famous for writing the epic poem, *Paradise Lost*, produced a pamphlet that attacked this renewed attempt to control the press: *Areopagitica; A speech of Mr. John Milton for the Liberty of Unlicenc'd Printing, to the Parliament of England*. It is a dense and complex work, drawing on imagery and vocabulary from Ancient Greece and the Bible, but it develops an ideology of liberty of expression that would eventually become widely accepted.

A CLOSER LOOK

The works of Milton provide insightful observations about the heart of London during this period. Where some saw chaos and disorder, he was excited by the rush of free thinking that the loosening of boundaries had enabled.

SOURCE 5

This extract from Milton's *Areopagitica*, published in 1644, first builds a case for allowing public debate and then begins to develop an ideology for religious toleration:

Where people are hungry for knowledge, there will be much arguing and many opinions because opinion in good men is simply knowledge in the making. We are terribly worried about some of the extreme sects we see around us but let us not lose sight of the fact that these are evidence that God is stirring up a sincere thirst for knowledge and understanding within *our city*. What some see as a sad development we should in fact celebrate. A little wisdom, a little forgiveness and a grain of goodwill might persuade everyone to join together, united in one general and brotherly search after truth. The real enemies are the professional churchmen who want to crowd free consciences and Christian liberties into Church law and rules devised by men.

However, it is not impossible that Truth might have more shapes than one. How many things might be tolerated in peace and left to conscience if we exercised a little kindness. Is it not pure hypocrisy on our part to be always judging each other?

ACTIVITY

Make notes on how, in Source 5, Milton links specific examples to his reflections. For example, his reference to 'sects' can be related to the independent congregations that were beginning to flourish in London or to Edwards' observations about radicalism in the New Model Army. This will help you to build a context within which to read Milton's writing accurately.

ACTIVITY

Summary

Many aspects of the mid-1640s can be considered 'radical' and, while this chapter has treated radicalism thematically, in fact, there are many connections between different aspects of radicalism. To help you see this bigger picture, create a mind-map for 'radicalism' and use this chapter to create branches for political and religious radicalism.

Then, reflect on other aspects of radicalism (especially considering its two meanings) and add to your mind-map.

Finally, look for links between different aspects and try to explain why radicalism was such a dynamic force in the mid-1640s.

STUDY TIP

In answering this question you will need to reflect on the radicalism that existed before 1642 and assess how far the Civil War created new radicalism or intensified the old.

A LEVEL PRACTICE QUESTION

To what extent was the radicalism of the years 1642 to 1646 a product of the First Civil War?

16 The end of the First Civil War

Fig. 1 *This painting from 1645 shows a gloomy and defeated King Charles with his army; dark clouds are looming above them*

LEARNING OBJECTIVES
In this chapter you will learn about:
- divisions among the Parliamentary leaders
- attempts at settlement
- the capture of Charles I.

KEY CHRONOLOGY

1645	June	Battle of Naseby
	Sept	Battle of Philiphaugh
1646	April	Charles surrenders to the Scots
	July	Propositions of Newcastle
1647	Feb	Charles handed to the English

Divisions among the Parliamentary leaders

John Pym, that expert Parliamentary manager, and John Hampden had both died in 1643 and no-one had emerged with the same blend of political skill to provide the leadership that might maintain unity in Parliament.

In Chapter 14 we traced the divisions that arose among the Parliament and army leadership in 1644–45, which resulted in the Self-Denying Ordinance and the formation of the New Model Army. Now we turn to consider new divisions that emerged in 1644.

ACTIVITY
Refresh your memory about the meaning of 'political parties' in this period by discussing this term with a partner.

Presbyterians and Independents

The configuration of war, middle and peace groups that was a feature of Parliament in 1642–43 shifted during 1644 into two new patterns of allegiance: Political Presbyterians and Political Independents. These terms are used by modern historians to highlight the difference between religious and political allegiances, which is to say that an MP could be a member of the Political Presbyterian grouping without being a Presbyterian by faith.

A CLOSER LOOK
Within the **Westminster Assembly of Divines**, the Parliamentary division was echoed by two groupings, the majority Presbyterians and a small but significant minority of Independents, called the 'Dissenting Brethren'. The Dissenting Brethren wanted a Church settlement that protected toleration which would allow Independency, where each church can choose its own structure and theological emphasis.

CROSS-REFERENCE
An explanation of the purpose behind the **Westminster Assembly** can be found on page 121.

	Political Presbyterians	Political Independents
Leading members	Denzil Holles Earl of Essex	Oliver Cromwell Oliver St John Viscount Saye and Sele
Approach to war	Conclude through negotiation.	Win by military victory.
Attitude to settlement with the king	Moderate (even minimal) terms.	Firm limitations to be agreed before the New Model Army would be disbanded.
Attitude to structural religious settlement	National Presbyterian Church in order to maintain the Scottish alliance and prevent religion becoming a disorderly force in society.	Greater religious freedom, possibly within a national Church structure which allows considerable latitude for Independency.
Attitude to Scotland	Positive: potentially the Covenant will lead to a unification of the two kingdoms.	Strategic: Covenant useful as a war tool but ongoing shared government is not desirable.

Overall, Political Presbyterianism was stronger in the country at large, outside Westminster as well as inside:
- The cost of the war was increasingly burdensome because of high taxation and rising inflation.
- With 1 in 8 adult males in England serving in the army, social cohesion was under threat, compounded by poor harvests in 1646 and 1647 which increased social tension and fears of disorder.
- Gentry and traditional local governing elites were finding their authority threatened by the dominance of Parliament's men, often of lower social status and greater religious zeal, in the local County Committees.
- Disorder was rising among the rank and file of the armies because they were being paid steadily less and with decreasing frequency. Army mutinies, looting and unrest were becoming more common.

Clubmen Associations

Just as the localities had generally tried to keep out of the war in its early months, they were crucial in bringing about the end of the war. Local gentry, particularly in the areas of heaviest fighting such as Somerset and Herefordshire, began to organise their peasantry into local associations to maintain order, often by ensuring that troops in the county were adequately fed and effectively policed to prevent looting and violence.

SOURCE 1

From the articles of association of the Wiltshire and Dorset Clubmen. Each association had its own specific terms but they were broadly similar:

The Resolutions of the Clubmen of Dorset and Wilts agreed at Gorehedge Corner on 25 May 1645 when there were present near 4000 armed with clubs, swords, bills, pitchforks and over several weapons… We want to achieve nothing but to preserve ourselves from plunder and all other unlawful violence and have therefore drafted these articles:
- Every town, tithing, parish and great hamlet shall contribute three or more of its most able men to be officers of the Association.
- A continuous watch will be carried out by these men, with at least two men on duty at all times, reporting to the Constable.
- Anyone claiming to be a soldier and found either plundering or carrying out unlawful violence shall have their weapons confiscated immediately.
- No person or persons shall be allowed to search a house or seize the person or goods of any of the Associated inhabitants of the County, on any pretext whatsoever.

ACTIVITY
What can you learn from Source 1 about the experience of rural England during the Civil War?

Gradually, these diverse associations began to join together in order to actually force the removal of troops from their regions and this tended to mean that they allied with Parliamentary forces, not through political allegiance but for pragmatic reasons. It tended to be the Royalist soldiers who were lingering on in the localities, causing disruption and, (being paid less regularly), looting and ransacking more than their Parliamentary equivalents. For example, the Devon and Somerset Clubmen helped General Fairfax defeat Lord Goring's army.

Attempts at settlement

Before the capture of the king in June 1646 there were four major attempts to negotiate a settlement between king and Parliament.

	Nineteen Propositions June 1642	**Oxford Treaty 1643**	**Uxbridge Proposals 1645**
Context	Just before Parliament raised its army.	During the Royalist ascendancy in the Civil War.	During the Parliamentary ascendancy.
Content	Regular Parliaments. Anti-Catholic measures. Parliament in command of army. Parliament approves key appointments. Reform of Anglican Church.	Slightly moderated version of Nineteen Propositions. Episcopacy abolished.	Influenced by Solemn League. King to swear to the Covenant. Presbyterianism in English Church. Army led by joint English-Scottish Commissioners.
Duration of deliberations	Presented on 1 June 1642. Rejected by Charles on 21 June.	Proposed in January 1643; revised in March; abandoned in April.	From January to February 1645
Reason for failure	Far too radical.	Too radical and Charles optimistic of complete military victory.	Too radical and Charles hoping to capitalise on divisions emerging within Parliament.

Context of the Propositions of Newcastle

Following the defeat of the king's main army at Naseby in June 1645 and the resulting propaganda coup when Parliament published *The Kings Cabinet Opened*, Royalist defeat was inevitable. There were several crucial Royalist defeats that followed:

- July 1645: defeat of the second largest royal army, commanded by Lord Goring, in Somerset.
- September 1645: Prince Rupert surrendered Bristol.
- September 1645: Royalist Scottish Army of the Earl of Montrose was destroyed at the Battle of Philiphaugh by Leslie's Covenanter army.

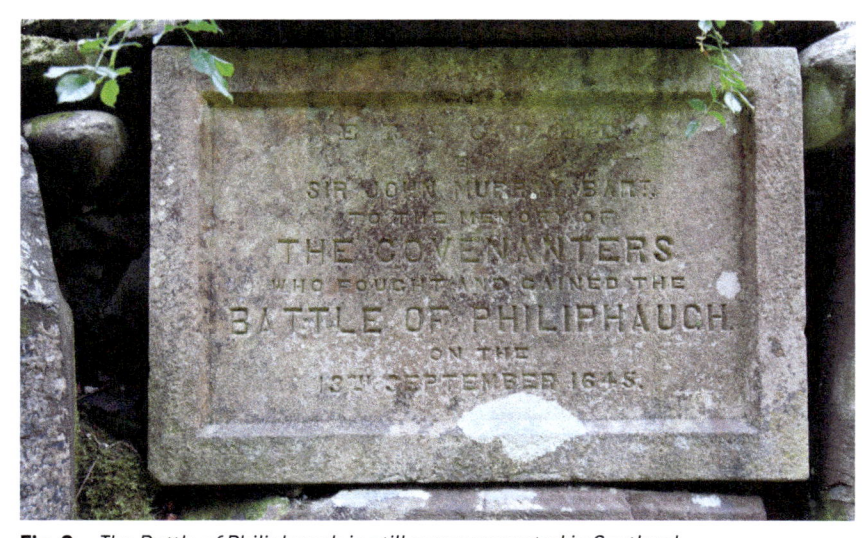

Fig. 2 The Battle of Philiphaugh is still commemorated in Scotland

The king's surrender to the Scots

By April 1646, Parliamentary troops were advancing on Oxford and the king fled in disguise, handing himself over to the Scottish Army at Newark. Charles gave himself up to the Scots having extracted promises from them to respect his conscience and ensure his safety, expecting that he would be able to benefit politically from the tensions between Scotland and England. In the custody of the Scots, he travelled up to Newcastle.

The Propositions of Newcastle, July 1646

The Propositions of Newcastle were drawn up by Parliament, with its majority of Political Presbyterians and despatched to Newcastle where they were given to the king.

CROSS-REFERENCE

See page 103 for the Nineteen Propositions, page 103 for the Oxford Treaty and page 124 for the Uxbridge proposals.

See page 131 for *The Kings Cabinet Opened*.

A CLOSER LOOK

The surrender of Bristol

Charles was horrified that his nephew had lost Bristol, and wrote harshly to him:

Nephew. Though the loss of Bristol is a blow to me, your surrender of it as you did caused me greater distress. What is to be done when one who is so near to me, both in blood and friendship, submits himself to so cowardly an action? On 12 August you reassured me that, if no mutiny happened, you would keep Bristol for four months. Did you keep it for four days? Was there anything like a mutiny? I desire you to leave England.

SECTION 4 | War and radicalism, 1642–1646

A CLOSER LOOK

The *Directory of Worship*

This was drafted by the Westminster Assembly and ratified by Parliament in 1645. It replaced the Book of Common Prayer, containing authorised prayers and liturgy for use within the Church of England. It was based on the Scottish Prayer Book whose replacement sparked the Scottish wars.

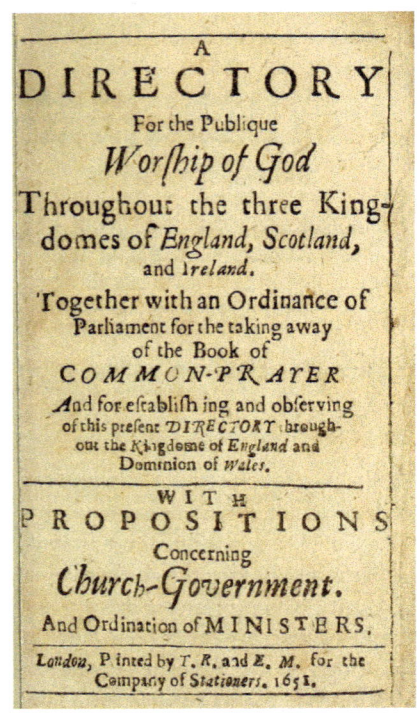

Fig. 3 *The* Directory of Worship *was a new prayer book to replace the unpopular English and Scottish versions*

SOURCE 2

From King Charles I's letter to the queen on 1 July 1646 after receiving the Propositions of Newcastle:

Dear Heart,
I was glad to receive your letter of the 28th June which arrived last Saturday. The same day I got an accurate copy of the Propositions which I have been told will arrive here within ten days. I can assure you that they are such as I cannot grant without losing my conscience, crown and honour. I will not be able to consent so I think the best thing to do is to delay making a flat denial for as long as I can and then try to make a denial that sounds as acceptable as possible, which will be difficult. To help me, I will take advice from **Montreuil** or the French Ambassador, so I will try to delay my reply (if I can) until one or both of them come. If I am pressed, I will say that I will not give an answer until I am back in London where I will be able to discuss the details of my answer with them in person and that I will not go to London until my freedom and safety there have been guaranteed. Trust me sweetheart, I have explained what I am thinking and I would value your opinion on my solution as soon as you can send it to me. I am eternally yours, Charles R.

A CLOSER LOOK

Jean de Montreuil was despatched to London in August 1645 as a diplomat, reporting to Cardinal Mazarin who had replaced Cardinal Richlieu as Chief Minister to King Louis XIV. Mazarin was concerned about the implications for France if the English Parliament became too powerful and hoped to persuade the king to ally himself with the Scots against the English.

Content of the Propositions

Religion: Charles was to accept the establishment of Presbyterianism in England for three years, as outlined in the Westminster Assembly's *Directory of Worship*.
Militia: Parliament was to control the militia for 20 years, this duration arrived at by considering how much longer Charles was likely to live.
Parliament: The Triennial Act was to remain, guaranteeing regular Parliaments to limit monarchical power.
Royalists: Fifty eight leading Royalists would be punished but the rest would be pardoned.

The king's response

Throughout the Stuart period, the Venetian Ambassador in London sent comprehensive reports back to Venice. Despatches from the autumn of 1646 describe Charles's attitude to the Propositions, which was to prevaricate rather than to give the inevitable negative response. Charles hoped, not without reason, that divisions in Parliament would create instability that would then help him reassert his monarchical authority.

SOURCE 3

Reports from the Venetian Ambassador to the Venetian oligarchs in November 1646:

London, 1st November
   The king has at last sent some peace proposals to London after Montreuil's arrival at Newcastle. There is little hope of these proposals bringing peace when the Houses have heard them.
London, 8th November

It seems certain that the sole object of the proposals sent by the king to parliament is to afford a pretext to some who still adhere to his Majesty to declare themselves. It seems to have produced the effect already, as the matter was hotly debated in parliament, waxing so hot that some even drew their swords in the house. To prevent any favourable impression that might be made on the people, they have stopped the printing which was beginning to circulate in the city, and have tried to withdraw the copies already issued.

It appears that the Scottish parliament has issued a decree to stand solid with the English in the treaty, but that the monarchy shall be maintained and the king's prerogatives and crown retained, a point which by no means pleases the English parliament.

Lord Digby has sailed from Ireland for France after conferring with the **Marquis of Ormond**. This conference has roused the suspicions of the parliamentarians.

All foreign soldiers have been dismissed from the armies, especially the French, as a nation suspected of lending a hand to trouble in this country rather than to peace.

ACTIVITY

Extension

The reports from the Venetian Ambassador in London are freely available online by searching www.british-history.ac.uk. Find and read his report from November 1646, from which Source 3 is taken, because it contains a lot of interesting detail about the roles of individual people.

CROSS-REFERENCE

Digby's actions prior to Naseby are covered on page 125.

The involvement of the Marquis of Ormond is covered in detail in Chapter 20, page 166.

KEY PROFILE

George Digby, 2nd Earl of Bristol (1612–77) was married to Lady Anne Russell, daughter of the Earl of Bedford. As MP for Dorset, he opposed the attainder of Strafford for which Charles I elevated him to the Lords as Baron Digby of Sherborne. He was a close, but not wise, adviser to the king and was involved in many of Charles's most disastrous decisions such as the attempted arrest of the Five Members. He became Secretary of State in 1643 and was a strong supporter of Henrietta Maria's advice to make foreign alliances and bring troops over from Ireland. His rivalry with Prince Rupert had catastrophic results at Naseby.

ACTIVITY

In pairs, reflect on the similarities and differences between the attempts of Scotland and England to reach a settlement with the king. Note down your ideas and return to them as more developments are discussed in later chapters.

By the winter of 1646, Charles's continued use of delaying tactics pushed both Scotland and England into more dramatic attempts to reach a settlement.

The capture of Charles I

The Scottish attempt to reach a settlement

In March 1646, Sir Robert Murray had put a peace treaty on behalf of Scotland in front of the king. As July progressed and it became clear that Charles was not inclined to accept the Propositions of Newcastle, Murray's treaty was brought back out for his consideration. Even Henrietta Maria counselled him to agree, despite the fact that one of its terms was that Presbyterianism should shape the religious settlement in England. His refusal exasperated the Scots and they began to consider how they could get him off their hands.

Reaching a deal with the English Parliament

In August the Scots decided to offer the king to the English in exchange for £400,000 of which half would be settled before he left their safe-keeping and half on his arrival into English custody. The money was to be used to pay their soldiers off. Having agreed on this idea, they nonetheless hoped that they could still reach an agreement with the king and efforts continued through the autumn to reach a settlement. On the 17 December 1646, the Scottish Parliament passed a final resolution:

- Scotland would promise to support the king and his descendants in their monarchical role.

SECTION 4 | War and radicalism, 1642–1646

> **KEY TERM**
>
> **deposed:** to be removed from office

> **A CLOSER LOOK**
>
> ### Charles's departure from Newcastle, February 1647
>
> There was a festival atmosphere when the Parliamentary forces took Charles I from Newcastle, with pipes and drums accompanying the soldiers as they marched out of the city. Not everyone celebrated though: some women called out 'Judas! Judas' to the Scots, and Charles himself managed to quip, 'They have sold me too cheap'.

- Scotland would continue to affirm the king's right to be King of England.
- The king had to subscribe to the Covenant and the Nineteen Propositions. The Scottish Parliament made it clear that if he did not agree then he would be no longer welcome in Scotland and the Scots would not come to his aid if he was **deposed** in England.

Immediate consequences of the king's response

The king still refused to reach agreement with the Scottish Parliament and so the Scots put their next strategy into operation:

- 16 January: The Scottish Parliament voted to return the king to England.
- 30 January: The first down payment of £100,000 was received from England.
- 3 February: The second down payment was received and Charles was handed over to the English Parliament's Commissioners.
- 11 February: All Scottish garrisons in England were handed over and all Scottish soldiers returned to Scotland.

> **SOURCE 4**
>
> From Robert Gordon's history of the Civil War, written in 1649. Gordon was a Scottish nobleman whose family were staunch Royalists. In this extract, he described the events of the winter of 1646/7:
>
> The Scots commissioners thought desperately about how they could make a lasting agreement between the King and his two Parliaments. I firmly believe that they were sincere and loyal despite the false and damaging lies that their enemies subsequently spread about them, saying that they recklessly sold their King. In truth, they managed to persuade him to things to which he would never formerly have consented and they got Parliament to yield to him as well. For example, he agreed to introduce Presbyterian Church governance and, regarding the militia, which was the main sticking point, he agreed to pass its control to Parliament for ten years after which it should revert to the Crown. The Scots agreed to send him to the English, on the absolute condition that they should not harm his sacred person nor in any other way injure him, and must still acknowledge him as their king and give firm assurances that neither he nor his heirs should be deprived of the Crown of England.

> **ACTIVITY**
>
> ### Evaluating primary sources
>
> Considering the provenance of Source 4, how reliable do you think it is as evidence of the Scots' intentions in 1646?

> **STUDY TIP**
>
> A timeline will help you to ensure that you are able to apply your own contextual knowledge in your answer. You will need to handle provenance carefully in order to assess the value of the sources.

> **A LEVEL PRACTICE QUESTION**
>
> ### Evaluating primary sources
>
> With reference to Sources 2, 3 and 4, and your understanding of the historical context, assess the value of these three sources to an historian studying the difficulties of making a peace sttlement in 1646.

On the journey from Newcastle to Northamptonshire, where he would be lodged at Holdenby Hall, Charles stopped to 'touch' sufferers of the 'King's Evil' and must have been cheered to see two miles of supporters lining the road as he approached Leeds. On arriving at Holdenby Hall, he lived in luxury, attended by 120 servants, allowed 28 dishes of food each day and enjoying playing bowls with Lord Spencer at his nearby ancestral home, Althorp. He was nonetheless guarded by a significant garrison of soldiers and Parliament refused to allow him an Anglican chaplain, offering Presbyterian ministers instead, so he did not attend church on Sundays.

CHAPTER 16 | The end of the First Civil War

Fig. 4 *Holdenby Hall was a relatively new manor house in 1646 and allowed the king to live in great comfort*

Now that Parliament was in direct control of the king's person, a new phase in the English Revolution had begun.

ACTIVITY

Summary

The significance of the English Civil War spread far beyond the confines of the English nation, touching France, Scotland and Ireland, as well as countries further afield.

Print out a map of Europe and use this chapter to help you plot personalities, journeys and key events onto it.

Do you think the term 'English Civil War' is a useful phrase? How could you improve on it?

A LEVEL PRACTICE QUESTION

'Charles's delaying tactics made it impossible to reach a settlement in 1646.' Assess the validity of this view.

A CLOSER LOOK

The King's Evil

Kings were believed, because of Divine Right, to possess special powers to cure a type of tuberculosis which was nicknamed the 'King's Evil', but which is known today as scrofula. Sufferers would implore the king to place his hands on them, to pass on a 'royal touch.' Scrofula causes sores to erupt on the chest and neck, so normally monarchs would only hover their hands over a victim.

STUDY TIP

Consider the events surrounding the attempts to reach a settlement. A timeline, or flow chart, might help you sort this information into a useful order. Thinking about the specific context can help you assess the failure to reach a settlement in order to fully answer this question.

141

5 The disintegration of the Political Nation, 1646–1649

17 Political and religious radicalism

LEARNING OBJECTIVES

In this chapter you will learn about:

- the politicisation of the New Model Army
- Lilburne and the Levellers
- Fifth Monarchists
- Ranters and other populist groups.

KEY CHRONOLOGY

1647 Feb	Disbandment of some New Model regiments
March	Purge of officer ranks
March	Publication of the Levellers' 'Large Petition'
25 May	Parliament voted to disband the New Model Army
31 May	Mutiny of two regiments
2 June	The seizure of the king
4 June	General Rendezvous of the army

KEY TERM

purge: the sudden removal of people who are deemed to be undesirable members of an organisation or institution; while modern purges, such as those in Stalinist Russia, have tended to be carried out by execution, this was not the case in the seventeenth century, where undesirables were simply dismissed from their posts

The politicisation of the New Model Army

The last significant pitched battles of the English Civil War were those of Naseby (June 1645) and Langport (July 1645). After these crushing defeats, Charles no longer had the means to win a military victory and had resorted, as we have seen, to political manoeuvring. However, neither the Parliamentarian army nor what remained of the Royalist forces had disbanded, which put enormous pressure on the civilian population because weeks were stretching into months with no action, little prospect of action, and yet no settlement. By mid-1646, the question of what to do about the large number of soldiers (over 20,000 New Model soldiers and more than 10,000 in the Northern Association) in England had become a matter of pressing political concern. The country was becoming increasingly restive, tired of quartering troops and paying heavy taxes. Among the soldiers, grievances were becoming more widespread, predominantly about pay.

Fig. 1 *The vicious cycle of pay arrears and dwindling tax receipts*

(Cycle diagram: Soldiers pay in arrears → Soldiers cannot be disbanded without full payment → Under-paid soldiers violent, looting and disrupting communities → Communities scared and angered by presence of soldiers → Communities do not want to pay for these soldiers so tax receipts go down → back to Soldiers pay in arrears)

Parliamentary attempts to disband the New Model Army

Parliament began to plan to reduce the financial burden of the army by redeploying some units of the New Model Army into Ireland to finally crush the rebels there and, in the process, shift quartering costs out of England. Political Presbyterians had additional reasons why they wanted to neutralise the influence of the New Model Army. They disliked its religious radicalism and its military efficiency, and they feared that it would hinder a rapid settlement with the king. Parliament began to move against the army. In February 1647, some New Model units were designated for Irish service while a decision was taken to disband the rest. In March 1647, Parliament ordered a **purge** of the officer ranks to exclude MPs and non-Presbyterians.

Response of the New Model Army
The Humble Petition of the Officers and Soldiers of the Army

Initially the New Model Army responded to Parliament's attempts to reduce their influence with 'The Humble Petition of the Officers and Soldiers of the Army' which was sent to General Fairfax on 20th March 1647 in his capacity as an MP and which summarised their grievances: 'We have brought about peace and yet our enemies are prospering while we are being condemned. The honest people in this Kingdom are being poorly treated.' The petition was moderate and deferential. It requested:

- Soldiers' pay to be brought up to date before disbandment.
- Provision to be made for widows, orphans and war-maimed.
- Indemnity to be granted for **acts committed in wartime** that would be considered criminal in peacetime.
- Volunteer troops to be allowed to refuse deployment outside England.

Divisively, Denzil Holles responded to the Humble Petition with a declaration on 30 March, which soon became known as the 'Declaration of Dislike' because it labelled the petitioners, 'Enemies to the State, Disturbers of the Peace.' The Declaration created an open fault line between the Political Presbyterian majority in Parliament and the New Model Army. Far from endorsing the Petition, Parliament voted to appoint only Presbyterian Generals to lead the army to Ireland and to carry out a purge of Independents from the **London Trained Bands**.

The election of Agitators

In April, eight cavalry regiments elected representatives, known as **Agitators**, to liaise with the officers and make sure the voices of the ordinary soldiers were heard. Their existence is noteworthy because it represented a grass-roots democratic movement forming among a significant proportion of the population. A royalist newspaper noted that the New Model Army 'now wants to see even more change in the Kingdom, because they think that Parliament needs to be regulated as much as the King. Further, they think that this regulation should be done by the people and they say that they are the people's champions and true representatives.'

At the end of April, a majority of army officers showed their support for the Agitators as representatives of the rank and file by publishing an endorsement of the Humble Petition, the *Vindication of the Officers of the Army*.

> **A CLOSER LOOK**
>
> ### Acts committed in wartime
>
> The presence of large numbers of under-occupied soldiers meant that criminal damage to property was an ever-present threat. However, what lay behind the demand for indemnity was the fact that soldiers particularly feared being hanged for stealing horses, which they were frequently ordered to do by their senior officers.

> **CROSS-REFERENCE**
>
> For more on the London militia which was known as the '**London Trained Bands**', see Chapter 13.

> **KEY TERM**
>
> **Agitator:** not a pejorative term in the seventeenth century: it had no negative connotations, but simply meant someone who spoke on behalf of others

SOURCE 1

The *Vindication of the Officers of the Army*, published in April 1647, was minuted in the Commons Journal and included in the Rushworth Collection.

We are keenly aware that some have caused you to think badly of us and make weighty expressions of displeasure against us. There could not be anything worse for us than this, because we have sworn on our Honour to stand by Parliament until you have completed your Work of removing every Yoke from the People's Necks and establishing those good Laws that you shall judge necessary for the Commonwealth.

Some have questioned whether we should have the Liberty of Petitioning. We hope that, although we are soldiers, we have not lost the rights of Subjects. We hope that in striving for the Freedoms of our Brothers that we have not lost our own.

For your sakes, we left our homes, our Jobs and Vocations and set aside the Contentments of a quiet Life, unafraid and not concerned about the difficulties of War. For all these reasons, we anticipated that you would not blink at our reasonable Request for our hard-earned Wages and would certainly not have accused us of grumbling, or even Mutiny.

SECTION 5 | The disintegration of the Political Nation, 1646–1649

A CLOSER LOOK

Disbanding the army

On 18 May 1647, Charles finally accepted a third draft of the Newcastle Propositions which required him to implement a Presbyterian settlement for three years and gave Parliament control over the militia for ten years. The prospect of renewed negotiations gave the Political Presbyterians the urge and confidence to crack down on the New Model Army, which they felt was too extreme and beyond Parliamentary control.

KEY TERM

rendezvous: a word for a meeting that derives from the French phrase, 'rendez-vous' which means 'present yourselves!'; it is frequently used in military contexts

KEY PROFILE

Edward Sexby (1616–58) was born in Suffolk and became an apprentice in London before the Civil War. He joined Cromwell's cavalry regiment as a trooper in 1643 and remained at the lowest rank of 'Private', but became an Agitator in 1647.

KEY TERM

Cornet: the lowest ranking officer class in the New Model Army

ACTIVITY

Check your understanding by explaining in detail why the rumours of an impending settlement pushed the New Model Army into action.

Parliament's response to the Vindication

Opponents of the *Vindication* in the House of Commons diffused its impact by arguing that it was a series of different demands from different regiments and therefore could not be dealt with as a whole. Instead, they required each regiment to send their own complaints in writing, to be considered individually. To prevent disorder breaking out, on 30 April 1647 they ordered Cromwell, Ireton and two other soldier-MPs to communicate their intention to settle outstanding pay and pass an Indemnity Act.

Tensions continued to rise. The Agitators demanded the impeachment of 11 Presbyterian MPs who they considered to be the masterminds of the Declaration of Dislike; in turn, the Presbyterians and the City of London began to consider raising an army against the New Model Army. On 25 May, Parliament voted to **disband the army** with just eight weeks' arrears: this vote catalysed the army into becoming a political force. Officers and rank and file stuck together and within four days, General Fairfax had declared a general **rendezvous** of the New Model Army to be held at Newmarket on 4 June. Notwithstanding Fairfax's move to defend the army's cause, two regiments mutinied on 31 May.

The seizure of the king

Fig. 2 *In this print from 1647, the king stretches out his hand to the pistol being carried by Cornet Joyce*

The Agitator **Edward Sexby** relayed rumours that the king was on the verge of making a deal with the Political Presbyterians and this news spurred the New Model Army into drastic action. On 2nd June, thirty-one year old Agitator **Cornet** Joyce led a troop of soldiers to remove the king from Holdenby House and take him to the headquarters of the New Model Army, at Newmarket. It is not known on whose orders he acted, although it is probable that the Agitators discussed such a move. One leading Presbyterian was convinced that it was Cromwell's idea supported by his son-in-law **Henry Ireton.** Whatever the exact circumstances, once the deed was done, Joyce wrote directly to Cromwell for urgent orders, 'Sir, we have secured the King. Let us know what we shall do.'

The Humble Remonstrance and Solemn Engagement

On 4 June, the first day of the army rendezvous, a 'Humble Remonstrance' was printed and signed by officers and soldiers. It listed the army's grievances and strongly criticised Parliament for its failure to rescind the Declaration of Dislike. While General Fairfax met with each regiment individually, Ireton and Cromwell put the finishing touches to a military covenant which was presented to the army on the next day as 'The Solemn Engagement of the Army'.

On 5 June, the Solemn Engagement of the Army was read to all the regiments and assented to by all officers and soldiers.

> **SOURCE 2**
>
> From the Solemn Engagement of the Army, drafted by Cromwell and Ireton and presented to the army on 5 June. This extract comes from a copy recorded by the nineteenth-century collector William Cobbett, who specialised in Parliamentary History:
>
> We the Officers and Soldiers of several Regiments do hereby declare, agree and promise, to the Parliament and Kingdom as follows.
>
> That we shall cheerfully and readily disband when required to do so by the Parliament as long as the Grievances we have presented to you have been resolved and guaranteed to the satisfaction of a **Council** which consists of general Officers of the Army, two Commissioned Officers and two Soldiers chosen by each regiment. These must all agree.
>
> And, because we have heard that many strange things have been suggested or suspected, which have done our cause very great harm, concerning dangerous principles, interests and plans in this Army, we shall very shortly present Parliament with a Vindication of the Army to prove our innocence. What is more we shall do our utmost to help establish widespread and equal rights and freedoms that everyone might equally share.

Following the Solemn Engagement, Fairfax's men began to march slowly towards the capital. Disorder in London was by now breaking out on a daily basis, heightening tensions and putting pressure on Parliament to do something decisive to maintain social order.

From 4 June onwards, mobs of soldiers in London virtually besieged Westminster, demanding pay and redress of grievances. On 8 June a motion to take their grievances seriously was rejected by one vote in the Commons and an opposite motion, to disband the army, re-take the king and raise a City cavalry regiment, was passed instead. Although the Declaration of Dislike was rescinded and an Indemnity Ordinance passed, relations between Parliament and army had reached a new low.

A Representation of the Army

On 14 June, the Army released another document, *A Representation of the Army*. It was principally drafted by Henry Ireton with the assistance of a twenty-eight year old Major General, **John Lambert** and some input from Cromwell. At its heart was an assertion that the New Model Army was not 'a mere mercenary army, hired to serve any arbitrary power of a state', but had been summoned by Parliament 'to the defence of [its] own and the people's just rights and liberties.' It outlined the army's fundamental demands with regards to Parliament:

- A purge of Parliament, intended to remove the army's opponents in the Commons.
- Future Parliaments of fixed duration.
- Guaranteed right of freedom of people to petition Parliament.
- Liberty of tender consciences, allowing freedom of worship.

The politicisation of the New Model Army had begun: it was turning into a political as well as a military force.

KEY PROFILE

Fig. 3 *Henry Ireton, Cromwell's son-in-law and one of his most trusted companions*

Henry Ireton (1611–51) trained as a lawyer and was a Puritan. He organised a Root and Branch petition within his home county of Nottinghamshire and became a cavalry officer in the Civil War and an MP in 1645. He married Bridget Cromwell in 1646 and became one of Cromwell's closest advisers.

A CLOSER LOOK

The **Council** outlined in the Solemn Engagement became known as the General Council of the Army.

ACTIVITY

According to Source 2, what 'satisfaction' was required? The Solemn Engagement established a new institution, the General Council of the Army. What was its membership and purpose to be?

CROSS-REFERENCE

See Chapter 21, page 180 to find out how the New Model Army reached the pinnacle of its political force in 1655, when its Major Generals were used as regional governors.

KEY PROFILE

John Lambert (1619–84) trained as a lawyer but became a cavalry officer on the outbreak of war. He proved himself to be a gifted commander and succeeded Sir Thomas Fairfax as Major General in commander of the army in the north in 1645.

SECTION 5 | The disintegration of the Political Nation, 1646–1649

Lilburne and the Levellers

John Lilburne, Puritan Pamphleteer, had continued to develop his radical ideas and by the mid-1640s, a loose collective of supporters, known by the pejorative term, '**Levellers**', had assembled around him. He was particularly aided by **Richard Overton** and William Walwyn: between them, they developed a wide-ranging although not particularly systematic programme of political, economic and social reform. Until the autumn of 1647, Leveller ideas floated alongside the New Model's politicisation. Some Levellers were New Model soldiers; some were civilians; not all New Model soldiers were Levellers. Lilburne was himself an Agitator and a famous tract issued from within the army, the 'Apollogie of the Souldiers,' referred to the unjust imprisonment of Lilburne and Overton 'who have shown themselves with us.'

> **A CLOSER LOOK**
>
> ### Demands for a purge of Parliament
>
> The army drew up impeachment charges against 11 MPs, with Holles at the top of the list, arguing that 'It is not the desire of the army to make themselves Masters of the Parliament but to make the Parliament Masters of themselves.' Ireton had himself challenged Holles to a duel because he so detested the Declaration of Dislike.

> **KEY TERM**
>
> **Levellers:** term used to describe the followers of Lilburne because of their desire to 'level' society, giving rights and liberties to all men, not just those of standing; this was seen by traditional Stuart culture as being unusual, abnormal and dangerous

> **CROSS-REFERENCE**
>
> Lilburne's activities in the 1630s are found in Chapter 6, page 53.

> **KEY PROFILE**
>
> **John Lilburne (1614–57)** became a Captain in an infantry regiment on the outbreak of war but he resigned his commission when ordered to swear to the Solemn League and Covenant because he fundamentally disagreed with Presbyterian model of Church governance on the grounds that it unreasonably restricted religious liberty. He began to develop deeper ideas about the rights that all humans are born with, which he described as 'freeborn rights'.

> **A CLOSER LOOK**
>
> ### Radical pamphleteers in 1646
>
> Particularly dismayed at the failure of the Long Parliament and Westminster Assembly to bring about radical-enough change, Lilburne, Overton and Walwyn published dramatic pamphlets urging further reform, including: *England's Lamentable Slaverie* (Walwyn, October 1645); *An Arrow against all Tyrants* (Overton, October 1646) and *London's Liberty in Chains* (Lilburne, November 1646).

Unsurprisingly, owing to their radical ideas, Levellers began to attract opposition from Parliament and the City authorities, who tried to supress the Leveller movement by imprisoning key members and repressing their tracts. However, opposition helped provide the movement with form and focus. The introduction to Richard Overton's 7000 word tract, *An arrow against all tyrants and tyranny, shot from the prison of Newgate into the prerogative bowels of the arbitrary House of Lords and all other usurpers and tyrants whatsoever*, is a startling expression of radical thought.

Fig. 4 *This engraving shows Newgate Prison still in use in the early nineteenth century as a place of public execution*

SOURCE 3

Richard Overton's 1646 tract, *An arrow against all tyrants and tyranny*, was drafted while he was imprisoned by Parliament for challenging the authority of the House of Lords:

To every individual at birth is given an individual personhood which cannot be removed or overcome by anyone else. An individual will be violated if anyone deprives them of their personhood, which captures the very principles of nature and the rules of equity and justice between man and man. Unless each individual has their own personhood, there can be no such thing as 'mine' or 'yours'. For, given by birth, all men are equally and alike created to enjoy rights of ownership, liberty and freedom. The hand of nature brings us into this world, as designed by God, each person having a natural, inborn freedom and right to property, and these freedoms are written deep into each man's heart in writing that cannot ever be erased. This surely means that we are to be allowed to live, everyone equally and alike to enjoy his birthright and the privileges that come with that; above all, we know that God desires us to be free.

KEY PROFILE

Richard Overton (c1610–63) began publishing pamphlets in the early 1640s that were initially to do with matters of religion (he was condemned by Thomas Edwards as a heretic in *Gangraena*), but became increasingly connected with politics and social order. He was imprisoned by Parliament in August 1646, but pressure from supporters in the New Model Army led to his release in the autumn of 1647.

The Large Petition

In March 1647, the Leveller leadership published the 'Large Petition', a significant articulation of their values and aims:

- The House of Commons was the true representative of the people. The House of Lords was an instrument of tyranny.
- Law courts should not be allowed to pursue 'godly, peaceable people for nonconformity' and the proceedings of the law should be in English.
- Trade monopolies should be abolished because they oppress the ordinary tradesmen, sailors and merchants.

CROSS-REFERENCE

Refer to page 126 to refresh your memory about why London was such a hotbed of radical ideas in the 1640, and remind yourself about *Gangraena* on page 129.

ACTIVITY

Create a Venn diagram with 'Levellers' on one side and 'New Model Army radicalism' on the other. Use the diagram to help you identify similarities and differences between the agendas of these two movements.

The Fifth Monarchists

Another radical political and religious grouping that was beginning to take shape in the mid-1640s was the Fifth Monarchy Men, or Fifth Monarchists. The name comes from a particular interpretation of the prophetic books of the Bible because some of the books which are collected together into the Christian Bible, particularly the Old Testament book of Daniel and the New Testament book, Revelation, speak prophetically of the future and point to the end of time, when Christians believe that Jesus will return and rule over a new heaven and earth. This is called **millenarian** theology and it was normal and accepted doctrine in the seventeenth century. However, quite how and when the establishment of the kingdom of heaven on earth would take place was a subject of hot debate and great interest, particularly because Daniel was clear that there would be four earthly kingdoms before the fifth, heavenly, monarchy would be established. Magic, astrology and outlandish folklore-derived prophecies led many people in different countries and contexts to claim that the Fifth Monarchy had either just arrived or was imminent.

KEY TERM

millenarians: they believed that a period of one thousand years was a significant measure of time in Biblical theology; they differed in their understanding of when it might occur: some thought that there would be a thousand-year period immediately preceding the Second Coming of Christ while others thought that his Second Coming would usher in one thousand years in which he ruled on earth

A CLOSER LOOK

Daniel's vision foretold a kingdom that would last forever and would follow four great earthly monarchies. In the seventeenth centuries these were typically identified as the monarchies of Assyria, Persia, Greece and Rome. Many stretched the meaning of the Roman civilisation to include the Holy Roman Empire, whose Emperor in 1647 was Frederick III and who was at this time embroiled in the last throes of the Thirty Years' War.

SECTION 5 | The disintegration of the Political Nation, 1646–1649

> **CROSS-REFERENCE**
>
> The beliefs of the **Fifth Monarchists** and the rise of the movement in the 1650s is examined in Chapter 22.

> **KEY TERM**
>
> **recruiter MP:** a term used by Royalists to refer to the recruitment of MPs to replace those who supported the king to maintain numbers in the Commons

The radical **Fifth Monarchists** were millenarians, who were certain that the turmoil of the Civil War presaged the arrival of Christ's kingdom. Their religious fervour imbued them with a determination to do everything that they could to hasten its arrival, by striving to lead spiritually pure lives and encouraging others to do likewise and they began to express this politically as the 1640s progressed. Chief among the developing Fifth Monarchy movement was **Thomas Harrison**, a **recruiter MP** and an evangelist of Fifth Monarchy theology among the New Model Army.

> **KEY PROFILE**
>
> **Thomas Harrison (1616–60)** was the son of a butcher who trained as a lawyer and became a Major in the Eastern Army during the Civil War. He became a recruiter MP in 1646 representing Wendover in Hampshire. Once he was in the Commons he lobbied for New Model arrears to be paid swiftly and in full and became known for his very radical views on religion as well as politics.

Ranters and other populist groups

While the Levellers had a predominantly social ideology, and Fifth Monarchy Men were developing a fusion of religious and social ideologies, other sects developed with a fervent focus on religious revival and reformation. These religious dissenting groups had roots that can be traced back through generations, but the mid-1640s saw them expressed increasingly openly and to greater extremes.

Ranters

> **CROSS-REFERENCE**
>
> Calvin's doctrine of **predestination** is discussed on page 22.
>
> The ideas of **Antinomians** are described on page 129.

> **KEY TERM**
>
> **libertinism:** being completely at liberty from a divinely ordained moral code, meaning that Ranters gained a reputation for sexual immorality, alcoholic excess and other forms of licentious behaviour

'Ranters' is a contemporary, pejorative, collective term for assorted groups and individuals who shared similar beliefs. Typically, they were Antinomians who took Calvin's ideas about **predestination** to an extreme, heretical conclusion. They believed that because God had already decided who would be saved to an eternal heaven after earthly death, their behaviour on earth was irrelevant for their future destiny. This meant that they endorsed total freedom without moral boundaries; in effect, they believed that could not sin because they were already selected by God for eternal life.

> **SOURCE 4**
>
> **Abiezer Coppe**, a leading Ranter, published several prophetic pamphlets. This excerpt is from his pamphlet, *The Fiery Flying Roll*, of 1649, which contains typical **Antinomian** theology, couched in millenarian language:
>
> Behold, behold the day of judgement! Jesus is now risen from the grave, to save his chosen people with vengeance. His mighty angel is proclaiming with a loud voice that sin is finished and ended. Instead, everlasting righteousness is being ushered in with the most terrible earthquakes and heaven-quakes and powerful demonstrations of God's power and might.
>
> Thus says the Lord, 'I tell you that I overturn, overturn, overturn and your turn is next! Whoever you are, whatever level in society, if you oppose me, the eternal God, I will overturn you. I am universal love and those who serve me receive perfect freedom and pure **libertinism**.'
>
> I have sweated blood and gone beyond being simply tormented in my efforts to receive this prophesy. Indeed, I feel that I have personally experienced the horror which will come when the angels pour out the plagues of God. In truth, it is far less offensive to me to hear a Ranter, swearing foul-mouthed oaths and ripping out his hair like a mad man, cursing and teaching others to swear than to be near a zealous Presbyterian or Independent, behaving piously, praying and preaching.

> **KEY PROFILE**
>
> **Abiezer Coppe (1619–72)** left his family farms to study theology at Oxford, where he became a member of Lord Brooke's circle of godly clergymen. Coppe became a chaplain to a Parliamentary regiment in the war. However, he began to develop increasingly radical Baptist beliefs and then, at the age of 28, had a series of mystical experiences which led him to the theological understanding that underpinned his Ranter beliefs.

Fig. 5 *Ranter behaviour was shocking in the culture of the seventeenth century*

Baptists

Anabaptists were typically fervent millenarians, but as the 1640s progressed their congregations were diversifying rapidly. Some groups such as the Particular Baptists were moderate in their theology and practice. They were keen to disassociate themselves from the more extreme Anabaptist sects who interpreted political turbulence as conclusive evidence that the end times were at hand and the apocalypse was imminent.

What is clear from these different expressions of radicalism is the extent to which the mid-1640s were years in which traditional ideas of religion, politics and society were being transformed at an unprecedented extent. Truly, the old world was being turned upside down.

CROSS-REFERENCE

For a description of **Anabaptists**, see page 129.

ACTIVITY

Summary

1. Copy and complete the chart below to show the radical spiritual, political and social ideas that emerged in the 1640s:

spiritual ideas	political ideas	social ideas

You could start by considering new ideas about the role of the individual and trace developments of individuality in the spiritual, political and social spheres.

2. What common characteristics do these three expressions of radicalism share?

STUDY TIP

You could use this question as an opportunity to consider the many and varied ways that a contemporary would have considered the turmoil of the mid-1640s and then use the sources to make specific comments about particular aspects of radical ideologies.

A LEVEL PRACTICE QUESTION

Evaluating primary sources

With reference to Sources 2, 3 and 4 and your understanding of the historical context, assess the value of these three sources for an historian studying the development of radical thought in the 1640s.

STUDY TIP

You could prepare for this question by listing different political ideas that were generated in this period and identifying their significance in the 1640s. Consider how modern hindsight can impact opinions compared to what a contemporary of the period would have thought. How does this affect your own perspective?

A LEVEL PRACTICE QUESTION

How serious a threat to the established order were the political ideas that emerged in the 1640s?

18 Political and religious divisions

LEARNING OBJECTIVES

In this chapter you will learn about:

- the attitude and actions of Charles I
- divisions within the opposition to the king
- the failure of attempts to reach a political settlement.

KEY CHRONOLOGY

Events of 1647

July	Council of the Army met at Reading
2 Aug	Heads of the Proposals
4 Aug	Army enters London
21 Aug	Solemn Engagement published by Londoners
Oct	The Agreement of the People
Oct	Putney Debates
11 Nov	Escape of King Charles
14 Dec	The Four Bills
26 Dec	The Engagement with the Scots

KEY TERM

iconoclast: someone who tears down religious symbols; ripping out Laudian altar rails was another form of iconoclasm

In 1643, Parliament had passed an ordinance 'that all Monuments of Superstition or Idolatry should be removed and demolished… in any other open place, before the said first day of November.' It took four years for the **iconoclasts** to reach London's famous Charing Cross, erected for Edward I in memory of his wife Eleanor, but during the summer of 1647 the monument was broken down and its stone used to pave a section of road in front of Whitehall. London continued to be a place of ferment, awash with radical political and religious ideas and perpetually tense because of competition between bands of underpaid soldiers. The demolition of Charing Cross was yet another visible sign of the 'world turned upside down'. It was during the events of summer 1647 that a rebellion against a king began to turn into a genuinely revolutionary era.

The attitude and actions of Charles I

Charles, in the custody of the New Model Army, was moved first to **Stoke Park** in early August and later that month taken to Hampton Court Palace where he lodged in considerable comfort in a suite of rooms overlooking the Privy Garden. Charles was allowed to retain a small number of close advisers, including John Ashburnham who was a relative of the Duke of Buckingham and William Legge, who had been Governor of Oxford during the Civil War.

Charles had not seen his wife since March 1644. Her safety was of particular importance to him because she was by then heavily pregnant and so she was carefully kept ahead of the advancing parliamentary army. She had left England for France in July 1644 and set up a court-in-exile at St-Germain-en-Laye. The following summer in 1645, Prince Charles joined her there. During 1647 she continued to try to raise support for the king on the continent and tried to persuade him to reach a settlement with the Scots but her influence was limited.

Fig. 1 *Charing Cross before it was demolished*

A CLOSER LOOK

Stoke Park in Buckinghamshire was the home of Sir John Villiers, 1st Viscount Purbeck who was the older brother of George Villiers, Duke of Buckingham. In 1617 he had married Frances Coke, daughter of Sir Edward Coke, despite fierce opposition from her mother Lady Hatton: the marriage was a disaster because Villiers began to suffer from an intermittent form of insanity and his wife started an affair with Sir Robert Howard. George Villiers pursued a case of adultery against her and she was convicted by the Court of High Commission: she fled abroad before she could be imprisoned. Robert Howard became a leading Royalist commander, while Lady Hatton became a staunch Parliamentarian, allowing her home to be used as a military rendezvous.

CHAPTER 18 | Political and religious divisions

While efforts to reach a settlement with him continued through 1647, Charles still anticipated that he would prevail because he would ultimately be able to exploit the intense divisions between his opponents. Although he appeared to be sincerely working to reach a settlement, those close to him knew otherwise: from her exiled court, Henrietta Maria gave letters of recommendation to John Berkeley, the Royalist Governor of Exeter, authorising him to act as an intermediary between the king and his captors.

SOURCE 1

From the private diary of John Berkeley, intermediary between King Charles I and his New Model Army captors, describing how he found the king. He published his diary as the *Memoirs of John Berkeley* in 1699:

The General granted me permission to speak to the King. I delivered my letters and verbal messages to his Majesty. His Majesty was very open to me, as he was to everyone he spoke with. He was indifferent to all in the army, which he said was because he had been unable to persuade any of the Officers to receive any Advantage from him. I shared his Majesty's opinion, that men whose hands were still warm with the dripping blood of his most faithful subjects ought not entirely to be trusted. I agreed that he needed to be careful what he says to his captors, trying to keep the upper hand and I suggested that he offer them some concessions. I recommended that he should allow the army's chaplain to preach in front of him. I also suggested that he should encourage soldiers to speak freely to him, and that he should work particularly hard to get on the good side of the most active Agitators. But his Majesty rejected all my advice.

ACTIVITY

Look back to earlier chapters and your notes to refresh your learning about other reasons why Charles would not reach a settlement, considering such things as religious radicalism, Divine Right and loyalty to friends.

Divisions within the opposition to the king

To a great degree, Charles was accurate in his analysis of the problems facing the Parliamentarian search for settlement. While he rested, conversed and spent carefully supervised time with some of his children at Hampton Court, divisions within the army and between the army and Parliament were intensifying.

A CLOSER LOOK

The royal children

While the king was in captivity and the queen was in exile in France, Parliament exercised considerable control over the younger royal children. Parliamentary records show the huge number of detailed decisions taken in the Commons about the children's whereabouts and care. During the summer of 1647 for example, Parliament voted to allow the royal children to visit their father for three days before returning them to St James's Palace in London.

Fig. 2 *The king's youngest children remained in England under the care of Parliament*

SECTION 5 | The disintegration of the Political Nation, 1646–1649

CROSS-REFERENCE

Ireton, Cromwell and Lambert's June document, the 'Representation of the Army' is discussed on page 145.

KEY TERM

electoral reform: any reform of the system by which people elect their representatives; the Heads of the Proposals called for a redistribution of Parliament's electoral boundaries to take into account shifts in population

A CLOSER LOOK

Who were the 'reformadoes'?

During June and July, Parliament was threatened by disturbances on numerous occasions. 'Reformadoes' were the most active, former soldiers who were still in arrears, but apprentices, sailors, butchers and porters and a significant number of women all took to the streets at varying moments.

Divisions between army and Parliament

In July 1647, the Council of the Army, made up of Agitators as well as officers, convened in Reading to discuss a document once again largely drafted by **Henry Ireton**, with the help of **Cromwell** and **John Lambert**. It suggested terms for a settlement that would be made directly between the king and the army although Lord Wharton and Viscount Saye and Sele were also present in Reading and the settlement broadly aligned with the goals of the Political Independents.

On 2 August, these terms were published as the 'Heads of the Proposals.' The key terms were:

- Biennial Parliaments, allowing a gap of no longer than two years from the dissolution of one Parliament to the recall of the next.
- **Electoral reform**, linked to changes in population and wealth.
- Parliamentary control over the militia and navy for ten years.
- Parliamentary appointment of great officers of state for ten years.
- A religious settlement that provided for a national Church with bishops, while legalising independent congregations and freedom of worship.
- An Act of Oblivion which granted widespread indemnity from crimes committed in war time, only excluding seven specified Royalists.

The Heads of the Proposals were considerably more moderate than the Newcastle Propositions. In fact, Berkeley noted that Ireton had spent a long evening with the king on 3rd July and had subsequently amended his draft version of the Heads. Ominously, a nickname was developing among the lower ranks of the army which described the senior members of the Army Council who had taken the lead on the Heads as Grandees, a term laden with social tension.

The Presbyterian reaction in London

While the army waited for the king to respond, it resumed its steady march towards the capital. London was extremely unsettled and, by late July, there was a rising clamour from within the London populace to reach a resolution with the king. On the 21st, hundreds of assorted Londoners put their names to their own Solemn Engagement to support the king and find a mutually acceptable settlement. On the 22nd, thousands of **reformadoes** rallied in St James's Field. Two petitions followed, urging the City to retain the Trained Bands, to provide some protection against the advancing New Model Army. On 26th, a huge mob surged into Westminster, terrorised the House of Lords into reinstating the London Militia Committee and then invaded the Commons, throwing excrement at the members and keeping them captive until a resolution inviting the king back to London was passed. Once they had left, the Lords and Commons adjourned themselves; the Speaker of each House, 57 Independent MPs and 8 peers fled.

A CLOSER LOOK

The role of Denzil Holles

Holles was believed to have helped coordinate the mob's actions, although he vigorously denied the charge. He almost undoubtedly knew what was being planned through his connections in the City and he certainly hoped to profit from it as the London mob's aims aligned with those of his Political Presbyterians.

Berkeley continued to try to broker a peace between the king and the army and Parliament but he was beginning to lose hope. The king's advisers suggested that he could rely on Scottish support, or incite the London Trained Bands to rise for him, or engender a new Presbyterian Royalist force as well as lawyers, pointing out the complex legislative issues that settlement presented. Charles was, crucially, certain that he still held the balance of power, complacently assuring the Grandees that 'You cannot be without me, you will fall to ruin if I do not sustain you.' It was a catastrophic misjudgement. By early August, the New Model Army had reached Hounslow Heath where they were joined by the refugees from Parliament. A disciplined rank of New Model soldiers over one mile long greeted them, cheering 'Lords, Commons and a Free Parliament!' The army's presence reversed the balance of power: the London militia dispersed, and, on 4 August, the army entered London unopposed and triumphantly accompanied the Independent MPs back to Westminster.

SOURCE 2

From the Venetian Ambassador in Paris, Gio Battista Nani, who received messages from London which he forwarded on to the Venetian doges. This extract dates from 6 August 1647 and comes from the Venetian archives:

The Presbyterians, seeing their party downtrodden, have incited the apprentices of London to push the City Council to prepare to defend London and the privileges of the realm. The City therefore proposed to form a league so that the King could return to London. When General Fairfax heard of this, he wrote to Parliament, offering all his forces to prevent such a destructive strategy. 10,000 apprentices proceeded to Parliament and presented a petition which pushed Parliament into both withdrawing a statement which had denounced them as rebels and also confirming their request about retaining the milita of London. When the apprentices saw the Speaker, they asked him if he was a good servant of the King. When he said, 'Yes', they told him to prove it by shouting 'God save the King.' Feeling very intimidated, he did so in a very low voice but they made him do it again in a loud voice so everyone could hear. After this, the Houses wished to end the session for the day but the people threatened to set fire to them unless they stayed there for longer. All is in confusion and upside down while the militia of London have taken up their arms.

Divisions within the army

The extent and intensity of the political division in the summer of 1647 was profoundly unsettling to the greater majority of the Political Nation. Divisions were beginning to spread within the army as well because, although remaining deeply divided from the Political Presbyterians, the Army Grandees including Fairfax, Cromwell and Ireton were undoubtedly keen to make a relatively conservative settlement with the king. During the late summer and autumn, this conservatism would create an open breach within the army itself.

The Agreement of the People

Leveller leaders within and beyond the army were dismayed at the Heads of the Proposals because the suggested settlement was so moderate. The arrival of the army into London's febrile atmosphere sparked a meeting of minds between Agitators, disgruntled army rank-and-file and civilian political radicals which threatened both the unity of the army (which the Grandees were striving hard to maintain) and the attempt to reach a moderate settlement with the king. John Lilburne had once again been imprisoned in the Tower of London in July 1646, this time because he had criticised the Earl of Manchester. He was incensed that the arrival of the army in London in the summer of 1647 did not lead to his release from imprisonment in the Tower and he began to attack the Grandees directly: 'Be sure not to trust your great officers at the Generalls quarters, no further than you can throw an Oxe'.

SECTION 5 | The disintegration of the Political Nation, 1646–1649

KEY PROFILE

John Wildman (c1623–93) was the son of a Norfolk butcher who attended Cambridge University as a low-status student who had to work as a servant in his college to pay for this training. He served under General Fairfax and swiftly became an adviser to his regiment's Agitators.

A CLOSER LOOK

A **representative Parliament** would represent the population as a whole, not just those of wealth or high status. At this time 'representative' did not include electoral rights for women, but the Leveller cause did come very close to a full adult male suffrage (vote).

Leveller ideas began to spread and gather pace. In October 1647, the Leveller **John Wildman** and new agitators from five cavalry regiments (including those of Cromwell and Ireton) published *The Case of the Army Truly Stated*, which merged together old army grievances about pay and arrears with new complaints, that the Grandees had betrayed the soldiers and were conceding too much to the king. A new political thread emerged too, arguments for widespread political reform based on a truly **representative Parliament**.

The *Case of the Army* was quickly reworked into *An Agreement of the People for a Firm and Present Peace Upon Grounds of Common Right and Freedom*.

SOURCE 3

An Agreement of the People was submitted to General Fairfax on 27 October 1647 for discussion by the General Council of the Army:

1. That the people of England being at this day very unequally distributed by counties, cities and boroughs for the election of their deputies in parliament, ought to be more fairly proportioned according to the number of the inhabitants…

3. That the people do of course choose themselves a parliament once in two years, upon the first Thursday in every second March… and to continue till the last day of the following September, and no longer.

4. That the power of this and all future representatives of this nation is inferior only to the people who elected them. The authority of the parliament extends to enacting, altering or repealing of laws; to the erection and abolition of offices and courts; to the appointing, removing and calling to account magistrates and officers of all types; to the making of war and of peace; to dealing with foreign states; and to any other general business that is not specifically dealt with under particular conditions. The nation's representatives do not need the approval of any other person or persons: the will of the people who elected them is sufficiently authoritative.

Fig. 3 *An Agreement of the People* was one of the key Leveller texts

The Putney Debates

Fig. 4 *St Mary the Virgin, in Putney, south-west London, is now overshadowed by offices and traffic, but it has a proud heritage*

ACTIVITY

Using your knowledge of early Stuart government, which elements of the 'Agreement' in Source 3 simply restated current conventions and which elements were innovative and radical? Draw up a table to help you arrange your ideas.

Faced with such strong evidence of dissent in the ranks, Fairfax put discussion of the Agreement onto the agenda for the next Army Council meeting which was scheduled to be held in late October. By now the army was headquartered in Putney and the council met on 28 October in the parish church of St Mary the Virgin. Cromwell and Ireton were the main spokesmen for the Grandees, urging settlement according to the Heads, while **Colonel Thomas Rainsborough**, John Wildman and **Agitator Trooper Sexby** acted as main spokesmen for the Levellers. Several themes emerged during the debates, including:

- **The basis of Parliament's authority:** Was the current system of king and Parliament an oppressive invention of the Norman kings that should now be overthrown and replaced by something better (the Leveller position) or was it an expression of ancient rights and liberties that could be modified but should be protected (the Grandee position)?
- **The right to suffrage:** Was property a necessary qualification for electoral rights (Grandees), or should there be an overthrow of the current system, to allow all men the opportunity to vote (Levellers)?
- **Cromwell's efforts to maintain unity:** Throughout the Putney Debates, Cromwell's voice stands out as endeavouring to hold all sides together, reminding them of their common purpose, appealing to their faith and softening extremes.

> **KEY PROFILE**
>
> **Colonel Thomas Rainsborough (1610–48)** was the son of a vice-admiral in the king's fleet. He travelled to the Providence Island Colony in the 1630s. During the Civil War he was a Colonel in the New Model Army and he became MP for Droitwich in 1647. He was killed by Royalists in 1648.

> **CROSS-REFERENCE**
>
> **Agitator Sexby's** role prior to the capture of Charles I can be found on page 144.

SOURCE 4

From the minutes of the Putney Debates, recorded by clerks during the proceedings:

Cromwell: It is so difficult to reach an agreement because even when something is evidently true, it is still possible to find something about it to object against. So, we need all honest men to really consider whether their objections are actually going to help us reach an agreement. I firmly believe that our faith will provide us with answers to all difficulties but I also know that sometimes we talk about our faith when really we are just wishing things were going our way, or worse, that we are trying to manipulate the truth. So, I have resolved in my heart and before the Lord that I won't say anything unless I am certain it will help us to become more united.

The open atmosphere of the Putney Debates was somewhat undermined by the publication of a Leveller tract on 29 October, 'A Call to all the Soldiers of the Army' which was anonymous, but probably authored by Wildman. It incited **mutiny** on the basis that Ireton and Cromwell had betrayed the army: 'They're as likely to be at Hampton Court as to be here because the Grandees and the king have become as one.' News began to arrive of disturbances and minor mutinies in a number of regiments, including that of John Lilburne's brother Henry.

In an attempt to break what had become a stalemate, the General Council appointed a committee to negotiate a solution in a less combative manner and the next few days saw a combination of closed committee sessions and open debates. Suddenly however, on the 8 November, all the agitators were ordered back to their regiments and Fairfax and Cromwell shut the debates down. Their motives were not made known but must have included:

- Growing evidence that Charles was plotting something.
- An increasing awareness that finding a negotiated compromise acceptable to the General Council was unlikely.
- Leveller agitation was spreading unrest into more regiments.
- The emergence of increasingly extreme attitudes to the king, including **republican** voices.

> **A CLOSER LOOK**
>
> **Religious fervour** ran throughout the entire debate process. At the end of the first day, one of the generals expressed his belief that the present quarrels were due to a lack of prayer and recommended that the next day should begin with a prayer meeting: 'We have had continuous trouble because God has not been with us as he has been in the past. We want to continue to be used by him, so let us seriously set ourselves before the Lord and seek him in prayer and wait for him to bring conviction to our spirits.' This suggestion was accepted by all parties, although Wildman was concerned that every minute lost was a minute closer to the king reaching an agreement with the Presbyterians.

> **KEY TERM**
>
> **mutiny:** when the authority of the commanding officer is wilfully disregarded by his subordinates
>
> **republic:** a state in which supreme power is held by the people and their elected representatives, with an elected or nominated president and without a monarch

The failure of attempts to reach a settlement with the king

Fig. 5 *King Charles was next imprisoned in Carisbrooke Castle*

Charles threw a lifeline to Cromwell and the Grandees by escaping from Hampton Court on the night of 11 November. He made his way to the Isle of Wight, where he presented himself to Governor Colonel Robert Hammond who promptly arrested and re-imprisoned him, at Carisbrooke Castle. Where unity had been evaporating and discipline breaking down, the king's action caused the army to re-bond against its common enemy. There is a palpable sense of relief in the House of Commons' Journal entry for 19 November 1647.

> **SOURCE 5**
>
> From a House of Commons journal entry, 19 November 1647:
>
> Lieutenant General Cromwell gave the House an Account of the Proceedings at the Rendezvous of the Army; and how that, by the great Mercy of God, upon the Endeavours of the General and Officers, the Army was in a very composed State of Obedience to the Superior Officers, and Submission to the Authority of Parliament.

Preparing for a renewed struggle against the king dealt a mortal blow to the attempt of many in the army to agree on a basis for settlement. More importantly, Charles's actions demonstrated to the army that he was not pursuing settlement in good faith and should not be trusted.

The Four Bills

On 14 December 1647, Parliament passed a new set of settlement terms to be sent to the king at Carisbrooke Castle. Known as the 'Four Bills', they outlined conditions under which he could come to London and negotiate in person:

- **Act for settling the Forces by Sea and Land** – handed military control to Parliament for 20 years
- **Act to justify the Proceedings of Parliament** – prevented the king from **revoking** Parliamentary business carried out in his absence
- **Act concerning the Adjournment of the Houses** – prevented the king from adjourning Parliament
- **Act concerning Peers lately made** – revoked recent honours made by the king

A CLOSER LOOK

Cromwell reasserts control

Cromwell acted swiftly to repress the Leveller threat. Prior to the king's escape the Levellers had begun to petition for a single army meet, in order to have rank-and-file input into the debates. Following the escape, Cromwell issued orders for three separate rendezvous and when mutiny broke at one of them, at Corkbush Field, it was brutally crushed. Followed by a resolution in Parliament on 23 November, to suppress Leveller ideology and actions, order was substantially restored.

KEY TERM

revoke: to cancel, specifically in terms of overturning legislation

In good faith, the next item on the statute book notes 'That these Instructions be communicated to the Scots Commissioners, by the Members of both Houses that are of the Committee of Both Kingdoms, this Afternoon.' What Parliament did not know was that the king had been secretly negotiating with the Scots. On 26 December, two days before rejecting the Four Bills, he published a treaty, the 'Engagement' with the Scots. A renewed period of war was approaching.

ACTIVITY

Summary

Find a map of London in the seventeenth century, and its outskirts, then print it and stick it in the centre of a large piece of paper, leaving a wide border around the edge. Use the information in this chapter to annotate it, with dates and events, to show movements of people and significant publications.

A LEVEL PRACTICE QUESTION

'By the end of 1647, the army was no longer a united force.'
Assess the validity of this view.

STUDY TIP

This question addresses change and continuity. You will need to reflect on changing circumstances in 1647 but a deeper answer might also consider the extent to which the army was united prior to 1647 so that you challenge the basic premise of the question itself.

A LEVEL PRACTICE QUESTION

Evaluating primary sources

With reference to Sources 1, 2 and 3, and your understanding of the historical context, assess the value of these three sources to an historian studying the reasons why settlement with the king was not achieved during 1647.

STUDY TIP

Provenance is of vital importance for answering this question effectively, particularly considering the purpose and authorship of these sources. Try to include analysis of the competition between rival factions as well.

19 The Second Civil War

LEARNING OBJECTIVES

In this chapter you will learn about:

- political causes of the Second Civil War
- local causes of the Second Civil War
- the Scottish invasion
- the reasons for the outcome of the Second Civil War.

KEY CHRONOLOGY

1647	Dec	Four Bills
	Dec	Engagement with the Scots
1648	Jan	Vote of No Addresses
	April	Royalist attack on Berwick
	25 Aug	Surrender of Hamilton's Royalist army
1649	March	Final Royalist defeat at Pontefract

A CLOSER LOOK

Christmas was killed

Although Cromwell has been blamed for banning Christmas, it was in fact the Westminster Assembly who originally ruled that Sundays should be strict holy days and that no other days could be designated as 'holy'. In June 1647, Parliament endorsed their decision by confirming the abolition of feasts including Christmas and Easter. As a form of compensation for hard-pressed servants, apprentices and labourers, the second Tuesday of each month was instead designated a secular holiday.

SOURCE 1

From a ballad, *The World is Turned Upside Down*, which was published in 1646:

To conclude, I'll tell you news that's right, Christmas was killed at Naseby fight:
Charity was slain at that same time, Jack Tell-truth too, a friend of mine,
Likewise then did die, roast beef and shred pie,
Pig, Goose and Capon no quarter found.
Yet let's be content, and the times lament, you see the world turned upside down.

By late 1647, war had been a feature of Charles's reign for eight years. It is worth pausing to reflect on the impact of such a sustained period of turbulence on a nation and its individuals. The main reasons for tension and anxiety in the mid-1640s were:

- the repeated failure to reach a political settlement with the king
- the displacement of population, both military and civilian
- the suffering of many: life-changing injuries and loss of loved ones
- steadily increasing financial burdens
- continued debate and change within the Church
- the imposition of new and unusual governmental structures
- radical zealotry and apocalyptic fervour.

A CLOSER LOOK

Economic problems

During the 1640s, the English economy struggled. This was partly because of problems caused by disruption of trade with Europe, which was a factor of the Thirty Years' War. In addition, people had to leave their businesses to fight, money was diverted from normal purposes to paying for military equipment and crops and property were destroyed during fighting. The economic problems which were the result of war were compounded by harvest failures which put pressure on particular regions such as the north-west.

ACTIVITY

In a group of four, imagine yourselves back into England in the 1640s and allocate roles of: urban tradesman, rural farmer, county gentleman, and a child. Each of you think through the different ways that your life might be being affected by the conditions listed in this Summary. Discuss and decide who you think is having to cope with the most significant changes.

Political causes of the Second Civil War

The Engagement with the Scots

Charles had secretly negotiated with the Scots while he was imprisoned in Carisbrooke Castle in 1647–48. These negotiations concluded in the creation of an Engagement between the king and his Scottish subjects.

SOURCE 2

From the personal collection of Edward Hyde, later the Earl of Clarendon, this extract of the Engagement with the Scots was incorporated into his *History of the Great Rebellion*:

An army shall be sent from Scotland into England with the following goals: to bring long-lasting order to religion; to defend His Majesty's personal safety and his constitutional authority; to restore the King to his government, restored to his lawful rights and his full revenues; to defend the privileges of Parliament and the liberties of the subjects; to make a firm union between the kingdoms, under His Majesty and his heirs and to settle a lasting peace. To these ends, the kingdom of Scotland will endeavour to ensure that a free and full Parliament will be recalled in England. His Majesty may then take his rightful place in honour, safety and freedom so that he issue Declarations that will restore order to his kingdoms. The Scottish Army shall be upon the march before he is able to issue these Declarations, to ensure that he is able so to do. It is further agreed that all in the kingdoms of England or Ireland who wish to join with the kingdom of Scotland in this endeavour shall be protected by His Majesty, both in terms of their lives and their property. Anyone of His Majesty's subjects in England and Ireland who is in support of these goals may come to the Scottish Army and join with them.

In return for the support of the Scots, the content of the Declarations referred to in the extract was to be in line with Scottish ambitions because Charles had agreed to impose a Presbyterian settlement on the Church in England for three years; unite the two kingdoms; disband the English armies; allow Scottish occupation of border towns including Carlisle and Berwick and suppress all religious Independency. He still refused to subscribe to the Covenant.

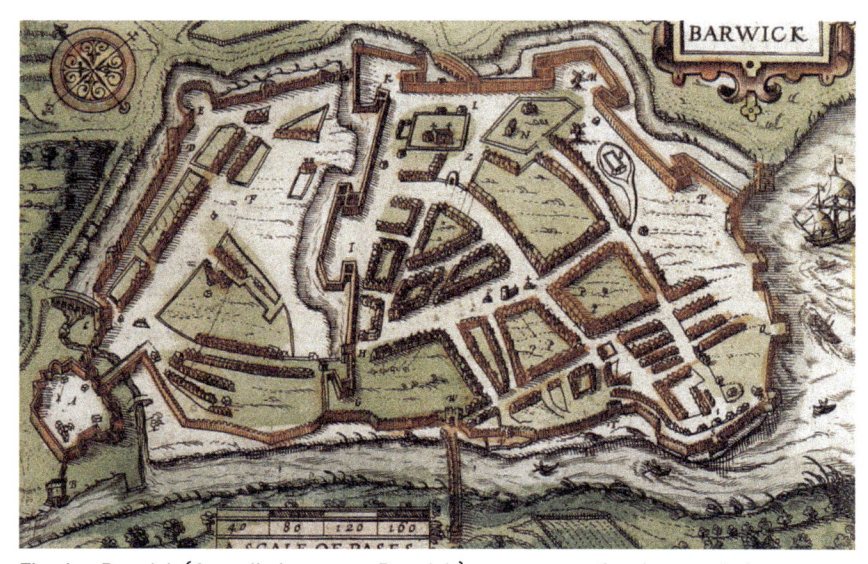

Fig. 1 *Berwick (formally known as Barwick) was a town of real strategic importance due to its location close to the Scottish border with easy access to the sea*

The Vote of No Addresses

Faced with concrete evidence of Charles's double-dealing and awaiting the impending Scottish invasion, on 17 January 1648, the Commons voted on a resolution 'That this House doth declare, That they will make no further **Addresses** or Applications to the King' by a majority of 141 to 90. Under pressure after a supportive resolution by the Army Council, the Commons' resolution passed through the Lords and onto the statute book.

KEY TERM

address: a polite request to be heard on a specific subject

SECTION 5 | The disintegration of the Political Nation, 1646–1649

SOURCE 3

From the Vote of No Addresses, January 1648, which was recorded in the Journal of the House of Commons:

1. That the Lords and Commons do declare that they will make no further addresses or applications to the King.
2. That no application or addresses be made to the King by any person whatsoever, without the consent of both Houses.
3. That any person or persons that shall make breach of this order shall incur the penalties of high treason.
4. That the two Houses declare they will receive no more any message from the King; and confirm that no person whatsoever may be allowed to receive or bring any message from the King to both or either of the Houses of Parliament, or to any other person.

ACTIVITY

With reference to your historical knowledge of the period, in what ways do you think the Vote of No Addresses would prove to be significant?

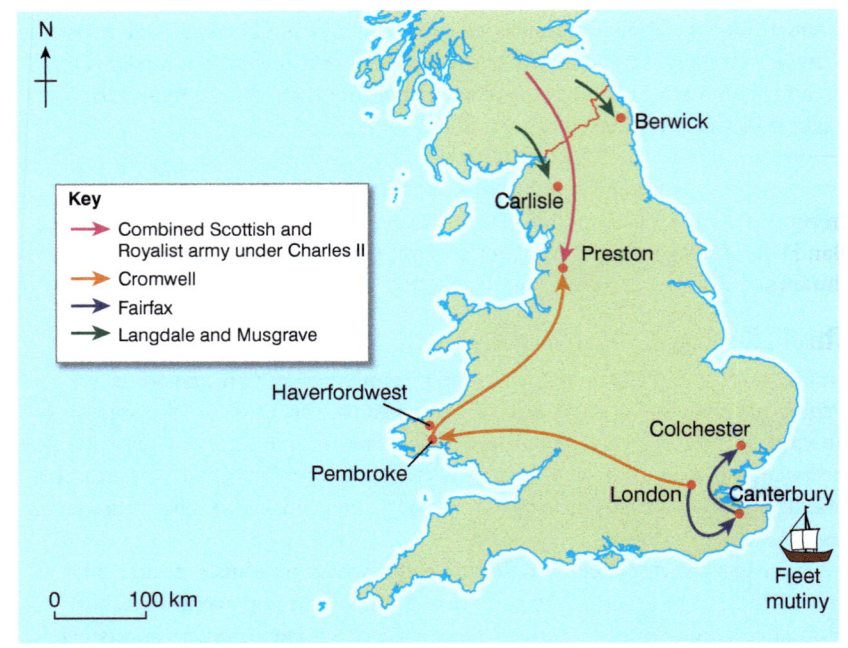

With this firm commitment confirmed by Commons and Lords, it was clear that no settlement would be reached with the king and that therefore both sides would need to resort to arms once again to attempt to prevail by military means.

KEY CHRONOLOGY

Events of the Second Civil War, 1648

11 April–July	Siege of Pembroke Castle
July	Cromwell orders Haverfordwest Castle to be destroyed
28 April	Langdale leads invasion force to Berwick
30 April	Musgrave leads invasion force to Carlisle
May–June	Kentish Rebellion
June–Aug	Siege of Colchester
Aug	Battle of Preston
25 Dec	Canterbury rising

Fig. 2 Major events of the Second Civil War

Charles had correctly identified a growing tide of anti-Parliamentarianism in the kingdom through 1647, with events such as the demonstrations in London in June and July which caused him to hope that more of his subjects were coming round to his side.

However, the Second Civil War differed considerably from the First because there was no coalescence of a focused Royalist party. Instead, until the Scots invaded in early July, there were few pitched battles and rather more skirmishes and localised, uncoordinated risings. Typically, these were rooted in specific grievances and not characterised by particular loyalty to Charles Stuart. In fact, it is possible to characterise some – such as **Lucy, Countess of Carlisle** – as anti-Parliamentarian rather than pro-Royalist.

The Canterbury Rising

On Christmas Day 1647, the Canterbury citizens, irked by the abolition of Christmas festivities and annoyed that they were being ordered to open their shops for 'business as usual', rioted 'For God, King Charles and Kent!' They expelled the small Parliamentary **garrison** from the town and published a Declaration, outlining their position.

SOURCE 4

From the *Declaration of many thousands of the City of Canterbury*, published in January 1648 and intended to defend their actions in expelling the Parliamentary garrison:

The Declaration of Many Thousands of the City of Canterbury, and County of Kent: Concerning the Late Tumult in the City of Canterbury, Provoked by the Mayor's Violent Proceedings Against Those who Desired to Continue the Celebration of the Feast of Christ's Nativity…: Together with Their Resolutions for the Restitution of His Majesty to His Crown and Dignity.

The two Houses have sat seven years to hatch basilisks and vipers. They have filled the kingdom with serpents, bloodthirsty soldiers, committees who commit extortions, men who rob others of their property, tax men; all the rogues and scum of the kingdom have been set on to torment and vex the people, to rob them, and to eat the bread out of their mouths… They have suppressed the true Protestant religion, suffered all kinds of heresies and errors in the kingdom, have imprisoned, or at least silenced, all the orthodox clergy, taken away the livelihood of many thousand families and robbed the fatherless and the widow.

In response, Parliament sent 3000 soldiers, (mainly from the London Trained Bands) and **besieged** the town. Canterbury surrendered without a fight and the country was once again broadly at peace.

The Rebellion in South Wales

On 23 March 1648, Colonel Poyer, the Parliamentarian commander at Pembroke Castle in South Wales who was also the local mayor, declared for the king. He was disgruntled because he had not received the financial reward he had anticipated for his loyalty to Parliament in the First Civil War and he was supported by other Parliamentarians who had refused to demobilise until paid.

Cromwell was despatched to South Wales (which was his first full army command) and besieged Pembroke Castle. It held out for seven weeks but capitulated when Cromwell's siege cannons arrived. He blew up the Castle's defensive towers and outer walls and moved on to Haverfordwest, where, on 12 July 1648 he gave orders to demolish the castle as a precaution against further rebellion. After a half-hearted attempt by the local people to blow up a wall, they wrote to Cromwell.

SOURCE 5

From the Mayor and Council of Haverfordwest to Cromwell and the Army Council on 13 July 1648:

Honoured Sir,
We received an order from your honour and the Council to demolish the Castle of Haverfordwest. In obedience to these instructions, we have today started some workmen on the task. However, in the absence of Powder, the job is so difficult it will exhaust an Immense some of money and will take an unfeasible

KEY PROFILE

Lucy, Countess of Carlisle (1599–1660) was a supporter of Thomas Wentworth during the 1630s. She later became aligned with the king's opponents after his execution in 1641. It is believed that she alerted Essex to Charles's attempt to arrest the Five Members. She did not approve of Parliament's growing constitutional opposition to the king and switched sides to support his cause in the Second Civil War, for which she was imprisoned in the Tower of London in 1649.

KEY TERM

garrison: a group of soldiers, stationed in a town or fortress to defend it

ACTIVITY

With reference to your historical knowledge of the period, how valuable is Source 4 to an historian studying the consequences of Civil War in England on the localities?

A CLOSER LOOK

Siege warfare was a legacy of medieval military tactics. Soldiers surrounded a town, preventing anyone from entering or leaving and cut off all supplies to force the town to surrender. Sieges were often effective but very costly because of the need to keep a large army around the besieged town. For this reason, Cromwell particularly preferred to try to storm towns instead.

SECTION 5 | The disintegration of the Political Nation, 1646–1649

amount of time to complete. As a result, we find ourselves having to ask your honour that a sufficient quantity of powder be spared out of the ships to carry out this work in a timely manner. We and the County will consent to pay for the gunpowder. This being the case, we ask you to make a formal order for the levying of a sufficient sum of money on all the hundreds of this County, to pay for the powder and the other costs of your commission. Acknowledging that we have been rather bold to ask these things of your honour and hopefully that we will shortly hear of your decision, we remain

Your honour's humble servants

Haverfordwest 13 July 1648

The castle was not demolished but slowly crumbled away.

Rebellion in Kent and Essex

Kent and Essex had been securely under Parliament's control since early 1642 and as such they had suffered more than most counties from heavy taxation and the imposition of Parliament's religious agenda. By May 1648, Kent was desperate for respite. At a special Sessions held in Canterbury, a 'Humble Petition of Knights, Gentry, Clergy and Commonalty' asked:

1. that 'our most gracious Sovereign' should be brought safely and quickly to London for the 'settling of the peace'
2. that the army should have its arrears audited and then be disbanded
3. that they should be governed 'by the English subjects' undoubted birthright, the known and established laws of the Kingdom and not otherwise'
4. that 'our property may not be invaded by any taxes or impositions whatsoever and particularly the heavy burden of the Excise'.

Fig. 3 *Haverfordwest Castle was ruined in the Second Civil War although in the eighteenth century, a part of the ruins was converted into a prison*

ACTIVITY

Why was it so important to Parliament that the army was back in a 'state of obedience'?

A CLOSER LOOK

The Siege of Colchester was one of the most devastating actions of the Civil Wars, beginning in mid-June and not ending until 27 August. Starvation forced its citizens to trade in dog flesh (six shillings a side) and maggoty horse meat. Rhetoric on both sides was intense and became increasingly extreme: *Another Bloudy Fight*, a news pamphlet, related how the town's commanders, Sir Charles Lucas, Sir George Lisle and the Earl of Norwich, 'began to grow into a great agony, vowing revenge and resolved rather to die like Sonnes of Mars in the field, than to submit basely to the mercy of an enemy, and to surrender the town upon dishonorable conditions.' The fact that Fairfax waged a siege rather storming the city, despite having adequate military strength is instructive. While the siege was devastating for its inhabitants, storming the town would have been worse because of wholesale rape and slaughter as the soldiers fought their way through the city. Nonetheless, Fairfax's actions after the Siege created Royalist martyrs. Using martial law he executed Lisle and Lucas, an act that ricocheted around ballads and pamphlets which described him as the 'Hangman Generall'.

Conversely, the poet and polemicist John Milton saluted Fairfax with a sonnet, 'On the Lord General Fairfax at the Siege of Colchester', in which he declared that his 'firm unshaken virtue brings Victory home'.

Initially 200 gentlemen signed the Petition; within days there were 20,000 signatories and a march was planned from Rochester to Blackheath to start on 29 May. The fleet off the coast of Kent declared for the king's son, Prince Charles, and forced their commander Rainsborough to disembark; a muster raised about 6000 men and 1000 horse. By the time the Kentish men had reached Blackheath, they numbered about 10,000 but they were pushed back by General Fairfax who had led an army to put the rebellion down. A pamphlet, *Bloody News from Kent*, described how the 'Kentish men [were] forced back from Deptford, Greenwich and Blackheath, went to Rochester and crossed the Bridge.' By June, the rebellion was over.

Committed Royalists who escaped Fairfax in Kent fled to Essex to join with rebels there. Fairfax pursued them and arrived at Colchester where he set up a devastating siege of the city.

Fig. 4 *The execution of Lucas and Lisle by firing squad*

The Scottish invasion

Sir Marmaduke Langdale, Royalist veteran of Marston Moor, had fled to Scotland at the end of the First Civil War. On 28 April 1648, he led a Royalist force from Scotland to seize Berwick on the north-east coast of England, an action followed the next day by Sir Philip Musgrave, another Royalist exile, who brought a force from Scotland to take Carlisle. The Scottish invasion was underway.

There were several weaknesses to the invading force:
- The Marquis of Hamilton had championed the negotiations with the king but he was only representative of a faction within Scotland. The Engagement did not have anything like the support nor the moral fervour that the Covenant had engendered among the Scots.
- Charles did not have the means to pay for the Scots in the foreseeable future and they were poorly funded by their Scottish supporters which meant that they were also ill-equipped.
- The Scottish Army was a disparate assembly of 10,000 Scots, 4000 English Royalist veterans and a further 3000 Scots fresh from fighting under General Monroe in Ulster. Monroe refused to fight under the command of the **Earl of Callendar** who in turn, refused to allow him an independent command.
- Hamilton was not a skilled commander, lacking tactical awareness as well as leadership ability.

ACTIVITY

The turbulent career of Callendar reveals the extent to which allegiances were fluid and responded both to national and local concerns as well as to personal loyalties and friendships. Create a timeline for Callendar's career, adding your own research to help illuminate his choices.

KEY PROFILE

James Livingston, 1st Earl of Callendar (c1590s–1674) was a Covenanter who fought under General Leslie in the Second Bishops' War, but who later signed the Cumbernauld Bond alongside Montrose. He was a Royalist participant in the Incident and became a Covenanter Lieutenant-General in the First Civil War, taking part in the blockade of Newcastle but preferring not to fight against Montrose. He took part in the negotiations leading up to the Engagement of 1647 and fled abroad after defeat of his army at Preston.

SECTION 5 | The disintegration of the Political Nation, 1646–1649

> **STUDY TIP**
>
> You will need to consider the influences on and attitudes within the Royalist risings and military encounters. You will need to evaluate the aims of the Royalists and the part played by loyalty to Charles as opposed to other factors in provoking these.

> **A LEVEL PRACTICE QUESTION**
>
> 'In the Second Civil War of 1648, the Royalists fought against Parliament rather than for the king.'
> Assess the validity of this view.

The Battle of Preston

With Cromwell in Wales and Fairfax in Kent, Major General John Lambert, still only 29, had led a Parliamentary army to the North to counter Langdale at Berwick. His cavalry engaged with Hamilton's army just outside Preston. Although Lambert was beaten back by Hamilton's superior numbers, he delayed the Scots sufficiently for Cromwell, marching north from Wales, to arrive. Cromwell's military prowess was supreme at Preston and by 19 August 1648, he had consummately out-manoeuvred Hamilton, cutting the Scottish Army into two and devastating it numerically. Langdale's entire infantry were annihilated; more than 1000 of Hamilton's soldiers were killed and 4000 taken prisoner. Hamilton himself escaped by swimming down the river Ribble. On 25 August, Hamilton surrendered and all that was left was for Cromwell and Lambert to wipe out the last few pockets of Royalist opposition. Cromwell steadily pursued Hamilton's retreating troops into Scotland where he allied with Hamilton's arch enemy the Duke of Argyll. By October, only Pontefract remained in Royalist hands: it was finally taken by Lambert in March 1649.

The outcome of the Second Civil War

In Carisbrooke Castle during August 1648, Charles received news of the collapse of his hopes for military victory and preparations began for a new round of treaty discussions to be held in Newport. It may have seemed to him that the endless cycle of negotiation and prevarication was going to resume.

> **ACTIVITY**
>
> **Summary**
>
> To help develop your understanding, create a table to compare the First Civil War and the Second Civil War in terms of similarities and differences. Consider leadership, aims, alliances and participants.
> Once this is complete, you will be able to reflect on the significance of the Second Civil War. Do you agree with the terminology of 'Second Civil War' or do you think a more appropriate name could be used for it?

> **STUDY TIP**
>
> Make sure you consider the provenance of these sources, particularly their dates so that your answer reflects the development of events and attitudes.

> **A LEVEL PRACTICE QUESTION**
>
> **Evaluating primary sources**
>
> With reference to Sources 2, 3 and 4, as well as your understanding of the historical context, assess the value of these three soures to an historian studying the Second Civil War.

20 The problem of Charles I

Divisions within the army and Parliament

As the Second Civil War unfolded, the question of what to do with the king began once again to open fissures between his opponents.

Charles I: 'the man of blood'

In April 1648, the Army Council had held a three-day prayer meeting at Windsor, during the course of which a belief was articulated that the king's continued war-mongering was evidence that he was himself God's enemy.

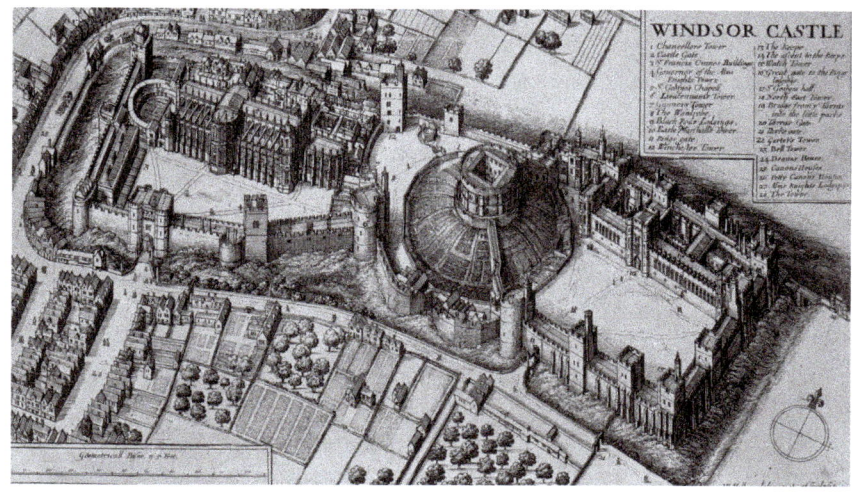

Fig. 1 *Windsor Castle was a substantial fortress in the mid-seventeenth century*

SOURCE 1

From a report by William Allen, an Agitator at the Council, in 1659 of the proceedings of the prayer meeting in: *A Faithful Memorial of that Remarkable Meeting of Many Officers of the Army in England, at Windsor Castle, in the Year 1648*:

The Lord directed our steps and led us to form a clear agreement among ourselves, without one voice of opposition. We recognised that it was our duty, with the forces we had, to go out and fight against our powerful enemies who had, in that year, appeared against us in a multitude of places. We had a humble confidence in the name of the Lord, that he would allow us to overpower them. We sincerely sought the will of the Lord and came to a clear and united resolution, all of us together. We had debated intensely and for several reasons decided that it was our duty, if ever the Lord brought us back in peace, to call Charles Stuart, that man of blood, to account for the blood he had shed and the mischief he had done to his utmost, against the Lord's cause and against the people in our sad nations. We acknowledged as well how the Lord had led and prospered us in all our undertakings this year.

The army was slowly but surely articulating a new perspective on the actions of God and king: in the First Civil War, king and Parliament had put God to the test and God had demonstrated that his judgement was against Charles. That the king had chosen to put God to the test again, 'against all the witnesses that God has borne', surely showed that he was beyond redemption. In turn,

LEARNING OBJECTIVES

In this chapter you will learn about:

- divisions within the army and Parliament
- the trial and execution of the king.

KEY CHRONOLOGY

1648	24 Aug	Parliament revoked the Vote of No Addresses
	18 Sept	Treaty of Newport discussions opened
	20 Nov	Remonstrance of the Army
	6 Dec	Pride's Purge
1649	4 Jan	House of Commons declares itself independent of king and Lords
	20 Jan	Trial of King Charles I commences
	27 Jan	Guilty verdict handed down
	30 Jan	Execution of King Charles I

A CLOSER LOOK

The man of blood

The phrase 'man of blood' was loaded with significance, deriving from 2 Samuel 16:7, an Old Testament book about King David. King David had disgraced himself by orchestrating the murder of an innocent man and forging an alliance with the enemies of Israel. The prophet Shimei was sent by God to expose David's sin: he cursed him for being a man of bloodshed and declared that God would pass the throne to another man.

> **ACTIVITY**
>
> Look back at previous voting statistics for Parliamentary business and plot a graph which shows the appetite for radicalism among the MPs. Can you see a correlation with other events?

> **A CLOSER LOOK**
>
> **Irish Confederates**
>
> In 1642, in response to the Puritan direction that the Westminster Parliament was taking, the Catholic 'Old English' and the Irish gentry created an alternative form of government for Ireland, which they called the Irish Confederation and which was headed up by a Confederate Assembly. This assembly had two houses, Lords and Commons, and met from 1642 to 1648 in Kilkenny. It was loyal to the king and determined to restore Catholicism throughout Ireland.

> **A CLOSER LOOK**
>
> **Ireton's role in 1648**
>
> Henry Ireton assumed a leading role in the army's political affairs during the autumn of 1648. Not only did he draft the Remonstrance but he also worked hard to manage the Leveller threat to army unity by instituting a renewed round of negotiations, based on a revision of the 'Agreement' which became known as the 'Whitehall Debates' in December. Although the same points that had caused division at Putney re-emerged, Ireton's actions meant that the Levellers continued to support the Grandees as the army moved back into London on 2 December.

this evolving perspective would shape the strategy and aims of Cromwell and the army in a way that would prove ultimately fatal for the king.

Parliament's attempt to reach settlement

As the Second Civil War drew to a close, some of the less radical Political Independents within Parliament began to move towards the Presbyterian position, driven by the need to bring order and stability back to the country. On 28th April 1648, the day before the Army Council began its prayer meeting at Windsor Castle, Parliament voted by 165 to 99 that it would not 'alter the fundamental Government of the Kingdom, by King, Lords and Commons'.

To the dismay of many within the army, Parliament revoked the Vote of No Addresses on 24th August, and preparations were put in hand for another peace conference with the king. This time, Parliament stipulated that the negotiations needed to be completed within 40 days.

The Treaty of Newport

Negotiations began in Newport, on the Isle of Wight, on 18th September 1648. The king negotiated directly with fifteen commissioners who represented the Lords and Commons, the Political Independents and the Political Presbyterians. For a while it appeared that progress was being made:

- The king agreed to a three year Presbyterian settlement while the Westminster Assembly drew up a permanent solution but would be allowed to continue to worship with episcopal ministers himself.
- All Royalists would be covered by an Act of Oblivion so they would not be punished for their role in the civil war
- The king would not swear the Covenant oath.
- Parliament would control the army and navy for 20 years
- Parliament would appoint state officials for 10 years
- The king would cease attempting to reach a settlement with the **Irish Confederates**.

Despite the 40-day stipulation, Parliament granted extensions to the negotiations and the talks dragged on.

Charles's actions

Once again, Charles continued to double-deal. Throughout the Newport negotiations, he was in secret communication with the Marquis of Ormond and told him that he would not be bound by anything he had agreed while in captivity. Events in Ireland were giving him some grounds for optimism because the Earl of Inchiquin, a successful military leader and formerly a Parliamentarian sympathiser, declared for the king in September and began to broker talks between the Royalists and Irish Confederates. Ormond, who had been in exile in France with Henrietta Maria, returned to Ireland in October with weapons paid for by the French king.

The army's response

Irrespective of affairs in Ireland, the New Model Army was growing increasingly dissatisfied with the Newport negotiations. **Henry Ireton** drafted a 'Remonstrance of the Army' which was discussed by the Army Council on 16th November and presented to Parliament on 20th November. In it, he reiterated the case that the king could not be trusted, affirmed the Vote of No Addresses, and demanded that 'the King be brought to Justice as the main cause of all, the author of that unjust war and therefore guilty of all the innocent blood split in the war and all the evils that occurred during or as a result of the war'. Equally radically, the Remonstrance recommended that a replacement king should only be appointed following an election held by a purged Parliament as the elected representatives of the people.

Pride's Purge

Parliament's response to the Remonstrance was to prevaricate, delaying discussion for a week, while on 5 December, it voted (129 for, 83 against) to continue the Newport negotiations. In late November, Fairfax had recalled Cromwell from Lancashire where he had been pursuing some last remnants of Royalist troops. By the time he returned to London on 6 December, a shocking and unique event in Parliamentary history had taken place. Earlier that day, one **Colonel Pride** had stood at the door of the Commons and prevented Political Presbyterians from entering, an event which became known as 'Pride's Purge'.

Fig. 2 *A depiction of Pride's Purge*

Pride's Purge was a well-planned and efficiently executed military coup. Ireton had led a committee of officers and MPs to create a longlist of about 180 MPs who should be excluded, and a shortlist of about 45 who should be arrested, including Holles (although he had fled the country) and William Prynne. Major General Philip Skippon, a popular New Model officer, persuaded the London Trained Bands to allow the army to act unopposed. Pride was supported by two officers who checked the identity of MPs as they arrived at Westminster.

With the excluded members held under armed guard in nearby Queen's Court, the remaining members passed a new Vote of No Addresses.

The response of the excluded members was to send in a Protestation on 11 December, entitled: *A Solemn Protestation of the imprisoned and secluded Members of the Commons House: Against the horrid force and violence of the Soldiers of the Army, on Wednesday and Thursday last*. The Protestation listed reasons for their utter outrage and dismay: 'That this appalling force and open violence upon our Persons, and the whole House of Commons… is the highest and most detestable force and breach of Privilege and Freedom ever committed against any Parliament of England… As a result, we consider ourselves duty bound to declare and publish to the world for fear our unwise silence should provide any tacit consent to this most detestable crime.'

The Solemn Protestation of the excluded members was rejected by the MPs who remained in Parliament, which became immediately known as the '**Rump.**' Attendees at Parliament for the rest of December averaged around eighty in the Commons with a peak of just eight peers in the Lords on 28 December.

A CLOSER LOOK

The army in London

The return of the army to London caused dismay among its citizens. Those who could leave the city did so, many removing all their wealth from government treasuries and causing what would be described in later centuries as a 'run on the bank'. Others remained in the capital, trying to defend their food and property and keeping out of the way. The army used St Paul's Cathedral as a stable, which shocked many moderate Londoners. Tensions ran high.

KEY PROFILE

Thomas Pride (unknown–1658) was a brewer in London just before the outbreak of the First Civil War and served under the Earl of Essex, reaching the rank of Colonel. Little else is known about his life.

A CLOSER LOOK

The Rump Parliament

William Prynne (see page 53) became MP for Newport, Cornwall, in 1648 and was one of the MPs who was excluded by Colonel Pride. In January 1649 he put the parliament's name into print by writing a pamphlet, *A New Year's Gift to the Rump Parliament*, which was a satirical attack on the MPs who remained in Parliament for betraying the ideals of Parliamentary democracy.

SECTION 5 | The disintegration of the Political Nation, 1646–1649

The role of Fairfax and Cromwell

Edmund Ludlow later claimed that he had informed Fairfax of the army's plan on the night before the Purge, but by December, General Fairfax was showing clear signs that he was feeling increasingly helpless and adrift. The furore that followed the executions after the Colchester siege and the continued failure to reach an agreement with the king led him to gradually withdraw from what had been his leading role. He later described Pride's Purge as 'that horrible attempt', and by the summer of 1649 he was living in retirement on his country estate. It is probable that he had little, maybe even no, influence over the events that led up to the Purge.

It is more difficult to shed light on Cromwell's precise role in proceedings. As Ireton was his son-in-law, it is probable that he knew what was being planned. However, he himself had remained in the north, despite the fact that he could have easily left military affairs up there to one of his subordinates, which suggests that he wanted to remain at a distance from events. In November, his cousin Robert Hammond (Governor of the Isle of Wight and therefore the king's main captor) had written to him to express anxiety that a purge by the army might be imminent. Cromwell's response reflects the influence of his religious beliefs on his political undertakings.

> **A CLOSER LOOK**
>
> **Viscount Saye and Sele** was another former activist who had reached the end of his radicalism by late 1648. He pleaded on his knees with the king to accept the terms of the Newport Treaty and thereafter retired from public life until 1660.

> **KEY TERM**
>
> **providence:** the protective care of God, thought by believers to provide good things for those who trusted him; Cromwell was a firm believer in providence, which meant that he interpreted successes in battle as evidence of providence, and worried that failures were evidence of God's displeasure

> **SOURCE 2**
>
> From Cromwell's letter to Robert 'Robin' Hammond, dated 25 November 1648, subsequently collected into a volume of his letters and speeches:
>
> Dear Robin, we are trapped by earthly and not godly reasoning. Was there not a little of this when Robert Hammond, through dissatisfaction too, desired retirement from the army and thought of quiet in the Isle of Wight? Did God not find him out there? Dear Robin, you and I were never worthy to be doorkeepers in this Service. If you wilt seek, seek to know the mind of God in all that chain of **Providence**, whereby God brought you thither and the King to you.
>
> My dear Friend, let us look into providences; surely they mean something. They hang so together; are so steady, so clear. Think about it - malice, real, sworn malice against God's people who are now called 'Saints', directed at crushing them. And yet, they, these Saints have been provided with arms and blessed with defence and more! All the Officers I know are finding themselves more blessed. Names, titles and authorities are all against us, and yet we are not terrified. We only desire to fear our great God and do nothing against His will.

> **ACTIVITY**
>
> Religious faith can be a powerful motivator. What are the possible advantages and disadvantages of a belief in providence? In what ways do you think that Cromwell's belief in providence influenced events in the autumn of 1648?

Clearly, whatever the nature of Cromwell's involvement in Pride's Purge, he had reached an understanding that it was God's will, displayed through providence, that was behind the rise of the army against the king.

The trial and execution of the king

On 15 December, the Army Council decided that it would use martial law to bring the king to trial. Cromwell insisted that they should first send one more set of settlement terms to the king, which they duly despatched in the care of the Earl of Denbigh. When the Earl of Denbigh arrived on 26th, Charles refused to acknowledge him.

In the meantime, the MP **Bulstrode Whitelock** noted in his diary that he and Cromwell spent the Christmas period endeavouring to persuade the king to abdicate in favour of a regency by his younger son Henry, Duke of Gloucester. (As Henry was aged just nine, and was being educated under

> **KEY PROFILE**
>
> **Bulstrode Whitelock (1605–75)** was a lawyer who brought his skills to bear in creating some of the key documents of the Long Parliament including the Act against Dissolution and the impeachment articles used against Strafford. He liaised closely with the king to try to reach a peace and was one of the Parliamentary Commissioners at the Uxbridge negotiations. He chose not to participate in the trial of the king.

Parliamentary supervision, this seemed as though it might be a workable compromise, but it came to nothing.)

By late December, undoubtedly keen to legitimise its authority, the Rump took over the reins of government from the Army Council and on 28th issued an Ordinance to create a special court to try the king on the charge that: 'By the fundamental Laws of this Kingdom, it is **Treason** in the King of England to levy War against the Parliament and Kingdom of England.'

The supremacy of the Rump

The House of Lords rejected the Commons' Ordinance relating to the king's trial, which posed a significant problem to the Rump. They shut the doors of the House and appointed a committee made up of, among others, the republican **Henry Marten**, Cromwell and Ireton. When they reported back later that day, they had reached another ground-breaking decision.

The Commons Journal for 4 January 1649 shows the unprecedented outcome of their deliberations. Based on the premise that the people were at the heart of the nation and the original source of power, the Committee explained that the House of Commons was the true representative of the people's collected will and that therefore the Commons on its own could create and pass laws, to be implemented with the full force of law, binding on everyone in the nation, without requiring the consent of the king or the House of Lords.

Clear of the king and House of Lords, the Commons independently created a High Court of Justice with which to try the king. They appointed 135 commissioners to sit as judges and set the trial date for 20th January 1649.

Preparations for the trial

The specially convened High Court of Justice was built on precarious legal foundations because, innovatively, it drew its legitimacy from the people rather than from the monarch, but the Rump did everything that they could to legitimise the appearance of its proceedings:

- The trial was to be held in the Great Hall at Westminster because it was the location at the heart of the justice system and it would be decorated sumptuously, with scarlet drapes over the benches and a crimson and gold chair for the **president**.
- Rails were brought in to create a viewing gallery so that the Court would be seen to reflect the will of the people.
- The College of Arms was consulted over what the participants should wear and the king's arms were removed from the walls and replaced by the Arms of St George. 'How like Judges they look for such a purpose, cloath'd in the scarlet of their rebellious sin, their Garments Roul'd in Blood; their ermin spotted with Carnation' was the judgement of the Royalist writer of the satirical paper, *Mercurius Pragmaticus*.

Even so, when the trial began, the novel proceedings caused some confusion as traditional practices were sometimes followed and at other times muddled up. One anecdote tells of the Serjeant-at-Arms, a soldier whose job included keeping order in the court. The Serjeant carried the **Mace** and one eye-witness described with some humour how he held it wrongly and put it on the wrong side of the king.

KEY TERM

treason: the crime of betraying one's country; this was a capital crime, which meant that a conviction automatically led to a sentence of death

KEY PROFILE

Henry Marten (1602–80) was an MP for Berkshire in the Short and Long Parliament, Marten was disliked by Charles, not least because of Marten's loose morals and reputation as a heavy drinker. Marten's radical views made him an enemy of John Pym, who engineered his temporary expulsion from the Commons in 1642, which lasted until 1645. He was one of the strongest backers of the Vote of No Addresses and a firm supporter of the Levellers, personally raising a regiment with a strong Leveller contingent for action in the Second Civil War.

KEY TERM

president: (High Court of Justice) responsible for ensuring that the trial would follow conventional legal processes; he controlled who could say what and at what point

CROSS-REFERENCE

There is a picture of the Commons' Mace on page 57.

ACTIVITY

According to this short source, what was the main objection of the writer of *Mercurius Pragmaticus* to the High Court?

SECTION 5 | The disintegration of the Political Nation, 1646–1649

Fig. 4 *Fearful of an assassination attempt, John Bradshaw wore a bullet-proof hat to the High Court*

Fig. 3 *The High Court of Justice turned the Great Hall at Westminster into a courtroom*

ACTIVITY

Thinking point

Using your knowledge of the historical context, why do you think the trial was controversial to the point that only half of the commissioners attended?

ACTIVITY

Conduct a class version of the trial of Charles I. Appoint a court president to manage proceedings and then divide into two groups and prepare prosecution and defence arguments relating to the items in the impeachment. Which are the easiest charges to prosecute or defend? Overall, which side has the stronger case?

The conduct of the trial

The President of the Court, John Bradshaw, used the example of King John and Magna Carta to provide a historical precedent for such an unprecedented event. He described how the honest barons of England saw their king acting like a tyrant and stood up to him, defending the liberty and assets of all Englishmen. Bradshaw challenged the Commons to do likewise with this king, even if the Lords were not as mindful of their honour and the good of the people as John's barons had been.

In reality, the extent to which the Commons could actually claim to be preserving English liberty was easy to call into question. While 135 commissioners had been selected, only around 70 actually attended the trial, while some, such as Fairfax, attended only on the first day and subsequently stayed away.

The legal arguments of the trial

The king was impeached as a 'Tyrant, Traitor, Murderer, and a public and unstoppable Enemy to the Commonwealth of England', because, 'while he was acknowledged as the rightful King of England and therefore entrusted with power to govern, limited only by the laws of this land, in order to use his power for the good and benefit of the people and for the preservation of their rights and liberties, nonetheless, he had implemented a wicked plan to create and maintain an unlimited and tyrannical power to rule according only to his will and thus to overthrow the rights and liberties of the people.'

The king's defence was straightforward and he made it clearly, without the stammer that had dogged him in his earlier years.

SOURCE 3

From the proceedings of the High Court of Justice at the trial of King Charles in January 1649, minuted by clerks in the courtroom and maintained in official records. In this source, the king set out the single issue on which he would defend himself:

I would know by what power I am called hither... I would know by what authority. Remember, I am your King, your lawful King, and you bring sins upon your heads, and the judgement of God upon this land. Think well upon it before you go further from one sin to a greater... I have a trust committed to me by God, by old and lawful descent, I will not betray it, to answer a new unlawful authority. I stand more for the liberty of my people, than any here that come to be my pretended judges... I do not come here as submitting to the Court. I stand as much for the privilege of the House of Commons, rightly understood. I see no House of Lords here, so this cannot be called a Parliament... Let me see a legal authority warranted by the Word of God, the Scriptures, or warranted by the constitutions of the Kingdom, and I will answer.

For two days the argument between Bradshaw and the king continued, as both tried to demolish the other's case about the legitimacy of the Court. Bradshaw could not draw the king into answering any of the charges brought against him because the king's default position was, 'I will answer the same as soon as I know by what authority you sent this.' Finally, Bradshaw changed tack. Accepting that the king did not acknowledge the authority of the court, he proceeded to bring witnesses and not allow the king to speak.

SOURCE 4

From an explanation by Judge Bradshaw by why he refused to allow the king to speak, recorded by the clerk and filed for posterity:

There is a contract and a bargain made between the King and his people, and your oath is taken: and certainly, Sir, the bond is reciprocal; for as you are their lord, so they are your subjects ... This we know now, the one tie, the one bond, is the bond of protection that is due from the sovereign; the other is the bond of subjection that is due from the subject. Sir, if this bond be once broken, farewell sovereignty! ... These things may not be denied, Sir ... Whether you have been, as by your office you ought to be, a protector of England, or the destroyer of England, let all England judge, or all the world, that has looked upon your actions ... You do not acknowledge us as a Court and therefore for you to address yourself to us, not acknowledging us as a Court to judge of what you say, it is not to be permitted. And the truth is, all along, from the first time you were pleased to disown us, the Court needed not to have heard you one word.

A series of witnesses was then brought to prove the king's guilt. One such witness testified to the king's presence at the slaughter of Edgehill, Naseby and Newark, which was taken as proof that the king had waged war on his subjects.

On the 27 January, the trial was brought to an end. The Clerk to the Court concluded with the sentence 'this Court doth adjudge that he the said Charles Stuart, as a Tyrant, Traitor, Murderer and Public Enemy to the good people of this Nation, shall be put to death, by the severing his head from his body'. Despite multiple protestations by the king, Bradshaw continued to prevent the king from speaking. He was led away, still protesting: 'I am not allowed to speak; how therefore can anyone be certain of justice in the future?'

Of the 135 commissioners who had been called to the trial, only 59 signed the death warrant.

ACTIVITY

Charles decided that his strongest line of defence was to challenge the authority of the court. Do you think this was his best option? Consider the charges brought against the king and use the example of Strafford's trial to help shape your thinking.

SECTION 5 | The disintegration of the Political Nation, 1646–1649

ACTIVITY

Pair discussion

In pairs discuss how a modern historian might feel reading the king's final words in Source 5 compared to a contemporary of the period, Royalist or Parliamentarian.

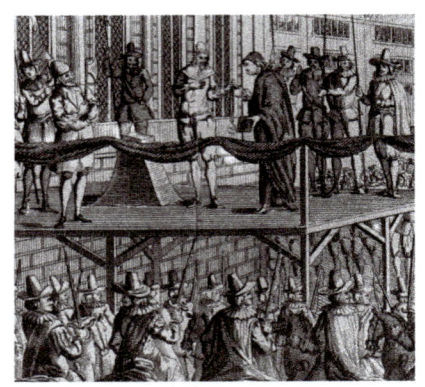

Fig. 5 *Charles I was executed on 30 January 1649 on a scaffold erected outside Whitehall Palace*

STUDY TIP

This question requires you to demonstrate your understanding of the provenance and content of some key sources relating to the trial and execution of Charles I. Don't forget to evaluate them in the light of your broader contextual knowledge.

STUDY TIP

To answer this question effectively, try to consider the religious arguments at the heart of the Civil War period, particularly the clash between ideas of Divine Right and the sovereignty of the people. It could also be useful to refer to 'other reasons' for Charles's execution in your answer.

The execution of the king

On 30 January 1649, Charles I was taken through the banqueting hall of Whitehall Palace, with its Ruben's ceiling that he had commissioned to glorify the Divine Right of Kings. Walking onto the scaffold, he composed himself for his last words.

SOURCE 5

From a report of the final words that King Charles spoken on the scaffold, 30 January 1649, from the Rushworth Collection:

I think it is my duty to God first and to my country to clear myself both as an honest man, a good king and a good Christian… I am not responsible for starting this war with the two Houses of Parliament and it was never my intention to encroach on their privileges. They began the war against me. … I only say this, that an unjust sentence that I have allowed to be passed against me is compounded now by an unjust sentence upon me. I have made it clear to you why I am an innocent man. As for the People, their liberty and freedom consists in having a Government over them: it is not necessary for them to have a share in Government. A subject and a sovereign are entirely different things. I am the Martyr of the people and I go from a corruptible to an incorruptible Crown, where no disturbance can be.

He knelt down: with one blow his head was severed and the period of English history known as the **Interregnum** had begun.

KEY TERM

Interregnum: a period represented by a lapse in the normal form of monarchy; in English history the period 1649–60, when England was governed as a republic

A LEVEL PRACTICE QUESTION

Evaluating primary sources

With reference to Sources 3, 4 and 5, and your understanding of the historical context, assess the value of these three sources to an historian studying the trial and execution of King Charles I.

A LEVEL PRACTICE QUESTION

'Charles I was executed because he refused to relinquish his belief in Divine Right.' Assess the validity of this view.

ACTIVITY

Summary

The pace of events from the collapse of the Newport Treaty negotiations to the trial of the king is quite breath-taking, particularly since the outcome – the execution of a reigning monarch – was so unprecedented. Using a detailed timeline will help you to identify the key drivers of these few short months. Start by plotting the main events onto it – such as Pride's Purge. Then, change colour, and incorporate people and their actions. Particularly note who pursued the trial and who withdrew and at what point.

6 Experiments in government and society 1648–1660

21 The Third Civil War

SOURCE 1

From the 31 January 1649 edition of the Royalist newspaper *Mercurius Elencticus*, which was published in London:

What terrible thing have the English to look forward to now that they have murdered their lawful sovereign, no tyrant nor an immoral and greedy King but the most generous, merciful and pious King found in **Christendom**? Let the justice of heaven pursue these bloody **regicides** to the pit of destruction for so cruelly, so inhumanly shedding his innocent blood.

The day he was brought to London, one of them told him thus, 'Sir' (says he), 'the Parliament are setting up scaffolds in Westminster Hall for your trial.' 'Well!' (said the King), 'I have no hope for I guess what they mean to do to me. If they murder me, I shall die with good company.'

But the man did not understand what he was saying and asked him what he meant by 'good company'. 'I mean', (says the King), 'true religion, law, prerogative, privilege and liberty, for those I think are good company, and I wish that I could be sure they will outlive me but I fear they will not.'

In the surge of pamphlets, papers, ballads and drawings that followed Charles's execution, extensive writings created powerful evocations of his dignity and deep forebodings of what might follow such a momentous act. One such **hagiographical** text, Eikon Basilike, ran to 46 editions within the year: allegedly the last musings of the king, it was a mysterious mix of prayer and political commentary that portrayed the king as the martyr of the English people, echoing the sacrifice of Jesus on the cross.

Fig. 1 *Frontispiece of* Eikon Basilike *from 1648; The text is a classic of the hagiographical genre*

LEARNING OBJECTIVES

In this chapter you will learn about:

- the attempted Royalist revival
- the defeat and exile of Prince Charles.

KEY CHRONOLOGY

1649	17 Jan	Second Ormond Agreement
	9 Mar	Execution of Royalist leadership
	Aug	Arrival of Cromwell's forces in Ireland
1650	Mar	Montrose Rising
	May	Treaty of Breda
	3 Sept	Battle of Dunbar
1651	3 Sept	Battle of Worcester

KEY TERM

Christendom: a collective term for Christian countries

regicide: the act of killing a king; also a person who takes part in killing a king

KEY TERM

hagiography: a genre of writing that focuses on the lives of the saints

SECTION 6 | Experiments in government and society 1648–1660

The attempted Royalist revival

Royalism in England

The execution of the king created an unprecedented governmental vacuum for which the country at large was not prepared. Broadly speaking, the majority of the Political Nation remained attached to the idea of monarchical government as witnessed by the fact that the charge against the king had been carefully limited to target the conduct of the one specific king and not the office itself. There was very little desire expressed to use the execution of this one king to create a republic. Even among the regicides, the men who signed the death warrant, the overwhelming majority had signed with a sense of weighty reluctance; very few were truly republican. This created a significant problem because there was no straightforward and obvious solution to the vacuum on the throne. **Prince Charles** had fled England in 1645. By 1648 he was living in The Hague at the court of his sister Mary and her husband, Prince William of Orange. Although he wanted to claim his birth right and become King Charles II, he was tarnished by his close involvement in the military and political manoeuvres of his father and the Catholicism of his mother.

With this in mind, it is true to say that while the army and the Rump were ready to embark on a republican experiment, the country at large was broadly monarchical in impulse but not supportive of Charles Stuart. There was nonetheless a small subset of the population wanting to actively promote the cause of Prince Charles, and these people formed the Rump of a Royalist party.

Execution of Royalist leaders

The likelihood of a military Royalist revival in England that would challenge the dominance of the Rump Parliament and bring about the accession of Charles II was dealt a catastrophic blow when five veteran Royalist leaders – including Henry Rich, Earl of Holland, James Hamilton, 1st Earl of Argyll and **Arthur Capell, 1st Baron Capell of Hadham** – swiftly followed Charles onto the scaffold, executed on 9 March for their roles in the Civil Wars.

Challenges faced by Charles Stuart

With the backbone of militant royalism in England broken, Prince Charles looked to his father's other kingdoms for support, but he faced particular challenges:
- From exile in the Dutch Republic, he found it difficult to co-ordinate military action.
- He had little financial support.
- He could not readily build a court because he did not have a permanent base.
- His ability to command authority was reduced and continued to dwindle as his difficult circumstances remained.
- The Irish and the Scots saw an opportunity to renegotiate their constitutional balance as the price for their loyalty to the Crown.

Royalism in Ireland

The Marquis of Ormond had been relatively successful in negotiating a settlement in Ireland on behalf of the king when he had returned to Ireland in October 1648. On 17 January 1649, he concluded an **Agreement** that brought together Confederates and Protestant Royalists into one movement, loyal to the Stuart monarchs. The death of Charles I did not therefore affect the Agreement as its terms were transferred to Charles Stuart who was immediately proclaimed rightful King of Ireland by Ormond.

A CLOSER LOOK

Prince Charles is known interchangeably as Charles Stuart. This is because his princely designation was not used by all contemporaries in England during the turbulent years after 1649, and so he was known by his Stuart family name. He was declared the Scottish and Irish King Charles II in 1649 but in this book he is not normally designated as King Charles II until his restoration to the English throne in 1660.

KEY PROFILE

Arthur Capell, 1st Baron Capell of Hadham (1608–49) was MP for Hertfordshire in the Long Parliament, where he offered mild criticism of the Personal Rule but he declared for the king and led the Royalist forces in Shropshire, Cheshire and North Wales. He surrendered to Fairfax at the Siege of Colchester 1648 and was kept imprisoned (despite a failed escape attempt) until trial on 6 February 1649. His wife petitioned Parliament for mercy but her request was refused and he was executed on 9 March 1649.

A CLOSER LOOK

The First Ormond Agreement was made in 1646 between Ormond, for King Charles I, and moderate Confederate Catholics, but its terms were not accepted by a powerful Catholic faction led by the papal nuncio in Ireland, and it was rejected by the Irish Assembly.

The terms of the Second Ormond Agreement included:
- 'Full assurance' that Catholics in Ireland would have equality with Irish Protestants, until the king could meet with them in a representative assembly to discuss all issues in full and reach an agreed and binding settlement. This included:
  - Freedom of worship for Catholics as well as Protestants
  - The lifting of the ban for Catholics of holding military and political office
- Dissolution of the Confederate government, to be replaced by 12 Commissioners, operating under Ormond, governing Confederates, Old English and Ulster Scots.
- Restructuring of the Irish-Royalist army, with Ormond at its head.

With this powerful bond created between Confederates and Protestant Royalists, Ormond began to press against the remaining Parliamentarian enclaves in Ireland. From The Hague, Prince Charles was encouraged by 'this great comfort to us in the midst of many and great misfortunes.' However, evidence of resurgent royalism from within Ireland was a significant security concern to the Rump because Ireland was a much-vaunted launching point for a foreign invasion and Ormond had close ties with Prince Charles and the French court. Fatefully, the English Parliament decided that the Irish problem needed, finally, to be resolved with force. Cromwell was offered the command, and accepted.

A CLOSER LOOK

Ormond counselled Prince Charles to be careful because his in-depth knowledge and experience of Irish political loyalties had taught him that the Agreement was a fragile instrument. As he wrote to the young prince, 'further new concessions may loose the hearts of the Protestants without whom your Majesties worke heere much less in England and Scotland is not to be done.'

ACTIVITY

Group discussion

Do you think Charles I would have accepted the Second Ormond Agreement, if he had lived?

Cromwell's Irish Campaign

Fig. 2 *Map of Ireland, 1649*

Cromwell maintained strict control over the 12,000-strong Parliamentary army which was, for once, adequately paid and properly equipped. Landing in August 1649, within nine months, he had comprehensively defeated Ormond's forces, but at the cost of a devastating and enduring legacy.

The massacres of Drogheda and Wexford

Bishop Nicholas French, a Roman Catholic leader among the Irish Confederates, later wrote, 'Cromwell came over and like a lightning passed through the land.' His strategy involved a rapid series of brutal sieges around key Royalist strongholds starting in early September with Drogheda, a town of considerable strategic value on account of its position to the north of Dublin. Controlling Drogheda cut Dublin off from help from Ulster. With the fall of Drogheda, the New Model Army moved on to Wexford, a significant port south of Dublin and the likely staging point for a Royalist invasion force boosted by troops from France or Spain. Wexford fell on 13 October 1649. Cromwell had, through decisive action, superior soldiery and excellent leadership, reduced Ormond's army to 3,000 men, secured his own ship-borne supply lines from England, and neutralised the threat of a continental invasion.

There is no greater example of Cromwell's willingness to act with utmost brutality for a cause that he felt was justifiable before God than his command of the sieges of Drogheda and Wexford. While he defended his actions to Parliament as 'a righteous justice... a just judgement upon them who [were] made with their blood to answer the cruelties which they had exercised upon the life of divers poor Protestants,' controversy has raged about the extent to which he broke conventions of seventeenth-century warfare (and basic human morality) by putting two entire towns, civilian and military populations alike, to the sword in a wholesale slaughter. While it may seem – especially to modern sensibilities – that his actions were unconscionable, in fact there was considerable recent military precedent for this strategy, an example being the brutal massacre of Protestants in Magdeburg, Germany, by a Hapsburg Catholic army in 1631. Moreover, memories of the 1641 Irish rebellion and particularly the brutal treatment meted out to the Protestants by the Catholics had already created an environment of savage brutality in Ireland.

The conclusion of the campaign

Cromwell's devastating efficiency threw Ormond's fragile coalition into turmoil. Among his soldiers, food and equipment were running out, and the reputation of the New Model Army caused a steady rise in desertions. Repeated rumours of the imminent arrival of Prince Charles, which never occurred, sapped confidence and also caused Ormond significant anxiety because he knew that reinforcements from Catholic Spain or France would be very likely to alienate his Protestant supporters. It was becoming clear that when pushed to choose between royalism and survival, many Irishmen were choosing the latter. Although skirmishes and some pitched battles continued, Ormond knew that he was losing the war because he could not maintain Royalist momentum. Communications from Prince Charles were so infrequent that in the winter of 1649, Ormond wrote to his contact at the court of Henrietta Maria: 'It made it incredibly difficult to maintain momentum because we were so in the dark about the king's intentions and his ability to act. In fact, this ignorance was to some degree a significant cause of our problems because without regular contact, reassuring us that the king was preparing to help us, our people felt that they had been utterly abandoned.'

Gradually Ormond himself became the focus of Irish discontent from virtually all quarters and his leadership was dealt a mortal blow in the summer of 1650 when Prince Charles secured an agreement with Scotland that

---

KEY PROFILE

Bishop Nicholas French (1604–78) was born in Wexford, and trained to become a Catholic Priest. He became one of the leading figures in the Confederacy and was a bitter opponent of Ormond's faction. In 1650 he tried to persuade the French Duc de Lorraine to bring a force to beat back Cromwell and then become Protector of Ireland. He did not succeed, however, and from then on lived in exile on the continent.

Fig. 3 *This later depiction of the Massacre of Drogheda captures the sense of horror that the assault generated*

required him to reject the Ormond Agreement. Ormond felt that he had no choice but to resign from his leadership position in the Confederation as, 'I have lost the meanes of Ballanceing the partys, or of bridging them to reason.' The fleeting Irish Royalist revival was dashed to pieces.

Ormond's increasing inability to lead an effective response to Cromwell and his eventual resignation caused him to be scapegoated as the central factor in causing Ireland's suffering, which was prolonged and deep.

> **SOURCE 2**
>
> From *The Unkind Deserter of Loyal Men and True Friends*, written in 1676 by the Irish Catholic Bishop Dr Nicholas French, who went into exile in Europe following Cromwell's invasion of Ireland:
>
> All our enemies used much cunning and cruelty in destroying Catholic Ireland but Ormond surpassed them all; …the holy Cromwellian crew did no less or more than we expected; after all, they were very powerful and they went all-out to be our mortal enemies. We never trusted them though, so at least they did not betray our trust.
>
> But Ormond betrayed our trust and so acquired a black stain of notoriety even though he was a peer of the highest status, of great lineage from Catholic and Noble ancestors. He did not prove himself to be a pillar of strength to his nation but became a bruised and rotten piece of straw, deserting us in our time of crisis. We deserved to share in the blame for allowing the ruin of our country, because we sinned by placing our trust in Ormond. Nations overseas were shocked at our devastation, not least because our King promised so much to us and yet gave us up as sacrifices to our enemies, without considering the innocence of the trust we placed in him.

Royalism in Scotland

In Scotland the situation was different. It is indicative of the ambivalence of the regicides that the Rump swiftly passed measures to abolish the monarchy in England and Ireland but not in Scotland. (The Rump's action will be discussed in greater detail in the next chapter.) The Scots rejected the English Parliament's proposal to break the union and to launch Scotland as an entirely independent kingdom without any ties to England, albeit under the rule of Charles I's son.

Instead, the Scots stuck to their Covenant, interpreting it as a moral and religious obligation that bound them to the restoration of Charles II as 'the righteous heir and lawful successor to the kingdoms of Britain and Ireland by the providence of God and by the lawful right of undoubted succession and descent.' As the Scottish Royalist James Graham, Marquis of Montrose, affirmed to Prince Charles, 'I desired to live only to serve your father and I swear I am prepared to die in your service.' The Scottish interpretation of their dutiful service would open a renewed war, this time between Scotland and England over the future of Britain.

Conditions placed on Charles Stuart by the Scots

The Scots were loyal to the Stuarts but bitter experience had taught them that loyalty needed to be moderated by good sense and legal guarantees. As a result, they simultaneously swore allegiance to their new king while innovating in the terms with which they did so. On 7 February 1649, two days after the Scottish Parliament proclaimed Prince Charles as King Charles II, it passed an act that defined his constitutional position. Until he agreed to these innovatory terms, he would be refused entry into Scotland – monarch in title but not yet 'admitted to the exercise of his royall dignitie':

> **ACTIVITY**
>
> Use this opportunity to revise your understanding of the National Covenant and Solemn League and Covenants. To what extent did Charles Stuart agree to terms that his father had resisted?

> **A CLOSER LOOK**
>
> **Scottish concern over Stuart Catholicism**
>
> The Scots believed that Charles I had wilfully disregarded their sound advice, which had led directly to his death, and were concerned that his son would display the same stubborn traits. They counselled Prince Charles to take care to manage his mother's Catholicism better, identifying it as having been one of the main causes of the trouble that had afflicted the Stuart kingdoms.

- Subscribe to and sustain the National and Solemn League and Covenants.
- Maintain the Scottish Presbyterian Church settlement.
- Establish a Presbyterian settlement in England and Ireland, which meant repudiating the Second Ormond Agreement.

The attitude of the Scots to their new King Charles provoked intense debate among members of his exiled court. Should he allow his royal authority to be so limited? Was Scottish support of greater value than Irish allegiance, since one would probably preclude the other? Like his father, Charles prevaricated and delayed the Scottish Commissioners, who had been sent to negotiate his return. Ultimately, as Cromwell fought his way through Ireland, Charles moved towards the Scottish solution.

The Montrose Rising

Charles Stuart hoped that a show of military force would improve his negotiating position and enable him to reach an agreement that preserved more royal prerogative and enforced a tighter definition of allegiance onto his Scottish subjects. In early 1650, hoping to ignite a traditional Royalist revival, the Marquis of Montrose led a small force of mercenaries in an attempt to raise the Highland clans and thereafter sweep Charles into a coronation in Edinburgh.

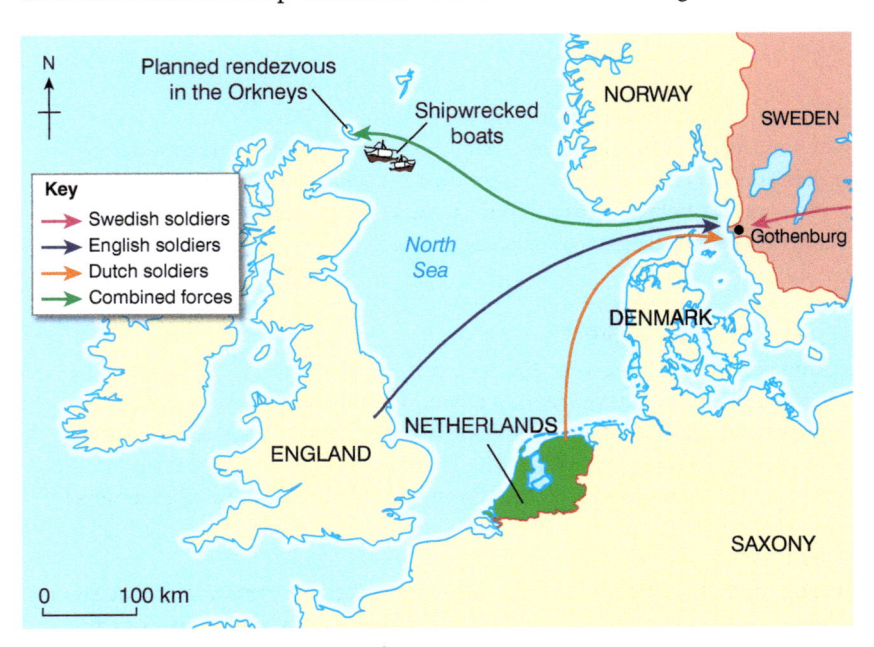

Fig. 4 *Montrose lost many men to the sea*

SOURCE 3

From a report of Montrose's expedition recounted by Sir James Stewart of Coltness, Provost of Edinburgh, in February 1650:

More of Montrose's men landed this week in the Orkney Islands but the greatest part of his men and vessels are spoiled and lost; for, of twelve hundred he shipped from the seaside, near Gottenburg in Sweden, there are no more than two hundred landed in Scotland. For when they had sailed about two leagues from the shore, they were shattered by sticking in the ice; many died, others afterwards got ashore and deserted, and they were much broken. There came only two ships, with two hundred soldiers and their officers; twelve small brass cannons, and a small number of arms, with a parcel of ammunition. Montrose himself is yet at Gottenburg, with some Scotch, English, and Dutch officers, waiting to see if he can get any monies for them; if not, they will desert him.

In March, Montrose's forces crossed onto the Scottish mainland but there was very little will to fight among the clans; his army was defeated at the Battle of Carbisdale and the Marquis himself was captured and would be executed on 21 May. Charles Stuart rapidly distanced himself from Montrose.

SOURCE 4

> From the official minutes of the Scottish Parliament proceedings of 25 May 1650, taken by the **Lord Lyon**, Sir James Balfour:
>
> Noted: Saturday, 25th May. A letter from the King's Majesty to the Parliament, dated from Breda, 12th May 1650, showing he was heartily sorry that James Graham, Marquis of Montrose, had invaded this kingdom, and how he had tried to persuade him against so doing; and earnestly desires Parliament to do himself that justice as not to believe that he was accessory to the said invasion in the least degree… Also a double of his Majesty's letter to James Graham, date 15th May commanding him to lay down arms and secure all ammunition under his charge. Also read in the House, a letter from the Secretary, the Earl of Lothian, which showed him that his Majesty was no ways sorry that James Graham was defeated, in respect, as he said, he had made that invasion without and contrary to his command.

A CLOSER LOOK

The **Lord Lyon** is a Scottish office of state rather than a person, with responsibilities that include registering new tartan patterns as well as the performance of administrative and clerical tasks. Sir James Balfour held the office between 1630 and 1654.

The Treaty of Breda

With the failure of the Montrose rising and the collapse of Ormond's resistance in Ireland, and despite significant misgivings, Charles considered the Scottish Parliament's proposal for a settlement which would place limitations on his prerogative powers. He was still in exile, now in the Dutch Republic city of Breda.

The Scottish Parliament's main terms:
- compulsory subscription to the Covenant
- king and family to become Presbyterians
- no toleration for Catholicism in any of the kingdoms
- recognition of the Covenanter-dominated Scottish Parliament and all its Acts since 1641
- all recent treaties to be annulled (this included the Ormond Agreement).

Negotiations over the settlement

Among many sticking points for Charles were the requirements that he should condemn his father, censure his mother and her Catholicism, lose control over political appointments, and accept that his subjects saw their loyalty to Presbyterianism as greater than their loyalty to their monarch. The Scots were nonetheless resolute: they insisted that Charles II should acknowledge that his father's catastrophe originated in his ill-advised 'opposition to the work of God', and required the son to demonstrate that he loved and honoured 'Jesus Christ more than father or mother.'

Confirmation of the Treaty of Breda

Ultimately, Charles's need for support outweighed his scruples and the settlement was signed as the Treaty of Breda on 1st May 1650.

The Battle of Dunbar

Having signed the Treaty, Charles was welcomed to Scotland and arrived in June 1650. Faced with the prospect of a king in the field, the English Parliament decided to despatch an army in a **pre-emptive** invasion of Scotland. For General Fairfax, the prospect of another war – this time against his old Scottish allies – was too much and he retired to his country estate.

CROSS-REFERENCE

Two significant documents were issued from Breda. The 1660 Declaration of Breda is discussed on page 210.

KEY TERM

pre-emptive: an action taken in order to prevent an anticipated event from happening

SECTION 6 | Experiments in government and society 1648–1660

Fig. 6 *Events of the Third Civil War*

KEY CHRONOLOGY

Events of the Third Civil War

1649	Sept	Storm of Drogheda; Cromwell neutralises threat of invasion from Ireland
1650	Sept	Battle of Dunbar; Cromwell delays threat of invasion from Scotland
1651	Sept	Battle of Worcester; defeat of Charles Stuart and Scots

CROSS-REFERENCE

Leslie's actions at Marston Moor can be found on page 197.

KEY TERM

scorched-earth policy: a military strategy of burning or destroying crops or other resources that might be of use to an invading enemy force

CROSS-REFERENCE

Religious radicalism of the sectaries in the New Model Army is discussed on page 128.

Fresh from victory in Ireland, Oliver Cromwell now replaced Fairfax at the pinnacle of the New Model Army. As the new Lord General, he led 7500 foot soldiers and 3500 cavalry up to Scotland where they were faced by the veteran army of **David Leslie**, the hero of Marston Moor.

Leslie commanded 22,000 men and swiftly gained the upper hand, denying provisions to the advancing New Model Army through a **scorched-earth policy**, and corralling them into the surrounds of Dunbar on the west coast, cutting off their line of retreat into England. Cromwell warned the garrison at Newcastle, commanded by Haselrig, to expect an invasion. Perhaps the Scots were complacent, but Cromwell planned a tactical masterstroke, outflanking Leslie's troops under cover of nightfall on 2nd September and attacking them at dawn. The Scottish Army, caught totally by surprise, fled in confusion while Cromwell rallied his troops with the Old Testament battle cry, 'Let God arise and his enemies shall be scattered!' It was an incredible victory for the New Model Army and was followed by the occupation of Edinburgh by Cromwell.

Defeat and exile of Prince Charles

Paradoxically, defeat on Scottish soil somewhat boosted the Royalist cause within Scotland. While skirmishes between the remnant of Leslie's army and Cromwell's troops continued sporadically, will was building for another aggressive thrust by the Scots. This time, the Church began to take a lead in warmongering in order to defend Scotland against the pernicious influence of the 'sectaries' in the New Model Army.

The Battle of Worcester

Following an act of the Scottish Parliament in December 1650, convicted Royalists were given leave to fight alongside Covenanters in a renewed Scottish Army. Hoping to avenge the defeat at Dunbar and trigger a Royalist revival within England, in the early summer of 1651 Charles Stuart (King Charles II of Scotland) himself led the invasion force, with an eventual target of reaching London.

On 3 September 1651, the first anniversary of the Battle of Dunbar, Charles Stuart and the New Model Army met at Worcester:

Table 1 *Royalist and army losses at the Battle of Worcester*

	Royalists, commanded by Charles Stuart	New Model Army, commanded by Cromwell
Forces	12,000 (mainly Scottish)	28,000
Losses (dead)	3000	200
Losses (captured)	7000	

Cromwell's strategy

The Battle of Worcester was a masterpiece of military strategy by Oliver Cromwell, requiring considerable co-ordination by different military units.

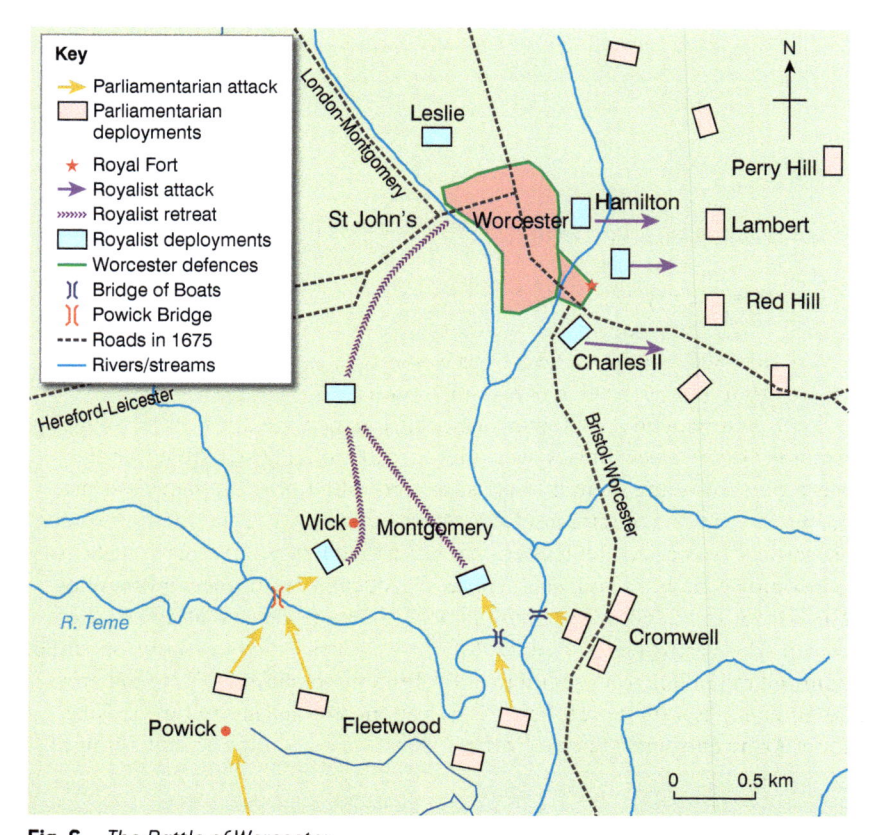

Fig. 6 *The Battle of Worcester*

The outcome of the battle

By the end of the day, most of the Royalist commanders and many Royalist rank and file were dead or captured, and Charles Stuart was on the run, desperately trying to avoid being taken prisoner. In stark contrast, losses in the New Model Army reached only about two hundred. Cromwell confidently credited providence for such a decisive victory and looked soberly towards the future.

SOURCE 5

From a report sent by Cromwell from the battlefield on 4 September to William Lenthall, Speaker of the House of Commons:

The dimensions of this mercy are above my thoughts. For all I know, this may prove to be the final, crowning mercy. If it is not quite that then surely we shall soon finally triumph, it my report causes everyone to be thankful and encourages Parliament to do the will of Him who has done His will for it, and for the Nation; God, whose good pleasure is to establish the Nation and the Change of the Government, by making the People so willing to defend it and so signally blessed in this great work. I am bold enough to humbly beg that everyone's thoughts might promote His honour because it is He who has provided such a salvation, and that we might take care to make sure that His mercy does not lead to pride or immorality in us. Instead, let the fear of the Lord keep His authority and His people blessed, humble and faithful. In this way, justice and righteousness, mercy and truth may flow from Parliament, as a thankful return to our gracious God.

The looked-for Royalist revival in England had not materialised. It took Charles Stuart six weeks to reach the safety of exile in France, during which time he disguised himself by dressing as a farmer and even hid in an oak tree in the grounds of Boscobel House in Shropshire. He would remain on the continent until 1660.

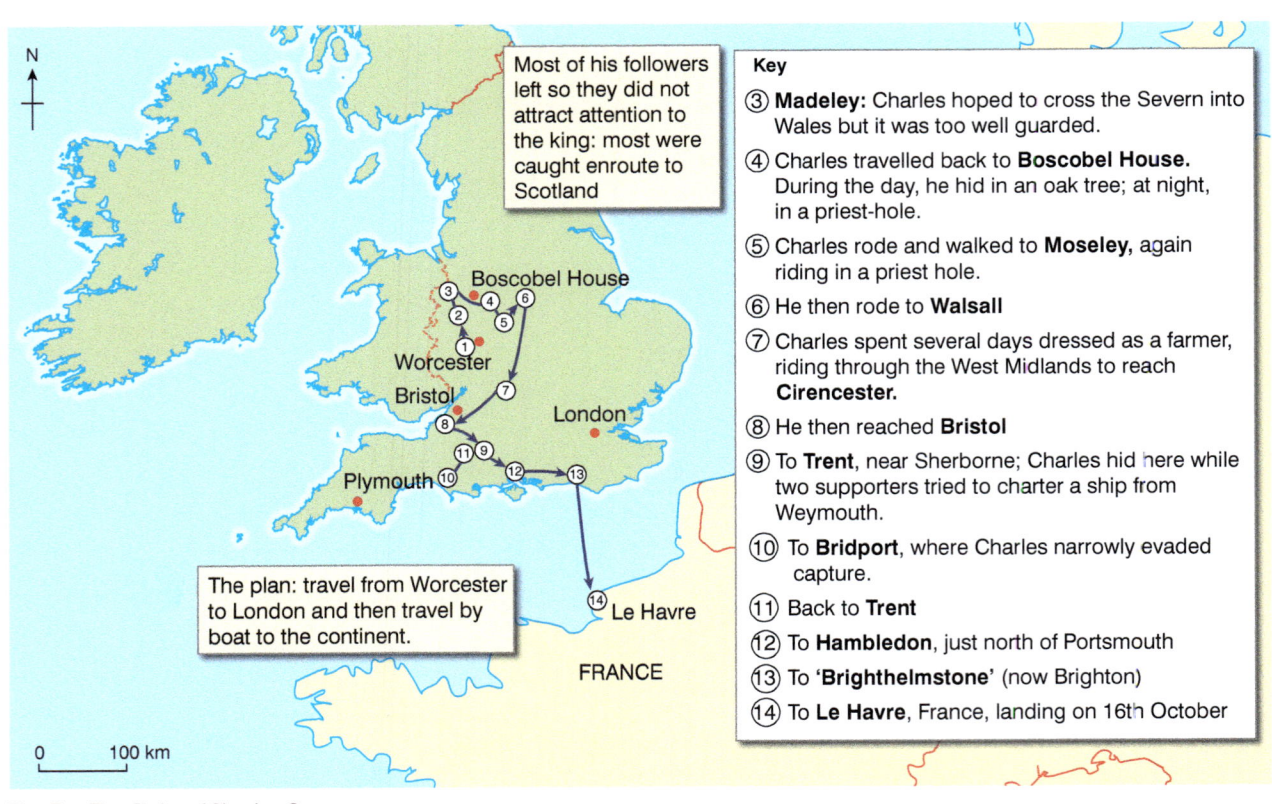

Most of his followers left so they did not attract attention to the king: most were caught enroute to Scotland

Key
③ **Madeley:** Charles hoped to cross the Severn into Wales but it was too well guarded.
④ Charles travelled back to **Boscobel House.** During the day, he hid in an oak tree; at night, in a priest-hole.
⑤ Charles rode and walked to **Moseley,** again riding in a priest hole.
⑥ He then rode to **Walsall**
⑦ Charles spent several days dressed as a farmer, riding through the West Midlands to reach **Cirencester.**
⑧ He then reached **Bristol**
⑨ To **Trent,** near Sherborne; Charles hid here while two supporters tried to charter a ship from Weymouth.
⑩ To **Bridport,** where Charles narrowly evaded capture.
⑪ Back to **Trent**
⑫ To **Hambledon,** just north of Portsmouth
⑬ To **'Brighthelmstone'** (now Brighton)
⑭ To **Le Havre,** France, landing on 16th October

The plan: travel from Worcester to London and then travel by boat to the continent.

Fig. 7 *The flight of Charles Stuart*

CHAPTER 21 | The Third Civil War

ACTIVITY

Summary

A valid interpretation of these turbulent years sees the Civil War period end with the execution of Charles in 1649; Cromwell's campaign in Ireland as a deliberate attempt at conquest by an aggressive Rump; and Parliament's war with Scotland as a fresh conflict between two sovereign powers. A different, but also valid, interpretation considers the Irish and Scottish campaigns of 1649 to 1653 as constituting a Third Civil War. Make notes to support these different viewpoints and then decide which you think is more historically valid, or propose your own interpretative model.

A LEVEL PRACTICE QUESTION

Evaluating primary sources

With reference to Sources 1, 2 and 4 and your understanding of the historical context, assess the value of these three sources to an historian studying the Third Civil War of 1649 to 1653.

STUDY TIP

Assess both the provenance and content of the sources to provide an evaluation that is supported by source detail and shows your own contextual understanding.

A LEVEL PRACTICE QUESTION

'The failure of the Royalist cause in the years 1649 to 1651 was the result of the conflicting alliances made by Prince Charles.'
Assess the validity of this view.

STUDY TIP

You could use your notes from the summary activity to help answer this question. It will be helpful to define what you understand by civil war and why or why not the term is appropriate for the 1649 to 1653 campaigns.

22 Political radicalism

LEARNING OBJECTIVES

In this chapter you will learn about:

- failure of the Levellers and Diggers and the 'Godly Society'
- Quakers, Baptists and other radical sects
- the Rump Parliament as an experiment in radical republicanism
- the Parliament of the Saints.

KEY CHRONOLOGY

1649	Feb	Establishment of the Council of State
		Publication of *England's Chains Discover'd*
	17 Mar	Abolition of the 'kingly office' in England
	19 Mar	Abolition of the House of Lords
	April	Establishment of the Digger Community in Surrey
1650	Aug	Blasphemy Act
1653	April–Dec	The Nominated (Barebones) Assembly

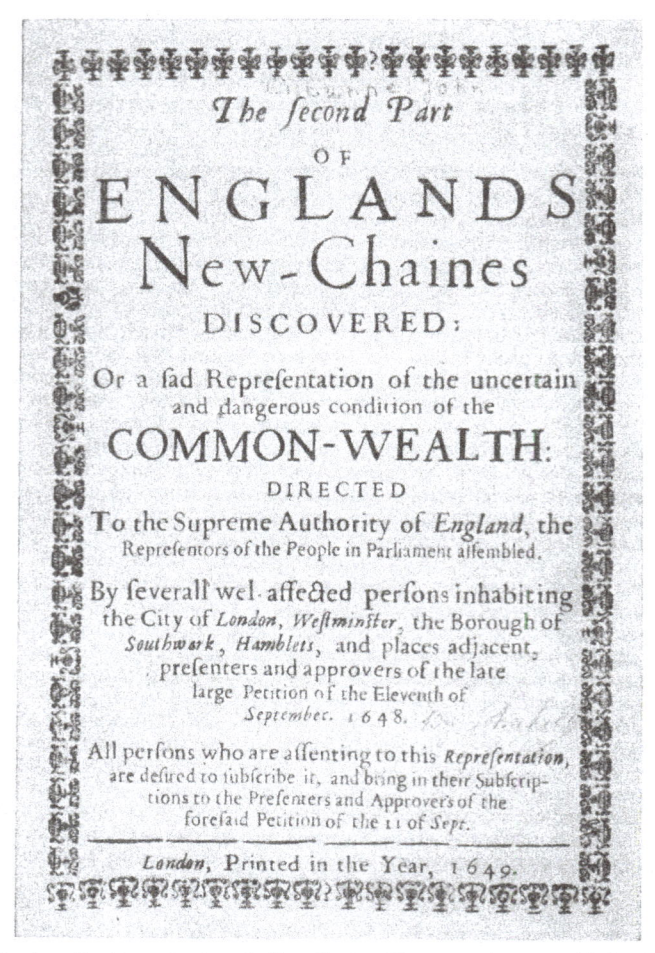

Fig. 1 *The Leveller Tract,* England's New Chains Discovered, *was published in 1649 and contained strong criticism of the Rump Parliament and the army Grandees*

ACTIVITY

Identify the key words in the tract in Figure 1 that indicate to you that this is a Leveller publication.

Failure of the Levellers and Diggers and the 'Godly Society'

The execution of the king was a unique moment in English history. It took the Commons a week to organise themselves to debate formally what to do next. The judgement on Charles I had declared that there could be no future king 'without the free consent of the people in parliament', but beyond that lay an empty slate. Initially they considered whether to hand the Crown on to one of the Stuart princes, but this proved practicably impossible and politically divisive. On 7 February 1649, Cromwell proposed a motion 'for abolishing the kingly office', which passed the Commons on 17 March. Two days later, the House of Lords was abolished. For the Levellers, the Rump did not do nearly enough.

The failure of the Levellers

Ireton had managed to maintain sufficient cohesion between the Levellers and Grandees of the New Model Army to get through the turbulent weeks of late 1648, but by early 1649 the breach between the Levellers and the Rump was widening to a point beyond which it could not be healed.

The Leveller complaint

The Levellers denounced the Rump because it did not address the fundamental issue of Parliamentary representation, which they saw as being the most important constitutional consideration. To the Levellers, unless representation was fair and equal, no constitutional settlement could be acceptable and they feared that the Rump was aiming to become equally as tyrannical as the king. In fact, unfounded rumours circulated in January that the Levellers were planning to join forces with Royalists to mount a challenge to the Rump. On 26 February, Lilburne published an aggressively critical pamphlet, *England's New Chains Discovered*. Speaking on behalf of the 'citizens of London and the borough of Southwark', he attacked the Grandees for betraying what people had fought for. He appealed to the army, Londoners and others to reject the rule of what he considered to be a new oppressor – the Rump Parliament.

SOURCE 1

From the pamphlet, *England's New Chains Discovered*, which was written by John Lilburne and published for widespread distribution in February 1649:

We have seen and heard many things recently which have made us worry about our present circumstances and fear that we are heading into a new period of oppression and ruin that will affect us all.

We are aghast and astonished about this because this nation has developed the highest notions of what freedom means than has ever been articulated, in this country or among any other people in this world. What is more, a vast expense of blood and treasure has been used to buy these freedoms and God has most definitely been pleased to honour us with many famous and even miraculous victories. Even the House of Commons itself has suffered more than once at the hands of its own members, with unprecedented complaints and real pains, all for the sake of obtaining these, our native liberties.

But what has been the purpose of all this effort, and where is the liberty that we so strove for, so dearly purchased? For now this House has voted itself the supreme authority, even taking onto itself the power of the House of Lords!

The Rump's response

Cromwell and Ireton were driving events in the Rump and they made use of its authority to disperse the Leveller threat. Lilburne and other leading Levellers were arrested on the orders of Parliament in March 1649 and charged with treason. Despite the imprisonment of their leaders, during the spring of 1649, the Levellers stirred up two significant mutinies in the army, angry that the Rump had not yet settled arrears of pay, resistant to being sent to fight in Ireland, and incited by the publication of a new Leveller pamphlet, *The Third Agreement of the People*.

The first mutiny started in Colonel Whalley's regiment in April, when soldiers refused to leave their quarters for a muster at Mile End Green, just outside London, prior to despatch for London. It took personal persuasion from Cromwell and Fairfax to disperse the mutiny, and the ringleader's execution (as inciting mutiny was a capital crime) was followed by a significant demonstration of Leveller support as a procession marched through London wearing ribbons in Leveller colours.

The second mutiny in May 1649 was more dangerous. Five cavalry regiments mutinied and a Leveller soldier led a mutiny among the militia of Banbury. Fairfax and Cromwell were again successful in suppressing the mutinies, this time by a night-time assault by Cromwell. The church at Burford was used as a temporary prison for several hundred mutineers, three of whom

A CLOSER LOOK

Leveller attacks on the Grandees

Lilburne singled out Cromwell for particular attack, as 'the pretended false Saint Oliver', finding him guilty of meddling, trickery and cynical politicking. He accused Cromwell along with the other Grandees, of hating 'the Liberties of England more than they do the Devil'. In a pamphlet of March 1649, probably drafted by Lilburne with Overton, entitled *The Hunting of the Foxes*, the Grandees were attacked as 'Wolves in Sheep's clothing, Foxes in the habits of Saints'.

ACTIVITY

Rewrite Lilburne's comments in modern-day language.

ACTIVITY

Discuss in pairs why the Leveller perspective, that the army Grandees were becoming new tyrants, could have been justified. Use your prior learning to ensure you are precise in your application of historical context and terminology.

CROSS-REFERENCE

The first Leveller Agreement of the People is discussed on page 146.

Fig. 2 This woodcut represents a Digger community

were subsequently executed in the churchyard, having been identified as ringleaders.

The Rump swiftly passed measures to pay army arrears which satisfied the discontent that provided the basis of Leveller support within the army. Although Lilburne was acquitted at his trial in September 1649, the Leveller movement was effectively over.

The Diggers

An off-shoot of the Levellers emerged in late 1648 under the inspiration of two former members of the Merchant Taylors' Company, William Everard and Gerrard Winstanley. These self-declared 'True Levellers' took the basic Leveller idea of equality, merged it with religious radicalism, and applied it not so much to politics as to property.

Overview of the Digger leaders

Gerrard Winstanley (1609–1676)	William Everard (1602–1651)
Born in Wigan, Lancashire	Born in Reading, Berkshire
Both men trained as tailoring apprentices in the London Merchant Taylors' Company, where they met and became friends.	
He was made bankrupt by the collapse of the cloth trade with Ireland during the economic turmoil of the First Civil War and moved out to Cobham in Surrey to find work on a farm.	Arrested and imprisoned in 1648 for causing a disturbance in Kingston, Surrey, which prompted Winstanley to publish a pamphlet in his defence.

SOURCE 2

From Gerrard Winstanley's tract, *The New Law of Righteousness*, January 1649, laying out his radical vision for the earliest Digger communities:

In the beginning of time God made the earth and he never said that one branch of mankind should rule over another, but selfish imaginations set up one man to teach and rule over another… So long as there are rulers like this who claim that they own the land, the common people shall never enjoy liberty nor will the land ever be free from troubles, oppressions, and grumbling, behaviour which offends and provokes the Creator of all thing. Sinful man thinks it is good that some men are particularly well provided for and, because they are rich (whether they became wealthy honourably or not), should be allowed to be magistrates, to rule over the poor. That sinful man also thinks it is quite justifiable that the poor should be servants, even slaves, to the rich. But the spiritual man, modelling himself on Christ, makes good judgements according to the light of equality and reason, so that all mankind should have enough for their bodily needs and freedom to live upon the earth and no man should have to slave or beg in the whole of God's holy earth.

ACTIVITY

Winstanley's vision for a model community was very radical for his time. Discuss in pairs what you consider to be the most innovative idea that he introduced, and then suggest how a critic might respond to his teaching.

KEY TERM

common land: land that belongs to a community as a whole, with shared ownership and protected rights, such as the right to graze sheep on its grass

In April 1649, Winstanley and Everard founded a community of True Levellers in the parish of Walton-on-Thames in Surrey. Occupying first St George's Hill and subsequently Cobham Heath, they began to dig vegetable plots on **common land**, so that they could, in the words that Winstanley had heard in a vision, 'Work Together. Eat Bread Together.'

Digger beliefs

Diggers focused on a line in the New Testament book of Acts, 'All who believed were together and had all things in common; they would sell their possessions and goods and distribute the proceeds to all, as any had need' to develop the idea that God had created the earth to be a resource equally shared among the whole of humanity, with no-one in authority over another. For this reason, they rejected the very concept of monarchy, reckoning it to be an instrument of oppression introduced into England by William the Conqueror. They saw the upheaval of the Civil War as being significant because it threw off this 'Norman Yoke' and they passionately hoped that a new era was going to be ushered in – an era of the Commonwealth. They thought that a first step towards this Commonwealth would be for poor and dispossessed people to group together into communities who would dig on common land, growing crops to share.

Opposition to the Diggers

The community at St George's Hill was dispersed within six months, mainly because of local pressure, particularly from the church minister and landowners, but by then the movement had reached a high enough profile to have been given the nickname 'Diggers' and for Fairfax to have visited the community to question Winstanley and Everard in person. Digger communities were established in nine other counties, including Nottinghamshire, Kent and Gloucestershire, but none survived for long. There were a number of reasons why the Digger movement did not thrive:

- Their approach to property caused anxiety among local landowners who feared their own property would be threatened if the movement spread. The church, with all its lands, would be particularly vulnerable.
- It was easy to attack them as being disorderly because they went against social conventions.
- They were easily (although wrongly) accused of being Ranters by people who misunderstood the nature of their communities.
- Winstanley in particular developed a heretical belief that all mankind would eventually enjoy eternal life in heaven.

Winstanley's political writings

Notwithstanding the failure of the Digger communities, Winstanley continued to espouse Digger ideology in tracts and pamphlets. In 'The Law of Freedom,' published in 1652, he challenged Cromwell to bring about genuine liberty or to accept that he had simply transferred the king's power into his own hands. He advocated regular elections, to keep officials from becoming corrupt and set out a vision of a genuinely communal society:

The earth is to be planted and the fruits reaped and carried into barns and storehouses by the assistance of every family. And if any man or family want corn or other provision, they may go to the storehouses and fetch without money. If they want a horse to ride, go into the fields in summer, or to the common stables in winter, and receive one from the keepers, and when your journey is performed, bring him where you had him, without money.

However, his political influence was minimal and, despite the popularity of his pamphlets, the movement was fleeting.

The 'Godly Society'

Underlying the political and religious radicalism of the era of the Rump was the concept of a 'Godly Society'. Whether Cromwellian Puritan, Leveller, Digger, Quaker or Fifth Monarchist, all shared some common beliefs, although they were expressed in different ways and took their supporters in different directions:

- Individuals can relate directly to God without the agency of a priest and can be influenced directly by the Spirit of God.
- Sin was a public as well as a private responsibility and, just as God had first judged and then removed Charles I for his sin, so it was incumbent on believers to do what they could to bring about a godly reformation.

> **ACTIVITY**
>
> Compare Leveller ideas with those of the Diggers by creating a diagram to help you compare similarities and differences. What do you think were the most significant differences between the two movements?

> **ACTIVITY**
>
> Turn these common beliefs into a diagram and trace as many consequences/related events to these beliefs as possible. How does the Ranter movement (see page 148) fit into your diagram?

SECTION 6 | Experiments in government and society 1648–1660

A CLOSER LOOK

The 1650 Blasphemy Act

This Act was designed to help spread the Christian gospel across the Commonwealth by itemising heretical beliefs and practices and setting out punishments for those committing offences relating to heresy. It was most certainly a response to the immoral excesses of the Ranters. A first offence would lead to six months in prison, and a second offence would lead to banishment overseas.

KEY PROFILE

George Fox (1624–91) was the son of wealthy Puritan weaver from Leicestershire and became an apprentice to a shoemaker. He suffered from depression and was very miserable in his teenage years but had a spiritual awakening when he was 23, coming to the sudden realisation that each person had an Inner Light through which God would speak to them directly.

A CLOSER LOOK

Attempts to overhaul the English legal code

Some in the Rump and beyond wanted to go as far as to enact Mosaic Law, turning the Ten Commandments, and more than 600 other specific laws that are found in the Old Testament, into English legislation. John Milton, for one, strenuously and successfully opposed such a move: in his tract, *De Doctrina Christiana*, he argued that Christian theology recognises that the Old Testament law has been supplanted by the New Testament words of Jesus, to 'do to others what you would have them do to you.'

Quakers, Baptists and other radical sects

The Quakers

Around 1647, the religious radical **George Fox**, together with other likeminded preachers, began to gain a following as they travelled around the country spreading the message that God's Spirit imparted an 'inner light' to all believers in the form of a purified conscience, which taught Truth to the soul. He identified his fellow believers as 'Friends of the Truth' and they became known as the 'Society of Friends', but they rapidly attracted the contemptuous nickname 'Quakers' because they tended to shake and quake during religious meetings – evidence that they were experiencing the workings of God's spirit. Quakers did not differentiate between the spiritual roles of women or men: as all could experience God for themselves, who they were to prevent women from teaching and participating in Friends' activities?

Fig. 3 *This later depiction shows George Fox preaching in a tavern*

The Quakers' main beliefs were:
- God spoke to every believer through an individual Inner Light; their interaction with God would make them more holy.
- There was no need for designated ministers or ceremony and there was neither a need for deference to those of a higher social class, nor a place for prejudice towards those of a lower class.
- Oath-taking was wrong because allegiance lay first and foremost with God.
- Services should be conducted with extended periods of silence, for individual contemplation.
- Military service was wrong, as soldiers had to be prepared to kill. Only God had the right to end life.

Fox was one of the first radicals to be tried under the new Blasphemy Act, for which he was sentenced to six months' imprisonment in October 1650.

SOURCE 3

From George Fox's journal, in which he recorded his spiritual experiences. Spiritual journals were a rising genre of published literature, designed to evangelise to non-believers, as well as to pass on religious instruction, in an anecdotal and accessible way. This extract dates from the time of Fox's imprisonment in 1650:

While I was here in prison a variety of professors came to debate with me. I had a sense, before they spoke, that they came to were actually on the side of sin and imperfection. I asked them whether they were believers and had faith. They said, 'Yes.' I asked them, 'In whom?' They said, 'In Christ.' I replied. 'If ye are true believers in Christ, you are passed from death to life; and if passed from death, then from sin that brings death; and if your faith be true, it will give you victory over sin and the devil, so purify your hearts and consciences (for the true faith is held in a pure conscience), and do what you can to please God, so that He will give you access to Him again.'

But they could not endure to hear of purity, and of victory over sin and the devil. They said they could not believe any could be free from sin on this side of the grave. I instructed them to stop babbling about the Scriptures, which were holy men's words, whilst it was clear that they were recommending unholiness.

PRACTICE QUESTION

Evaluating primary sources

With reference to Sources 1, 2 and 3 and your understanding of the historical context, assess the value of these three sources to an historian studying political and religious radicalism in the years 1649 to 1653.

STUDY TIP

You need to consider not only what these sources say but who wrote them. Try to use your own knowledge of political and religious radicalism to judge each source's value.

ACTIVITY

Thinking point

Considering Quaker beliefs and practices, why do you think that the movement spread so rapidly in the 1650s?

The development of the Quaker movement

The Quaker movement grew rapidly, because it had a missionary, evangelistic vision, which it organised effectively. Quakers would travel in pairs, crossing the country and, in particular, targeting towns to ensure that the message of personal spiritual fulfilment reached the widest possible audience. They were also competent in their use of the press, producing large numbers of pamphlets that spread a consistent and readily understandable message.

By 1660, there were upwards of 20,000 Quaker converts in England, with missionaries at work across the British Isles and in North America.

Baptists

The different branches of the Baptist movement continued to grow in strength during the period of the Rump, during which time a genuinely innovative organisational structure emerged that provided a new alternative to Anglicanism or Presbyterianism. Lifting a concept from the New Model Army, the General Baptists grouped their churches into Regional Associations, sending a representative of each to London and a General Assembly, the first of which was held in 1653. Associations had multiple purposes:
- Christian fellowship and accountability for ministers
- Quality control of teaching, with regular meetings to elucidate and then communicate orthodox theology
- Monitoring and maintenance of Baptist doctrine and practice

> **CROSS-REFERENCE**
>
> The early years of the Fifth Monarchy Men are discussed on page 148.

> **KEY PROFILE**
>
> **Major General Thomas Harrison (1606–60)** was a lawyer who served in the Earl of Manchester's army in the First Civil War before joining the New Model Army as a Major General. He became MP for Wendover in 1646; sat in the High Court of Justice and signed the king's death warrant. He commanded the army in England while Cromwell was in Scotland, and fought at the Battle of Worcester.
>
> **Nathaniel Rich (unknown–1701)** Rich also served under the Earl of Manchester and then became a cavalry Colonel in the New Model Army. He helped draft the 'Heads of the Proposals'. He became MP for Cirencester in 1649.
>
> **Sir Henry Vane (1613–62)** became a fervent Puritan as a young man and travelled to Massachusetts in search of a godly community, becoming governor in 1636. On his return, he became MP for Hull. He did not fight in the war but became one of the leaders of the War Party in Parliament and helped draft the legislation that led to the formation of the New Model Army. He refused to attend the trial of the king but returned to Parliament and ensured that the army was adequately supported.

> **KEY TERM**
>
> **Trinity:** the collective term for the Christian God in his three component parts: Father, Son (Jesus) and Holy Spirit

- Group action such as the creation of Statements of Faith and political lobbying for religious liberty.

Other Baptist sects followed the lead set by the General Baptists so that within a decade, the association model was creating a homogenous movement that was developing into what we would now describe as a denomination. In the religious turmoil of the 1640s and 1650s there was not a clear division between what was within and what was beyond the reach of the Anglican Church, except at the extreme, heretical ends. The legal settlement that would allow for denominations to exist outside the Anglican Church was still over a decade away.

Other radical sects

Fifth Monarchists

Theologies with a particularly millenarian thrust continued to thrive, and the Fifth Monarchy movement in particular reached its peak around 1650, developing detailed plans for government and society while they awaited the apocalyptic return of Jesus:

- Government should be based on the model of the Jewish Sanhedrin, a governing body that had developed in ancient Judaism in which 71 wise men, drawn from the key cities in Israel, met together to make law and distribute justice.
- The legal profession could thus safely be abolished.
- Mosaic Law would be imposed.

From 1651, Fifth Monarchists began to meet weekly at the church of All-Hallows the Great, with other congregations forming elsewhere in London and, to a much lesser extent, in East Anglia, Devon and Cornwall. Congregations were typically formed of a majority of tradesmen (especially cloth workers) and apprentices but some notable Parliamentarians were also dedicated members of the sect, including **Major General Harrison** and **Nathaniel Rich**. **Sir Henry Vane** was certainly sympathetic if not fully committed.

Muggletonians

In 1651, Ludowicke Muggleton and his cousin John Reeve claimed that God had sent them two revelations for which Reeve was to be the messenger and Muggleton the mouthpiece. They claimed that they were the two 'witnesses' of the Apocalyptic book 'Revelation', whose job was to usher in Judgement Day by prophesying for 1260 days. Muggleton was convicted for blasphemy in 1653.

The Muggletonians had an eclectic set of beliefs, including:

- Denial of the **Trinity**, a key orthodox Christian doctrine.
- The mortality of the soul, believing that the soul died when the body died and then both were brought back to life.
- The devil is simply man's sinful thoughts.
- God is a man of between 5 and 6 feet tall, living 6 miles above the earth.
- Doctors are akin to witches.
- Pacifism.
- Hostility to magistrates, lawyers and church ministers.

Muggletonianism was not an evangelistic movement; instead its followers waited for new believers to find them by visiting a particular shop in London. They had an extravagant annual feast to celebrate the revelations that had started the movement, and they met more frequently to debate and sing together. It never became a widespread belief, although it did persist with a small number of members into the twentieth century. It is of significance rather as evidence of the bizarre nature of some expressions of religious radicalism in the 1650s than because of any particular impact it made.

The Rump Parliament as an experiment in radical republicanism

ACTIVITY

Definition is crucial when deciding whether the Rump Parliament was a genuine experiment in radical republicanism. To ensure you develop an authentic, historically sound approach, have these questions in mind:
- What did 'republicanism' mean in 1649?
- Did the Rump define itself as an instrument of republican government?
- Would the Rump MPs have considered themselves to be radical republicans?

From Republic to Commonwealth

In the constitutional melee of February 1649, a new body was introduced to replace the vacuum caused by the loss of the **executive powers** of the king. Known as the 'Council of State' it was made up of 41 councillors, elected by the Rump, including peers, Commons MPs and magistrates (including John Bradshaw, who took on the role of President of the Council). Elections to the Council were held annually for the duration of the Rump. Attendance at the Council was poor, with rarely more than fifteen members and sometimes falling below its lower limit of nine.

Incoming members to the Council had to swear an oath of allegiance, 'to the government of the nation for the future, in way of a republic'. However, this is one of the very few times in which the term 'republic' was used by the Rump to describe the English constitutional arrangement. Instead, very swiftly, the term 'Commonwealth' became the key term.

Why 'Commonwealth'?

Commonwealth was an established term within England already, with a very loose meaning which could be extended as far as being any country or state, irrespective of its constitutional structure and was connected with Christian virtues, service, devotion and the common good. Until 1649, it had been used interchangeably for 'kingdom' and 'realm' in Long Parliament legislation so the Rump could continue to use it, while simply dropping its monarchical synonyms. Significantly, the new coins issued by the Rump used the words 'Commonwealth of England' and the joint symbols of England (the St George cross) and Ireland (the Harp) with 'God with us' on the reverse.

It was precisely because 'Commonwealth' was so vague a term that a complainant about the Rump could write that all the change in government had achieved was to remove the king: in all other ways, the term 'Commonwealth' was applied to what had previously existed. As a leading historian of the Rump, Blair Worden, notes, 'It was the most unrevolutionary term available'.

The relationship between Parliament and Commonwealth is also illuminating. While the Rump MPs had certainly had the opportunity to elevate themselves to a new, higher status, they actually took pains to continue to promote the primacy of Parliament in its role as the preserver of ancient liberty and custom. Their outright rejection of Leveller ideology and their continued reliance on precedent and tradition demonstrated innate conservatism, not republican zeal. As Bulstrode Whitelocke noted:

ACTIVITY

Create a quiz about the different forms of radical religion discussed in this chapter. Take it in turns to challenge other members of your group.

KEY TERM

executive power: the ability to administer government on a day-to-day basis, ensuring that Parliamentary legislation is carried out across the country; it also includes responsibility for foreign policy and defence

A CLOSER LOOK

The reforming agenda of the Rump

The early 1650s reached a high watermark in centralised efforts towards creating a 'Godly Society.' Closer regulation of the press, attempts to enforce Sabbath law more strictly, an Act of May 1650 for 'suppressing the detestable sins of Incest, Adultery and Fornication', and a new blasphemy law which was passed in August 1650, all indicate the extent to which the Rump tried to take seriously its role as the harbinger of godliness.

CROSS-REFERENCE

For a profile of **Henry Marten**, see page 169.

For more details on **Cromwell's rejection of the Crown**, see Chapter 23.

'unavoidable necessity hath put us upon these courses which otherwise perhaps we should not have taken.'

Radical Republicans

It is difficult to identify many genuinely radical republicans during the Rump period. **Henry Marten** stands out – a committed republican throughout the Civil War period, vigorously pressing for regicide, and a keen participant in the Rump. He, and a small group of likeminded men, did have an influence on proceedings. However, in the absence of a credible candidate for the throne, the Rump and the army endeavoured to find a workable republican settlement that would bring stability to the country. In the context of the times, this desire to find a republican solution was genuinely radical because it was so different to centuries of monarchical precedents and it was certainly a factor in **Cromwell's rejection of the Crown**.

The Parliament of the Saints

On 20 April 1653, Oliver Cromwell strode into Parliament, called 30 soldiers in behind him and dissolved the Rump.

Reasons for the Dissolution of the Rump
Had the Rump failed?

The Rump proved to be a much more conservative political force than many of its early opponents might have feared.
It had many strengths:
- The Rump's Navigation Act of 1651 boosted national morale. Even though it led to war with the Dutch Republic over commercial rivalry and fishing rights, it was popular because it brought England back onto the continental stage as a major player after a lull of a decade and the opening stages of the Anglo-Dutch war went very much in England's favour.
- Careful handling of local circumstances prevented serious opposition from the localities. Royalists were typically treated gently with minimal purges from county office.
- The Rump managed to maintain stability and order even in the face of economic distress, religious radicalism, threat of invasion from Ireland and actual invasion from Scotland.
- There was no good alternative and the Rump held off the threat of the army's political ambition.
- Some much-needed legislation was passed including the easing of laws relating to debtors and the change of language for legal documentation from Latin to English.
- The Rump managed to raise enough money to finance the army (mainly through the sale of Church, Crown and Royalist lands)

It also had a few weaknesses:
- Taxes, of necessity, remained very high.
- Attendance at the Rump was always low, with only about 70 active MPs out of 210, and average attendance of 50 to 60.
- The passage of new legislation (an indicator of constitutional vigour) dropped steadily throughout the Parliament.

The electoral question

Membership of the Commons had been steadily decreasing as the Long Parliament continued and the seats left vacant from Pride's Purge had not yet been filled. The issue of new elections rose to the fore in 1653, but details are sketchy and historians are divided over the question of whether Cromwell welcomed or feared new elections:

- Perhaps he feared the election of even more conservative members, losing forever the opportunity to complete the creation of a 'godly society'.
- Perhaps he feared that the Rump might perpetuate itself indefinitely, only filling vacant seats and never again holding a general election.

What is certain is that the army became a significant political force again in 1653.

The ambition of the army

By 1653, the New Model Army had defeated the Irish and the Scots and was brimming with confidence and power. Its supreme Lord General Cromwell had an in-depth understanding of its grievances against the Rump and shared its exasperation with the slow pace of godly reformation.

The Dissolution of the Rump

It was in these circumstances that Cromwell led a troop of soldiers to Westminster on 20 April 1653. He entered the Commons Chamber and began lecturing the Members about how poorly they had performed. Finally, he declared 'You have sat too long for any good you have been doing lately… In the name of God, go!' and ordered the soldiers in to forcibly dissolve the Parliament.

The Nominated Assembly

Cromwell's power was unassailable: formulating a plan with Fifth Monarchist Thomas Harrison, he gathered the Army Council together to select 140 men from England, Wales, Scotland and Ireland, and he summoned them to Westminster. The Assembly met for the first time on 4 July 1653.

Barebone's Parliament

Fig. 4 *This woodcut pokes fun at Praise-God Barebone's humble origins*

The Nominated Assembly was not a Parliament but it rapidly gained a derogatory nickname based on the outlandish name of one its members, Praise-God Barebone who was a Fifth Monarchist. This nickname served to support a lazy stereotype that the assembly was an assortment of religious zealots and oddities: 'The Parliament of Saints' was the preferred term of the Godly.

> **A CLOSER LOOK**
>
> ### The New Model Army and the Rump
>
> The army had specific grievances with the Rump on account of its failure to provide adequate pensions for war widows; its apparent lack of respect for Cromwell (his home of Hampton Court Palace was under threat) and its efforts to disband New Model regiments. Religious radicals also shared the frustration of Cromwell's chaplain in Ireland, John Owen, who had proposed the formation of a broad national Church, with such loose Articles of Faith that it would secure freedom of worship for all but the most outlandish sects in order to break the deadlock in Westminster, from which no religious settlement was forthcoming.

> **A CLOSER LOOK**
>
> ### Who was in the Nominated Assembly?
>
> The Army Council sought local advice, usually from separatist congregations, in order to identify suitable candidates to nominate and the assembly was castigated by men such as Clarendon for being 'the major part of them inferior persons, known only for their gifts in praying and preaching.' In actual fact, although some were religious radicals, the majority came from the same background as normal MPs. Thomas Fairfax, for example, was nominated but declined to take part.

SECTION 6 | Experiments in government and society 1648–1660

A CLOSER LOOK

The **Court of Chancery** was a long-established court designed to hear complex cases relating to matters such as land and estates and disputes that could not be solved within the normal court system. It also made sure that children who were 'wards of court', meaning that their parents had delegated their care to a guardian who was legally accountable to Chancery. Although Chancery should have performed an important function, by the mid-seventeenth century it had a backlog that had been problematic for decades and it had almost completely broken down.

In five short months, the Nominated Assembly pushed through a small amount of significant legislation:

- measures aimed at the promotion of godly reformation, including:
  - reform of marriage law
  - abolition of lay patronage of church livings (not concluded)
  - abolition of tithes (not concluded) Reform of debtor law
- more humane treatment of the insane
- tougher measures against highwaymen and thieves
- abolition of the Court of Chancery.

The Nominated Assembly ran into real trouble when it passed measures to carry out a purge of the Justices of the Peace to remove men who had been conservative members of the Rump. This measure caused dismay in the localities because it cut across regional sensibilities; religious moderates were scared by the efficient organisation of the radical sectarians within Barebone's and the army officers were threatened by proposals to stop their pay for a year. Fears began to grow that, in Cromwell's words, the Assembly would soon usher in 'confusion of all things.'

The removal of the Nominated Assembly

Very early on 12 December 1653, Major General Lambert, Cromwell's second-in-command and a member of the Assembly, led what was effectively a military coup. Co-ordinating with political moderates, proceedings opened very early in the morning, before the usual arrival time of Assembly members. Lambert brought in a vote to disperse the Assembly and to hand power directly to Cromwell. With the radicals not yet present, the vote passed and soldiers closed the Assembly down.

ACTIVITY

Summary

So much of constitutional importance happened during the period that it is crucial that you have a clear understanding of the chronology and content of each facet. Create a flow-chart that takes you from the execution of the king to the removal of the Nominated Assembly. Include notes at each stage in the constitutional journey undertaken by England in this period.

Then, look for connections to the religious radicalism of these years and annotate your flow-chart to show the significance of these links. For example, the ideas of the Fifth Monarchy Men found an echo in the structure of the Nominated Assembly.

STUDY TIP

You will need to be certain you understand the meaning of 'Godly Society' so that you can ensure your answer is specific and detailed. You may want to consider the extent to which a 'Godly Society' was attempted as well as the extent to which it was successful.

PRACTICE QUESTION (A LEVEL)

How successful was the attempt to create a Godly Society in England in the years 1649 to 1653?

23 Oliver Cromwell and the Protectorate

KEY CHRONOLOGY

1653	Dec	Investiture of the Lord Protector
1654	Sept	First Protectorate Parliament
1655	Jan	Dissolution of First Protectorate Parliament
	March	Penruddock Rising
	April	The Western Design
	Aug–Dec	Rule by the Major Generals
1656	Sept	Second Protectorate Parliament
1657	Feb	Humble Petition and Advice
	April	Cromwell rejects the Crown
1658	3 Sept	Death of Oliver Cromwell; accession of Richard Cromwell

LEARNING OBJECTIVES

In this chapter you will learn about:

- Cromwell's personality and approach to government.
- the limits of religious toleration
- the Major Generals
- Cromwell's refusal of the Crown
- the problem of the succession to Cromwell.

On 16 December 1653, Cromwell was taken by coach from Whitehall to Westminster Hall, the scene of the trial of Charles I, to be invested as **Lord Protector**. He was accompanied by a mounted guard with soldiers lining the route. In front of Cromwell were coaches taking other leading figures of the new regime. In the carriage with Cromwell was Lambert. He carried the sword of state and preceded Cromwell as they entered the Hall. The articles of the Instrument of Government, Britain's first written constitution, drafted by Lambert and issued by the Army Council, were read out before Cromwell took an oath to uphold them. Another constitutional experiment had begun.

KEY TERM

Lord Protector: the title given to the head of the government in 1653, and this period is known as the Protectorate

Cromwell's personality and approach to government

The contradictions inherent in the constitutional experiments of the 1650s can only be understood in the light of Cromwell's own personality and particularly, in his religious beliefs. By upbringing, he was a social conservative, keen to preserve traditional county values and promote what he described as the 'healing and settling' of the divided English people. At heart he was a Parliamentarian, identifying the representatives of the people to be the cornerstone of liberty. He was a religious zealot, which led him to take measures apparently at odds with liberty and conservatism as well as to take advantage of circumstances which he would label as evidence of **providence** at work.

Cromwell as a man

Cromwell was undoubtedly a complex man. His private writings reveal him to be humble, often very harsh on himself, and yet he behaved with supreme confidence on the public stage. He was sober, deeply religious, and sometimes overly introspective, yet he commanded loyalty on a grand scale at the head of (normally) triumphant armies. He resisted public adulation, famously demanding to be painted 'warts and all', and yet he believed that God had given him a unique and weighty commission.

Fig. 1 Cromwell's 'warts and all' portrait

> **CROSS-REFERENCE**
>
> Cromwell identified the work of **providence** in three critical events that led up to the Protectorate: Pride's Purge, the dissolution of the Nominated Assembly, and the drafting of the Instrument of Government. He claimed to have had no foreknowledge of these events and interpreted the way that each raised his status and power as evidence that God was propelling him onwards. Providence is discussed further on page 168.

> **A CLOSER LOOK**
>
> **The Four Fundamentals, September 1654**
>
> In response to the lobbying of the Commonwealthsmen, Cromwell issued 'Four Fundamentals' which would make his work of 'healing and settling' possible:
>
> 1. Government by a single person and Parliament
> 2. Non-perpetuation of Parliament against the will of the Protector or the terms of the Instrument
> 3. Liberty of Conscience
> 4. Control of militia by Protector, Council and Parliament.
>
> All MPs were required to swear an oath of recognition of the first Fundamental: about one hundred Commonwealthsmen resigned as a result.

The Instrument of Government

Lambert's constitutional settlement was fundamentally conservative despite its innovatory nature:

- A Lord Protector would hold executive power in a role akin to a modern president of the USA. Cromwell was granted this role for the duration of his lifetime, after which it would become an elected office.
- A Council of State of up to 21 members would handle finance, appointments and control of the armed forces.
- A Parliament (one with only a single chamber) would sit for at least five months and be subject to re-election every five years. It would be made up of 400 English and Welsh MPs and, for the first time, 30 each from Scotland and Ireland.

The settlement also tackled key areas of contention:

- Liberty of worship for all but Roman Catholics and extreme sectarians was guaranteed.
- Electoral reform maintained a property qualification but extended suffrage down towards the emergent middle classes
- Funding for the army and navy was set at 10,000 cavalry horses and dragoons, 20,000 foot and a 'convenient' number of ships.
- An annual budget of £200,000 was allocated to the Lord Protector to cover costs associated with administering justice.

The First Protectorate Parliament

Elections for the First Protectorate Parliament were called by Cromwell after the Instrument was approved and it sat between September 1654 and its dissolution (by Cromwell at the earliest opportunity) on 22 January 1655. Cromwell dissolved the Parliament in considerable disgust because:

- The Parliament brought forward repeated attempts to amend the Instrument in order to return executive power to itself.
- In particular, a powerful minority faction of 'Commonwealthsmen,' led by Sir Arthur Haselrig, strongly opposed Cromwell's dissolution of the Rump and saw his subsequent actions as a dangerous drift towards arbitrary kingship. The Commonwealthsmen developed recognisably republican constitutionalism.
- 'Godly reformation' was not pursued and instead it appeared that toleration would be narrowed, mainly due to the influence of the Presbyterian majority.
- Electoral reform had redistributed power away from towns and into the counties so it became much more difficult to manage Parliamentary business as county MPs were a more dispersed and diverse group.
- No legislation was enacted during the whole duration of the Parliament

The Major Generals

Following the dissolution of the First Protectorate Parliament, Cromwell decided to try a different form of government: rule by some of the New Model Army's Major Generals. This was significant because it was an official attempt to establish military government but it came under the constitutional umbrella of the Instrument of Government.

Reasons for military government

Between dissolution in January and the beginning of rule by the Major Generals in August 1655, two events occurred that caused Cromwell to believe he needed take decisive action to prevent a descent into tumult, insurrection and rebellion.

- In March 1655 Colonel John Penruddock attempted a Royalist rising in Wiltshire which was easily put down but caused great alarm.

- In April 1655 there was a compaign, known as the Western Design, to take Hispaniola (Cuba) from the Spanish for England in order to secure a strong base in the Caribbean. It was repelled. Cromwell interpreted this as showing God's displeasure in a form of reverse-providence.

Penruddock's Uprising

After Charles Stuart fled into exile, some of his supporters continued to press his cause and planned a general rising to take place across England in 1655. In the event, few Royalists took part. About 100 arrived at one of the planned rendezvous points, Marston Moor, ready to march on York; fewer turned up at Morpeth to attack Newcastle. The only remotely successful rising took place in Wiltshire, under the command of a local gentleman called John Penruddock. They held Salisbury for a few hours but the rebels were defeated by a small cavalry force who pursued them into Devon. Penruddock was executed in May 1655.

The Western Design

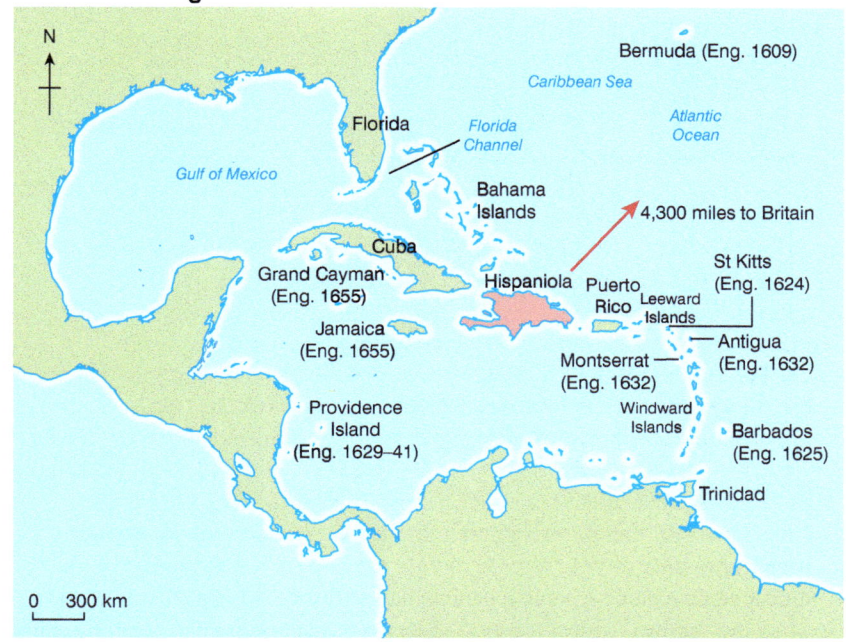

Fig. 2 *The West Indies in the 1650s; dates show when each colony was founded*

Cromwell initiated a foreign policy in which he generally allied with France against Spain, both Catholic countries. The reason for this alignment was pragmatic: Spain was commercially a greater rival than France, particularly in the Americas. In December 1654, a British naval force was sent to the West Indies, tasked with seizing Hispaniola (Cuba) from the Spanish as the first step in securing the West Indies for Britain: this campaign was called the Western Design. The Spanish were able to repel the invading force which was a devastating blow to the overall strategy.

Rule by the Major Generals

Lambert was again a guiding light in developing the rule by the Major Generals. Ireland was already governed by Major General Henry Cromwell and Scotland by Major General George Monck. Now England itself was divided into 11 districts, each under a Major General who was supported by 500 soldiers and who was responsible for ensuring that local magistrates were vigorous in crushing resurgent royalism and zealous in their pursuit of godly reformation. Lambert himself was a designated Major General, but he appointed a deputy so he could remain at Westminster.

A CLOSER LOOK

A rising tide of anxiety

Major General John Lambert expressed an increasingly widespread anxiety that Royalists were secretively regrouping:

I have been guilty of applying the Act of Oblivion too much to my own memory. I have done my best to build bridges with the Royalists, to win them over so we can forget the past. But they are as careful to breed their children to remember the quarrel as it's possible to be. They are, even now, making merry over their Christmas pies, drinking the King of Scots' health, or our confusion. The Act of Oblivion was supposed to work both ways but they are not trying to keep their part: it's a bad bargain for us.

ACTIVITY

Extension

The 1650s were a decade in which there were a series of significant wars and lesser military engagements. To develop your contextual knowledge, find out what was happening between England and France, the Dutch Republic and Spain in these years.

Fig. 3 *In 1653–55, England was divided into 11 districts, each with a Major General (whose names appear in red)*

Unpopularity of the Major General experiment

Overall, the rule of the Major Generals was unsuccessful. They caused social disruption, as typically the Major Generals were of a lower social status than the Justices of the Peace over whom they had authority, and, although they tried to work alongside local infrastructures, they were not averse to removing obstructive commissioners. Many interpreted their rule as unnatural because it was against the established social order.

The dubious legality of martial rule in a country that had only recently overthrown a king to protect the privileges and liberty of Parliament undermined the Major Generals experiment from the start, providing a focal point for growing dissatisfaction. As an MP observed in 1659, 'Any government is better than no government, and any civil better than a military government.' Another reason why they were unsuccessful was the huge financial burden. The cost of maintaining the standing army of five hundred troops per Major General added yet another fiscal burden onto the already weighed down population. In order to try to meet this additional cost, a Decimation tax was levied on Royalist estates worth more than £100 per annum, removing 10% of their annual revenue. This was directly contrary to the 'healing and settling' that Cromwell needed to achieve and it did not raise enough money anyway to solve such a pressing problem: by 1656, annual expenditure was exceeding income by £230,000. However, by far the greatest reason for the unpopularity of the Major Generals was the way in which many of them took seriously their responsibility for godly reformation.

> **ACTIVITY**
>
> What parallels can you draw between the aims and methods of Thorough, the governance of the New Model Army, and the rule by Major Generals? Use the information presented in this book to create a chart comparing all three.

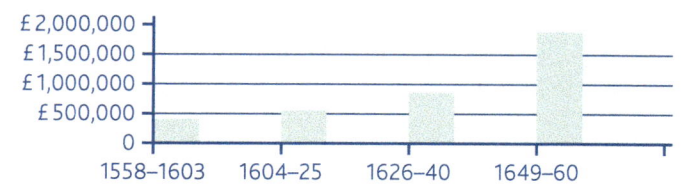

Fig. 4 *Average annual taxation, 1558–1660*

> **SOURCE 1**
>
> From the Instructions of October 1655, filed in the official Parliamentary records, setting out the mandate for government by the Major Generals:
>
> 17. No house standing alone and out of a town is to be permitted to sell Ale, Beer or Wine, or give entertainment. Licenses for such activities that have been given out will be withdrawn and no longer issued.
> 19. For bringing about more decisively a Reformation of London and Westminster, all gaming houses and houses of evil fame [brothels] be industriously sought out and suppressed within the cities of London and Westminster and all the liberties thereof.
> 21. That all alehouses, taverns and victualing houses towards the outskirts of the said cities be suppressed, except such as are necessary and convenient to travellers' and that the number of alehouses in all other parts of the town be abated, and none continued but such as can lodge strangers and of great repute.

Using the power of the army, vigorous Major Generals typically enforced a rigorous campaign in their districts, combating drunkenness, applying blasphemy laws and punishing indecent behaviour. They closed down theatres and brothels and enforced rules against gambling, outlawing bear-baiting, cock-fighting and horse-racing. To the conservative majority, the Major Generals' heavy-handed application of central directives into local contexts created fear and fury that their traditions and pastimes were being eroded.

The beginning of the end of the Major Generals

In September 1656, Cromwell was forced to call a Second Protectorate Parliament because he could not afford to finance the war against Spain which had resulted from the Western Design. In order to try to control its output, Cromwell and the Council of State excluded more than one hundred MPs, notably those who had tended to oppose Cromwell's measures in the First Protectorate Parliament, and indeed, it was for a short time relatively compliant and notably effective. It supported the Spanish war effort, tackled legal reforms and passed some 'godly' measures. However, it swiftly encountered the divisive issue of religion.

The limits of religious toleration

'Liberty of conscience', the third Fundamental of the Commonwealth, was the most provocative and divisive of all the issues facing England during the Interregnum. It is not synonymous with toleration but is intrinsically connected. Liberty of conscience is the right of an individual to their own faith. Toleration expresses what a governing state defines as acceptable practice of that individual faith.

The three main positions on tolerance

It is possible to identify three broad positions with regard to toleration although of course, definitions are only useful for creating generalisations and there were variations between individuals and groups.

A CLOSER LOOK

Zeal for 'godly reformation'

In Lancashire, Major General Worsley closed two hundred alehouses in one small region of his District, around Blackburn. He was so over-committed to 'godly reformation' that he had to be instructed to moderate his actions lest his District rebel. Some Major Generals were known to be less zealous. Major General Whalley in the Midlands was a local man, with powerful connections that helped him to keep order without recourse to harsh measures; he achieved less in the way of reformation.

SECTION 6 | Experiments in government and society 1648–1660

> **KEY TERM**
>
> **secular powers:** belong to governing authorities that are not explicitly religious, such as criminal courts

A CLOSER LOOK

Cromwell and toleration

Blair Worden argues that Cromwell's drive for liberty of conscience did not spring from what we would recognise as 'modern liberalism' but from his understanding of 'the godly'. In 1648 Cromwell wrote to Robert Hammond, 'I profess to thee I desire it in my heart, I have prayed for it, I have waited for the day to see union and right understanding between the godly people (whether they be found among the Scots, English, Jews, Gentiles, Presbyterians, Independents, Anabaptists, and all).' This emphasis caused him to be frustrated at the way that individual sects attacked each other and encouraged his preoccupation with establishing who was within the godly and who was 'diabolical', beyond the ranks.

	Anti-tolerationists	Conservative tolerationists	Radical tolerationists
Keywords:	Uniformity, discipline, order	Independence, orthodoxy	'Primitive' Christianity
Preferred structure:	Established Church	Established Church with toleration for the Churches meeting certain criteria, known collectively as 'the gathered Churches'	Religious faith and practice to be entirely removed from oversight by **secular powers**
Included:	Royalists who wanted to uphold an Anglican settlement Presbyterians who wanted to extend a Presbyterian settlement across Britain	'The godly': those mainstream movements that dissented from Anglicanism, such as Baptists and Presbyterians	Quakers, Socinians, and radical Independents
Advocates:	William Prynne, Thomas Edwards, Robert Baillie	**Oliver Cromwell**, John Owen	George Fox, Henry Vane

A CLOSER LOOK

Secular powers

The demand of the radical tolerationists for removal of religious matters from the jurisdiction of the secular powers was explained in terms of the role of the magistrate. Radical tolerationists said that magistrates (those who apply the law) gained their authority from the consent of the people, an application of the theory of Natural Law. They argued that God had not devolved authority over religious matters to the magistrates and therefore they could not legislate in that area.

Liberty but not toleration

Ideas about liberty of conscience also led to a re-evaluation of Catholicism and the status of the Jews in Cromwellian England.

Catholicism

As a Protestant Independent, Cromwell was anti-Catholic but his commitment to liberty of conscience led to a reconsideration of the relationship between Catholics and the state. As an example, in 1654, the Jesuit John Southworth was tried under Elizabethan anti-priest legislation for which he was hanged, drawn and quartered. Cromwell had protested against his execution and arranged that his corpse would be sewn back together and sent abroad for decent burial. He also allowed Catholics to celebrate mass within the Venetian Embassy.

Two Paris-based English Catholics, Henry Holden and Thomas White (the **Blackloists**) sought to shape a distinctively English Catholic Church which would loosen its relationship to the Papacy and come to terms with the Protectorate.

In 1655, Thomas White outlined a proposal in *Grounds of Obedience and Government*:
- acceptance of Cromwell as Protector
- Parliamentary Oath of Allegiance for all English Catholics
- six English Catholic bishops, appointed by the Pope, but with limited powers.

In effect, the Grounds of Obedience made provision for Catholics to build a state-approved pastoral structure but not become a missional, evangelistic movement.

A CLOSER LOOK

Blackloists

Thomas White wrote under the pseudonym Blacklow, hence Blackloists. He became mired in a controversy with the Jesuit priest Robert Pugh: under the Blackloist approach, Jesuits would be prevented from entering England as they were primarily evangelistic in focus. The Restoration in 1660 ended the influence of the Blackloists.

Judaism

In shameful circumstances in 1290, Edward I expelled Jewish people from England. During the Interregnum, an Amsterdam Jew called Manasseh ben Israel petitioned for their re-admittance, with freedom to worship and trade. His cause was taken up by Cromwell, who insisted that the Protectorate Council should hear the petition and discuss it at a Conference which took place at Westminster Hall in December 1655 with four Protectoral councillors, church ministers and lawyers present. Although the petition was rejected, Cromwell nonetheless ensured that Jews were quietly allowed back into England.

Challenges to toleration

The crucial religious problem faced by English lawmakers in the 1650s was to define the limits of 'godly' faith. All but the ultra-libertarian sects such as the Ranters had their defined own sense of what was orthodox and what was blasphemous or heretical but it was the blasphemy legislation of 1648-1650 which provided the most up-to-date legal definition of orthodoxy and its terms were more narrowly Presbyterian than the prevailing climate of the Protectorate. Cromwell had managed to create a larger space for religious practice than was officially defined by the blasphemy legislation but in 1654, a test case threatened to unbalance this practical equilibrium.

John Biddle

John Biddle was a **Socinian** who had been able to hold church gatherings quietly in London in the post-war period. In 1654 he published 'A Twofold Catechism' which outlined his Socinian beliefs and brought him to the attention of the distinctly conservative First Protectorate Parliament, which initiated proceedings against him in line with the Blasphemy Act. While under arrest, it became clear that a floodgate had been unleashed: William Kiffin, a staunch Cromwellian, was threatened with arrest for 'preaching that baptism is unlawful' and groups on the radical fringes began to gather together, prepared to defend themselves against what they saw as a new wave of persecution.

While Cromwell held different views and had to agree that the Blasphemy Act still had legal force, he nonetheless acted in order to protect the 'godly' who might be caught up in the unfurling net. It was substantially to end the Biddle action that he dissolved the First Protectorate Parliament, complaining 'where shall we have men of a Universal Spirit? Everyone desires to have liberty but none will give it,' and then despatched Biddle to the Scilly Isles, beyond Parliament's reach.

James Nayler

It was another religious case that was one of the chief catalysts behind the breakdown of the Second Protectorate Parliament in 1657. James Nayler was a former soldier who became a dedicated Quaker. In 1656, he set out on a mission to the West Country and rode into Bristol on a donkey in a dramatic re-enactment of Jesus's triumphal entry into Jerusalem. This was not acceptable to the Protectorate Parliament and they brought the Blasphemy Ordinance against him, convicting him in December and punishing him by boring a hole in his tongue, flogging and branding him, and sentencing him to life imprisonment. Cromwell himself found Nayler's behaviour distasteful, particularly because Quakers were seen as socially disruptive. They refused to pay tithes, disturbed church services by publically rebuking ministers, and showed disrespect to secular authorities by, for example, refusing to doff their hats to magistrates and other social superiors.

What the Nayler case demonstrated to Cromwell was that the Instrument of Government did not provide enough protection to religious liberty, and the conservative nature of the Parliamentary classes meant that this liberty was perpetually under threat.

A CLOSER LOOK

Cromwell and Jews

Cromwell's desire for Jews to return to England was rooted in his millenarianism. He understood the Bible to say that Jews needed to be converted to Christianity as part of the apocalyptic process. For that, he needed them back in England so that they could be brought into the 'godly' society.

A CLOSER LOOK

Socinians believed that there was a single divine being, God the Father, who was supported by the Holy Spirit, a divine force but not God, and an exceptional sinless but not divine man, Jesus Christ. This is an anti-Trinitarian belief, because it denies the 'Father-Son-Spirit' doctrine of the Trinity and it is described as Unitarian belief because it holds that there is one, single God.

CROSS-REFERENCE

A definition of the Trinity is found on page 190.

Major General	Region
James Berry	Herefordshire, Shropshire, Worcestershire, Wales
William Boteler	Bedfordshire, Huntingdonshire, Northamptonshire, Rutland
John Desborough	Cornwall, Devon, Dorset, Gloucestershire, Somerset, Wiltshire
Charles Fleetwood	Buckinghamshire, Cambridgeshire, Essex, Hertfordshire, Norfolk, Oxfordshire, Suffolk
William Goffe	Berkshire, Hampshire, Sussex
Thomas Kelsey	Surrey, Kent
John Lambert	Cumberland, County Durham, Northumberland, Westmorland, Yorkshire
Philip Skippon	Middlesex; including the cities of London, Westminster
Edward Whalley	Derbyshire, Leicestershire, Lincolnshire, Nottinghamshire, Warwickshire,
Charles Worsley;	Cheshire, Lancashire and Staffordshire
George Monck	Scotland

KEY PROFILE

Major General John Desborough (1608–80) had married Cromwell's sister Jane in 1636. He was trained as a lawyer; became a cavalry commander in the Civil Wars and became an MP in the Parliaments of 1654 and 1656, in addition to being one of the 11 Major Generals. He was a blunt-speaking and down-to-earth man, mocked by Royalists as a 'rustic'. He was firmly republican and vigorously opposed offering the Crown to Cromwell.

John Claypole (1625–88) married Cromwell's second daughter Elizabeth in 1646. During the Second Civil War he raised a cavalry troop in Northamptonshire and was promoted by Cromwell to the ceremonial position of 'Master of the Horse'. He was an MP in both Protectorate Parliaments and opposed the Major Generals experiment. In 1657 Cromwell awarded him the rank of Baronet, entitling him to be known as Lord John Claypole. Elizabeth died in 1658.

Cromwell's refusal of the Crown

By early 1657 it was clear to Cromwell that the current constitutional experiment was neither bringing about the 'healing and settling' that he knew was necessary for stability, nor enshrining liberty of conscience.

The Humble Petition and Advice

In February 1657, a new constitutional proposal was brought before the Second Protectorate Parliament, in the form of a 'Humble Petition and Advice.'

Background to the Petition

The Nayler case had again exposed the problem of liberty of conscience. The final days of the Instrument and Major Generals began on Christmas Day 1656. **Major General Desborough** chose that very quiet Parliamentary day to introduce a Militia Bill which would turn the Decimation Tax from a temporary measure into a permanent tax. By now, as we have seen, the Major Generals were unpopular and the Decimation Tax was a high watermark in their unpopularity. Desborough's Bill pushed the growing polarity between civilians and military men into the open.

Faced with a choice between the radical army position and the more moderate Parliamentarians, Cromwell now found himself on the side of the civilian gentry. He threw his weight behind his son-in-law **John Claypole's** attack on the Militia Bill, signalling a death knell to the Major Generals and the Instrument of Government.

The offer of the Crown

The Humble Petition and Advice originated among Cromwell's civilian supporters and was presented to Parliament in February 1657. Most of its terms were conservative but acceptable to Cromwell:
- A new definition of religious liberty and tolerance.
- The establishment of a national Church with a wide Confession of Faith.
- The reduction of the Council of State to a small group more reminiscent of the Privy Council.
- The creation of a new Upper Chamber whose members would be nominated by Protector and Council.
- The right of the Lord Protector to nominate his successor.

Overall the Humble Petition was somewhat conservative and moderated some of Cromwell's executive power. Dramatically however, the Humble Petition called for the reinstatement of the office of monarch, with Oliver Cromwell as the first office holder. It was debated for several weeks before being finally submitted to Cromwell.

Opposition to the Humble Petition
Civilian republican opposition
Sir Arthur Haselrig led a faction of republicans who were aghast at the Humble Petition and vigorously fought against it. Specifically, Haselrig was implacably opposed to the introduction of an upper chamber, despite being offered a place on it: he had been part of the Rump that had abolished the House of Lords, and ideologically he did not believe that there could be a higher authority to the Commons.

Army opposition
Many in the army were particularly opposed to the idea that Cromwell should become king.

> **SOURCE 2**
>
> From an Officers' Petition, 1657, from army officers opposed to offering the Crown to Cromwell. It was probably drafted by Lambert:
>
> We have hazarded our lives against the monarchy, and were still ready so to do in defence of the liberties of the nation; but they now observe in some men great endeavours to bring the nation under the old servitude by pressing their General to take upon him the title and government of a king, in order to destroy him and weaken the hands of those who were faithful to the public. We therefore humbly desire that Cromwell would discountenance all such persons and endeavours, and continue steadfast to the good old cause, for the preservation of which we for our parts are most ready to lay down our lives.

While Desborough and Major General **Charles Fleetwood** accepted the Humble Petition, Lambert found himself unable to support the Protectorate any more and, temporarily, retired from public life.

As it happened, Cromwell's continued links with the army prevented the petitioning officers from being able to spread their influence very far and neither the civilian republicans nor the army opposition were able to derail the Humble Petition.

The Humble Petition and Advice
On 3 March 1657, the revised Remonstrance was presented to Cromwell. Despite long consideration, on 13 April he rejected its offer of the Crown and the Humble Petition was sent back for another redraft.

Why did Cromwell reject the Crown?
Cromwell could not reconcile kingship with Christian faith and specifically his understanding of providence. As we have seen, he was anxious that God might turn against him if he committed sins of pride and ambition.

> **SOURCE 3**
>
> From a speech Cromwell made to a committee of MPs on 13 April 1657. The text was preserved among Cromwell's papers:
>
> God, with severe discipline, has not only eradicated a whole family and thrust them out of the land but he also brought about the eradication of their title. It was not done by me, nor by the government I now act in: it was done by the Long Parliament. It is providence at work, to strike at the family and also the name. I will not seek to set up what providence has destroyed and laid in the dust. This is a matter for me alone, and my judgment and my conscience. I would rather I were in my grave than that I become an obstacle to anything that

---

A CLOSER LOOK

The use of the word 'civilian' does not necessarily imply that those in the civilian faction had never been or were not currently army men. However, it reflects an ethos, that the civilian Cromwellians supported a Parliamentary settlement and wanted to reduce the power of the military.

CROSS-REFERENCE

A Key Profile of **Arthur Haselrig** can be found on page 97.

KEY PROFILE

Charles Fleetwood (1618–92) worked his way through the ranks of the New Model Army and although he was not a particular effective soldier he was an excellent military administrator. He married Bridget Ireton (Cromwell's widowed daughter) in 1652. He became Major General for the eastern counties, but he did not cope very well with the stress of the 1650s and had a tendency to weep with anxiety in public.

ACTIVITY

Create a family tree for Oliver Cromwell, to illuminate his family connection to key figures in this period. How does understanding the relationships that surrounded Cromwell deepen your understanding of the Interregnum?

SECTION 6 | Experiments in government and society 1648–1660

ACTIVITY

Thinking point

Do you think Cromwell should have accepted the Crown? Make a list for and against and decide how you would have advised him.

STUDY TIP

Before you focus closely on the sources in the question, you should aim to reflect on what you think was happening in the 1650s. Don't forget to consider the provenance of the sources, as well as their context.

might help bring settlement to this nation. For the nation needs settlement, never more than now! And therefore, out of the love and honour I bear you, I am forever bound to acknowledge you have dealt most honourably and worthily with me, and most lovingly, and have had respect for one who deserves nothing.

A LEVEL PRACTICE QUESTION

Evaluating primary sources

With reference to Sources 1, 2 and 3 and your understanding of the historical context, assess the value of these three sources to an historian studying the Protectorate.

With the Humble Petition and Advice amended to remove monarchy from the new constitutional mix, Cromwell agreed to its conditions in June and was invested as Lord Protector, this time using St Edward's Chair, which was also known as the Coronation Chair because it had been used for the enthronement of monarchs since Edward II in 1308. The presence of the military was much more muted than at his previous investment. Cromwell rode to the Investment service with his third son, **Richard**.

The problem of the succession to Cromwell

Cromwell died on 3 September 1658, the anniversary of his great victories at Dunbar and Worcester. The accession of Richard to the role of Lord Protector was relatively uneventful – in part because he was much more of a civilian than an army man, so his installation was broadly accepted by the majority of the gentry who feared destabilisation more than anything. He had some powerful supporters from within the civilian faction, including his brother Henry Cromwell and **General Monck**. In November 1658, Richard Cromwell called the Third Protectorate Parliament, which convened in January 1659. However, his inability to manage the powerful divisions within the Political Nation soon put the entire Protectorate under threat.

ACTIVITY

Summary

Debate the extent to which Cromwell was a king in all but name during the 1650s. Divide the class into two groups, one group to argue he was a king, the other that he was not. Individuals should consider his actions in particular periods during the 1650s, for example, during the rule of the Major Generals. Structure your debate to consider each particular period in turn.

STUDY TIP

Questions like this require a coherent overall argument showing the ability to respond to a provocative interpretation, displaying a secure grasp of terminology and perspective. Before constructing on answer, it is necessary to identify what is meant by 'absolute ruler'. You could judge Cromwell's theoretical and actual position and actions against this definition.

KEY PROFILE

Richard Cromwell (1626–1712) was a Justice of the Peace for Hampshire in the early 1650s and became an MP in the First and Second Protectorate Parliaments. His father began to involve him more in political affairs and he became a member of the Council of State in December 1657. Cromwell nominated his son as his successor under the terms of the 1657 Humble Petition and Advice, probably only a couple of days before his death.

General George Monck (1608–70) gained military experience on the continent in the 1620s and 30s. He was a Royalist commander in the First Civil War but, between 1647 and 1649, he served Parliament as a Major General in Ulster. He fought alongside Cromwell at the Battle of Dunbar and was appointed Governor of Scotland in 1654, where he was both moderate and effective. He pledged his support to Richard Cromwell.

A LEVEL PRACTICE QUESTION

'Cromwell was an "absolute ruler" in the 1650s.'
Assess the validity of this view.

24 The monarchy restored

KEY CHRONOLOGY

1659	Jan	Third Protectorate Parliament
	22 Apr	Dissolution of Third Protectorate Parliament
	7 May	Recall of the Rump
	13 May	Humble Petition and Address of the Officers
	Aug	Booth's Rising
	Oct	Dissolution of the Rump
	26 Dec	Recall of the Rump
1660	1 Jan	Monck's army crosses into England
	21 Jan	Recall of the Long Parliament
	16 Mar	Dissolution of the Long Parliament
	4 Apr	Declaration of Breda
	25 Apr	Convention Parliament
	8 May	Charles Stuart declared King Charles II

LEARNING OBJECTIVES

In this chapter you will learn about:

- political vacuum after the death of Cromwell
- negotiations for the return of the monarchy under Charles II
- the legacy of the English Revolution by 1660.

Fig. 1 *Richard Cromwell, Oliver Cromwell's third son, was nominated by his father to succeed him as Lord Protector*

The political vacuum after the death of Cromwell

The Humble Petition and Advice required the Lord Protector to nominate a successor and from 1657 onwards, Oliver Cromwell involved his son Richard in the day-to-day government of the country in order to prepare him for the task. Richard had played very little part in events up to that point; he had not fought in any of the Civil Wars and had kept away from London, raising a large family and working as a JP in Hampshire. His first political role was an MP in the First Protectorate Parliament but he did not play a significant part. Oliver Cromwell may well have chosen Richard to succeed him precisely because he had not previously been enmeshed in the events of the previous decade and so was not attached to any one particular faction. The disadvantage of this approach was that Richard was not a politically minded man, and while he was not particularly opposed, nor was he strongly supported.

Weaknesses of Richard Cromwell's Protectorate

Finance

The cost of war had once again put the governmental system under strain: income was being consistently outstripped by outgoings and army pay was once again falling into arrears.

Divisions

Richard had been unable to exclude MPs from the Third Protectorate Parliament so it was a heady combination of diverse political opinions, including civilian Cromwellians, army men, republicans and many MPs of shifting loyalty. The division into civilian and military factions ran right through Parliament and the Council of State and was further complicated by the ongoing machinations of republicans such as Haselrig who continued to oppose the constitutional settlement as being too monarchical.

A CLOSER LOOK

Charles Fleetwood headed up a faction known as the 'Wallingford House Faction', named after his London home. This group included Desborough and a number of other army Grandees. While they had originally been supportive of Richard Cromwell, they began to sense the power of the army waning. They campaigned for proper payment of army arrears but their ambitions reached further: they wanted the Grandees recognised as an ongoing political force in the nation.

A CLOSER LOOK

A new wave of religious radicalism

The collapse of the Protectorate unleashed another wave of religious radicalism. Quakers were at a high tide after their big evangelistic campaigns, and Fifth Monarchists held a huge rally in West Sussex.

CROSS-REFERENCE

Speaker Lenthall is introduced in Chapter pages 98–99.

A CLOSER LOOK

Prynne's final militant act

William Prynne (of the shorn ears) had been a member of the Long Parliament before Pride's Purge. He tried to force his way into the new session of the Rump but was turned back by soldiers. Two days later he sneaked back in and launched a verbal attack on the Rump and called for a return to the full Long Parliament. Haselrig and Vane adjourned the Commons for lunch and had Prynne forcibly removed and barred. After a very long and active career, Prynne finally retired.

Civilian faction	Military faction
John Thurloe	Charles Fleetwood
General George Monck	John Desborough
Major General Goffe	John Lambert
Henry Cromwell	

The end of the Protectorate

Richard did not have the leverage within the army that his father had enjoyed and he rapidly began to lose contact with the Grandees, even those who were less overtly hostile to his Protectorate than the Wallingford House group. He allowed his Parliament to discuss reducing the army and limiting religious toleration, both abhorrent to old New Model men. It was the final straw for the Grandees and they mobilised the London-based soldiers. Richard tried to call the soldiers to rally to the Protectorate but without success. On 22 April, Major General Desborough forced Richard to dissolve the Third Protectorate Parliament and placed him under house arrest. A new crisis loomed.

Richard Cromwell had proved himself unable to maintain his authority in the face of the might of the army: next the army would see if it could manage without a Cromwell at its head. The nub of the problem was that Cromwell had been able to maintain power by bridging both the civilian and military factions. After his death, power was fought over between those factions.

The recall and expulsion of the Rump

The first problem the army faced was that it was divided about whether or not to support a continued Protectorate. Fleetwood and Desborough had opposed the civilian Cromwellians but they were not ideologically opposed to the Protectorate system. The recall of John Lambert to the Army Council, now the de facto Council of State, began to raise the question of whether Lambert himself could replace Richard as Lord Protector.

However, others within the army had opposed the Protectorate because it was too monarchical and they yearned for the days of the 'purer' authority of the Rump. This faction stirred up dissent among the latent religious radicalism of the lower ranks, the Fifth Monarchists and other sectarians and forced the hand of the Grandees to recall the old Rump Parliament which opened on 7 May 1659 with Speaker Lenthall in the chair again. The Rump MPs immediately abolished the Protectorate constitution. Richard was still Protector in name but he resigned when he was presented with paperwork to sign and a promise that his considerable personal debts would be cleared.

The Rump itself was a fraction of its former strength: 42 MPs sat on 7 May, out of a total of 78 who were eligible to attend. Some never attended at all. Its legality was dubious because it had been formed as the result of an army coup and was now recalled because of the army, whereas the Protectorate system, though innovative, had nevertheless been established by a Constitution that had been agreed in a more conventional way.

The Humble Petition and Address of the Officers

John Lambert presented another new constitutional proposal, the 'Humble Petition and Address of the Officers' to the Rump on 13 May. It contained 15 articles of the 'Fundamentals of our Good Old Cause' and recommended the restoration of a 'Commonwealth, without a king, single person or House of Lords' but did endorse the creation of a Senate, made up of 'able and faithful persons, eminent for Godliness' which would, in effect, be able to represent the army interest in the heart of government. Haselrig led the opposition to the Address on the basis that it tended to reduce the authority of the Commons: he counter-argued for a purge of the military. The Rump had, by the end of May, broken into civilian and military factions and was in a deadlock. Worse still for stability, the army was also fracturing into those who would accept a degree of oversight from Parliament and those who resisted, desperately trying to retain independence.

George Booth's Rising, August 1659

Opposition to the Commonwealth had grown steadily throughout the 1650s, whether focused directly against Cromwell or diffused into more general opposition to the **Interregnum** governments. Penruddock's Rising of March 1655 (see page 197) was only one of a series of attempts to overthrow Cromwell's regime, including numerous assassination plots, which rose in frequency as the decade progressed. As the end of the decade neared, Charles Stuart was beginning to develop something close to a meaningful military force on the continent which encouraged him to despatch the Earl of Ormond on a clandestine mission to test the likelihood of a successful rebellion being kindled in England Plans were indeed afoot. A rising was planned for August 1659 which required simultaneous action across England. Near Guildford in Surrey, a fanatical Royalist called John Mordaunt was to take the lead while in Oxfordshire, a separate faction was preparing to rise. In Cheshire, Sir George Booth mobilised an army and smaller risings were planned around the midlands and west country. However, at the last minute, the Surrey and the Oxfordshire risings failed to materialise, triggering a loss of confidence elsewhere. Only Booth led men decisively into action.

On hearing news of the rising, Charles Stuart travelled to Brest on the French coast in order to set sail to take charge of Booth's army. However, local militia rose against Booth, and Lambert marched an army up to Cheshire which decisively put the rebellion down at the Battle of Winnington Bridge on 19 August. News of the defeat reached Charles and he turned back to regroup with his two principal aides, Sir Edward Hyde (later Earl of Clarendon) and the Marquis of Ormond.

A CLOSER LOOK

Booth did seek the restoration of Charles Stuart but only on limited terms. His first aim was to secure the recall of a new and free Parliament which could negotiate acceptable terms for the return of the king, in keeping with his early Parliamentarianism.

The dismissal of the Rump

With peace restored, the Rump began to discuss how to add members without calling fresh elections. The regime was again penniless and in arrears with army pay. Junior officers, in tune with the rank and file, petitioned Parliament to restart 'godly reform' and protect the status of their senior officers and the army's role in politics as it looked probable that Parliament would replace the New Model Army with a more conventional militia that swore its allegiance to the Commonwealth. With tensions reaching fever pitch, Haselrig ordered the closure of the doors to the Commons, manoeuvred the Rump into expelling from the army those he considered to be ringleaders, and summoned army regiments who he believed to be loyal to the Rump to come to the defence of Parliament. Lambert by now had returned to London and, finding himself expelled from the army and threatened with arrest, called on the troops nearby to rally behind him instead, which they did. Assembling around Westminster on 13 October, Lambert's men prevented the members of the Rump from entering Parliament, and locked the doors.

ACTIVITY

What similarities can you see between the idea of a Senate and the Nominated Assembly?

A CLOSER LOOK

The 'Good Old Cause'

This phrase was loaded with significance in the late 1650s and referred to the republicanism and religious radicalism that had characterised the early Rump Parliament. It had been used in verbal attacks against Oliver Cromwell in 1658, and by 1659 the army were pushing the 'Good Old Cause' in widely disseminated tracts and pamphlets, with the aim of embedding it into the constitution itself.

CROSS-REFERENCE

For a definition of Interregnum, see Chapter 20, page 172.

KEY PROFILE

Sir George Booth (1622–84) had fought for Parliament in the Civil Wars and had sat in the Barebones Parliament and the First Protectorate Parliament, but by 1659 he had become disenchanted with the course of Protectorate politics, not least because he had been an excluded member in Pride's Purge and was not allowed to take up his seat in the recalled Rump Parliament. Despite being a staunch Presbyterian, his attempted Royalist rising in early August swiftly swept across Cheshire, Lancashire and North Wales.

A CLOSER LOOK

Expelling army ringleaders, October 1659

The vote to expel Lambert, Desborough and eight others was passed on 12 October by 50 to 15, and was swiftly followed by confirmation of new appointments to the role of Army Commissioner for seven men including Charles Fleetwood, Arthur Haselrig, George Monck and Edmund Ludlow: their authority was to be subordinate to that of Parliament.

KEY TERM

secluded members: a term used to describe the MPs who had been excluded by Colonel Pride by 1659

KEY PROFILE

Edmund Ludlow (1617–92) fought in Haselrig's cavalry regiment during the Civil War and became MP for Wiltshire in 1646. He was closely allied with Henry Marten and the political Independents and was a Baptist who had strong apocalyptic views. He supported Pride's Purge, tried the king and signed the death warrant. He took command of the army in Ireland after Cromwell left and Ireton died. He retired from public life because he refused to acknowledge the Protectorate constitution under Oliver or Richard Cromwell and became a member of the Wallingford House faction. He sat in the restored Rump, who despatched him again to military command in Ireland.

CROSS-REFERENCE

The gunpowder factory owned by Evelyn's family is featured on page 108.

The Committee of Safety

On 27 October, an interim government was put into place as a 'Committee of Safety.' This was the second such Committee in 1659, the first having held power for only two weeks in May. Under the leadership of Fleetwood, members were swiftly called to join, including Bulstrode Whitelock, Henry Vane Jr, Ludlow, Desborough, Lambert and John Ireton, brother of the late Henry Ireton. Within two months, the country was close to renewed civil war. London was descending into anarchy as conservative forces became increasingly active in their opposition to the Committee, with significant rioting on the streets and attacks on the New Model forces. The judicial system was breaking down, not least because the Committee was surprisingly reluctant to pursue its opponents through the courts, allowing them to continue to stir up dissension instead of crushing them as had Cromwell and others before him. Tax revenues had dwindled to next to nothing, and demands were growing for a return of the **secluded members** of Pride's Purge of 1648. Division in the army was solidifying into action, with Monck's Scottish Army, Fairfax's forces in Yorkshire, the army in Ireland and the Navy off the south coast all declaring for a 'free Parliament'. By December, it was clear that the Committee had failed to create a viable governmental alternative and Fleetwood resigned: now the initiative swung back to Haselrig.

Pride's Purge reversed

The Rump returned on 26 December 1659 but found itself increasingly and rapidly out of step with public sentiment, which was now reflecting a desire for an end to turbulence. Presbyterians and Royalists were equally vocal and once again the printing presses were working hard. Henry Vane grumbled that everything was going wrong and the House, City and army were looking towards the king.

General George Monck, commander of the New Model Army in Scotland and one of the Commissioners appointed by the Rump prior to Lambert's coup, crossed into England on 1 January 1660. A moderate man who represented steadiness and order, he linked up with Fairfax's Yorkshire forces and continued to march towards London. Lambert raised a force to push back these unwelcome soldiers but this time the rank and file showed their weariness of continued instability and gradually drifted away. Haselrig expected that Monck would support the Rump and led Parliament to issue him with 'Letters of Thanks from the Parliament… acknowledging his faithful Service, and high Deservings'. In actual fact, he proved to be of quite independent mind.

Recognising that civil disorder was still climbing, seeing unbridgeable strife between Rump and army, and equally convinced that the army could not hold a middle ground acceptable to the wider Political Nation, Monck allowed the Rump to reinstate the excluded members from Pride's Purge. He was in a position to do so because his friend and political ally Anthony Ashley Cooper was working within Parliament, and Monck's forces were exerting pressure outside Parliament. At the same time, he himself was appointed Captain General, and Commander-in-Chief, under the Parliament, of all the Land-Forces of England, Scotland, and Ireland.

SOURCE 1

From the diary of John Evelyn, from Wotton in Surrey, who wrote a diary between 1641 and 1697. He was a prolific writer with many published pamphlets, but his diary was kept privately, unpublished until 1808. In this extract, he gives an insight into events around the reinstatement of the excluded members:

3rd February, 1660. General Monk came now to London out of Scotland; no man knew what he would do or whether he would declare for king or parliament; yet he was met on his way by the gentlemen of all the counties which he passed with petitions that he would recall the old long-interrupted Parliament, and settle the nation in some order, being at this time in such total confusion, and under no government, everybody wondering what would be next and what he would do.

10th February, 1660. Now General Monk entered the city and all the old army of the fanatics put out of their posts and sent out of town.

11th February, 1660. A significant day. Monk marched to Whitehall, dispersed that nest of robbers, and convened the old Parliament, the Rump Parliament (so called as retaining some few rotten members of the other) being dissolved; and for joy whereof were many thousands of rumps roasted publicly in the streets at the bonfires this night, with ringing of bells, and universal jubilee.

A CLOSER LOOK

A case study of changing allegiances

Anthony Ashley Cooper (1621–1683), later 1st Earl of Shaftesbury (1672) earned the nickname the Dorsetshire Eel because he was so very flexible in his allegiances throughout his life, although there was integrity in his pursuit of moderation. He was a mild Puritan who became MP for Shaftesbury in the Short Parliament and Downton in the Long Parliament, although this was a disputed election. He was a member of the Nominated Assembly (July–Dec 1653) and the Council of State (July 1653). He backed the Instrument of Government and was an MP in all the Protectorate Parliaments. He was initially excluded from the recalled Rump because the disputed election of 1640 was still unresolved but the recalled Rump confirmed his election and finally took his seat in 1660.

Fig. 2 *General George Monck*

The end of the Long Parliament

The recall of the members who had been excluded by Pride's Purge meant that the session of Parliament that began on 21 February 1660 included all surviving members of the original Long Parliament. Overall, the recalled Long Parliament retained its Presbyterian flavour from the early 1640s, although its members were of course considerably older.

SOURCE 2

The diary of Samuel Pepys reveals a sense of cheerful optimism (although that may have been just his own personal exuberance) as this extract from 2 March 1660 reveals:

This morning I went early to Mr. Crew's. Here were a great many come to see him, as Secretary Thurlow who is now by this Parliament chosen again Secretary of State. There were also General Monck's trumpeters to give my Lord a sound of their trumpets. Then going home, I had two brave dishes of meat, one of fish, a carp and some other fishes. After that to Westminster Hall, where I saw Sir G. Booth at liberty. This day I hear the City militia is put into good posture.

I understand that my Lord Lambert did yesterday send a letter to the Council, and that to-night he is to come and appear to the Council in person. Sir Arthur Haselrigge do not yet appear in the House. Great is the talk of a single person, and that it would now be Charles, George Monck, or Richard Cromwell again. Great also is the dispute now in the House, in whose name the writs shall run for the next Parliament; and it is said that the MP Mr Prynne, in open House, said, 'In King Charles's.

KEY PROFILE

Samuel Pepys (1633–1703) attended the same grammar school in Huntingdon as Oliver Cromwell, although he was by some years his junior, and early on in life attached himself to Edward Montagu, the Parliamentary army commander who was also a Huntingdon boy. He worked for Montagu and rose to a senior position in naval administration. He wrote his diary, in a secret code, over a 10-year period.

ACTIVITY

Why do you think that Pepys thought it noteworthy that William Prynne declared his allegiance to the king in Parliament?

Certainly change was afoot and the Long Parliament had gained a renewed sense of purpose.

SECTION 6 | Experiments in government and society 1648–1660

ACTIVITY

1. Why was it necessary for this Bill to refer specifically to the House of Lords?
2. How long was the Long Parliament?
3. What do you think the Bill might have meant by 'manifold Sins and Provocations'?

KEY PROFILE

John Mordaunt (1627–75) was Baron Mordaunt of Reigate and Viscount Mordaunt of Avalon from 1659. He was a devoted Royalist who was tried for treason for his part in Booth's rising. Colonel Pride was supposed to attend as one of the judges but was ill: Mordaunt's wife successfully bribed as many of the judges as she could to acquit him. He continued to support the Royalist cause and formally welcomed Charles Stuart when he landed at Dover in May 1660.

CROSS-REFERENCE

Be careful not to confuse the Declaration of Breda with the Treaty of Breda, found on page 179.

SOURCE 3

On 16 March 1660, the reconvened Long Parliament published a Bill of Dissolution and made arrangements for a fresh election for a new parliament. The Bill and subsequent remarks were filed in the Commons Journal:

A Bill for Dissolving the Parliament begun and first held at Westminster, the 3rd of November 1640; and for the Calling and Holding of a Parliament at Westminster, on the 25th Day of April 1660.

A proviso was attached: 'While the Long Parliament is acting out of one single chamber in creating this Bill, its intention is not to infringe and certainly not to remove the ancient native Right of the House of Lords to be a part of the Parliament of England.'

Resolved, That Friday, the 6th Day of April 1660, be set apart for a Day of public Fasting and demonstrations of humility, to be conducted solemnly throughout the Nation, under the Sense of the great and manifold Sins and Provocations that this nation has presented to God; and to seek the Lord for his Blessing upon the Parliament, that the Lord will make them Healers of our Breeches, and Instruments to restore and settle Peace and Government in the Nations, upon Foundations of Truth and Righteousness.

New elections for a fresh Parliament were called, using the traditional electoral process and excluding no one on the basis of their activities over the past decades.

Negotiations for the return of the monarchy under Charles II

While Charles Stuart had abandoned his attempt to take the country by force, news of the collapse of the Committee of Safety encouraged him to envision a political takeover instead. Plans were even mooted that he might marry Lambert's daughter to bridge the great divide with the army but as it became clear that Monck's actions were beginning to open a very promising door, Charles's contacts in England began to seek links with Parliamentarians instead. John Mordaunt, now Viscount Mordaunt, and to a significant extent, his wife Lady Mordaunt, based in London, began to woo the excluded Presbyterian faction of 1648, including the Earls of Northumberland, Manchester, Bedford and Clare as well as Denzil Holles and Sir Harbottle Grimston, whom he collectively nicknamed the 'Presbyterian Knot'. These men still desired what they had wanted in 1648: a settlement with the king who was bound to honour the liberty and privileges of Parliament and would govern with wise counsellors.

Monck also began to build contacts with Charles Stuart and negotiated with him via Sir John Greville. He kept fairly clear of parliamentary constitutional issues and instead focused on the army's requirements, requesting indemnity, prompt payment of arrears and moderate religious toleration.

The Declaration of Breda

Charles Stuart, working with just three advisers, Edward Hyde, the Marquis of Ormond and Sir Edward Nicholas acted on a sound piece of advice from Monck and moved his court from Catholic Spain to the Protestant Dutch Republic. He proceeded to draw up a proposal for his restoration, which he issued from Breda on 4 April 1660 and despatched to the Lords and Commons, the army and navy and the City of London.

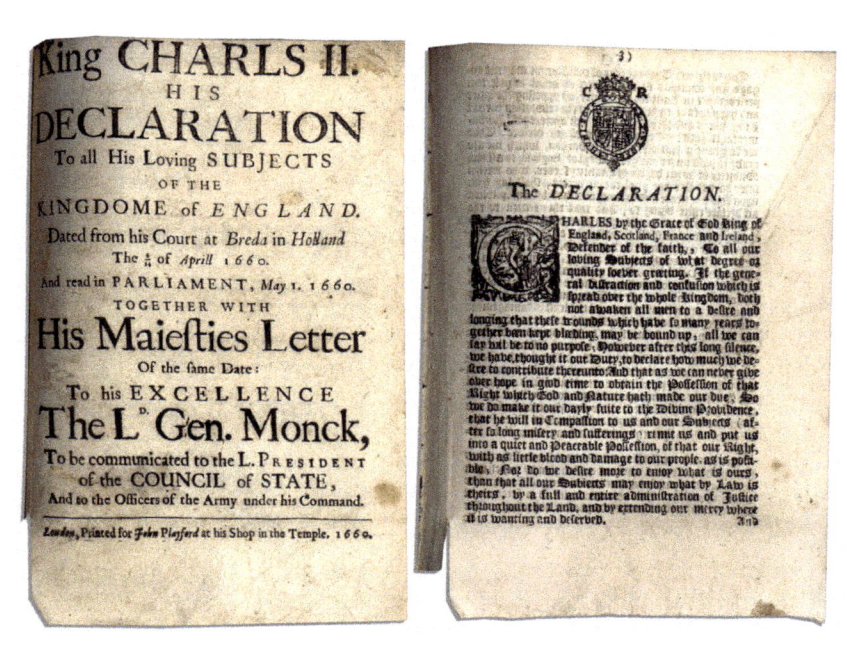

Fig. 3 *The Declaration of Breda 1660*

KEY PROFILE

Sir Edward Nicholas (1593–1669) was a royal officer under Charles I, with particular responsibility for the administration of Ship Money. He travelled with the king during the Civil War and went into exile in France when Charles surrendered. He moved to The Hague, where he endeavoured to serve Charles Stuart who made him Secretary of State in 1654, a position that was reconfirmed in 1660.

The Declaration was a clever piece of political writing because it covered all the significant topics that would be issues in a restoration of the monarchy without committing Charles to any specific course of action.

SOURCE 4

From the *Declaration of Breda*, From drafted by a small group of loyal supporters of Charles Stuart and issued from Breda in the Dutch Republic on 4 April 1660:

Charles, by the grace of God, king of England, Scotland, France and Ireland, Defender of the Faith, &c.,

We pray daily that God will put us into a quiet and peaceable possession of our right, with as little blood and damage to our people as possible, so that all our subjects may enjoy what by law is theirs, through a full administration of justice and our extension of mercy where it is wanted and deserved.

Therefore we declare that we grant a free and general pardon to all our subjects (except those named by Parliament), provided that they make it known that they require our pardon within 40 days.

We declare a liberty to tender consciences and affirm that no man will be questioned about his religious opinions as long as these do not disturb the peace of the Kingdom. We will consent to an Act of Parliament to make this commitment binding.

Furthermore, we will ensure that all arrears will be paid, to all officers and soldiers under General Monck, and they shall transfer into our service on the same good pay and conditions as they now enjoy.

PRACTICE QUESTION

Evaluating primary sources

With reference to Sources 2, 3 and 4, and your understanding of the historical context, assess the value of these three sources for an historian studying the Restoration.

STUDY TIP

This question requires you to consider the interplay of the short-term context, personalities and long-term causes of the Restoration.

SECTION 6 | Experiments in government and society 1648–1660

The Convention Parliament

On 25 April 1660, fresh elections returned a new House of Commons to Westminster. Technically it was not yet a parliament as it had not been called by a king, so it began life as a 'Convention' and then legitimised itself as a Parliament in June, in an Act to which the king gave his assent. In terms of membership, about half the Parliament were old-style parliamentarians and the rest were a mixture of new MPs and Royalists. The Convention debated the terms of the Declaration of Breda and on 8 May, declared Charles Stuart to be King Charles II. Parliament's terms allowed the new king to take up the English throne on terms more favourable to monarchical power than his father Charles I had agreed with the Long Parliament in 1641, most particularly because no control was exerted over the king's choice of ministers, and his control of the militia was unquestioned.

> **ACTIVITY**
>
> List the main terms of the Declaration of Breda into one column of a table and in the other column, cross-reference them with the measures to which Charles had agreed during the 1641–42 sessions of the Long Parliament. What do you think was the most significant difference? Would Charles I have approved of his son's negotiations?

Fig. 4 *Charles had to wait until 23 April 1661 for his coronation*

The Indemnity Act

Those who signed the death warrant of Charles I were incontrovertibly excluded from the Indemnity Act that was promised in the Declaration of Breda and they were executed as traitors. The body of Cromwell itself was disinterred, hanged, drawn and quartered on the orders of the king. Some non-signatories were also caught up in Charles's careful pursuit of vengeance, including Sir Henry Vane the Younger. Despite initially being pardoned by the king, he was charged with treason by Parliament. Attempting to defend himself against a predominantly Royalist jury, he spoke at great length about the problem of loyalty during the Interregnum: his case was that he had consistently stood for the sovereignty of Parliament as the enactment of the authority of the nation, from whom a king derives his power.

> **A CLOSER LOOK**
>
> ### Events in Ireland
>
> The Rump's final act echoed what had happened in Ireland, where in December 1659, conservative forces in the Irish Army seized Dublin Castle and brought about the Irish Convention, which declared for Charles Stuart.

> **SOURCE 5**
>
> This excerpt from Sir Henry Vane Junior's defence during his trial for treason comes from the official court records of his trial:
>
> I do humbly affirm that in the great changes and revolutions from first to last, I was never a first mover, but always a follower., It is very apparent by my

conduct when that great Violation of Privileges happened to the parliament, during which, by force of arms, several members thereof were debarred coming into the House and keeping their seats there. Because of this I boycotted Parliament from December 1648 to February 1649. I can also say that I had neither consent nor vote at first in the Resolutions of the Houses, concerning the Non-Addresses to his late majesty, so neither had I in the least any consent in, or approval of his death. In like manner, the Resolutions and Votes for changing the government into a Commonwealth or Free State were passed some weeks before my return to parliament. I steadfastly opposed the introducing of an arbitrary regal power, under the name of Protector, by force and the law of the Sword. Furthermore, I was disappointed that the removal of the Protectorate and the return of the original members of Parliament was carried out under the power of the army. (Cited in Cobbett's Complete Collection of State Trials and Proceedings, Volume 6)

Despite wavering from Charles (and the recent example of John Lambert, who escaped the death penalty by pleading for mercy), Vane was beheaded on 14 June 1662.

The legacy of the English Revolution by 1660

The Restoration settlement dated the start of Charles II's reign to January 1649 and many would argue that more was achieved in 1660 to reverse the legacy of the Interregnum than to negotiate a progressive settlement between king and subjects.

While parliamentarians could justifiably be aggrieved at the broad and generous terms of the return of a Stuart to the throne, Royalists were also quite reasonably disgruntled at the lack of reward that they received for their long and often dangerous loyalty. The king returned with the English constitution substantially intact and with most of the problematic issues of the 1640s still unresolved. Most notably, Crown finances and religious settlement remained at the forefront of governmental business for the duration of Charles II's reign.

Revolution reversed

The Restoration swept away the undoubtedly revolutionary aspects of England's constitutional experiments:
- A quasi-federal state in which a Westminster-based executive Council, headed by one man, was supported by administrative councils in Ireland and Scotland, who each had representation within the Westminster Parliaments of 1654–8, well in advance of the Acts of Union of 1707 (Scotland) and 1801 (Ireland).
- The concept of Parliament as the prime authority based on natural law, with guaranteed sessions lasting at least five months every three years.
- Centralised practice of law and the legal process across the three Stuart kingdoms.
- Religious tolerance in which all but the most extreme were allowed access to public life and office.
- Revised and broadened franchise: an increased number of county seats, the demotion of borough seats, a wider county franchise, and Scottish and Irish representation.

Revolution sustained

Outside the narrow constitutional sphere however, some developments which had been catalysed by the turmoil of the Interregnum were most definitely not lost:

A CLOSER LOOK

Regicides and other traitors

The 33 surviving regicides were brought to trial following the passage of the Act of Indemnity and Oblivion. Most were executed but a few had their sentences reduced to life imprisonment. In addition, the Marquis of Argyll was executed in 1661 for leading the Scottish Covenanters. John Lambert's death sentence was commuted to life imprisonment, and Sir Arthur Haslerig died in prison while awaiting trial.

ACTIVITY

Make a copy of the excerpt of Vane's defence in Source 5 and use it as a revision exercise, identifying the events that he makes reference to.

Fig. 5 *Female preachers continued in the Quaker movement*

Polemic

By 1660, pamphleteering, newspapers and other polemic expressions were an established part of the cultural life of the nation and were fiercely defended in the novel climate of the renewed monarchy. Thus George Wither, in his 1661 tract, *An Improvement of Imprisonment*, stood up for the right to free speech which he felt was under threat, writing 'We are in danger shortly to become the truest slaves throughout all Christendom'.

Religion

The genie of religion was not put back into the bottle in 1660. While Charles's woolly indications of tolerance in the Declaration of Breda came to little, nonetheless the English religious landscape at the end of Interregnum was filled with diverse expressions of faith, from the smallest sects to the emergent denominations including the Baptists. What is more, a vocabulary for the defence of individuality within the Christian faith had been cemented and continued to provide an Independent balance to the conservative drift that accompanied the Restoration.

Gender politics

The role of women in public life was permanently changed by the higher status they attained in many of the more radical religious sects, and especially among the Quakers. While forces of conservatism began to pull the tide back from these radical outposts, nonetheless women consolidated their position as active players in the nonconformist churches that remained.

The 'Good Old Cause'

As the regicides were brought to trial and executed in the early months of the restored monarchy, the concept of the 'Good Old Cause', which had first appeared in the late 1650s, began to take a permanent shape. Thus Daniel Axtell, convicted for commanding the parliamentary guard during the trial of Charles I declared from the scaffold, 'If I had a thousand lives, I could lay them all down for the Cause' and Milton wrote, 'What I have spoken, is the language of that which is not call'd amiss the good Old Cause,' and went on to write, The Parliament of England, assisted by a great number of the people who rose up and stuck to them faithfully in the defence of religion and their civil liberties, judged kingship to be proven burdensome, expensive, useless and dangerous and so abolished it. They turned bondage to royalty into a free, glorious and ever-progressing Commonwealth.

Two dramatic decades

There can be no doubt that the decades between 1640 and 1660 were among the most turbulent ever experienced in British history, both in terms of the amount of change that was experienced and the long duration of the period of change. It is no wonder that the years of the so-called English Revolution are seen as such a turning point in our history.

ACTIVITY

Summary

Looking back across the two decades leading up to 1660, the question arises of whether the term 'revolution' is the best choice to describe the events of these turbulent years. Reflect on the question below.

- The Restoration was fundamentally conservative, returning England substantially to the conditions offered to the king in 1660. Does this mean that a better term than 'revolution' would be 'rebellion'? Remember that Edward Hyde's book was entitled 'The History of the Great Rebellion'.
- What did contemporaries mean when they used the term 'revolutionary'?

STUDY TIP

There are a number of possible positions you could take in your answer. You could make a list of the other key figures of the period and analyse their roles and responsibilities. Try to use your contextual knowledge to assess what other factors may have been responsible for the instability after Cromwell's death.

PRACTICE QUESTION

'John Lambert bears the greatest responsibility for the instability that followed the death of Oliver Cromwell.'
Assess the validity of this view.

Conclusion

Fig. 1 *King Charles II*

SOURCE 1

From a joint statement by the House of Commons, the House of Lords and the Mayor and Aldermen of the City of London, 8 May 1660:

We, the Lords and Commons assembled in Parliament, together with the Lord Mayor, Aldermen and city councillors and other freemen of this Kingdom do, according to our duty and allegiance, heartily, joyfully and unanimously acknowledge and proclaim that, immediately upon the death of our late sovereign lord King Charles, the Imperial Crown of the realm of England and all the kingdoms, dominions and rights belonging to the same, did by inherent birthright and lawful and undoubted succession descend and come to his most Excellent Majesty Charles the Second as being by lineage justly and lawfully the next heir of the blood royal of this realm and the most potent, mighty and most undoubted King and Defender of the Faith.

Eleven years of English history were seemingly wiped away in 1660 as King Charles II took the throne. Monarchy restored, Lords and Commons back in their traditional forms, London settled, the army back under the control of its royal Commander-in-Chief: on the surface, the constitutional clock was reset somewhere close to 1625. A visitor arriving in London for the first time in 1660 would have been forgiven for seeing a country united in affection for the monarchy. Nevertheless, the 'English Revolution' had left its legacy.

The changing role of Parliament

King James I had arrived in London in 1603 with the expectation that the Westminster Parliament would operate in the same way as its Scottish equivalent, as an extension of his royal court, biddable and relatively compliant. That he encountered immediate difficulties shows that the English Parliament at least was already beginning stretch its constitutional wings under the direction of MPs who were well-grounded in the law. The Civil

War and Interregnum catalysed this process and spread it into Scotland and Ireland. In all three kingdoms, initiatives such as the Ormond Agreement, the Scottish Engagement and the Instrument of Government developed the sense that government had a contractual basis, replacing a patriarchal idea of kingship with new notions of a contract between the state and the people. In the process, Divine Right was swept away: no king would ever again be able to use God as a defence against the people's will. Although the monarchy was ostensibly restored in 1660, it rested on new foundations.

What is more, although Parliament in the form of Lords and Commons was restored in 1660, another change was underway in the balance of power between those two houses. In 1625, members of the Lords dominated the Political Nation by virtue of their wealth, their status and influence in the regions and their proximity to the king. By 1660, the Commons had shown they could govern independently, without need for a House of Lords. What is more, under Cromwell, government had been able to push forward into radically uncharted waters with such experiments as the rule by Major Generals. Although the Restoration brought governmental authority and power back from the furthest reaches, the seat of Parliamentary power had decisively moved from Lords to Commons.

The development of the modern nation state

The years 1625 to 1660 also saw other elements of transition towards a modern state.

Modern state finance

Financial trouble is a thread that runs throughout these years. Whether this was Charles I's need for money to finance his foreign policy, or the Commonwealth's need for money to pay New Model Army wages, what is self-evident is that money posed a governmental problem in the first half of the seventeenth century that began to be resolved during the latter half of the century. The demands of the state had, by 1600, clearly outstripped traditional means of raising revenue. Salisbury's Great Contract was an abortive effort to resolve this problem; Charles I made a catastrophic attempt to make the old system work. The issue began to be effectively addressed in the Protectorate through the medium of the annual allowance of £200,000 that was provided for the Lord Protector and maintained in the Restoration settlement which made an annual allowance of £1.2m to the monarch. Although neither of these sums was actually adequate for the required expenditure, the principle behind the allowances was sound and new. Furthermore, taxation, controlled by Parliament, had become a more normal feature of everyday life through the Civil War and Interregnum, mainly because of the ongoing expense of keeping soldiers in the field. Taken together, governmental finances were being put onto a modern footing.

A modern standing army

In the old feudal system, soldiers were gathered by knights and brought to the service of the king. At the beginning of the Civil War, this was still the model, as both king and Parliament vied for control of the county militia. Yet by the end, England had developed a model for an efficient and professional standing army of soldiers who were not bound to any particular region or noble commander but worked for the government and gave their allegiance to the state.

Centralised government

In 1625, local government was the medium through which the monarch's will was enacted. Hindsight and the benefit of our modern awareness of economics and demographics shows that the growth of centralised government was becoming necessary in the Stuart era as commerce and industry were creating significant regional interdependence and there was a population drift from rural areas into towns. Without such understanding, Charles I was quite right to see that his realms were in need of more efficient government, and Thorough was a sound, if poorly executed strategy. Cromwell also had to grapple with the growing gap between central and local government, although he was no more successful in his attempt to find a solution, with martial law under the Major Generals an example of one such flawed endeavour. In this respect, a concrete legacy of the English Revolution by 1660 is less easy to identify, but a process was underway.

Changing relations between the three kingdoms

Whether the term 'English Civil War' should be replaced by 'War of the Three Kingdoms' is a topic of historiographical debate. What is true is that Charles I was king of three kingdoms and all three were affected immensely.

Scotland

Although Charles I was born in Scotland, he was most distinctly an English king at the start of his reign, evidenced by the fact that his 1633 visit to Scotland was his first such in 30 years. Scotland was also lower in status than his English kingdom, by virtue of such things as wealth, population and proximity to the king's royal person. During the 1640s however, Scottish affairs became of the highest significance to English affairs in a manner entirely unprecedented, with a Scottish agenda reaching a point of near-dominance of English matters of state, defence and religion. Yet by 1660, Scotland had become once again the junior partner, its soldiers under the English General Monck and its religious demands for Presbyterianism unheeded in the Restoration settlement. Charles II was, like his father, an English king who also had kingdoms elsewhere.

Ireland

In contrast, despite arousing substantial fear, which was critical in the turbulence of 1641, affairs in Ireland did not have much material impact within England, but the legacy of England's involvement in Ireland endures far beyond 1660. James I's policy of plantations, maintained under Charles and managed under Wentworth's iron grip, set up the devastating sieges of Drogheda and Wexford under Cromwell that permanently polluted Anglo-Irish relations. It is difficult to describe these events as a specific legacy of the English Revolution because it was religious tension between Catholic Ireland and Protestant England dating from the sixteenth century that set up the chain of events that led to the massacres. However, it is only fair to say that it was Cromwell's military skill and the New Model Army, both creations of the Civil Wars, that contributed heavily to these events.

From state Church to religious diversity

In the religious sphere it is easier to identify the legacy of the English Revolution. Censorship and strict enforcement of conformity had kept the lid on different religious expressions up until the 1630s, and those beliefs and practices that diverged from mainstream Anglicanism, such as Anabaptism, were most definitely in the extreme minority and always at risk of persecution. However, the turmoil of the early 1640s released a surge of religious radicalism that is not entirely traceable back before that decade. Ranters, Quakers, Muggletonians and Fifth Monarchy Men emerged and indelibly changed the religious landscape. While each movement has its own significance, collectively they indicate a dramatic (although incomplete) shift from a single, state-defined religion to which adherence was a test of patriotic loyalty, to the beginnings of a multi-denominational environment within which the

A CLOSER LOOK

Historiography

Historians such as Jenny Wormald, who specialises in Scottish history, tend to draw out the commonalities and connections between England, Scotland and Ireland during the Civil War period. Others such as John Adamson have developed new perspectives that illuminate the English Civil War as the central point of the crises of the 1640s. An abridged version of Adamson's characterisation is that the Revolution was driven by a group of noblemen who were aiming for the creation of a constitution more akin to the Venetian oligarchy. A further area of historiography focuses on the radicalism of ordinary participants, with a strong emphasis on the extent to which revolutionary ideas, disseminated across London and into the provinces, changed history from the bottom up. The years 1625–60 are a period alive with historiographical debate!

people represented in Parliament, and not a divinely ordained monarch, set wide parameters for religious toleration. Given that it was not until 1829 that Catholicism become officially tolerated in England, it goes too far to say that this was the beginning of a secular state, but there are indicators of the direction of travel.

From community to individual

The Earl of Clarendon described the Civil War and Interregnum period as the time of 'The Great Rebellion'. Looking at the themes of this era, his interpretation can be seen as valid; many of the events that emerge pre-date the outbreak of 'rebellion' against King Charles I and had not been resolved by the time of the Restoration. It is possible therefore to suggest that deeper changes were underway in the nation during the seventeenth century that were not created but only catalysed by the consequences of the king's decisions, particularly those of the 1630s. In this reading, first John Pym and then Oliver Cromwell's own particular charisma and political skill disrupted normal government: once they had exited the scene, the 'Rebellion' was over and the normal English constitutional arrangement continued to grapple with a changing world. There was no 'Revolution,' just turmoil and civic disobedience.

However, stepping outside personalities and individual events, and with the benefit of a long view that Clarendon could not possess, the Civil Wars and Interregnum years were genuinely revolutionary. Driven undoubtedly by Puritan theology, which propounded the individual's ability to interact directly with God, concepts of the innate qualities shared by all human beings began to form that were new, unprecedented and genuinely revolutionary. In the political sphere, such ideas kindled the revolutionary theories of the Levellers, who articulated theories of natural right and individual freedom that exploded underneath the old, established paradigm in which people of high birth status and property were superior to those without. In the religious sphere, the emergent primacy of the individual expression of faith threatened to sweep away centuries of obedience to Church discipline and dogma that was the preserve of a clerical elite and even began to usher in possibilities of question and doubt. English society and culture by 1660 was still fundamentally traditional, moderate and conservative but radical seeds had been planted and taken root that would mean England would never be the same again.

The legacy of the English Revolution

In the 1630s, Thomas Wentworth had said that a king is the 'keystone which closes up the arch of order and government'. Perhaps the most significant legacy of the English Revolution by 1660 was the achievement of consensus within the Political Nation that Wentworth was right. Having tried a multiplicity of different ways to keep order and administer effective government, Commons, Lords, army and Aldermen had decided that monarchy was England's best constitutional arrangement.

Glossary

A

annus horribilis: first used by Queen Elizabeth II, the term means a 'horrible year' and has entered our vernacular to describe a period dominated by one catastrophe after another

address: a polite request to be heard on a specific subject

Agitator: not a pejorative term in the seventeenth century: it had no negative connotations, but simply meant someone who spoke on behalf of others

aldermen: high-ranking members of a city or borough council, next in status to the Mayor

apotheosis: 'to make divine', i.e. to elevate someone to the rank of a God; Rubens' work depicts James being carried towards God on the wings of a huge eagle and represents the close alliance between his royal and God's divine authority

Arminianism: a denomination of Protestantism whose members did not want Puritan reformation within the Church of England

arsenal: a large store of weapons; in the 1640s there were significant arsenals in London, Hull, Oxford and Bristol

B

billeting: the placement of soldiers into private houses where they would receive food and a bed; billeting was used to solve a logistical problem of what to do with soldiers when they were away from home

C

Canon Law: the laws that apply within the Church

canons: rules that apply within the Church (see Canon Law) and are made up of a number of articles, which each cover a specific topic

Caroline: a term used to describe the period when Charles I was King of England

catechism: a summary of the principles of Christian religion in the form of questions and answers used for religious instruction

Christendom: a collective term for Christian countries

civilian: anyone who is not a member of the armed forces

common land: land that belongs to a community as a whole, with shared ownership and protected rights, such as the right to graze sheep on its grass

commonwealth: a term which contemporaries would have understood to have evolved from 'the common wealth' which signified the general wellbeing of the people in a community. When used in a political sense, as 'The Commonwealth', it meant a system of government in which the ordinary people of England were well cared for

conscript: to enlist someone into an army by law rather than by their own decision

constitutional: refers to matters relating to a constitution, the rules that state how a country should be governed and who exercises power

cornet: the lowest ranking officer class in the New Model Army

D

deposed: to be removed from office

dogma: the set of religious beliefs that inform one's religious practice. To become more dogmatic means that you insist on being able to pursue your beliefs to the full, which in 1630s' England meant that religious divisions began to sharpen in focus

dowry: a sum of money and other goods that a bride's family gave to her husband upon marriage

dragoons: infantrymen who rode to battle on horses but then left their horses behind the front line to fire their muskets

E

electoral reform: any reform of the system by which people elect their representatives; the Heads of the Proposals called for a redistribution of Parliament's electoral boundaries to take into account shifts in population

embezzlement: the theft of money that belongs to one's employer

episcopal: a Church structure that includes bishops

excommunication: a well-established religious punishment which meant that a person was excluded from attendance in church and would automatically go to hell when they died

executive power: the ability to administer government on a day-to-day basis, ensuring that Parliamentary legislation is carried out across the country. It also includes responsibility for foreign policy and defence

F

Feudalism: was the organisation of society imposed on England by the Normans after 1066

fiscal: Fiscal is another word for financial

front: the point at which one army engages with another; fighting on more than one front at a time puts enormous pressure onto an army because it effectively means that two or more complete armies, with equipment, food and manpower, have to be created out of one

G

garrison: a group of soldiers, stationed in a town or fortress to defend it

H

habeas corpus: literally meaning 'you have the body'; it is an ancient legal principle that prevents the punishment of anyone without making formal charges and allowing the person to defend themselves; at its heart is the assumption of innocence until proof of guilt

Glossary

hagiography: a genre of writing that focuses on the lives of the saints

hundreds: administrative units made up of a number of parishes within a county; a parish is the smallest administrative unit of local government and is formed of the dwellings that are serviced by a particular church

I

iconoclast: someone who tears down religious symbols; ripping out Laudian altar rails was another form of iconoclasm

impeachment: refers to an accusation against someone in public office, claiming that they have acted unlawfully, even treacherously, in their conduct while in that office

infantry: soldiers who fight on foot, as opposed to cavalry – soldiers on horseback

Interregnum: a period represented by a lapse in the normal form of monarchy; in English history the period 1649–60, when England was governed as a republic

J

Jacobean: a term used to describe James's rule

Junto: a political grouping and a precursor to our modern idea of political parties

L

Levellers: term was used to describe the followers of Lilburne because of their desire to 'level' society, giving rights and liberties to all men, not just those of standing; this was seen by traditional Stuart culture as being unusual, abnormal and dangerous

libel: the offence of writing something that harms someone's reputation

libertinism: being completely at liberty from a divinely ordained moral code, meaning that Ranters gained a reputation for sexual immorality, alcoholic excess and other forms of licentious behaviour

Lord Protector: the title given to the head of the government in 1653, and this period is known as the Protectorate

M

mace: a ceremonial rod made of either wood or metal which was carried in front of the king or a royal official to represent their authority

martial law (or military law): this was declared by the king and overruled normal legal processes such as trial by jury; sentences could be handed down with right of appeal

millenarians: believed that a period of one thousand years was a significant measure of time in Biblical theology; they differed in their understanding of when it might occur: some thought that there would be a thousand-year period immediately preceding the Second Coming of Christ while others thought that his Second Coming would usher in one thousand years in which he ruled on earth

Mount Calvary: the location in Jerusalem where Christians believe that Jesus was crucified, on a cross alongside two thieves

muster: when troops gather together for inspection or to go into battle; it is expensive to muster troops because you have to pay for them and their food; musters normally lead swiftly to battle

mutiny: when the authority of the commanding officer is wilfully disregarded by his subordinates

P

Parliamentarian army: specifically the army raised by the Parliamentary opposition to the king

patronage: the support of a wealthy or influential person for someone of lesser wealth or status; a patron might commission (and pay for) works of art, or help someone find a good job; the king acted as a patron when he gave out titles such as 'Lord' and 'Duke'

polemicist: someone who makes powerful attacks on ideas or people in a carefully constructed format filled with argument and counter-argument

pre-emptive: an action taken in order to prevent an anticipated event from happening

prerogative: the exclusive rights of a sovereign, which are subject to no legal restriction

Presbyterian: a Church structure that does not have bishops

Presentment Bills: reported directly to the Archdeacon and listed failings in church buildings, conduct of clergy or behaviour of parishioners

president: (High Court of Justice) responsible for ensuring that the trial would follow conventional legal processes; he controlled who could say what and at what point

propaganda: information, often misleading or biased, that is used to promote a particular cause

providence: the protective care of God, thought by believes to provide good things for those who trusted him; Cromwell was a firm believer in providence, which meant that he interpreted successes in battle as evidence of providence, and worried that failures were evidence of God's displeasure

purge: the sudden removal of people who are deemed to be undesirable members of an organisation or institution; while modern purges, such as those in Stalinist Russia, have tended to be carried out by execution, this was not the case in the seventeenth century, where undesirables were simply dismissed from their posts

pyrrhic victory: a victory that is so devastating for its victor that it is, in a way, a defeat

R

recruiter MP: a term used by Royalists to refer to the recruitment of MPs to replace those who supported the king to maintain numbers in the Commons

recusancy: not attending your local parish church for services, which carried a financial penalty

regent: a person who leads a state because the monarch is too young or incapable of ruling

regicide: the act of killing a king; also a person who takes part in killing a king

Glossary

remonstrance: a strongly worded protest

rendezvous: a word for a meeting that derives from the French phrase, 'rendez-vous' which means 'present yourselves!'; it is frequently used in military contexts

republic: a state in which supreme power is held by the people and their elected representatives, with an elected or nominated president and without a monarch

revoke: to cancel, specifically in terms of overturning legislation

Root and Branch petition: called for the abolition of the episcopacy from the 'roots' and in all its 'branches', and was signed by 15,000 Londoners; it led to the Root and Branch Bill

Royalist: supporters of the king during the Civil War period

S

scorched earth policy: a military strategy of burning or destroying crops or other resources that might be of use to an invading enemy force

Scottish Kirk: the Church in Scotland; 'kirk' is a Gaelic word

secluded members: a term used to describe the MPs who had been excluded by Colonel Pride by 1659

secular powers: belong to governing authorities that are not explicitly religious, such as criminal courts

sedition: the offence of stirring up a rebellion against the established order; so, seditious libel means writings that threaten governmental order

settlement: in this sense, the resolution (or an attempt to find a resolution) of an issue of governance

Ship Money: a prerogative form of income that a monarch could levy on coastal towns to provide emergency funds in time of conflict or threat, in order to defend coastal regions and equip the fleet

siege warfare: a legacy of medieval military tactics whereby soldiers surrounded a town, preventing anyone from entering or leaving and cut off all supplies to force the town to surrender; sieges were often effective but very costly because of the need to keep a large army around the besieged town and for this reason, Cromwell particularly preferred to try to storm towns instead

slander: when someone makes a false verbal statement that damages another person's reputation

smallpox: a viral disease with a mortality rate of between 30 to 90 per cent; depending on precise variation, smallpox symptoms (like severe chicken pox) emerge after about 12 days, and most deaths occur within 16 days from infection, it was common during the sixteenth and seventeenth centuries

steward: a servant (who may be nonetheless of a high status) who is given responsibility for looking after an absent master's affairs; there is a touch of irony in the description of Ann Wentworth as a 'careful steward', when it was to be Wentworth's vigorously careful stewardship that led to his death

stigmata: meaning 'sign'; mystical markings on the skin, in the same location as where nails were struck in the hands and feet of Jesus on the cross; medieval Christianity in particular believed that stigmata were a special sign of God's favour

stutter: a speech disorder in which sounds, syllables, or words are repeated or prolonged, disrupting the normal flow of speech; Charles I would have found it a confidence-denting hindrance in his public role, because people then tended to think that a physical problem reflected a mental problem in the seventeenth century

T

the king's word: a solemn promise, backed up by personal honour and not by legislative force

the king's peace: refers to peace and order being maintained in the kingdom, because of the correct application of law and justice, which has the king at its head

tithe: the tax that everyone in the parish had to pay in order to finance their minister; tithes were generally collected by the clergy

treason: the crime of betraying one's country; this was a capital crime, which meant that a conviction automatically led to a sentence of death

Trinity: the collective term for the Christian God in his three component parts: Father, Son (Jesus) and Holy Spirit

V

vagrancy: the state of being a vagrant, which means a homeless person who survives by begging and often travels from place to place looking for shelter and food

Venetian doges: the Venetian Republic was famous for its system of government, where a group of wealthy, powerful citizens known as oligarchs elected a leader from among their ranks whose title was the Doge

vestments: the special clothes worn by clergymen; under Laud, use of vestments became more ornate than the Puritans felt was appropriate, increasing fears of insidious Catholicism

vicissitudes: a change in life and fortune; it tends to have a negative connotation – unwelcome moments; ups and downs

visitations: made by bishops to each of the parishes in their diocese on a regular basis; bishops had to check that the churches were in good order, well maintained and with the altars in the right place

Z

zealot: someone with a powerful enthusiasm in pursuit of a cause or an objective

Bibliography

Students

Ackroyd, Peter, *Civil War: The History of England Volume III*, Macmillan, 2014

Farr, David, *Stuart Britain and the Crisis of Monarchy 1603–1702*, Oxford University Press, 2015

Fraser, Antonia, *Cromwell, Our Chief of Men*, Orion Books Ltd, 2002

Hibbert, Christopher, *Charles I*, Palgrave Macmillan, 2007

Hunt, Tristram, *The English Civil War at First Hand*, Penguin Books Ltd, 2011

Morill, John, *Stuart Britain*, Oxford University Press, 2000

Purkiss, Diane, *The English Civil War, a People's History*, Harper Perennial, 2007

Teachers and extension

Adamson, John, *The Noble Revolt*, Orion Books Ltd, 2009

Coward, Barry, *The Stuart Age*, Routledge, 2011

Cressy, David, *Charles I and the people of England*, Oxford University Press, 2015

Hill, Christopher, *The Century of Revolution*, Routledge, 2001

Hutchinson, Lucy, *Memoirs of the life of Colonel Hutchinson*, Phoenix Press, 2000

Hyde, Earl of Clarendon, Edward, *The History of the Rebellion*, Oxford University Press, 2009

Kenyon, J.P., *The Stuart Constitution*, Cambridge University Press, 1986

Lockyer, Roger, *The Early Stuarts*, Longman, 1989

Manning, Brian, *Aristocrats, Plebeians and Revolution in England, 1640–60*, Pluto Press, 1996

Marvell, Andrew, *The Complete Poems*, Penguin Classics, 2005

Milton, John, *Paradise Lost*, Oxford University Press, 2004

Morrill, John, *Oliver Cromwell and the English Revolution*, Longman, 1990

Morrill, John, *Revolt in the Provinces: The People of England and the Tragedies of War, 1630–48*, Routledge, 1998

Roberts, Keith, *Cromwell's War Machine*, Pen & Sword Military, 2009

Roots, Ivan, *The Great Rebellion, 1642–60*, Sutton Publishing Ltd, 1995

Royle, Trevor, *Civil War: the War of the Three Kingdoms 1638–1660*, Abacus, 2005

Russell, Conrad, *The Causes of the English Civil War*, Clarendon Press, 1990

Sharpe, Kevin, *The Personal Rule of Charles I*, Yale University Press, 1992

Underdown, David, *Revel, Riot and Rebellion Popular Politics and Culture in England 1603–1660*, Oxford University Press, 1987

Woolrych, Austin, *Commonwealth to Protectorate*, Phoenix Press, 2000

Worden, Blair, *The English Civil Wars*, Orion Books Ltd, 2010

Worden, Blair, *God's Instruments: Political Conduct in the England of Oliver Cromwell*, Oxford University Press, 2012

Worden, Blair, *The Rump Parliament*, Cambridge University Press, 1977

Wormald, Jenny, *The Seventeenth Century*, Oxford University Press, 2008

Websites

British Library:
www.bl.uk

The History of Parliament:
www.historyofparliamentonline.org

British History Online:
www.british-history.ac.uk

Open University English Civil War hub:
www.open.edu/openlearn/tags/english-civil-war

Index

A
Absolutism xiii, 18, 26
Agitators 143, 144, 146, 152, 155
Arminianism 14, 22, 23, 33, 46–50

B
Baptists 149, 189–90
Bastwick, John 45–6, 52, 53, 54, 82
Bedford, Francis Russell, Earl of 77, 79, 80–1, 84, 89–90
Bishop's Wars 66–71
Bristol, Earl of *see* Digby, George
Buckingham, George Villiers, Duke of 7, 8, 32–3
    attempted impeachment of 19, 20, 25–6
    relations with Charles I 11, 12, 15
    role of 22, 23, 24–5, 26
Burton, Henry 45–6, 52, 53, 54, 82

C
canon law 38, 50, 73
Catholicism 2, 8, 13–14, 51, 177, 200
Cavendish, William *see* Newcastle, William Cavendish, Earl of
Charles I
    advisers 15–16
    attitudes and actions 150–1
    capture 139–41, 144, 156
    character and aims 10–11, 17
    chief ministers 36–8
    church conflict 22–4
    failed settlement attempt 156–7
    government 19–26, 38–9
    and Henrietta Maria 10, 12, 105, 113, 150
    Long Parliament 89–91
    opposition to 28–35, 165–8
    Personal Rule 34–5, 36–43
    profile of 8, 109, 135
    strengths and weaknesses 74–6
    trial and execution 138–72
Charles II 174, 212, 215
    defeat and exile 180–2
    negotiations for return as monarch 210–13
    and Scotland 177, 178–9

Charles, Prince *see* Charles II
Clarendon, Edward Hyde, Earl of 61, 83, 102, 159, 210
Coke, Edward 7, 29, 30, 31, 33
Commonwealth 34, 56, 191–2
Cromwell, Oliver
    government 195–6
    personality 118, 195
    political vacuum on death 205–10
    refusal of the Crown 192, 202–4
    succession to 204
Cromwell, Richard 204, 205–6
Crown, relations with 3–5, 32, 60–1

D
Devereux, Robert *see* Essex, Robert Devereux, Earl of
Digby, George, Earl of Bristol 25, 112, 125, 139
Diggers 186–7
dissolution of Parliament 32–4, 74, 78, 152, 193, 196, 210
Divine Right 17–18, 74, 113, 141

E
Eliot, John 25, 26, 28, 29, 30, 34
England 3, 56–8, 61
English Revolution, legacy of 213–14, 218
Essex, Robert Devereux, Earl of 77, 105, 109, 111, 114, 120, 122
Evelyn, John 108, 208–9

F
Fairfax, Thomas 114, 124, 144–5, 155, 160, 162, 168
Fiennes, William, Viscount Saye and Sele 53, 68, 74, 79, 135, 152, 168
Fifth Monarchists 147–8, 190
financial policy 19–21, 40–3
First Civil War 102, 104–14, 116–25, 135–41
Five Members 98–9, 103
foreign policy 5–8, 24–6

G
'Godley Society' 187
government 19–26, 38–9, 195–6
Graham, James *see* Montrose, James Graham, Earl of
Grand Remonstrance 85–8, 102

H
Haselrig, Arthur 97, 98, 117, 203, 205, 207
Henrietta Maria 10, 12–15, 25, 67, 105, 113, 150
Holles, Denzil 28, 29, 34, 77, 79, 98, 123
Hyde, Edward *see* Clarendon, Edward Hyde, Earl of

I
Independents 129, 135–6, 143, 152, 166
Ireland 58–61, 95–7, 174–7, 212, 217
Ireton, Henry 144, 145, 152, 166, 169
Irish Rebellion 96–7

J
James I/James VI 1–8, 16

K
king's word 31

L
Lambert, John 145, 152, 164, 194, 197
Laud, William 37, 83, 91, 129
    relations with Charles I 11, 12, 75
    role of 33, 56, 63, 73
Laudianism 46–50, 52–3, 59
legacy of English Revolution 213–14, 218
Levellers 146–7, 153, 154, 184–6
Lilburne, John 52, 53, 146–7, 153, 185
local grievances 99–101
London 87–8, 116
London Mob 87–8

223

Index

Long Parliament 73–4, 87–8, 89–91, 209

M

Major Generals 196–9
Manchester, Henry Montagu, Earl of 37, 39, 123, 124, 128
martial law 30, 31, 162, 168, 217
military preparations, First Civil War 104–5
Militia Ordinance 99, 103, 104, 117
monarchy 10–18, 205–14
Montagu, Henry see Manchester, Henry Montagu, Earl of
Montrose, James Graham, Earl of 71, 90, 91, 137, 177, 178–9

N

National Covenant 65
New Model Army 122–5, 128–31, 142–5, 152, 153–5, 166–8
Newcastle, William Cavendish, Earl of 108, 109, 114, 118, 125
Nominated Assembly 193–4

O

opposition 28–35, 77–9, 80–2, 135–6, 151–5
Overton, Richard 63, 146, 147, 185

P

Pacification of Berwick 69
pamphlets 131, 133, 134, 146, 214
Parliament
　dissolution of 32–4, 74, 78, 152, 193, 196, 210
　divisions in 135–6, 152, 166–8
　opposition to 77–9, 80–2, 151–5
　recall of 61–2, 72–4
　relations with Crown 3–5, 28–35
　representative 154
Parliament of the Saints 192–4
Parliamentarian army 116–25, 142
Personal Rule 34–5, 36–43
Petition of Right 31–2, 55
Political Independents 129, 135–6, 143, 152, 166
Political Nation, 1640 72–82
political radicalism 142–8, 184–94
popular radicalism 88, 126–8
popularist religious groups 148–9
Presbyterianism
　Ireland 58
　political 135–6, 137–8, 142–3, 144, 152–3
Pride's Purge 166–7, 208
Scotland 2, 50, 121, 139, 178
Pride's Purge 167–8, 208
propaganda 131–4, 146
providence 168, 195, 196
Prynne, William 45–6, 52, 53, 54, 82, 167, 206
Puritanism 50–1, 52–3, 100
Pym, John 29, 31, 74, 83–5, 98, 135
　Strafford's trial 92, 93, 94

Q

Quakers 188–9, 201, 206, 214

R

radical republicanism 191–2
radical sects 190–1
radicalism 63–4, 88, 126–34, 142–9, 184–94
Ranters 148, 188
religious radicalism 63–4, 88, 128–31, 147–9, 190–1
religious sects 129, 148–9, 214
religious toleration 199–202
Root and Branch petition 78, 79, 81–2, 88
royal authority 16–18, 28, 98, 102–4
Royalist Party 91, 102–4, 106–14, 174–80
Rump Parliament 167, 168, 185–6, 191–3, 206–7
Rupert, Prince 109, 110, 111, 113, 125, 137
Russell, Francis see Bedford, Francis Russell, Earl of

S

Saye and Sele, Viscount see Fiennes, William
Scotland
　by 1660 217
　Laudianism in 49–50
　religious radicalism 63–71
　Royalism 177–80
　Second Civil War 158–9, 163–4
　settlements 90–1, 139–40
Scottish Covenant 64–6, 80, 114, 120, 122
Second Civil War 158–64, 166
Self-Denying Ordinance 122–5
settlements, attempts at 2, 136–9, 156–7
Ship Money 42, 43, 44, 53, 61, 78
Solemn League and Covenant 120–2, 124, 178
Spain 24–5, 26, 40, 90, 197, 199
St John, Oliver 43, 53, 80, 81, 135
Star Chamber 16, 39, 49, 51, 79
Strafford, Earl of see Wentworth, Thomas
Stuart, Charles see Charles II

T

Third Civil War 173–82
Thorough (policy) 49, 56–61, 65, 91, 217
tonnage and poundage 19–20, 30, 33, 34, 78

V

Vane, Henry 81, 92, 190, 208, 212, 213
Villiers, George see Buckingham, George Villiers, Duke of

W

Wentworth, Thomas, Earl of Strafford 33, 59, 84, 91–4
　recall of Parliamnet 73
　relations with Charles I 11, 75
　religious radicalism 63
　role of 37, 55, 56, 57, 58, 218
Westminster Assembly of Divines 121, 135, 138, 158, 166